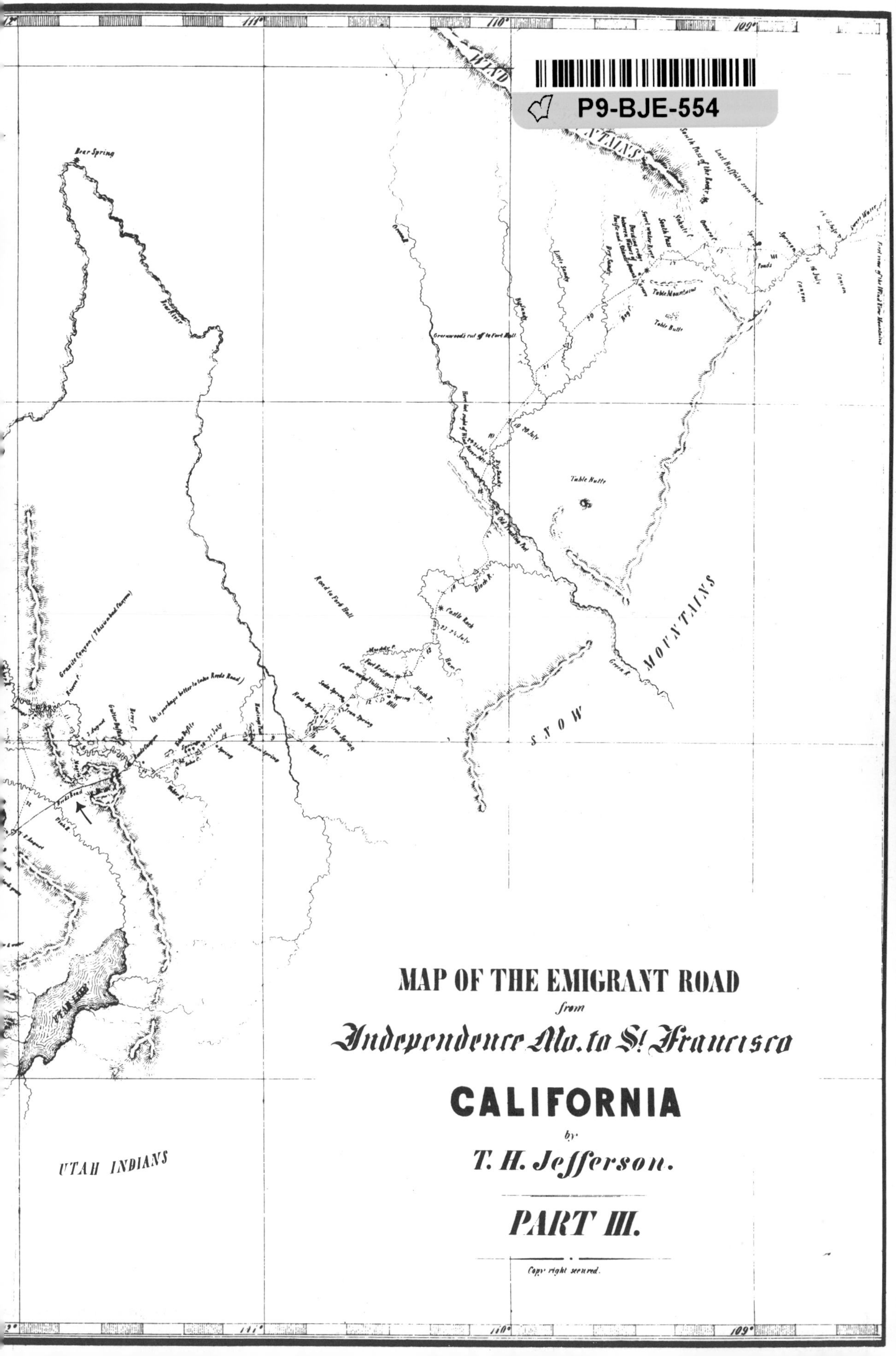

MAP OF THE EMIGRANT ROAD

from

Independence Mo. to St Francisco

CALIFORNIA

by

T. H. Jefferson.

PART III.

LEFT HAND TURN

LEFT HAND TURN

A STORY OF THE DONNER PARTY WOMEN

By Jeannette Gould Maino

Jeannette Gould Maino

Dry Creek Books
P.O. Box 1359
Modesto, California 95352

First Printing 1987
Second Printing 1988
Third Printing 1989

Library of Congress Card Catalog Number 89-063221
ISBN 0-941885-05-4

Published by
Pioneer Publishing Co.
Fresno, California 93704

Manufactured in the United States of America

Dedication

For those who have cared
criticized and encouraged.
For those who called
from the past.

Plaque on "This Is The Place" Monument, at Salt Lake City, representing the struggle of the trail blazers through the Wasatch Mountains in 1846.

Photo courtesy of the Utah State Historical Society

Preface

In 1846, two Donner brothers, George, 62, and his ailing older brother Jacob, 65, joined with James Frazier Reed, 42, and their large families to emigrate to California. Although gold was not discovered until two years later, the emigration that year was large, partly because of detailed guide books such as the one written by Lansford W. Hastings, sometimes satirically referred to as California's first real estate promoter. He described the climate as ideal, free from the agues and fevers of what were then the "western states."

The first part of the journey over the great rolling prairie was much like life at home. Each party was a village of people traveling together. Companies formed and reformed as unmanageable numbers separated into smaller parties. Captains were elected, deposed, supplanted by others until a sort of balance was attained. As at home, people married, gave birth, became ill and died. The people celebrated holidays, played fiddles and banjos and danced in the evenings when they weren't too tired, sang, quarreled and forgave.

Among the many companies, the one including the Donners and Reeds was larger and slower than most. What was the worry? California would be waiting at the end of the trail; they were well equipped with food and supplies for the trek which was to last four months, more or less. Gradually, however, they began to realize that the distance they must cover was farther than they had expected. Reaching Fort Laramie the day before the Fourth of July, they knew they were roughly half-way on their trip, but they had used more than half the time allotted. The Donners and Reeds and several other families determined to take a new cut-off suggested in Hastings' book which promised a saving of some 200 miles or more. Despite the warning of James Reed's old friend from the Black Hawk War, a mountain man named James Clyman, they started off on the new route.

The decision was argued even until the night before the southern turn toward Salt Lake. After camping overnight at the Little Sandy the Reed-Donner contingent, comprising twenty wagons, led off for Fort Bridger where Hasting had promised to conduct them through the Wahsatch Mountains, then across a 'dry drive' to rejoin the California trail far ahead of the others. Hastings deceived them twice. He did not wait, but went ahead to guide the Harlan-Young party; he gave them false information. James Clyman was right. This was no trail for wagons ... mules perhaps, but never the large family wagons. Hacking a trail over rough mountains higher than any they had ever seen before consumed almost a month in which they advanced only 35 miles. The 'dry drive,' purported to be 40 miles, was actually closer to 90. Hardships multiplied. The party was fragmented. Fright took over as the frantic men and women struggled to reach California before the dreaded snows. Reaching the eastern base of the Sierra Nevada at the end of October, desperately low on food, they were caught by an unseasonably early snow fall, and were trapped at Truckee (Donner) Lake.

Once heard, the story of the Reed-Donner Party cannot be dismissed from the mind. It is, as Stewart has said, a microcosm of human life. I first read about it at the age of nine, having discovered C.F. McGlashan's HISTORY OF THE DONNER PARTY, reprinted in 1907, in our family library. I had devoured most of it before my parents realized that I was reading it and felt that it must be frightening for a girl of that age. It was.

In a sense, it has haunted me ever since. The truths in that dark blood-colored book followed me for years. Every crust left on our table made me wish I could somehow spirit it away to those suffering people. That people could actually eat each other was beyond belief. I had never been that hungry.

As I grew older I continued to read other accounts. More questions rose in my mind. Why had this happened to those people? Was there a curse on the Donner Party? Later still, I searched for a hero, a heroine and a villain. Certainly there were some of each in the grim tale. I tried to dismiss the story as one concerning stupid people making stupid decisions, digging the holes that were to trap them.

Yet I could not forget, and my interest grew. My grandmother knew some of the party that had settled in the Napa Valley, and at the library in Calistoga, where I went to borrow the Thornton Burgess books, Elizabeth Wright, a relative of the Graves family, was the librarian. On the place next to my Aunt Irene's prune orchard was a small private cemetery containing the graves of some of the party. Our beloved neighbor, Alice Crouch was, I discovered, the daughter of Sarah Fosdick, whose husband Jay died in her arms during the last days of the march of the Forlorn Hope. My Aunt Beatrice told me that she remembered little children pointing and screaming at an old man named Keseberg. "You eat children!" they would taunt him.

Many books followed, each with its own point of view. The ghosts along the trail would not stay buried. Where was the truth? I realized at last there were facts that hadn't been discovered, and never will be. To me it became a mystery story with no ending.

Almost all the accounts were written by men, although in 1856, an early feminist, Eliza Farnham in CALIFORNIA INDOORS AND OUT made women angels and men cowards or worse. I knew that was not the truth. I knew that the men were equally brave and strong, and that the women were stoic and resourceful, and that more of them had survived.

Each reading of a new book, and every re-reading of an old created wonder. What had the people thought as they crossed the plains to a nebulous new life in a fairy-tale country? Had they, as they passed the point of no return, ever wondered what they were doing there or how they had got themselves into such a fix? How had they managed their women's duties and trials day after day? In the dark snow-covered shanties through the long dismal days of winter what thoughts, regrets, disappointments had occupied their minds? I knew that Tamsen Donner was unhappy at the decision to take the short-cut. Was she alone in her feeling, or was she the only one who dared show how she felt?

A simple statement in A SHORT HISTORY OF CALIFORNIA by Rockwell Hunt and Nellie Van De Grift Sanchez caught at my mind. "It was July 20 when the Donner Party broke camp and took the left hand trail for Fort Bridger." The left hand "being the weaker hand in most persons, clumsy, awkward, insincere, sinister, malicious; the left hand wrong, as springing from indirection ...." woman sits at the left side of the male. From the left hand turn, tragedy was inevitable. Horror begins and grows. Quarrels start, tempers are taut to breaking. There is no turning back, and the "Grim Journey" as Hoffman Birney called his book, is inevitable. Disintegration of the party increases as tense days pass futilely, one by one.

The Reed-Donner Party are real men and women who meant no harm to no one, let alone to themselves. They were moving west as some of them had done before, always farther west in the American tradition. They weren't mountain people; they did not listen to the advice of hardened mountain men. For the most part they were farmers, small business men, young people looking for something better. They were certainly ignorant of the perils of the crossing and they were stubborn in their credence in the published words of Hastings. They were *not* stupid.

Personalities evolved in my mind. I began to love these people. Little Stanton, fine-spirited, handsome, trustworthy, heroic; William Eddy, the man who never gave up, who was always the first to offer help when an axle broke or a wagon needed repairing; the giant of a man, William McCutchen, spouting Shakespeare and profanity, a man to trust in an emergency. Patrick Breen and his big Irish family, who depended on God and his sturdy wife Peggy. Genial George Donner, good to the core, who accepted leadership without a shred of real leadership in him. James Reed, impatient, high-strung, rich, intelligent, resourceful, lover of animals and his family, who forgave as quickly as he was quick to anger. The strange puzzle of Louis Keseberg. Was he evil personified or was he the whipping boy for a group of desperate people who needed someone to hate? John Snyder, handsome and brave, who broke under pressure. The two sons-in-law of Lavina Murphy who helped her across the plains with her large family.

I admired them, loved them and suffered for them and the women and children they had brought willy-nilly into misery and suffering ... poor children who had nothing to say about the trip. The women ... oh, the women! Had they wanted to come, to be taken from their homes, friends and relatives? What did they think about as they jolted in the creaking wagons into that vast wilderness? What sad thoughts hovered in their minds when darkness came and their hearths were far away, whether they looked to the east or the west? They cooked, washed when there was water, knitted, mended, changed diapers when they could, wore the same dusty foul-smelling dresses every day, suffered menstrual periods in silence, nursed their babies until their breasts refused to give milk, made shrouds for the dead, sometimes took turns driving the teams. They wrote in diaries, walked in the dust beside the wagons to save the weary animals, listened to their children whimper in the night, held their heads when they vomitted, counted graves along the way, and wondered if the trip would ever come to an end and they could settle down again, make new homes as much like the comfortable ones they had left behind.

In many ways, I crossed with them. I knew now what I would try to do. I would let them talk.

TABLE OF CONTENTS

MAPS

Note: The fictional sections of LEFT HAND TURN are printed in English Text.

The sections printed in italics are the author's opinions based strictly on research.

Direct quotes from recognized authorities have been placed in boxes.

CAST OF CHARACTERS
REED-DONNER PARTY

REED FAMILY

James Frazier Reed, 46, from Springfield, Illinois; of Polish-Irish descent, rumored aristocratic forebears. Prosperous. A town named for him in Illinois. Lately owner of a cabinet shop where his spectacular 'Pioneer Palace Car' was built to his specifications.

Margaret Keyes Backenstoe Reed, 32, his wife. Her first husband, Lloyd Backenstoe died, leaving her with their infant daughter, Virginia.

Virginia Backenstoe Reed, 13 years old.

Martha Jane (Patty) Reed, 8, daughter of Margaret and James.

James Frazier Reed, Jr. 5 and Thomas Keyes Reed, 3, sons of James and Margaret.

Mrs. Sarah Keyes, who died on the trail, widowed mother of Margaret Reed.

GEORGE DONNER FAMILY

George Donner, 62, wealthy farmer from Springfield.

Tamsen Eustis Dozier Donner, 45, George's third wife. A New Englander, well-educated school teacher, amateur botanist and painter. Her first marriage to Tully Dozier ended tragically with his death and that of their two small daughters in an epidemic, probably cholera.

Elitha, 14, and Leanna, 12, daughters of George and his second wife.

Frances, 6, Georgia, 4 and Eliza, 3, daughters of George and Tamsen.

JACOB DONNER FAMILY

Jacob Donner, 65, older brother of George, also well-to-do farmer from Springfield, in failing health.

Elizabeth (Aunt Betsy) Donner, his wife, 45. A sister to George Donner's second wife, making her a double aunt of Elitha and Leanna.

William Hook, 14, and Solomon Hook, sons of Elizabeth by a former marriage.

George Donner, 9, Mary M. Donner, 7, Isaac, 5, Samuel, 4 and Lewis, 3, children of Jacob and Elizabeth.

WILLIAM EDDY FAMILY

William Eddy, 28, from Belleville, Illinois, a carriage maker.

Eleanor Eddy, 25, his wife.

James Eddy, 3, and Margaret Eddy, 1, children of William and Eleanor.

PATRICK BREEN FAMILY

Patrick Breen, 40, an Irishman from Keokuk, Illinois.

Margaret (Peggy) Breen, 40, his wife.

John, 14, Edward, 13, Patrick, Jr., 11, Simon, 9, Peter, 7, James 4, and Isabella, 1, children of Patrick and Peggy.

MURPHY FAMILY

Lavina Murphy, widow, from Tennessee and Missouri. Rumored to be a Mormon.

John Landrum, 15, Mary M., 13, Lemuel, 12, William G., 11, Simon P., 9, Lavina's unmarried children.

Sarah Murphy Foster (Sally), 23, married daughter.

William Foster, 28, Sally's husband.

George Foster, their son, nursing babe.

Harriet Murphy Pike, 21, married daughter.

William Pike, Harriet's husband.

Naomi Pike, 2, and Catherine, nursing babe, the children of Harriet and William.

KESEBERG FAMILY

Lewis Keseberg, 32, from Germany. A mysterious character, possibly because of the language barrier, although he spoke French as well as German.

Phillipine Keseberg, 32, his wife.
Ada, 3, and Lewis, Jr., born on the trail, their children.

WOLFINGER FAMILY

Mr. and Mrs. Wolfinger, first names and ages unknown. From Germany.

GRAVES FAMILY (joined Reed-Donner Party at Weber Canyon)

Franklin Ward Graves, 57, from Illinois. Formerly from New England. Called Uncle Billy; name changed to Uncle Frank to avoid confusion.

Elizabeth (Lizzie), 47, his wife.

Unmarried children: Mary Ann, 19-20, William (Billy), 18, Eleanor, 15, Lovina, 13, Nancy, 9, Jonathon, 7, Franklin W., Jr., 5, Elizabeth, Jr., nursing babe.

Married children: Sarah Graves Fosdick, 27, newly married Jay Fosdick, 23, her husband.

McCUTCHEN FAMILY

William McCutchen, 30, (Big Mac) from Missouri, via Tennessee. Tall, strong, forthright in speech and action. He and his family joined the party at Fort Bridger.

Amanda, 24, his wife.

Harriet, their nursing babe.

SINGLE WOMAN

Eliza Williams, serving as a mother's helper to the Reed family.

SINGLE MEN

Milford Elliott, 28. Head teamster for the Reeds, treated almost as a member of the family. Long time employee of Reed's in Springfield.

Charles Tyler Stanton, 35, from Chicago. Bachelor, traveling alone.

Patrick Dolan, 40, from Keokuk, Illinois. Born in Ireland. Friend of the Breen family, but traveling independently.

Luke Halloran, 25, from Missouri. Invalid who joined the Donner family at the Little Sandy.

Mr. Hardcoop, 60, from Belgium. On the trip to California before returning to Belgium.

John Snyder, 23, teamster for the Graves family. Said to be Mary Ann's fiance.

Hiram Miller, age unknown, from Springfield. He left the emigration at Fort Laramie with Edwin Byrant and others to travel faster. A friend of both the Donners and Reeds, he returned twice to Truckee Lake to assist in rescue efforts.

Teamsters John Denton, 28, English; Walter Herron, 25, Springfield; Baylis Williams, 24, Springfield, a brother of Eliza Williams. An albino, he was useful for night duties.

Joseph Rhinehardt or Rinehart, 30, German and his possible partner Augustus Spitzer, 30, also German; James Smith, 25; Noah James, 20; Charles or Karl (Dutch) Burger, 30; Samuel Shoemaker, 25; Juan Baptiste Trubode, under 20, teamster hired at Fort Bridger to take Hi Miller's place; Antonio (Antoine), age unknown, also taken on at Fort Bridger.

Lewis and Salvador, two Indians from Fort Sutter, who accompanied Stanton on his relief trip.

FELLOW TRAVELERS

Edwin Bryant, 39, editor of a Louisville, Kentucky newspaper. Well educated, with skills in botany and medicine, etc. Traveling alone, taking notes for his book "What I Saw In California." At Fort Laramie he sold his wagon and went forward in a mule train with Miller and others in the interest of speed. He took Hastings' Cut-off.

Lillburn Boggs, Ex-Governor of Missouri. Captain of the large party taking the Fort Hall Road, with his wife and family. Boggs had been governor during the Mormon troubles in 1838.

William Henry (Owl) Russell, deposed captain of the larger party. Given to speeches and drink.

Colonel Andrew J. Grayson and his wife, fellow botanists with Tamsen. Became famous for his botanical studies. Founded the town of Grayson in California.

Jessy Quinn Thornton and his wife, Nancy, who recorded accounts of the Donner Party in 1848. Well educated lawyer, friend of Stephen Douglass, and Thomas Benton; from Quincy, Illinois.

Aquilla Glover, member of the Boggs train, who later volunteered to return to go to the relief of his friends.

Reasin (Dan) Tucker, another member of the large train who returned to help.

Lansford Warren Hastings. The elusive author of "The Emigrant's Guide," in the party just ahead of the Reed-Donners. For a sketch of his character, see Notes page 240.

Part I: THE NIGHER WAY

A SHORT DISTANCE beyond the south pass of the Great Divide a slow, winding wagon train came to a halt at the Little Sandy River. It was already past the middle of July in the year 1846.

Preparations for the night were made as usual: the cattle put to graze, the camp fires lit, babies fed. Women prepared the evening meal, men mended harnesses and checked wagon wheels against the next day's drive. It was the last night many of these emigrants would camp together.

Most of the wagons would continue on the well-marked trail bearing north to Fort Hall where they would separate, some going to California, some to Oregon. However, a resolute few had determined to turn southwest on the faint trail to Fort Bridger, there to take a new route to California. Publicized in a guide book written by Lansford W. Hastings, guaranteeing a savings of many miles of travel, the new route would go directly to Salt Lake, cross a stretch of desert, and rejoin the California Trail on the Humboldt River.

Even though it was late in the season, most emigrants headed for California had chosen to take the known route. However, tempted by the two hundred mile short-cut, a splinter of the train decided to try the new way. Why shouldn't it be safe? Hastings had written in *The Emigrants' Guide to Oregon and California:* "The most direct route, for the California emigrants, would be to leave the Oregon route, about two hundred miles east of Fort Hall; thence bearing west southwest, to the Salt Lake; and thence continuing down to the bay of St. Francisco." This treasured book was with them, and had not failed them this far. Some of the emigrants considered the short-cut far too risky, but these few were willing to take the chance. Likely, they would reach the Humboldt before the others.

However, as the women cooked their last meal with those they had traveled with from Independence, Missouri, many of them had a bittersweet sadness in their hearts for friends they would part with tomorrow morning at sun-up.

Tamsen Donner held Hasting's slim book in her hands. "Listen to me, George, please! Only for a minute. It's easy to say things in a book. Why, George, we've talked to people going back home and they tell things differently..."

"Sore heads, Tamsen. People who couldn't make it..."

"Maybe ... once in a while. Don't you see, California can't be that perfect. Nowhere can. Lansford Hastings sounds like a man selling snake oil at the county fair! And when he said these things about the short-cut, he hadn't even seen it! He lied about that."

"Tamsen, the fact is we're far back in the emigration. We've got to make up some time, and Hastings' route will do it for us."

"But George! Jim Clyman himself said maybe we could get through on horses, but it wasn't fit for a wagon trail! You heard him just as plain as day. And so did James Reed!"

"Hastings will wait for us at Fort Bridger. That ought to convince you, my dear. He'll personally conduct us through the mountains."

"Why should you believe Hastings? You take his word as if it came straight from the Bible."

"He knew enough to write a book. It's right there in print."

"In print! James Clyman stood right at our camp fire and told us not to go that way if we wanted to get to California before the snows came." Tamsen could still hear the concern in his voice and she remembered how his eyes looked, troubled and truthful back at Fort Bernard as he stood twisting his ragged hat in his hand, his leather coat fringed like an Indian's. Strange that she had believed him, put his information above Hastings'. Jim Clyman didn't look like a man who could read a book, much less write one.

"I've never liked this book, from the very start. Now that we've talked to Mr. Clyman I have less use for it than ever. It's too easy, too full of grandiose words. Cattle that require no care, oats eight feet high, clover growing to five feet, two crops a year of wheat! It never made sense to me, and now it makes me afraid ... afraid to believe a word the man says. Sending that man Bonney toward us galloping as if the devil were after him, waving his message about war and staying close together."

George Donner watched her, a half-smile on his genial face. A tall strong man, no one would have guessed he was already in his sixties. Only a few gray hairs threaded through the black. "My dear wife, you worry too much. Don't tell me you take those words of that dirty codger as truth, and the printed account of Mr. Hastings as a lie. That 's not like you, my honey-girl." His voice was patient, as if he had gone over this argument many times. Tamsen couldn't repress a tone of scorn in her voice.

"Yes, I liked that old codger, as you call him. Granted he wasn't clean and dressed as I'd like, but his eyes were very truthful..."

"Ah, now we have it," George said with a laugh. "It's his eyes that have convinced my little wife, is it?" He put his large hand gently on her shoulder. She was only five feet tall; he was a giant beside her.

"You must trust me, Tamsen. We men have thought this over carefully, and we are determined to take the shorter way. We need every bit of the 200 miles the new trail will save. We are late, almost the last of the emigration. We start tomorrow. Now smile at me, my girl, and tell me you love and trust me."

Tamsen attempted a smile. "Of course I love you, George. Of course I trust you, but..."

"Well then, that's all that needs to be said."

With a final spurt of rebellion, Tamsen said, "Something tells me this is the wrong way ... that we are gambling with more than we dare lose..."

"Women are always having little ideas like that, Tamsen. If men paid attention to mood, we'd never get anywhere. I've not disappointed you before, have I?"

Why was George so stubborn? Usually she could persuade him if she were careful not to injure his pride.

"You just get some supper for us all, my dear, and I'll take care of the road we choose."

The nature of the prolonged conversation was revealed by Clyman years later:

"We met Gov. Boggs and party at Fort Laramie. It included the Donner Party. We camped one night with them at Laramie ... Mr. Reed was inquiring about the route. I told him to 'take the regular wagon track (by way of Fort Hall) and never leave it — it is barely possible to get through if you follow it — and it may be impossible if you don't.' Reed replied, 'There is a nigher route and it is of no use to take so much of a roundabout course.' I admitted the fact, but told him about the great desert and the roughness of the Sierras, and that a straight route might turn out to be impracticable.

"The Party when we separated took my trail by which I had come from California, south of Salt Lake, and struck the regular emigrant trail again on the Humboldt."

James Hewitt, "Eye-witness to Wagon Trains West" p. 89

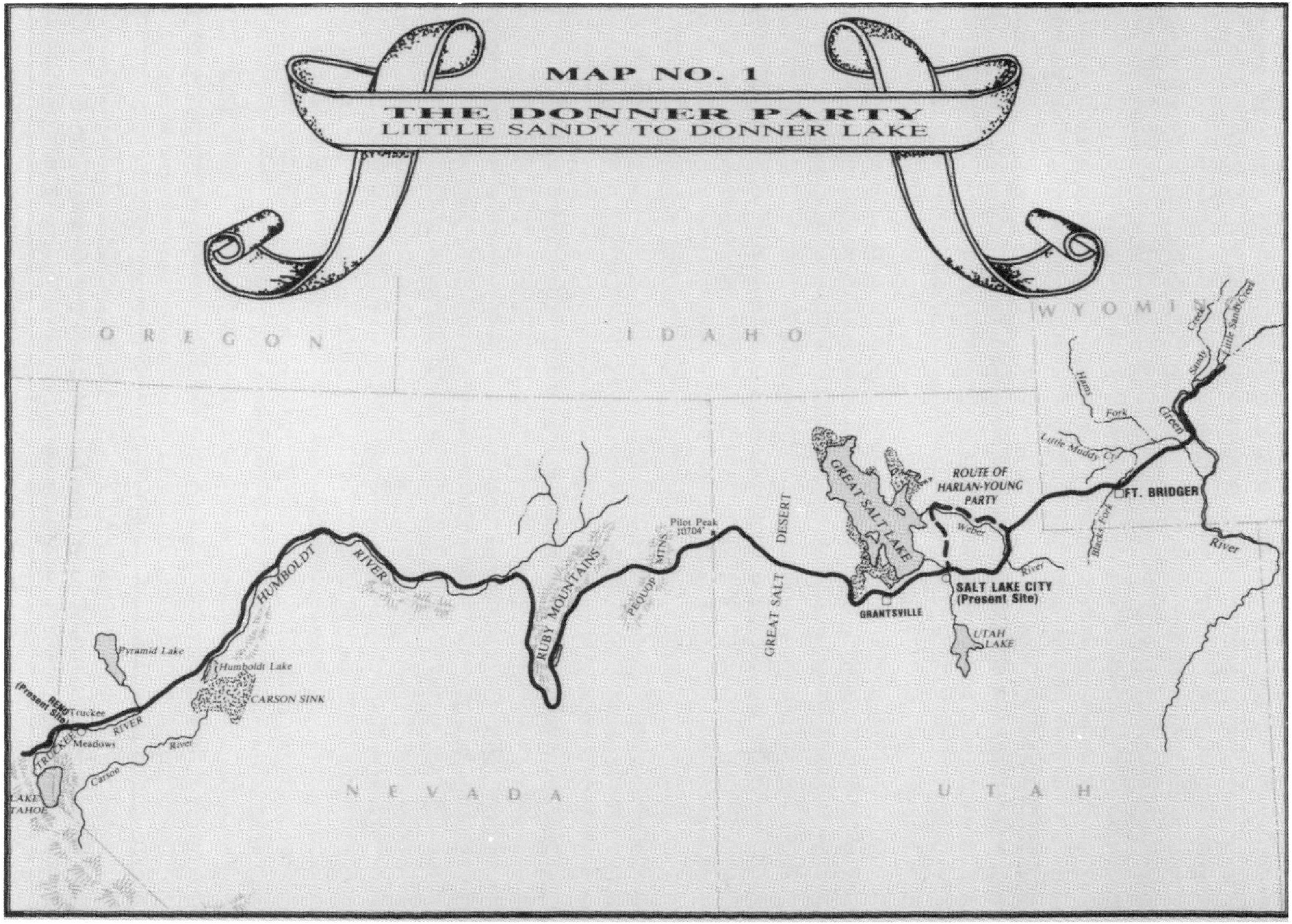
MAP NO. 1
THE DONNER PARTY
LITTLE SANDY TO DONNER LAKE
OREGON
IDAHO
WYOMIN
NEVADA
UTAH
Sandy Creek
Little Sandy Creek
Green
Hams Fork
Little Muddy Cr.
FT. BRIDGER
Blacks Fork
River
ROUTE OF HARLAN-YOUNG PARTY
Weber
River
SALT LAKE CITY (Present Site)
UTAH LAKE
GREAT SALT LAKE
GRANTSVILLE
GREAT SALT DESERT
Pilot Peak 10704'
PEQUOP MTNS
RUBY MOUNTAINS
HUMBOLDT RIVER
Pyramid Lake
Humboldt Lake
CARSON SINK
RENO (Present Site)
Truckee
Meadows
TRUCKEE RIVER
Carson River
LAKE TAHOE

She had lost. No use to make any more protest about the left hand turn. Tamsen's good friend Margaret Reed had had no more luck than she. As a matter of fact none of the women she had heard talking were anxious to try the new Hastings' route; they were for going the safer way through Fort Hall. A cold chill ran through her even while she was standing over the camp fire that night tending the antelope steaks.

Nothing more she could do, unless she did as that other pioneer woman had done, when she saw that the great divide had been reached. Determined, she had turned and started walking back east again. They had tied her to the wagon with a rope. Now that would be a strange item for Allen Francis' Springfield paper: "Mrs. George Donner, former schoolmistress and wife of one of Illinois' wealthiest farmers, was dragged all the way to California." She smiled at her thought, but the smile faded quickly, and she gazed into the coals until the smell of roasting meat aroused her and she turned the steaks. Goodness, look at her hands! She'd have a hard time persuading anyone she wasn't a farmer-woman herself. Her nails were blackened with soot and sun, her arms rough. Lucky she had given in to wearing one of those useful if silly-looking sunbonnets, or her face would be as dark as an Indian's.

Margaret Reed, who had her handy-girl Eliza to help her with the cooking, walked up to the fire.

"Well, it's decided," she said. "We take the nigher way, as James calls it."

Tamsen smiled wanly. "I know."

"Mr. Bryant took that way ... he's already gone. Maybe it won't be as bad as we fear."

"But he isn't dragging a wagon ... and he's in a party of men."

"You are sad, aren't you, Tamsen?"

"I think we're making a mistake."

"But there's a wagon party ahead of us, with Mr. Hastings leading them."

"*Hastings!*" Tamsen's contempt made the name sound evil.

"He'll wait for us at Fort Bridger ...."

"I shall be interested in seeing this man Hastings. I'd like to hear what he has to say for himself, after what Mr. Clyman told us ...."

"Well, we start early tomorrow. Soon you'll find out."

The next morning started as usual, with first light. The trumpet blared and was followed by wake-up calls echoing from wagon to wagon. The corralled cattle were herded out of the camp circle to graze. Fires were struck, pans and pots rattled, smoke rose in blue plumes, babies cried, dogs barked. The smell of frying bacon and side-pork mingled with that of pine trees, onions, sweaty clothes and cow dung. While bacon sizzled, women prepared food to serve at the nooning: left-overs from breakfast, dried fruit and bread to be eaten out of hand. After the early breakfast, the cows were milked, children washed and dressed, usually by their older sisters and brothers, while the mothers nursed their fretful babies, rinsed out diapers and hung them on a line stretched inside the wagon. They cleaned dishes, packed them for the night's meal, and sent children out to play until it was time to go. Now men brought in the oxen to be yoked and chained to the wagon. Women hurried into the trees for a bit of privacy before starting.

Only the single man Luke Halloran was not riding his horse as usual. As they were yoking up, he approached George Donner to ask if he might ride in one of his wagons. For the last weeks, Luke had been poorly, and this morning he could not face riding his horse. Thin and pale, he stood there, his whole body imploring the Donners to take him and his small trunk, his saddle and bridle. He'd been traveling with another wagon and they no longer wanted to carry his trunk and the new way tempted him with its promise of 200 miles of shortened trail.

George Donner looked doubtful. "We've already got Charlie Stanton's effects with us, and a few things Ed Bryant left." Tamsen, looking at this young man, so obviously ill and lonely, interrupted. His hard rasping cough had caught her attention all during the prairie crossing.

"Of course there's room for him, George. We've depleted some of our supplies. We can shift some of the flour barrels now."

"True. He does look miserable," George whispered. "It don't look like he's got much longer, as a matter of fact."

"Poor motherless boy."

"Fetch your things, lad. Mrs. Donner says it will be all right."

With a smile and a "thank you, and God bless you," which sent him into another spasm of coughing, Luke climbed aboard, and Tamsen made him comfortable, bringing him a cup of milk left over from breakfast, and a piece of cold biscuit liberally spread with butter. She hardly looked up when the wagon lurched forward and the wheels started their slow turning and squeaking.

Margaret Reed, sitting in the rear of the lead Reed wagon with her three youngest children, looked for the last time at the wagons going the Fort Hall way. Goodbye, Nancy Thornton! Goodbye Owl Russell, Governor Boggs, goodbye friends ... Rebecca, Abigail, all you good women who've sat knitting comfortably in the Palace car since way back when we had left Independence last May. Goodbye Delia, Annabelle, Faith ... may we meet again! Good luck to you, and good luck to us! This morning, she was not as afraid as she'd been in the weeks before. In spite of fears, she felt hopeful. With James and her children with her, she would go anywhere. James had always been good. Nothing would happen to him. Only a few days ago, Edwin Bryant had gone this way with four friends, a light cart and mules. He was a most intelligent man, Tamsen said. Bryant had been concerned with the slowness of the large party and the lateness of the crossing, and he had chosen to go on unencumbered. Perhaps even so, they could catch up with him from time to time. When Bryant came to bid Tamsen farewell, he warned her to do all she could to keep the train traveling fast. "Winter snows are not to be trifled with, and we are among the last of the emigration this year."

At this moment, Tamsen also was thinking of the young editor from Kentucky. Perhaps she would see him again, that kindly young man, so interested in everything along the way. They might meet at Bridger, if they went fast. She hoped so. He said he'd leave a letter for her there if he had news. Now that there were fewer wagons, their progress would be swifter. Everyone seemed so happy that the decision to take the nearer way had finally been made. Well, Tamsen must be wrong. She must.

"To the right the wheel tracks, scarcely to be called a road, bore away from the Oregon and California over Greenwood's route. To the left was the way to Fort Bridger, leading to the new cut-off south of the Great Salt Lake. With last farewells said, Governor Boggs, Mr. Thornton, and the greater number of the emigrants turned their wagons off to the right, but Mr. Reed, 'Uncle George' Donner and his brother Jake, the 'Dutchmen' and a few others kept to the left. The day was July 20, 1846." *Ordeal by Hunger* by George Stewart, page 7-8

"The Californias were generally much elated, and in fine spirits, with the prospect of a better and nearer road to the country of their destination. Mrs. George Donner was, however, an exception. She was gloomy, sad, and despirited, in view of the fact that her husband and others could think for a moment of leaving the old road and confide in the statement of a man of whom they knew nothing, but was probably some selfish adventurer." *The California Tragedy*, J. Quinn Thornton p. 5

As the big train divided and the smaller group left the main Oregon-California route the women stood with eyes full of tears, blurring the wagons in the early morning air, great lumps of fear and loneliness clogging their throats. They lifted their hands in a farewell wave. "Goodbye! Till we meet again." But the men in the departing southbound wagons yelled triumphantly, "See you later. We'll leave you a note when we reach the Mary's River afore ye! Git on, men, let's roll west!"

The wagon train, compared by one writer to a "giant white caterpillar" had started from Independence, Missouri in the great emigration of 1846. Gold had not been discovered in California, and those who took the westward trail early in May were another kind of adventurer. Many were heading for Oregon and its fertile valleys; as a matter of fact, the trail was usually known as the Oregon Trail. At Fort Hall, roughly located in the southern part of Idaho, the transcontinental route broke off to the south, toward California via the Humboldt River. This was called the California Trail, and was far less traveled in 1846 than the northern route to Oregon. Tales of California's mild climate had filtered back to the states. Also there was an almost unspoken feeling among those who followed the government that the internal troubles in California might result in its acquisition by the United States. Had this influenced the migration?

Most of those in the giant white caterpillar were going for non-political reasons. The climate of Illinois, with its resulting agues and fevers was certainly a factor; reaching out for new horizons most definitely was. Business failures sent many a single man west for a new start. George Donner had had only to advertise for teamsters in the Springfield paper to find young men glad to have a free passage to the land of promise. Most of the emigration before the Gold Rush of 1849 was made up of family groups, women and children going with their men, for whatever reason.

At one time, the party at the Big Sandy numbered more than one hundred wagons. Early in the trek, the travelers realized the enormity of managing such cumbersome groups, and split into smaller companies. The emigration was like a river in flood. Eddies caught some parties while the others rode past them on the crest. Then an illness or death or a birth would slow that group for a time. Single wagons broke down and when repaired, joined other companies; people broke off like debris from flooded banks and bobbed ahead, only to be caught on a snag. However, by the time the people of the '46 emigration had reached the Rockies, the interweaving had stopped and the companies were fairly constant. The party at the Little Sandy this day was close to the end of the migration for the year. Some who had started from Independence at the same time were already in California; some were crossing the barrier of the fearful snowy mountains of California, others were crawling along the Humboldt River. In a letter to the states only a few weeks before, Mrs. George Donner had noted that there were only twenty wagons coming behind.

The first night after they made the turn George Donner was elected Captain. There hadn't been much trouble deciding. Organizing a company was no longer a novelty. Electing a leader ... a man you had met two weeks or two days or two hours before was an act of trust. How did you judge a man, by his height, the wealth of his wagon, or the cut of his jaw? In the past, with no experience to guide them, the emigrants had made frequent errors in choosing captains. You elected a man and the next day he ordered a stop-over because his wife needed to wash her clothes. If you disagreed, you called a meeting to protest. It was like town politics at home, but faster, and men were more impatient when things went wrong. Some men whipped up their animals and went ahead to catch up with friends. But if the choice were a good one, you went at a steady, even pace of between sixteen and twenty miles a day. Now, late in the season, the proclaimed stops for Sunday worship had been abandoned in the interest of speed, and muttered personal prayers had taken the place of an organized service on the Sabbath. The party, veterans now, were used to facing broken equipment, encounters with Indians, rattlesnakes, turned-over wagons, river crossings, even deaths and births. What could possibly happen that they were not already familiar with? They were hardened travelers. What was there for a captain to do except see that the rotation of wagons kept steady, and to call necessary meetings? The people did the deciding, after all.

Known as "the people from Springfield," or the Reed-Donner party, both men had been a part of a decision-making group since they had joined the great train back in May. Was it to be James Reed or George Donner?

Both had prospered. Both were tall and well-built. That George Donner was 62 and had made other trips by wagon ... from North Carolina to Kentucky and from there to Illinois made him a veteran; others added that there was that trip to Texas and back a few years ago, besides. James Frazier Reed was twenty years younger, but he was a man of property, certainly; a town in Illinois was named for him. Look at the maid his wife had brought, and the Palace car and the pony for his daughter Virginia to ride, to say nothing of his mare, Glaucus, the fastest and best bred horse in the train. But there was something biggotty about James Reed. He was short-tempered, curt-proud, you might say, and he'd made enemies. It was a wonder that the German, Keseberg wanted to come with this party, now wasn't it? Easy to see he hadn't forgotten the flare-ups between the two men; his face showed it. Handsome son-of-a-gun, though.

In the end, the election was merely a formality. Since the two men were great friends, it didn't really matter which put his name to the party. It was only right to give the honor of Captain to George Donner ... he being older than James Reed. Jake Donner was ailing ... had been ever since that cold he caught fording a creek back on the Blue.

Although the far less traveled road to Fort Bridger was narrow and poorly marked, it wasn't the bad road some had predicted. For the first few days the twenty wagons traveled along rivers over fairly level ground, the willows along the water marking the way. Grass had not been heavily cropped along the side, so cattle had enough feed. Although it was late in the season, wild flowers that had been in full bloom on the prairies were just beginning to blossom. The artemisia continued, affording them hot, fast fire in the evenings. Strangely, although the days were almost too warm, nights were colder than expected.

The emigrants crossed and recrossed rivers, laughing at the shrunken, shallow courses they would have called "cricks" at home. Why, the water barely wet the wheels of the wagons, and a man wearing boots hardly bothered to find a rocky place to walk across. Game was plentiful; they had their first taste of mountain goat. Antelope, which many preferred over buffalo meat, was fairly easy to obtain if you were quick and like Will Eddy, a dead shot. There wasn't the variety of food they'd had earlier, but there was plenty. Sow-belly, pickled pork, hominy, dried fruit. It was good to be free of that toper, Owl Russell and his speeches. Good to be traveling with a captain so easy-going and not given to making an oration out of every announcement he made.

On the 28th of July, a week and a day after the parting at the Little Sandy, the Don-

ner Party reached Fort Bridger. Expecting a settlement as large as Laramie, they were surprised at seeing only two cabins and a corral. There was a blacksmith shop and supplies for sale: barrels of vile-tasting whiskey for the Indian trade, flour, cornmeal, salt, sugar, some clothing, including Indian moccasins which they bought to augment their worn, broken-down shoes, all at exorbitant prices. Jim Bridger and his partner Vasquez were delighted to see another emigrant train come in ... sixty wagons had left a week or so ago with Hastings on the new road.

The Donner Party was shocked.

Hasting's hadn't waited for them! The message ran through the train, outraging everyone. Tamsen's lips tightened, and George avoided her eyes.

Don't worry folks. Hastings left directions for them to follow. Good time to rest a bit and fix the wagons and repair harness. Feed's good, too. Nice meadow for the cattle ... remember, friends, this is the last bit of civilization you'll see till you get to California. James Reed needed a new yoke of oxen, George Donner was looking for a man to replace Hi Miller who'd gone on with Bryant.

They added another wagon, too. William McCutchen and his wife Amanda and their baby daughter. Since there were already so many Williams, Bills, Billys and Wills in the outfit, they called him Big Mac — he was more than a six-footer. His language wasn't always fit for the ears of the ladies, but he was good-natured and strong. His size would be a help if the going got hard.

Another wait ... this time four days. Women sighed. They were anxious to get the trip over and done with, but it would be good to start clean and the wagons straightened. Out came the wash tubs, board and the soft soap. The bedding was spread to air, provisions reorganized. It was a lovely vacation for the children. They could run as they pleased. Jim Bridger said the Indians around here weren't dangerous ... and when they were ready to go again, the road was smooth all the way, no bad canyons, and plenty of water. The dry drive? Oh, yes ... maybe thirty-five - forty miles. Take maybe a day and a half driving straight through.

MARGARET REED

Margaret Reed had a moment to herself. The Reed wagon was beside the river. The children were playing on a sandy beach. Margaret took her mending and a cushion so she could lean against a tree and watch the water. The gleeful shouts of the children were far away. Behind her, the big Palace car, which James was so proud of, had made it this far, and after hearing the men at Fort Bridger talking, she was sure it would make it the rest of the way. She took out her darning thread and her egg and began on James' socks. For a moment she felt as if she had never left home, but was under the big elm trees back in Illinois. The water made a soft chuckling sound that set her mind adrift, though her fingers moved swiftly on the darning. She knew they should be hurrying on. James was already fretting about each delay, she could tell that by the impatient way he handled things ... his nerves were frazzled. But she, herself? She looked at the trees around the meadow. This was such a pleasant place, so clean after all the dust of the last weeks. She wouldn't mind staying right here ... letting the rest go ahead, make a little home and wait out the winter. She was tired of the call in the morning to chain up, the first creaking of the wheels, the first puffs of dust that grew and grew with every turn of the many wheels. Tomorrow they wouldn't be here ... they would be fifteen more miles down the road, with all the jostling, bumping, shaking ... the supper to fix over a new fire, wood to be chopped, dishes to wash. How lucky she was that deaf Eliza, Baylis's sister had followed them down the pike, carrying a change of clothes and that was about all, begging to go along with them. Eliza had heard there were husbands for the asking in California ... she was twenty-nine already, and she'd never been asked by anyone. Poor thing. She acted more stupid than she probably really was ... it was just that she didn't hear well ... Baylis was her albino brother, not much use in the day time, but a great help at night. Margaret supposed their family was glad to have them both go. Eliza was down by the water having as much fun as the children.

They had enough food to stay here. They could butcher the oxen. The nearby fort had a good supply of flour. It would be cold, but they could make a warm little cabin with a fireplace ... there was plenty of wood for the chopping ... it was a race against time, wasn't it? By next spring, they could start for California early — ahead of next year's emigration ... maybe they wouldn't even want to go farther. Why not stay here?

She was used to making a home wherever she was; she visualized the house they would build ... small at first and plain, but larger as the years passed than the big house in Illinois. They could raise corn in this meadow. They had all their books and furniture. She could teach the children herself. Just so long as she had James and the four children ... you'd never think that Virginia was James' stepchild; he loved her as much as he did his own. Then a thought occurred — if they stayed more than just the winter, where would Virginia find a husband? Not that she wanted to rush things; she herself had married far too young for the first time. Still Virginia was taking notice of young men now ... there was that lad she danced with at the Fourth of July celebration a few weeks ago. She'd seen Virginia crying when his family's wagon kept on toward Oregon. Margaret smiled to herself. Wasn't this just like her? Dreaming of things she couldn't have. James would be more than impatient if she even suggested staying here for the winter.

She finished the socks, rolled them into balls and put them in the basket. It was time to start supper and Eliza'd never think of it without being reminded. The sun was dropping toward the western mountains. She rubbed the darning egg between her fingers. It would be pleasant to remain here until the autumn leaves started to turn, to hear the river rushing past, cold and clear, never to have to move on again. She could wander through the woods, play the organ in the evening. Oh, she missed her home, she needed a place to put down roots ... California was so far away! Would they ever get there?

The children's voices calling to her made her stand, brush the grass off her skirt, "Ma, Ma, where are you?" It was Patty's voice. "Eliza says we have to come back now, do we?"

"Yes, it's time to start supper, children," Margaret called back, and walked to meet them. Virginia was helping Jimmy, Patty was coming slowly with little Tommy. Suddenly a breeze shook at the trees, and she shivered. "Hurry children, let's not catch colds. I hope you aren't sopping wet."

There was plenty of food tonight, and food cooked for tomorrow, too. James would be wanting his supper. She could hear the sound of men chopping wood for the fires. What would tomorrow bring? Margaret sighed. Oh, James, James. You're a good man, a brave man, and I love you, but you're never a quiet, peaceful man ... always ready for a change. And then, her mind went back as it so often did suddenly to her first husband, Virginia's father, Lloyd Backenstoe. If he had lived, would she be here now, on her way to California in the finest wagon ever seen on the prairie? No, she would be back in Illinois, safe and comfortable, with no reason to hear "Chain up, boys" at seven tomorrow morning. Then as suddenly she realized as she saw James riding toward her through the trees, tall, straight and eager, that she would never have known what it was to love as she loved James.

James had news. Bridger said that the short cut they were taking might save them as much as 350 miles, instead of the 200 that Hastings had mentioned. That was about 23-25 days off traveling time.

"What about that dry drive?"

"A day and a half ... before we reach it there will be grass to cut and water to fill the casks ...."

"We're still starting tomorrow?"

"Early. Every wagon is in good shape. These men here at Bridger couldn't be more helpful."

"Then we're not going north to the Fort Hall road? There's a turn, Tamsen says, a few miles down the road."

"And lose all this time we've wasted? Not a chance. We'll reach the trail on Mary's River before the others do."

Margaret saw Virginia smile happily. "And we'll see all our good friends again?"

Patty said, "I know what good friend you're thinking of, Puss. You can't fool me."

TAMSEN

The next morning, the last day of July 1846, the Donner Party left Fort Bridger. As they had on the prairie, the wagons alternated; the leading wagon went to the rear and the others moved up. George Donner was once again in the lead, and there was no hesitation as he took the second left hand turning, although everyone knew his wife Tamsen was still suggesting he take the Fort Hall road. She had spoken with Jim Bridger, asking him how far ahead Bryant and his friends were. "Oh, I don't know for sure ... some time ago."

"He left no word for us?" "No ma'am. Not that I recollect."

Strange, thought Tamsen. Had he forgotten them all? He had said he'd leave messages whenever he could. It wasn't like him to forget.

Now the road changed significantly for the worse. Up and down it went, through ravines, between boulders, back and forth across creeks plugged and matted with vines and brush, along side hills where the wagons looked ready to topple over. The teamsters walked beside the oxen, yelling "Gee" and "Haw" adding colorful adjectives and suggestions. Wagon wheels were locked; logs dragged behind them as they skidded down steep slopes. With all that, they managed to advance about twelve miles a day. They were following a stream that ran west into a canyon so deep that they had to stretch their necks to see the top ridges. After the weeks of being on fairly flat ground, it was frightening to be so deep in the mountains that sounds echoed and reechoed until they became a confused cacophony. When the emigrants finally emerged from that canyon, they found the Red Fork of the Weber River, the one that Hastings said ran into the Great Salt Lake. Down this trail, faintly marked with wheel tracks, they rolled, encouraged now. Four miles ahead, the lead wagons halted. There, impaled on a forked stick was a letter.

Hastings again. This time he wrote that the Weber Canyon ahead was bad; his party had barely made it. They were told to wait, send a man forward to overtake him, and he would return to guide them through.

The party convened, and three men were appointed to go ahead. Reed of course volunteered, and so did little Charlie Stanton, only five feet five tall. Both Pike and McCutchen raised their hands. Pike was chosen. In three hours, the men were mounted and ready to start away on their horses.

This time the site of their camp was uncomfortable. Mountains shut out the sun and made them feel trapped; ravines led nowhere, the river was lined with prickly vines. The cattle seemed uneasy too, for feed was scarce. If there should be an Indian raid, they had no way to escape. They had seen snow on some of the high peaks, in August, imagine that! The early mornings were as cold as autumn at home. Still and all, they must make the best of it. This was only to be a short wait. The men would be back with Hastings tomorrow ... or the day after, for sure.

MARGARET

Margaret Reed asked the ladies to the Palace Car for a mending bee. "There won't be much of a collation," she said, laughing, "because we must all be terribly careful with food, but we can get acquainted with Amanda McCutchen." Most of the women accepted, except for Phillipine Keseberg, whose husband wouldn't let her leave her new baby. Mrs. Wolfinger did come, though, dressed as always in her finery that was becoming a little less imposing as the days went by. She sat with them without talking, occasionally smiling when they did. Poor lonesome thing, not knowing the language, perhaps not even knowing why they had stopped. The talk was mostly of home, of children, of illnesses and the remedies for them, of the bravery of the little Breen boy who had broken his leg. *That* had been a scare, hadn't it? That filthy, dirty man from Fort Bridger who was sent for to amputate. He actually became abusive, if you can imagine that, when the boy begged his mother not to let him saw off his leg. "You'll be damned sorry you didn't, when he'll be screaming harder than he is now with the blood poisoning" the old man had said, walking away in anger. Peggy Breen said, "Well, ladies, I just took things into me own hands and told him to git. And it's glad I am that he's getting well after all. It all comes from prayin' to our blessed holy Mary, mother of God."

"It was a hard choice," Tamsen said.

"Who wants a lad with only one leg? That's what I thought, to tell ye the truth. I put him in God's hands."

"And good hands they are," Lavina Murphy said.

The talk fell to Indians ... what kind they were. Margaret told of the Indian mother and her children who had squatted down outside their fire circle and watched everything she had done — preparing the meal, washing the dishes — all the while picking lice out of her papoose's hair and cracking them between her fingers ... "and eating them!" she added, almost in a whisper.

"Every day seems long and tiresome," Eleanor Eddy said. "August is slipping by, and we haven't gone as far as we should, have we? Will is worried."

"Well, as soon as the men come back, we'll be on our way again. They'll bring Hastings with them."

"What good will Hastings be to us all if he *does* come back?" Tamsen said in a rare explosion of anger. "He's led 66 wagons down a trail he never went down himself! When he comes, if he has the courage to, I've a few questions to ask of him, I can tell you that!"

When, on the fifth day, James rode into camp, Hastings was not with him, nor were the other two men. He was alone.

"Now what has happened?" Tamsen groaned. Where was the elusive Hastings?

James Reed's story was simple, stark in its meaning. Yes, all three men had overtaken Hastings. Stanton and Pike had stayed to rest their worn out animals, while Reed, accompanied by Hastings, started back, Reed on a new horse. Hastings had refused to come all the way back, but he had stood with Reed on a high peak, and pointed out the way they should come, to avoid the dangers of the route he had taken. Reed left him there and rode on alone, blazing trees as he went, following the best he could the way Hastings had indicated. It roughly approximated the Indian trail, which Hastings had taken just lately when he had come east with Jim Clyman. All three of the volunteers had agreed that to take the trail Hastings had just cut with the sixty-six wagons would be disastrous. There were many able-bodied men in the larger group; even so a wagon had slipped off a cliff and been broken to pieces. Double and triple teaming had been necessary.

Reed added, "Hastings' route is extremely dangerous, perhaps impossible. The alternative way will be very hard. Only if we all work together can we make it at all."

When he had finished there was deep silence. Then a burst of indignation came. People talked all at once, and every voice was angry. Hatred of Hastings and his lies, the desperation of their position made the fear erupt. Because it was Reed and the Donners who had urged them to take this new trail, the vituperation was transferred to their leaders. Reed stood composed and silent while they cursed everyone and everything, his face drawn and weary. When a vote was finally taken, the emigrants chose to abandon the narrow canyon and take the course Reed had rudely blazed.

Some of the women wondered privately among themselves whether there wasn't another choice ... to turn back and take the Fort Hall road, late as it was. When they mentioned it to the men, they were met with the irrefutable fact that the season was too late; they could not make it to the California mountains before snow came. And of course there was the time-honored precept "no man, having put his hand to the plough...."

"We've been tricked," men said, again and again. "There's nothing to do but make the best of a bad bargain."

The next morning, ignoring Hastings' whispery trail, they made a third left hand turn, following a creek. The going was slow; they had to break a new road. The next day, after scouts had been sent forward, they did not chain up at all, but worked all day clearing a path through briars and boulders.

Reaching the top of a divide, they saw nothing but mountains and more mountains ahead. The downhill drive was harder on the wagons than the climbing had been. They reached what Hastings had called Bossman Creek. Named Beauchemin, the irony of its name was not lost. The beau chemin was nothing but a tortured, intertwined impermeable knot of willows, aspen and alders stitched together by the wild rose and service berries.

Here the party camped, day after day, while the men who were able to work went forward to cut a path. This was the third protracted halt since they had left the main Oregon Trail, and by far the most dismal. Children had nowhere to play. To keep them busy, mothers sent them out to gather the mountain berries which were growing everywhere, and would add a fresh touch to the side pork and bean diet. Deeply frightened, now that any semblance of civilization was gone, frantic with the passage of time and the consumption of food during days when no progress was made, the women became irritable. The men called this Mad Women's camp, and laughed among themselves, only to break their own tension. Provident women began to use any food they found such as wild greens, berries, even rose hips as a supplement to the monotonous diet, and to conserve rigidly the provisions for the long drive into California.

There were not enough strong men for the heavy work of breaking trail. Hardcoop, Jake and George were too old for the constant lifting and cutting. Patrick Breen sent his older boys but sometimes refused to work himself, saying he had the gravels again. Luke Halloran was far too ill now to leave the Donner wagon. He seemed to get more transparent every day. Stanton and Pike had not returned and two men had been sent out to find them. This brought the work crew to about 22 able-bodied workers. When rest per-

iods, injuries and blistered hands too sore to use were taken into account, only twenty men were working at one time. The axe work went on slowly; there was little talk, much grumbling and no merriment. Discouragement hung like a miasma over them all, men, women, children; frayed nerves led to quarrelling.

Pat Dolan, cheerful Irishman that he was, Will Eddy and James Reed fought to keep the men going. Dolan sang his merry songs, trying to bring a rhythm to the labor. Keseberg scorned the work as being beneath him; this angered the teamsters, who had been hired to drive oxen, not to build roads.

Worries and fears swarmed about them like gnats, small irritations grew into angry scuffles which ended in black looks and vituperation when the men were finally pulled apart. There wasn't a man who didn't wish he were on the Oregon Trail, hardly a woman who didn't wish herself back in Missouri, or Illinois or Kentucky, far from the mess they found themselves in. Only the nursing babies seemed contented. So far there were milk and warmth and encircling arms.

TAMSEN

At the enforced camp, Tamsen did her best to keep up her spirits. After she had taken care of poor Luke, she gathered up as many of the children as she could and took them berrying, meanwhile pointing out flowers and plants she knew, asking them to guess about others. It was hard to keep their attention, for the older children had absorbed the fears that hung over the group.

On the third day of their encampment the boredom ended suddenly. Echoing down the canyon behind them were the sounds of moving wagons and men's voices. Around a bend came three wagons. "Halloo! Hey! There they are! We've found 'em."

A greying man drove the lead wagon. The woman beside him, a babe in her arms, waved. Tousled heads appeared behind her. Dogs barked, cattle slowed. The other wagons were driven by two younger men. Walking at the side of the group, leading a youngster by the hand, was one of the most beautiful women Tamsen had seen on the trail.

"Halloa, there. This the Reed-Donner party?"

Tamsen said, "Indeed it is."

"Franklin Graves is the name. This is my family. We're hoping you'll let us join up."

Tamsen thought to herself, "What would you do if we didn't? Go back to the Little Sandy?" But she said only, "Of course we will. Most of the men are ahead breaking trail. I may as well tell you now we've had bad luck ever since we left Fort Bridger."

"We heard about you from Jim Bridger. He said about 20 wagons come down this way all alone. We're 'bout the last of the emigrants this year, and we decided to foller you." He turned to his wife, the one holding the baby. She was old to be having a baby herself, maybe it belonged to one of the other women who climbed out of the wagons. "Elizabeth, ain't it good to be with other folks again?" The woman smiled, and Tamsen said, "I'm Mrs. George Donner."

Mrs. Graves said, "Let me make you acquainted. These here are my family, Sarah Fosdick, her new husband, Jay, he's the one with the second wagon. Mary, Billy, Eleanor, 'Vina, Nancy, Johnnie, Frank, Jr. and the baby."

"Ma, don't forget to make her acquainted with John Snyder," Sarah indicating the handsome man they had first noticed. Fosdick said, "He's the one drivin' Pa's wagon." John lifted his hat politely and asked, "What're you people doing stalled here like this?"

George and his brother Jacob, now joined the group. "Well, Mr. Graves, you might say we've been tricked by everyone who told us about this short-cut. Jim Bridger had no business tellin' you to come this way. Hastings never came this way himself."

Little by little, with everyone contributing a share, angry, discouraged or resigned, the story came out. "The men is hacking away at the damnedest bunch of brush you ever did see. They'll be back about dark. They'll be purely glad to see four more men to help 'em. They've been axing out a trail for three days now, hardly a mile a day."

Some of the party had met the Graves family earlier on the Oregon Trail, and all had heard of the narrow escape Mary Graves had had when an Indian brave had tried to kidnap her. When they had settled their three wagons with the rest, someone mentioned the incident, and immediately all the children wanted to know more. They had never met anyone who had really truly been taken by Indians, though stories around the camp fire were full of such things. The children begged her to tell them all about it.

"Were you scared?"

"I should say so," Mary said, laughing. Women drew near. Mary was indeed a beautiful girl. Long heavy dark hair, black sparkling eyes and a full mouth that seemed ready to smile at the least opportunity, tall and slender, she moved as if she were hearing music.

"Did they shoot you with bows and arrows? What did they say to you? Were you scalped?"

"Does it look like I'd been scalped?" she teased.

"How'd you get away?"

"My brother Billy ... see that fellow over there? He and my Pa saved me. They were going to shoot, but they were afraid they'd hit me. When the Indians saw Billy's gun, they left me and took off ...."

The attention of the little boys was immediately transferred to Billy, a man of 18. He was an instant hero. Virginia Reed looked at him. "My, he's handsome too, isn't he?"

Many of the women who had come up to meet the new famly were wishing they could ask questions as the children were doing. The kind of questions that meant a great deal to women. How long had the Indians had Mary? Had any ... harm ... come to her? Had she ...."

Peggy Breen, rough as the bark of a tree, spoke for them all. "You wasn't after being harmed in any way, was you?"

Mary looked at her kindly. Her expression said that she knew what they were thinking, and she didn't blame them for asking. "No. I was rescued in time. Nothing happened."

Virginia said, "Well, that's good. Grandma used to tell us stories about the Indians back east and some of them ...."

"Hush, Virigina. That's enough." Mary smiled, and at that Tamsen said quietly, "Now you youngsters start gathering some berries for these people and make them welcome."

The boys followed Billy Graves around the camp all the rest of the day, worship in their eyes.

That night, the Graves family built a big fire after supper and asked everyone to join them. The singing started ... the first singing they'd had for weeks. Something about the addition of the Graves family had made them forget their weariness and aching bones and blistered hands. Curiosity brought them out too, to sing some of the old songs, to look at new faces (especially that pretty Mary Graves). Pat Dolan, tired as he was from the hours of chopping, began joking and telling stories in his Irish brogue, and the whole encampment was laughing before he was finished. Old Patrick Breen, who had been sulking and complaining about his health brought out his fiddle and began to play. The Graves family made coffee for everyone, and Mary Graves passed it around, smiling as she poured it into their tin cups. Then the handsome teamster, John Snyder, grabbed her by the waist and whirled her around to the music. The rumor was that they were engaged and were going to be married as soon as they reached California. The sight of such a handsome pair, in love, dancing, brought a memory of tenderness that covered over, for one evening at least, some of the hurt of the last desperate weeks.

"Let's give a whoop and a holler for the Graves family!" someone yelled, and Pat Dolan added, "And for bringin' us the purtiest girl we've seen!"

Mary, rosy from her spin with John, chose her brother Billy for a whirl, and suddenly everyone wanted to join the dancers. Eleanor Eddy put her baby down in someone's lap and spun around with Will. Leanna Donner and one of the Breen boys joined. The men without partners stood clapping to the rhythm. Eliza Williams grabbed Milt Elliott and away they went, Milt's face as red as his bandana, for he knew he was in for a kidding from the men. Twelve year old Virginia Reed was chosen by Pat Dolan. Around and around they all went, half intoxicated with the fiddling and singing and the yelling for a do-si-do. By the time Pat Breen, exhausted, put down his fiddle, Mary's hair was falling down around her shoulders. For the first time since Reed had returned from his trip to find Hastings, they were a warm group again, though Louis Keseberg and his wife stood apart. He scowled when his little daughter clapped her hands in glee. From the Donner wagon, Luke Halloran peered out, pale but smiling. He feebly called for another tune.

"Even Luke feels better tonight!" Virginia said. "Three cheers for Luke!"

Luke waved once more, and broke into a hard dry cough.

"It's done us good to have new blood," George Donner said to his wife that night. Perhaps better times will come, now we have four more men to cut trail. That Mary Graves is a pretty girl."

"You keep your eyes to yourself, George Donner," Tamsen teased.

If Mary had made George feel young again, it was a good sign. George wasn't George when he was heart-heavy.

"Now, you bitty little woman, don't you worry. She's no older'n my daughters."

"And neither am I, don't forget."

"You needn't be jealous of old Uncle George."

"Uncle George is a young man again tonight ... and it's good to see a smile on his old whiskered face." Tamsen herself felt cheerful. Something had brought people together again. Perhaps all the dissention would cease.

I, MARGARET

I was afraid of the tension that had been building up in James ever since his return from the meeting with Hastings. He drove the men unmercifully to build the road. He tried to soothe them and held in his tongue patiently, at least on the surface. Grumbling, complaining and the fear of slow progress were constant worries. If he slept in the wagon, he tossed all night, keeping us all awake. After Patty said something about this, he started sleeping outdoors under the wagon with the men. No matter how early we rose, and we were up by first light, he was pacing, hurrying the men with their breakfasts, pushing them and himself as hard as he could. I knew how anxious he had become at the long delay, but the men didn't like the way he ordered them around. I tried to talk with him. "Who's going to order them if I don't?"

I didn't know. George Donner was his sweet genial self, completely unable to be severe with anyone. I thought how wonderful it would be if we could combine George's amiability with James' leadership.

I knew him so well. Inside he was churning with impatience and frustration, boiling inside like some of the springs we'd seen. And he was blaming himself. He had urged this short-cut. I wondered how I could drain off this boil that was about to burst.

"James," I said one morning, "I want to ask you ...."

He pulled away impatiently. "There's no time to talk, Margaret, After I get home tonight ...."

"Please ... only a moment ...."

He looked at me, and his eyes changed as he suddenly saw me, really saw me as a person. "Forgive me, honey. I guess I can't stop for a second. I'm going crazy, maybe with worry about how to get us out of this mess."

"What can I do?"

That opened up a flood. "I can't get the men to stop quarreling among themselves, I can't get them to work hard. I try. They seem to hate me. They don't hate George the way they hate me. George won't put pressure on them, he suggests instead of ordering. He's a good man, Margaret, too damned good. He ought to bull-whip some of the men into working. These weeks we've been spending whacking a road through wilderness are making our chances mighty slim to get through in time. Why do the men resent it when I tell them what there is ahead of them? When we get through these mountains, there's a desert to cross. George smiles and says 'We'll make it through, Jim, don't worry so much.' Tamsen has more sense. She knows. She wishes ...."

He stopped. "I can't get people to believe me. I've been across this batch of mountains, and I know what is ahead. George shouldn't be so easy-going."

"What did Tamsen wish?"

"I shouldn't have mentioned that ...."

"I can be silent."

"Of course you can, my dear. I forget to trust you as I should. I've protected you so long that I had no idea of your strength. You've never complained, or blamed me .... Well, Tamsen wished that I'd been elected leader instead of George. She thought that George was too easy on the men ... then she felt sorry she'd criticized him. I said I couldn't hurt a man as fine as George. After all, I think perhaps I was the one who persuaded him to come, though he was as eager as I in some ways ... but at his age ... I don't think people would stand for me to be leader, anyway. And without an election and some sort of a fight which would divide us even more, I haven't any real authority. You can't let people treat a leader as a friend as George is to everyone. He never speaks up. To lead one must make enemies. George can't do that."

"Can't you get a group together and make people see what a chance they're taking?"

"Maybe, Margaret. Will Eddy understands ... he'd be a good leader, and people would accept him better than they do me. I'm bossy, I'm too rich, I have the biggest wagon, the most men working for me. They don't like my clothes, they don't like Virgina's pony nor my mare Glaucus. I have their hate without having got their respect first, that's the whole of it."

I said, "I think you worry too much, James ...."

He almost broke down. "I'm afraid. I pray every night we'll make it through." He had tears in his eyes and he was struggling to keep his face from shattering. "I shouldn't frighten you this way, my darling ...."

With my new strength firm and strong inside me, I answered, "James, you must lean on me a little, as I've leaned on you all these years. I'm no invalid any more. I'm not a child ... I don't even get my old headaches ...."

He put his arms around me in a new way, almost as if I were as strong as he. "I know you're no child, my beloved. You've become my strength." He kissed me hard, and then slowly pushed me away. "And that means, build roads as fast as we can. Time's my worse enemy. Time ... time ...."

I felt very proud. James had always consulted me and told me what he planned to do, and asked my opinion, but usually did just what he'd wanted to do in the first place. For a strong, lovely moment, I felt as if we were truly married, truly partners. "Try not to keep all your hurts inside, James. Lean on me a little."

The trail breaking continued. The jolly welcome to the Graves family, with John Snyder, Jay Fosdick, young Billy and Franklin himself, at 57 strong and able to work, put heart in them for a few days. They cut a tortuous path, barely wide enough for the wagons, and because of the overhanging trees, too low. Some of the osnaburg tops were ripped, one almost pulled off. Reed's wagon tipped over; luckily, it wasn't the Palace car. No one was hurt, and as soon as things were put to rights again, they lumbered on. By the 20th of August they had hauled, jerked and double-teamed the wagons to a new summit.

What a sight! There lay the lake they had read so much about in Hastings' book, with what seemed only a few small mountains between. With reckless haste, they pushed on down toward the water, wheels locked. At the bottom a great yell of delight rang out. Good old Charlie Stanton and Will Pike had been found. The two volunteers had become lost, had run out of food and were about to slaughter their horses when the searchers found them.

The joy did not last long.

Stanton reported that there was still a far round-about way to go; they must take yet another left hand turn and cross another steep watershed.

It was too much. Unable to weep as the women did, the men cursed. Reed was blamed once again. What was the matter with the fool? Couldn't he even follow his own blazed trail?

The women clustered together, some of them wiping tears from their eyes with their dusty aprons, wide-eyed children beside them, reflecting their fears but not quite understanding.

Margaret and Tamsen moved among them as if they wished they were invisible. Tamsen said quietly to a group, "I'm sure it will be all right."

"Mrs. Donner, you may as well let us be," one of them replied. "We're tired of promises and your cheerful face. Margaret Reed, you git and let us have our cry."

"It ain't your fault that your husbands ain't got a speck of sense in their heads," one remarked, trying to be kind.

Tamsen's face pulled in sternly, and she walked away. Margaret ran to her wagon to hide her tears. Patty followed. "Don't you worry, Ma. They'll feel different in the morning."

That night Tamsen sat a long time in front of the dying camp fire, looking into the coals, until a feeble groan from Luke brought her to her feet. She was glad to have something to busy herself with. It didn't look as if Luke would make it to the far-away place he'd been promised would cure him.

MARY GRAVES

That day, Mary Graves was late coming into the camp. She wanted to wait till the dust died down. She made a game of picking berries with the children who were as usual walking with her. Shouts and cheers ended the game. Now what had happened?

From above, she saw the party grouped around strangers, and guessed who they were just as Patty Reed yelled "There's Uncle Charlie and Uncle Will. They found them! Hip, Hip, Hooray!" She ran down the hill as fast as she could.

Two bedraggled men, one short, one tall, were the center of a group of men. The smaller must be the Stanton she'd heard so much about since she joined the train. Well. Heroes come in all sizes, don't they? Imagine a man that size and everyone praising him. He didn't look much bigger than her little sister Nancy. By the time she reached the bottom of the hill, there were no more cheers. People's faces were dark and closed. There must be more bad news. Except for that one first night when they arrived there'd been nothing but worry, worry, worry, all day and night. Even her John Snyder wasn't as happy-go-lucky as he used to be on the prairie, where there wasn't this kind of back-breaking work.

Sure enough, when she joined her family, Ma said that the lost men had brought bad news. Someways, they'd all missed the trail Hastings had pointed out to James Reed. The last ten days' work was about to start up all over again, just when they thought everything was going fine. "Pa's purely discouraged, and he's not been at it as long as the rest, at that," Ma said. "They's plenty of grumblin' and cussin' from the men and the women folks are all broke up, crying and puttin' their aprons over their heads like a bunch at an Irish wake."

Mary handed her the berries she'd picked and walked slowly back to the group of men. She stayed a discreet distance away. Men were down at the mouth, for sure. One of the teamsters said in a loud voice, "Well, if we didn't join up with one of the orneriest bunch of donkeys anywheres around I'd like to know."

"I'd just as soon sit right down here and starve than go cuttin' brush again. Thought we'd be in California long afore this. Hirin' out to a party with no more sense than a passel of sheep."

"I'll be double-danged if I'll work like I been workin'. Let 'em cut they own way out of these here mountains. They got us into 'em."

"We'd do better walkin' and carrying a fry-pan. What'd they do if all us bullwhackers took off I wonder?"

"I'm damned tired of usin' an axe. Looka them hands, covered with cuts and blisters!"

Poor fellow. Mary knew their hands were sore. She would fetch some of Ma's medicine, later on. Now they had to get their anger out and say their say.

The returned men were eating some of Tamsen's bread and butter while the talk continued. James Reed was talking to that little man Stanton. His face was a study, for sure.

Some of the teamsters were sittin' on the ground, saying they'd never get up again. Her John and that Milt Elliot that always looked at her so sheepish-like were standing to the side, watching. What kind of a group had the Graveses met up with, Mary wondered? Back on the prairie there had been quarrels, knives had been drawn and threats made, but there wasn't this discouragement, this black down-hearted feeling; there had always been someone to bring them around before things got bad. These men looked like the animals she'd seen caught in a trap; their voices even sounded like the snarls of foxes when the dogs had 'em. They had had just too much.

Then, to her surprise, that bitty little man Stanton started to speak.

"Wait a minute men, before you start trouble you can't stop."

"Hell, we've had trouble enough for six million," a teamster shouted. "All you give us is talk, talk, talk and wait a minute."

Stanton raised his arm. The giant man they called Big Mac shouted, "You Mars of malcontent, you parlous boy!, stop your blatherin' and listen to the man."

"Let him have his say," John Snyder said.

"It better be some say."

"Afterwards we can all have our say-so. None of us likes this trouble we're in," Stanton continued in a quiet voice that carried well even among the muttering men. "If we aren't all to die here, we've got to go back or go ahead. It's that easy. We have got to get out of this canyon somehow. It leads nowhere and you just talk to Pike about that if you don't believe me. Now what we made note of as we came is this: we've got to chop our way down this stream a little farther, bad as it is. No way to go over that ridge just here. When we do get over it, which looks to be about six miles downstream, there's a meadow which leads down to another stream, and that canyon's the last before we reach the lake."

A man groaned. "We can't do it. There's no way."

"By the great horned spoon we damned well can make it and we will," yelled Big Mac.

"All right, men. Talk it over. Talk all you want. Get everything out of your systems. We'll have a vote when you're done. But just to make it clear, the Reeds, the Donners, the McCutchens, the Eddys and any or all that want to follow along and take the chances we do, can prepare to start tomorrow morning after we've had our meal."

Mary heard her father call out, "You can include the Graveses in them that's goin' with you."

The Murphy clan, their spokesman good looking Will Foster, agreed. "Count us in. I guess me and my brother-in-law can hold an axe a couple of days more."

The German, Keseberg, standing off by a tree, looked more beaten than any of them. It must be hard for him to understand everything, Mary thought. He shrugged. "Is not goot. Nodding is goot."

Big Mac shouted in his great voice, "Moving is better'n sittin' here waitin' for the wolves to close in on us, you Phrygian Turk!"

Mary listened to the arguments that flew back and forth, but she was watching Charlie Stanton. He looked as tired as any of them, certainly dirtier. After all, he'd been lost in the wilderness of thickets and vines. His clothes were torn, his sleeve half off his shoulder, his face grimy. How had such a man influenced them at all? He just seemed to carry an air with him, of trust, of honesty, of endurance. He had large brown eyes and a handsome profile. On a big man they would have made any girl look twice. He was down off the stump now, and walking to the outside of the circle where she still stood, half-hidden. As he came closer, she could not take her eyes off his; there were strange depths in them of loyalty, of caring, like the eyes of a trusting animal.

He did not look past her; he stopped. "Ma'am, you must be one of the family that joined while I was away."

"I'm Mary Graves," she said simply.

"Charlie Stanton's the name." That was all. But he stood looking at her. What was he thinking, she wondered? His eyes had lost their distant look.

OVER THE TOP

Five more days of trail-making followed. Men worked automatically, without much talking. Those who worked did not grumble ... they hadn't the energy it took. "It's root, hog, or die. I hope it ain't gonna be die." There were those who were too tired to move; some took days off to heal blisters, and to let Mary Graves bring them her mother's remedy. Some could not forget anger. Was it God's fault, Reed's fault or just plain ornery bad luck? Arguing and swearing, they shirked work and made trouble for those who didn't. Most of the men worked for two, not sparing themselves. Discouraged as they were, their women made hot meals for them on their return, rubbed their backs, tended their cuts, and washed the flesh torn by briars.

Afterwards, as they tried to sleep, women worried about the food that was disappearing with such huge appetites.

The wagons reached the divide at last, and on the sixth day they reached the second meadow. This led to a canyon, the canyon emptied into a plain, Stanton said. Scouts went forward to report that another vine-tangled thicket through a narrow pass was ahead; other scouts were sent across the creek where a spiky arete loomed.

None of them had heart or strength for another week of brush-cutting. They gazed across the creek and lifted their eyes to the cliff; they peered downstream into the darkness of the narrow canyon. If they chanced the cliff, oxen would be doing some of the work; if they hacked on downstream, they would have to do it all. A vote was taken. "Let's try the cliff. Cross the creek, take our chances, we've had enough of this busting our gizzards. Up and over and one day's hard work will end it all!" It was a crazy choice, but by now, it seemed time for a gamble.

The next morning they chained up. It was a hard day, and as dangerous as any they ever had. But at least there was no brush-clearing.

To the other side of the stream they went, double-teaming the wagons to haul them up the steep slippery rocks. No one who could possibly walk was to ride. Women gathered their children and prepared to climb after the wagons if they made it.

Teamsters threw ropes up, fastened them to trees above, and with men on the downside of the wagons, steadied them in the most dangerous places. Wagon tops were removed and the bodies taken across, then the tops, by ropes. There were 23 wagons now, and more men. Because no one wanted to be left behind, there was also almost total cooperation, every man out to do his best.

The women and children were bunched under trees half-way up the slope, where they had a wide view. As each wagon was eased and pulled and steadied to the top, some women closed their eyes, praying, some watched with a hypnotized gaze and all clutched the hands of their children. Everything they had was balanced in the wagons.

The hulking Palace car was one of the first to reach the top, for the men felt that if it could make it up, they all could. Margaret Reed, Tommy on one side and Jimmy on the other, held fast and watched the heavy wagon roll ahead, shudder, heard the shouts as men ran to steady it. It recovered and rocked on up, and finally, with the ropes holding taut, men yelling, oxen grunting and pulling, crawled to the top like some huge white beast.

Patty screamed, "Hip, hip, hooray!" and Margaret took a deep breath. "Your Papa got over all right. Now we can start climbing ourselves, but keep out of the way of the wagons." Dogs were everywhere, but the loose cattle, herded by the younger boys, were munching on the meadow grass, unaware of any crisis. Margaret picked up Tommie, and told Jimmy to stay with Patty and Eliza.

Up and over went a second wagon, and another mother let out a breath and whispered, "Thank God!"

Waiting women watched and nodded as others passed, almost afraid to talk for fear it would break the luck. A child yelled, "There goes Pa, up the side. Ma! We made it!" Another woman picked up her babe and started the climb.

A long, long day. Tamsen, following with her three smallest girls, saw George's and then Jacob's wagons begin the climb. "You girls must pray hard and help Papa out. That's about all we can do, pray." Her shoulders were straight and eyes as clear and as calm as she could make them. "The good Lord helps those who help themselves."

Patty Reed, who was just passing by, said, "Well, He surely ought to help us. We've been helping ourselves for a long, long time."

Virginia suggested, "Ma, couldn't I take the little kids, one at a time, and let them ride behind me on Billy?"

"Do you think you ought to try that?"

"Pa said I could. He knows Billy is sure-footed. Come on, Ma, let me take Tommie. He's heavy to carry. Aunt Tamsen, I'll come back for your little Eliza."

"We'll see," Tamsen said. "You may not want to take another climb."

"I'm not afraid, Auntie Tamsen. Nothing's going to happen to me!" Margaret and Tamsen looked at each other. The confidence of the young! their glances said.

"If the wagons make it, Virginia can, I guess." Margaret Reed fastened Tommy tightly in front of Virginia with a sash. "I'm not sure I could carry him all the way ...."

Mary Graves passed, herding her little sisters and brothers as usual. "Sarah, you help Ma ... she's got the baby. I'll see to the rest." Sally Foster, her son by the hand, started on with her sister Harriet carrying her baby. Naomi was toddling along with her grandmother. Eleanor Eddy, her son by her side, carried her little girl, followed by Phillipine Keseberg, white-faced and eyes wide with fear, with her two. She cradled her newborn in her arms and the man from Belgium, Old Hardcoop, walked with her, back bent. Mrs. Wolfinger climbed alone, her once fine dress torn at the waist.

Although they worried as much as the men, women were not so tired. During those weeks of hard labor there were times when they would have welcomed work if it would get them there sooner. Shut up in the narrow canyons with each other, talking, cooking, washing, waiting, they had nothing else to do but watch how the food was disappearing. The eggs were all gone from the cornmeal barrel, the pounds of flour and potatoes were diminished. Some dried fruit remained, but women saved them for special days. Sea biscuits they had brought had begun to have weevils; earlier on the march these would have been discarded. Not now.

Waiting for the men to return from the day's trail-breaking, they would say sometimes how hard it was to be a woman. Most were puzzled and ignorant of how they had come to this desperate situation. Each morning they woke, having no idea of what the day held for them until their husbands or fathers told them. Most of them accepted what had happened as the way the world was when you cast your lot with a man bent on wandering, determined to move over this endless expanse of country to a place they could only dimly imagine: a place of sunshine and flowers and warmth and no illnesses, where they would build another home. They were resigned, as men were not, who had never had to learn to be resigned. That did not mean there were no rats of doubt and fear gnawing at them every step of the way. They herded their children, sustaining them as they could, following the men they had promised to love, honor and obey. Any questions they had of their men were made in private; no woman would be so bold as to question her husband's decision in public. This was the way of life, the way their mothers had done before them. They had no choice but to forsake all others and go where their men led.

TAMSEN

On the way up, Tamsen said more to herself than to the girls, "I feel like one of the oxen. They go on, lie down and die alone. No one asks them if they like it or not."

"Nobody asks us children either," Patty said quietly. "But we don't worry like the mamas do."

As if she hadn't heard Patty, Tamsen exclaimed, "Look, girls! There's a little flower here, growing on the ledge! A pretty flower, clinging to a bit of earth on this stony place, right over that terrible drop! I want you to notice it."

Patty said, practically, "It has a root to hold it there."

"You remember that, Patty. You're a very grown-up little girl. What would any of us do without a root, I wonder?" There was a lesson in reasoning that she would jot down in her notebook later on.

It was not until they all reached the top and saw the gentle slope leading down, with no mountains between them and the lake they had spied earlier that they realized that at last they had crossed the mountains. It was August 27. They had taken the left turning July 20, more than a month ago. Some estimated that in those 38 days they had gone 36 miles. If it weren't for the haunting fear of passing time ... time they had wasted so lavishly in the springtime trek across the plains, they could rest here, build up the tired animals, work on the wagons that had almost been shaken to pieces by the crude trail, and perhaps think things over ... maybe even smooth out the hard feelings that always seemed to sprout up when the going was hard.

TAMSEN

Tamsen sat that evening looking through her diary, counting the days they had stopped here and there on the trail ... sometimes for no more reason than women needed to wash clothes, or that someone had a fever, or had died — for broken equipment, for strayed cattle, sometimes just for a whim. The place was pretty or the water good, the feed plentiful. Rest days were far too many. No one had any idea what the cost would be. She remembered a sense of inner disdain she herself had when she'd seen people start out early on a morning when she was of a mind to explore the area a little more. "Do they think California is going to run away from them?" she had commented once as she saw a party roll at dawn. Mr. Bryant had been right ... he had noticed their slow pace as early as May. Nineteen, twenty, twenty-one went the relentless count. Oh, if they had those days back again! Even a week ... a little inconsequential week, that they had squandered here or there because it had been such a joyous, simple excursion, a "second honey moon," "an outing that the children will never forget!" Oh, George, George, where have you brought us? What is to become of us now? One of the flowers she had pressed from that lovely place, the camp by Fort Bridger, fell from between the pages, and she picked it up gently and replaced it.

MARGARET

The Salt Lake valley at last! James had told Margaret how easy the trail was there, almost as level as the prairie had been, and it was. The men of the party were agreed once again on one thing: keep on moving. When they came upon the trail left by Hastings and the 66 wagons, it was suddenly as if they were on a fair pike at home. In that first day of liberation after they left the Wahsatch mountains behind, they rolled more miles than they had in the whole of the ten days before. Tired as they were, elation shone in all faces. Of course, they all reminded themselves, there was that dry drive ahead; they must not forget that. But nothing could be as bad as the last days had been.

This land also looked as if a family might make a living from it. Again Margaret started putting down little roots in her mind, hoping to stop this hurry and wait out the winter here. It wasn't the lush land of Illinois, but it was tillable, James said. They could make it through the winter if they slaughtered some of the animals. But what about the others?

Margaret was frightened by the thought of a dry drive, and after that a long half-desert. There ... there, by that boulder, they could build some sort of home against the cold that was coming. There was snow on the peaks behind her, and in the mornings the air was as sharp as if it were already winter. Salt Lake was little more than half the way ... four months to go half-way. Four more months would be September, October, November, December. Of course it couldn't take that long, James wouldn't allow it.

After the repair to their wagon, they came into camp late that night. James' axle had broken — wood was hard to find. The Donners were later, having stopped on the trail while that young man, Luke Halloran died. The camp was silent.

VIRGINIA

Virginia was out and about the wagons, talking, finding out what had happened. Luke had been a hero to her, his illness romantic and sad. It seemed mystical to her that he was to be buried by the very same black rock where Papa had met Hastings so many weeks ago. She tried to remember things she had said to Luke when she took him food Ma and Eliza had cooked for him. His eyes had looked so hungry. She wondered where he was now, and tried to imagine what heaven was like. She felt a strange bitter-sweet sadness. It lacked the reality that Grandma's death had for her. Poor man, far away from home and friends! She sat in the open bow of the Reed wagon until late, thinking of death, watching the clear stars.

They buried him the next day, right beside a man who had died in the Hastings party. Luke was a Mason, just like her Pa, and he left all he had to the Donners to repay them for their loving care. Only a trunk, his horse, saddle and bridle. Virginia wondered if he had a sweetheart back home. If he did, perhaps she should write a letter and tell her about Luke. Aunt Tamsen would surely write to his mother. Virginia lived in a strange romantic dream.

In the trunk were his Mason emblems, and underneath his clothes, a lot of money. $1500, Uncle George told Pa. Who would have thought that lonesome man had so much money? Virginia wondered if he were the long-lost son of a wealthy man. How sad. Poor Luke Halloran. They day after they buried him, she made Billy walk slowly in his honor.

After a few days, Luke Halloran faded in her thoughts. It still was strange he was not with them, that Aunt Tamsen didn't have to hush them when they talked too loudly, that he wasn't lying on the bed Auntie had made for him, feebly raising his hand to wave when she went by on Billy.

There began to be new things to think about. The Twenty Wells where pools were everywhere. None lowered when you drank, none spilled over if you didn't. They were so deep that a seventy foot rope wouldn't reach bottom. The next day, a pretty stream so salty it burned your mouth for hours when you tasted it. And a sort of desert place, and then another meadow. Oh, it was good to be out in the open again! All the awful waiting in that dark canyon! Even Billy felt released ... he could gallop as fast and far as she dared go. Now everything was go, go, go! The mothers weren't so cross and the fathers not so tired and angry. For once they stopped blaming her Pa and Uncle George for their troubles. She knew it wasn't their fault, really, but it hurt her when the men made awful remarks. Patty talked back and scolded them, but she herself was too old to talk back as Patty did. Patty was forgiven everything because she was just a child, Mama said. Virginia wondered if Mama heard all the nasty things men said about the family. If she did, she'd get another one of her headaches again for sure. Come to think of it, Mama hadn't had a headache for a long time now ... funny she hadn't noticed before this.

How long had it been? Let's see ... had Mama had headaches and not mentioned them?

For the life of her, she couldn't remember any since they left Fort Laramie.

There had been so many things happening every day, new things ... not like crossing the big prairie when every day was alike ... just broken axles or lost horses or a sick ox, a river crossing or a buffalo herd, or some Indians ... that had all ended at Fort Laramie. Oh, hadn't that been a lovely Fourth! She'd become one of the older girls ... and she'd danced with that Jackson every dance and he'd kissed her. Mama didn't seem to notice the difference in her. She said she wasn't old enough to put up her hair yet nor wear longer skirts. She was just about as grown up as any of the girls on this trip. "I'll look you up when I get to California, wait and see!" he'd said that night; she hoped he would. But wasn't California pretty big and how would he find her when Pa wasn't even sure where they were going to settle? Were there post offices in California? There were lots of people in that train she'd like to see again. But she wasn't going to get married right away ... not she! She'd like to have a lot of fun at dances and parties before she settled down and had a family. Most married ladies didn't have much fun. Some of the older women were upset because Eleanor Eddy had danced with her husband, imagine! What could be wrong with that? Weren't you supposed ever to dance after you were married and had a baby? Mrs. Foster danced with her husband, and with Uncle Will Pike, besides. Her Ma just held the baby and smiled. Mrs. Breen said, "It ain't respectable!" What was respectable, and what wasn't, she wondered? She wanted to be grown-up like that Mary Graves with her black hair and her smiling face. *That* was who she'd like to be ... Mary Graves. The women said she was "getting along" and had better grab that John Snyder before someone else did ... he had an eye for the pretty girls ... or else she'd be a spinster like Eliza. Virginia didn't think Mary cared about getting married and settling down. She had that handsome John Snyder to spark with any time she wanted, and besides that the other young men stood around and wanted talk to her, every chance they got. She didn't blame them. Aunt Tamsen and Mama were talking once. Aunt Tamsen had said, "Honey draws more flies than vinegar." Virginia thought that was funny, but it must mean that Mary was all honey.

For herself, she was going to laugh a lot and dance with all the boys that asked, unless they were too smarty, and make eyes at them ... well, not really make eyes ... that might be going too far, but be friendly and make them laugh with her. Maybe it was the friendliness that made Mary so special, and not just the pretty hair and smile. She'd seen Milt look at Mary once in a while, and then look away ... everyone knew Mary belonged to John Snyder. Oh, it was going to be fun being a girl and have the boys look at you as if you were grownup enough to be married, and not care too much about marrying.

Now what had started her off on all this? It had been a long time since they'd had a good time, but lately people had perked up a little and stopped quarreling. Now that they were through the mountains, everything might go back to the jolly days on the prairie. Maybe Uncle Breen would bring out his fiddle and play tonight ... oh, but tonight was too soon after Luke Halloran had been buried! Maybe that wouldn't be respectable. How long after Luke died would it be respectable to have a good time? She didn't think Luke would mind very much if they had a dance or sang. He used to peer out the back of the wagon and his eyes looked as if he wished he could be dancing. he'd looked as wistful as she'd felt when she was too young to spin out at a dance. Poor Luke. She hoped that wherever he was, he'd remember her. It wouldn't hurt to sing a few songs tonight, would it? They could sing some of the sad ones, if that was more respectable. Singing made people feel better.

Up ahead, the wagons had stopped ... it wasn't time to make camp yet ... what had happened now? Had someone fallen out of a wagon? She touched Billy's flanks gently and he started forward at a fast lope. Funny how Pa had taught her to ride without ever being mean to Billy. Now it was as if Billy knew what she wanted by the slightest motion. Pa hated people to be cruel to animals. "Virginia, talk to him and just barely touch the whip, and he'll do as you wish." Lots of people didn't think that was true, but it was. She'd never had to whip Billy in her life. Pa was good with animals.

In no time she'd caught up with the train. Pa was right up front with the men as usual, and Auntie Tamsen with him. What were they holding?

It was a board. It had some scraps of paper still clinging to it. Auntie was saying, "If you'll all help me find every single piece of paper around here, I'll try to piece out what this is all about." Sure enough, there were slivers of paper on the bushes. Virginia jumped off Billy.

"What's happened, Pa?"

"I don't know yet, Puss. Probably another of Hastings' letters ... but the animals or Indians or someone have torn it all up, and we can't read it."

"I'm good at finding things, Auntie. Come on, all of you, help! I'll hunt till we find every piece!"

Men scowled, but they started gathering up the pieces ... all they could find. Auntie Tamsen was right in the middle of them, almost as if she were happy she was doing something. "Every piece, mind you ... don't miss a one!" It was her school-teacher voice, and the teamsters, just like little boys in school, obeyed.

"I bet I can find the most!" Virginia yelled. "Hey, you Patty Reed, come on. We've got a new game going!"

TAMSEN

It was too early to make camp, but they must. Tamsen sat with the board and the pieces of paper before her, a group of men and women behind her watching.

It wasn't hard to guess that this was Hastings' writing, and it wasn't hard to surmise it meant trouble. Everything connected with Hastings meant trouble of some sort. Tamsen thought back to the night in Illinois when George had brought Hastings' book home. If she'd known then what she knew now, she would have torn it into as many little pieces as the ones she had before her now. George wouldn't have read the book and they wouldn't be here, on the edge of an unknown desert following the wavering, uncertain whimsey of a man who didn't have his head put on right to begin with. Just because he wrote a book and had it in print ... she wondered how James Clyman had managed to be so mild, so calm, knowing what he did about the trail that Hastings had advised. He must have thought they were passel of idiot farmers from nowhere. They weren't idiots, but they were stubborn ignoramuses not to listen to a veteran like Jim Clyman, and to put their trust in a faker like Hastings. Sorry-looking as the old mountaineer was, he had the sound of truth in his voice. She had seen the dismay in his eyes when they refused to listen to what he had to say. "The nigher way," James Reed had kept saying. "The nigher way." No wonder the men taunted him with that phrase. At the time, however, they too had believed there was a "nigher way"; they had cheered and waved their hats and told the others they would be in California before anyone.

She'd like to get her hands on the man. A slick liar he was. There! Another piece fit into place. Certainly this was Hastings' hand. She searched through the collected fragments for something that might connect, make a sentence.

All she was doing was decyphering their doom. She'd had enough of the man. Now they were wasting more precious time piecing out another lie.

"Virginia, my dear, will you go to Uncle George and ask him to have the teamsters start cutting hay for the desert? No reason for them to be sitting idle." Then she looked up. "You, Baylis Williams, go give Mr. Donner my message." What am I thinking of, sending Virginia?

"I can go, Auntie."

"Uncle George wouldn't take kindly to a young girl making suggestions. Reach me that wrinkled piece over there, will you dear?"

"This is fun, isn't it, Auntie? This the one you mean?"

Fun. A child like Virginia thought everything was fun. Young people had no idea of the price they might have to pay. Yes, this was a puzzle, putting pieces together, like piecing a quilt, but it wasn't fun. The message would be dire, she knew in her heart.

The whole trip had been a puzzle, when you thought of it. One after another. So far, they hadn't made one right decision, not one, since George Donner had been elected captain. Yet he had made trips like this before, as everyone knew ... but crossing an entire continent wasn't quite like the moves from North Carolina to Kentucky to Indiana to Illinois, and then to Texas and back. This was a much bigger, a much more permanent move.

April, May, June, July, August, all had slipped by, and they were only a little past the half-way point. Was there enough time for the rest of the trip to California? How far had Hastings said it was from the Salt Lake to the coast? Why was she even asking such a question? There was no truth in Hastings' black heart.

"There ... this is beginning to take shape." Tamsen stuck another piece of paper on the board. "We're making some progress ...."

"Ma'am," Baylis Williams said, "Mr. Donner's coming to see how things is going ...."

"Thank you kindly, Baylis." Inside she was seething. Why didn't George make decisions? Why wouldn't he heed a simple suggestion from her? Baylis Williams, you're as bad as that sister of yours. No brighter. Nice of the Reeds to bring them along; they were reliable help. Eliza, the ninny, so sure of finding a husband in California when she hadn't caught one in Illinois. Hadn't an ounce of sense in her head, poor girl. A woman of 29. Perhaps though, to be fair, her deafness made her seem duller than she was.

Hastings made the whole of California sound like heaven itself. Returning travelers had another version; it wasn't all that wonderful, not that rich, not that easy. Well, if they ever got there, she wouldn't step one foot forward to return to Illinois. She'd never see this trail again. Nor would Luke Halloran, poor soul.

Not a word about the money in his chest, never a word about where he came from nor who to notify of his dying. All alone with his Mason's accreditations. Thank goodness, for then they knew how to bury him. Money enough for a start in California. Hastings again, with his promises of a good climate, health for everyone. Luke thought he'd make it, but dead he was back under alien sod.

They'd been responsible too. George had advertised in the Springfield paper for men willing to drive team and go to California free, where there was land for all. It didn't seem to be on his conscience, either, but it was heavy on hers. Oh, to be back in Illinois and start all over again from that night George brought that evil book home. How she wished she'd thrown it in the coals and watched it curl and burn, page by page. Whatever message was hidden in these scraps of paper would be only another lie.

"Thank you, Virginia ... that's the one I need now. Look for a piece that has a word ending in y, will you? Way, maybe. Day, perhaps? Virginia, do you see what a help spelling can be to you?"

They ought all to be readying themselves for what tomorrow might bring. Women cooking for the days ahead. They had sense enough to know what men must eat, whether or not. Men standing idle made her angry. They should be cutting grass, filling water casks, but she couldn't tell them that, and George ....

"What's the letter say?"

He came up behind her. "My fine girl. Thinking every minute, just like the school marm she is."

Tartly she answered. "No matter what it is, it will be bad news. I hope you've got the men out preparing for tomorrow."

Two more pieces fit into place.

"Some think Hastings has found a way around the dry drive ... maybe that's in the paper."

Always hoping, always trusting George. Always unable to think ill of any man. "You'd better do some praying then, George. It'll help as much as anything. Virginia ... look there ... reach me that one."

The pieces were going in faster now. "See here, George ... two days and two nights ... that part's clear."

For once George looked discouraged. "Why, he said it would be forty miles ...."

"If the fool says two days and two nights ... that's eighty miles, isn't it, if we go as fast as we can?"

"The oxen aren't in the best of shape. Two days, two nights! Best we can do has been 16-18 miles a day. Double that, going steady day and night. You're right, Tamsen. Finish it! There's got to be some other meaning!"

"I'll finish it as fast as I can, George," she snapped at him. "But you may as well know it's bad news. Make up your mind to it, and get started. Make the men cut hay."

Bewildered, and for once his broad shoulders stooping, George Donner walked away.

There! I've hurt him. He's discouraged. He doesn't know how to accept defeat. He's never lost before ... he hasn't felt the heavy hand of fate yet. He hasn't sat beside a bed and watched the one he loved die ... oh, yes, he has, twice before. He's done that and gone on. I suppose for a man to lose a wife isn't like a wife losing a beloved husband. There are always women around to cheer a widower. When I lost Tully Eustis, I lost everything in life, all I'd hoped for, all we'd dreamed of together, our little school where we would see to it that children had a good education, as we had both had, thank goodness. My dreams ... our dreams, dying before my tear-swollen eyes while I prayed and hoped and inwardly knew it was already too late ... just as I am sitting here piecing together a note, with no hope. Inwardly screaming at God, beating my own spirit with anguish. I saw Tully laid in the ground, my heart as torn as this evil letter ... then when I was still broken from that, my two little girls ... everyone said they would be my comfort in my loss ... one after the other, in two weeks of pure hell. They'd caught it from Tully. Has George known agony like that? He's seen only my spunky side, my determination to forget evil and the cruelty of the Lord. Oh, what have I said! Blasphemy ... the cruelty of the Lord, when I meant to think the power of the Devil in this sad world. Hastings, evil as Satan.

George, George, George, where have you brought me? Why am I in this endless wilderness, putting together a note that will bring us only more agony? My Lord, why hast thou forsaken me?

"Virginia, run and tell your Pa that I have fitted all the pieces I can together. Tell him to come."

"What does it day, Auntie?"

"It says we have a long and hard way to go. Now, go along with you."

There were a few people standing, watching her. "Read it to us, Mrs. Donner. I'm not much for book-learnin' nor writing, neither."

"The crossing of the desert will take much longer than we thought. Two days and two nights of hard driving."

A man groaned. "We can't do it ma'am. There ain't that much git up and go in the oxen, and my wagon's falling apart ...."

"You'd better do something, then, instead of standing around here gaping," Tamsen said dryly. "The devil finds work for idle hands...."

She walked away, leaving the board where George and James Reed could find it. She would not let anyone see her cry.

I, MARGARET

I am knitting, as the dry drive across the salt lake desert begins.

There is something frightening building up in James. I can't name it. He cannot remain still for a moment. He looks across this great white wilderness and his face is hard, determined, but more than that ... I can see some kind of rage that frightens me. The girls notice too, and have been especially tender toward him. Oh, not that he hasn't been kind; he is as good to us as he has always been. I hope when this dreary dry drive is over some of his anger will be appeased.

There is nothing but white ahead, a blinding white land that burns the eyes, with a crust that breaks when the wheels go over it. Hard walking, almost impossible to save the oxen our weight by walking. Poor animals ... perhaps that is what bothers James. He hates to see animals suffer.

"Let them ease themselves along, Milt. Talk to them, encourage them. If you whip them they'll give up sooner."

Milt answers in his slow way, "You always think the beasts have brains like us, don't you, Mr. Reed?"

"Poor things ... they didn't ask for this ...."

James is the leader now, though people don't realize it. He often scouts ahead, making each mile twice. He's trying to make up for taking the new road. If I tell him it isn't his fault, that it's Hastings' or those people at Fort Bridger, he looks as me, pity in his eyes, and something else ... what? I wonder what would have happened if no one had turned off with us back there at the Little Sandy? "Anyone who is of a mind to follow our wagons, come alone, you're welcome. The Donners and the Reeds take the left hand trail."

People forget that he went ahead to bring back Hastings. People forget that he worked harder than anyone cutting trail. His hands were blistered clear through the gloves he always wears ... the gloves worn to nothing. He's always cared for his fine slender hands. Encouraging the rest, pushing them while they called him a fool, calling him "Nigher Reed." Listening to Patrick Breen grumbling like an old bull ready to charge, listening to that German Keseberg cursing him (I'm sure it's cursing ... he spits the foreign words out so hatefully ...). Only dear Will Eddy and Milt on his side ... sometimes Pike and the Fosters ... of course, the Donners, both of them, are for him, but they don't back him up. George just says that God will get us out of this since he got us into it. Oh, I don't blame the Donners. Good men, the best in the world. But they don't take a firm stand, as James does. They'd rather be friends with everyone. James has always been firm. Firm, and fair and kind ... and hard to persuade. He listens, but he always goes his own way in the end, straight and direct.

I think he's taken this harder than anyone. Will Eddy said the other day, "Margaret, can't you ease him a little? He blames himself too much. It's eating at him." "So it has," I answered, "It's eaten clear into his soul. Nothing will ease him except getting us all through." "I think Jim Reed knows what we're up against better than George. Why didn't they make him the captain?" "Because, Will, we started out with too much. Too big a wagon ... they don't realize it was for mother. Too many horses and dogs and drivers, too much money, wine, clothes, gloves, furniture. And you know James ... he has that curt way with him, he rides a horse that's too well bred. Why, Will, people even envy Virginia's pony."

"You're right, I suppose. But he's the man for me."

"He may be for you, Will, but they don't like to listen to him."

I guess that's what's building up inside James. He feels he's beating his head against an unforgiving wall. People simply won't believe that we're in the danger he knows we are. I've never seem him more patient, but inside he's the same man, irritable of delay, fuming at stupidity, and raving mad at shirking. High-strung when he thinks of his own stupidity at taking this "short-cut" ....

Another thing about James. When there are decisions to make, he sees a solution right away and speaks up. That makes people angry — they don't figure things out as quickly.

For instance ... even in the family. James tries to teach young Jimmy to do his sums. James goes too fast, and Jimmy's confused. "Five and six, Jimmy." "Uh ... five and six? Five and six is ...." "Eleven. Don't hem and haw. There's no question about sums. Five and six are eleven. Nothing more or less. Say it straight out."

"I try, Pa."

"He hasn't had time to learn it fast yet, Pa," Patty says in her calm way, "but he will. We'll practice it today, won't we, Jimmy?"

"Well, learn your numbers, young man ... you'll not regret it. So that one day you won't have to stop to think. You'll just act."

Even little boys like Jimmy resent him at times. He's too quick, and doesn't see what it does to people. I think maybe they resent that more than the Palace car and Virginia's pony and his fine gloves. He makes them feel lesser'n they are .... He used to do that to me when I first knew him. Telling me right off that he was well off, that he had done well in America. Proud of that fine family in Poland ... of being real Irish, not shanty Irish. He was like that peacock at home spreading his beautiful fan to show off before the peahen, I suppose.

I didn't care about money ... I didn't care about whether he was from a great family or not. I just like the way he made me feel ... taken care of, when I had little Virginia and nothing much more than that, except Mama's money. Cherished and loved. I was never cherished before, I suppose ... even with Lloyd. Oh, we were in love all right, no question about that, but we were just two young people starting out with nothing but love and good looks between us ... having Virginia right off. I was left a widow before I learned much about being a wife. Then here comes this handsome tall man wearing fine clothes, with an Illinois town named after him and a big cabinet shop ... I felt like a lump of sugar melting in his mouth ... I didn't know him then as I know him now. He was a god then, older, wealthy, a "good catch," people said. I didn't find out till later how *very* good he was, how splendid, how brave and afraid of nothing. Nor even did I know how much I would love him. Taking Virginia as his own. Adding our three to her. Treating my mother like a queen. Lots of men grumble about their wives' kin, but James? He took us to his heart, he said, because he'd never known a real family. I thought he was devil-may-care, maybe a woman-chaser, who knows, but he's the finest family man in the train ... no, I guess I can't say that; people don't come on a trip like this if they're not family-people. Some said, "You'll get a touch of his fine Irish temper one day, Margaret Keyes Backenstoe, and you'll sing another tune!" But in all these years he's never raised his voice at me. Never once ... if only there wasn't this strange rage building up in him, make him pace back and forth like a tiger ... night and day.

And then, slow-talking Jacob Donner, half-ailing, but with a smile always, and George hopeful and trusting and unworried .... No wonder people chose George to be captain.

The heat! Last night it was so cold there was ice on the water buckets, and now, the blazing sun glancing off the white heat, and water so scarce we daren't waste a drop. Waste ... that's what James hates too. It doesn't go with the money, but maybe it does, because he had to make his own way in a new land, and he a half-orphan with a mother to provide for.

"Don't waste a drop of water, Margaret. Don't waste a morsel of food. Not even a bean nor flour with weevils. A day may come when a bean or two will look pretty good to us. People throw away food as if there was always going to be more where that came from. Save everything useful against the day you may need it." Waste not, want not.

Oh, but it's hot. Tommie asleep, his fine hair wet, pasted against his flushed cheek. His dog Cash next to him, panting. We've been going a day and a night and a day. There is no end to this. Two days and two nights, and we are no closer to the end of this white hell. No one said there would be hillocks to climb, nor that the white surface turns to mush when the animals break through it. No one told us of the dunes, and the wind that blows it into a fine salt spray. We taste salt on our lips if we lick them. Salt in our hair, making it like hemp.

The other wagons are ahead. Ours is the last in line. The biggest, and hardest to pull through sand. James begins to think we should put our possessions in the two lighter wagons, and leave the cumbersome Palace car behind.

The visions we have! Other wagons seem to be on the horizon, going as we are going. Cattle, dogs, drivers, multiplied by hundreds. The first time it was noticed Patrick Breen said it was a miracle. Hastings come back to escort us across this wilderness, praise the Lord! Will Eddy proved it was a trick of the eye ... he walked forward, so did the vision, walked backward, they did too. So much for praising the Lord.

Today the children are listless and quiet. Virginia tries to keep them awake, playing guessing games. Patty takes most of the care of Tommie for me. Eliza moans and cries out how thirsty she is and how hot. Talking about it only makes the children feel it more. I have told her to be still, that we are all in this together.

Perhaps the far away mountain that serves as a goal is running away from us. We never seem to come closer to it. Maybe it also is a vision. Maybe we are the Israelites crossing the desert ....

The faster wagons are far ahead. In the heat they look like great gravestones. Wavering trembling gravestones. The Donners are the closest, but they seem to float on a sea of salt.

"No, children, it isn't time for a drink of water ... not quite yet. In a little while." We have to save the oxen; without them, what would we do? Tamsen says to give the children a bit of sugar, with peppermint in it, but they complain that it makes them more thirsty. Tamsen also gives her girls squashed down bullets to suck. She says that keeps the mouth from being so dry. Oh, I am afraid.

It isn't easy to explain to the little boys what is happening. Tommie calls out in his sleep for wa-wa. Virginia wipes his face with a slightly dampened towel, and he drifts off again. Jimmy only looks puzzled. "Why can't Papa find water, Ma? Doesn't he know where any is?" How can you explain without making their father look improvident to them? "Papa knows where water is, but the oxen are tired, son, and they can't move fast enough."

What day is it now? We started Thursday. Thursday, Thursday night, Friday, Friday night (we expected to be across by then), Saturday, Saturday night ... the oxen look ready to fall; when the sun comes up tomorrow and it is hot again, they will surely drop. Only the Donners are in sight. The rest have left us far behind.

James is planning to go ahead on Glaucus to find water and bring some back for us. Milt is to drive the poor beasts until they cannot move further, and then unhitch them and drive them on to water.

He is saying, "I depend on you, Margaret, to make the right decisions for the children. I'll be back. Don't be afraid when the men leave you to drive the oxen in. You must trust me to come. If something should happen, and I cannot return to you, you must start out and follow ...."

"Can't we follow now?"

"My only hope is in the speed of the mare. No, you are better with the wagons."

He kissed me, hugged me hard and kept his hand on my shoulder until he left. We all watched him until he was only a moving speck on the white.

We have been walking as much as we can to save the oxen. Milt says they will give out soon.

Virginia asks, "What can I do?" and Patty answers, "Poor Ma, she doesn't know any more than we do." Jimmy is terribly silent and watches the place where his father disappeared from sight. His eyes are large. Tommie sucks his thumb. I suppose that will keep him from feeling so dry.

Now Milt tells us that we must stop. He's driving the beasts ahead. He says the oxen can smell water before we can ... that they will surely find it. "Don't worry none, Ma. Mr. Reed will be back soon, don't you worry. If there's anyone that can save us, it's Jim Reed." I nod.

"Mind you take care of yourself, Milford Elliott!" Patty calls out, "and bring us back a pail of water. Jack and Jill went up the hill, mind you don't fall down and spill it!"

"You're being silly," Puss says.

"I might as well be silly as scared," Patty answers.

Did I sleep that night? I don't remember. It seems I did in fits and starts. Never enough to forget where I was. Every sound woke me. It was a full moon and I watched for movement. Nothing stirred. It was as cold at night as it was hot in the day. I would see James coming on the horse, and then he would disappear, and I'd drift off and hear the children muttering in their sleep. Patty sits beside me when the boys settle down. Funny child. She talks to me in her matter-of-fact way, and I feel as if everything is all right. Then she drops off. Looking over the white waste, the moon so bright it almost shuts out the stars, I wonder if I am asleep or awake. This cannot be me, Margaret Keyes Backenstoe Reed, alone in a desert with just a little water remaining, no husband, my children dependent upon me for help. Not the Margaret Reed that started out four months ago as a semi-invalid, to be cherished and helped across this great span of land to a country I've never seen ... and may not see. This must be a nightmare, the after-affect of a terrible headache that has made me irrational. Virginia stirs. "Has Papa come yet?" "No," I answer, peering forward once more. "What day is it, Ma?" "It's Sunday night." "Is it *still* Sunday night, Ma? Eliza says we are all going to die here and dry up like paper and just blow away. She's crying back there in the wagon."

"Don't pay attention to her, Puss. You can trust your pa to come."

"Eliza wishes she hadn't made us take her ...."

"Well, I don't blame her for that. But she's not strong like you are, Puss."

"She's taller'n me, and lots older. Stronger, too, I bet."

"You're stronger in your mind. So is Patty. Comfort poor Eliza. She can't hear things as we can, and she doesn't rightly understand things."

"What doesn't she rightly understand?" Patty demands, sitting up suddenly.
"I didn't think you were awake, child. She doesn't understand why this had to happen."
"Do you, Ma?"
I have to say no. "Not completely. But I trust."
"In God?"
"In God, and in your father. He'll do his best. His best has never failed us yet."
"Look back there, Ma. The sky is getting lighter. The moon's almost down."
Dawn is coming. Another day. This must be Monday morning. Dare I give the children some water? If it would rain ... I look to see if there are clouds. I see none. Clouds would make the heat more bearable. How fragile the sky looks at dawn! I search the waste for some moving thing ... for James, and then doze. I dream of swimming in a river at home when I was a child. The water feels beautiful against my skin, it washes off the salt. Cool and sweet. I open my mouth to let the river run down my throat and ease its dry tightness. I try to swallow, but it hurts. I hear a shout. Am I awake now from my dream? Virginia calls in delight. It is not a dream. It is James, back at last.
"Papa! Papa! Papa!" the children are screaming in glee, Virginia jumps from the wagon and runs toward him. Patty follows, and I go forward too, saying a prayer of thanksgiving as I do, my heart so full of happiness that it hurts. How great thou art, God. James looks worn out, and well he might.
He talks with Walt Herron, who has stayed with us. Walt starts the way James has just come, leading Glaucus. "After what she's done for me, I can't let her die," James says, and then tells us what has happened. Thirty more miles, perhaps, lie ahead. A spring with plenty of water.
"I can taste it already," Patty says.
"There's water in my canteen. Share it equally, but don't take more than you need." The wagons ahead, James says, are strung out ... some have already reached the spring. Eddy left his wagon and was on the way back to it with water for his animals.
"Did you meet Milt?"
"Just before midnight. I told him to watch that the cattle didn't panic when they smelled water ... others have. Jake Donner is taking his animals in ... he's the nearest ahead. Milt and the boys will be back with the oxen as soon as he can."
I urge him to rest. It is daylight now. He has not slept since he left us. "I was at the spring only long enough to water and rest Glaucus, to fill the water bags and my canteen, and to talk to Will Eddy. I trust that man, Margaret. He has strength. We started back together."
"How are the rest? Are they safe?"
"Most of them are within a mile or so of the spring. We're the farthest. They're mad as the devil ... better to be angry than discouraged, Margaret. They swear they'll get to California if only to shoot Hastings' head off. At least they're not blaming me any more for this mess."
"Get some sleep, James. You're running on your nerves alone."
He lies down and closes his eyes. The sun warms the wagon until it is like a bake-oven. Virginia and Patty and I take turns fanning him as he sleeps. He twitches and moans, like one of the dogs. As soon as he wakes, he looks off into the direction where Milt should appear, his keen eyes troubled. There is not much water left. We daren't wet a towel to wipe his dusty face. Somehow the children have begun to realize what trouble we're in; they are speaking quietly to one another. I see Virginia fold her hands and whisper a prayer when she thinks she's not being watched.
When evening comes, James tells me to pack some bread, put on my moneybelt. We

take shawls and what is left of the water and start to walk. Jimmy does well, plodding along by himself, imitating his father's erect stride. Patty, Virginia and poor bewildered Eliza, who is sobbing, walk together. James carries Tommie, and whistles for the dogs to follow.

I don't know how far we walk. In the bright moonlight we are dark dim figures moving against the white, filing along like refugees from a fire or a pilgrim family going to church. Finally the children are so tired they can walk no farther. James says, "Lie down for a short rest, then." It is so cold they can't sleep. James puts a blanket on the ground for them, huddles the children together, covers them with another, and herds the dogs so they sleep close to them outside the cover. Then he and I sit together, our backs to the bitter wind, sheltering them. James holds my hand, but we don't talk, for fear of disturbing them. Poor things. There are so many questions I want to ask James, things I need to know but that I don't want the children to hear. I think even this is better than the night I was alone with them. James caresses my fingers and I squeeze his hand. It is a kind of talking, a kind of making love. I feel desperate, but think how can I feel desperate when I am not alone? My head falls upon my knees and I doze.

The dogs are barking wildly. Where are we? What time is it? What has happened? A huge raging animal looms out of the night, throwing sand and salt and bellowing, almost upon us. The dogs rush at him and he turns. It is one of our steers, crazed by thirst, stampeding.

Without thinking James says, "The beast is mad!"

The children are wildly awake. James has told them often how dangerous mad animals are. Eliza screams and the children are all crying.

"Don't worry, don't worry ... he's gone now," James says. He is more worried about why the oxen have stampeded and what it means than about the children's fears.

Too excited to sleep any more that night, we move ahead slowly. At last, about first light, we come to Jacob Donner's wagons. In the silence we think they have been abandoned, but then we hear people rising from sleep. Betsy's sweet calm voice in the dawn welcomes us as if she were on her stoop at home.

Jake has managed to go much farther than when James last saw him. This means we are closer to water than we had estimated. It is not enough joy to make up for the bad news we hear next. Milt and men have lost all our nine yolk ... they are looking for them. That is why they didn't return to our wagon. Jake says that the oxen weren't yoked together; the men had been driving the stock, and when a horse failed, they stopped to help him up, and the cattle took off.

"Oh Milt, damn it, that's what I told you not to do," James says. He clenches his hands together, and I see a look of tired despair on his face, only for a moment. Then he looks at Jake, who is unhappy to bring bad news.

"Jake, may I leave my family with you while I go ahead? We *must* find the animals, or I cannot go farther ... which way did they go?"

Slow-talking Jake nods his head and begins to talk, but Betsy interrupts. "Of course, James. Whatever we have you're welcome to."

"Bless you all. Margaret, see that the children help," James says and is gone again. So here we are with Jacob, Betsy, her two Hook sons and her own brood, and enough water for small sips for us all. Nothing in the world ever tasted better than that water they gave us to drink. Betsy, dear soul, makes a fire, fries bacon, stirs milk gravy to go over the salt rising bread, brews a hot cup of tea, and shares it all with us. Now the children recover from their weariness and fear, and think all is well again. Only Virginia looks puzzled and asks how we are to move the wagons if the men don't find the oxen, and I answer that I don't know. Eliza perks up and stops sniffling, the children begin to play together. Only I have black terror in my heart. Only Jake and Betsy and I realize what this may mean.

Jake and his men take his cattle to water the next day, and tell James, who is searching everywhere for lost oxen, that he will bring us in with the Donner wagon. Dear, good Jacob. He and I have been the invalids of the party, and we sometimes commiserated together in a teasing sort of way. Once I asked him why he hadn't turned back when he could. He said that it was his only hope to get Betsy and the children to a better place. He never mentioned getting there himself. That dreadful cold he caught after the men worked so hard to get us over the Little Blue River,the day my mother died, had never really left him. Sometimes he coughed as harshly as Luke Halloran. Still, he never complained. Later, I thought it strange that what had made me stronger ... the loss of Mother and the hardships and the graves ... had only made him worse.

After Jake and Betsy got us to the spring where the others were waiting we spent many days trying to locate cattle and deciding how to manage the wagons with what few there were left.

The first thing Patrick Breen said was, "We are all safe, thank the Almighty One. None has died. It is God's blessing!" Of course he was right. Even the dogs made it.

But not our cattle. James was away looking for them when Indians came to our encampment, and made signs they had seen animals. With their fingers they showed the number, which agreed with our losses. The Indians were driven away, although I begged the men to let them remain until James could talk with them. He would have been glad to buy the cattle back.

I did not cry. James had enough without woman's tears. Even the girls who set such store in the things Mother had left to them, were stoic. "Well, I guess we can do without; we've got Billy and Cash and Papa's Glaucus, and ourselves."

Well, Patty puts life in neat columns, valiant child, I thought. A Greek myth I had read once had said, "My children are my jewels," or something like that. Well, I have my jewels. The children and dear James.

The Donner party had crossed the desert with no human deaths, but with losses that staggered the mind. Thirty-six oxen, half of them belonging to Reed, had been crazed by thirst and had disappeared. The Reeds were reduced to one cow and one ox. Days followed, days they could not afford to spend looking vainly for animals that were gone and never found. The remaining cattle, however, recuperated beside the stream. The men worked long and hard, bringing in wagons, searching for cattle, mending wagons that were falling apart, dried by the desert crossing.

Here James Reed underwent another loss. His great Palace car was left behind, cached in the white sand, the provisions stowed in the remaining lighter wagons. There was more food than he could carry, and James Reed divided the supplies among the other families, for now the party began to be desperately low in food stuffs. So bad was the spirit between them all that no one would carry any of Reed's provisions without demanding a large share for himself. From the wealthiest man in the party, Reed descended to being the poorest.

Out on the white salty waste, abandoned wagons looked like graveyard monuments and indeed they were. To many of the party, they were tombstones for their hopes of the year before. Two horses remained for the Reeds, but both were worn and tired. Billy Graves and the sorrowing Milt Elliot had gone far afield looking for the lost livestock, which were never found. Weary of another wait, the party started on. Nineteen wagons rolled on west, without waiting for young Graves and Milt. There was no joy in the morning call "Chain Up, Boys!"

Without consulting the Donners, James Reed began to take inventory of the food supplies that remained.

They followed Hastings' trail a short way before they halted once more. Now what had the fool done? The trail turned south. Why? With no map of their own to follow, there was nothing to do but to turn south, also, keeping to the tracks of the will-o'-the-wisp Hastings.

To add to the dismal prospect, that day the desert heat made a sudden drop and snow began to fall. In September? What was the matter with this God-forsaken country? California would have to be a paradise to compensate for the horrors of the crossing. Slogging through mud the temperamental snow had left, they met Milt and Billy. Great news! A spring was ahead. But beyond that, another dry drive, maybe forty miles across. Stopping at the spring, they added only five miles to the total they had traveled since May.

MARY GRAVES

What has happened to us all? Mary thought. Everything has changed ... there is no love any more ... only fear, distrust, suspicion and even hate. Since the desert crossing, the terror of being alone on the trail was all that was keeping them in any order at all. They had been told that George Donner was the captain of the party; what had happened to him? No one doubted his goodness, his generosity, his friendliness; he would listen to troubles and sympathize with everyone, but orders he gave were in a tentative voice, almost as if he were saying, "Tell me what to do?"

At least James Reed had plans. He'd started making a list of all supplies left to them ... it was easy to see James Reed was worried. He had reason enough, with nothing left to him but his one ox and one cow and borrowed animals to keep him going. There was panic in the air. Mary could feel emotions on her skin, like mosquito bites; when there was a clash between the men, she heard it as if brass were beating upon brass. Where had love gone?

John had changed, too. Oh, he was still putting up a face, and at nights the party liked to see him smile, spin out with the girls once in a while, sing in his great voice. She saw him so briefly. Every able-bodied man was busy and exhausted when night came. The frantic hurrying, the strange mapless land, the hard work, made the men cross and weary, ready to blame anyone and everyone. John was jolly with everyone else but her ... he teased that Virginia Reed, made Leanna Donner think she was a grown woman, led Eliza Williams on till she giggled like an idiot, but he was abrupt with Mary, whom he wanted to marry.

Pa was no better. He wasn't sleeping. He fretted about the long barren stretch to California. Mary tried to help. "Pa, don't take on so, we've just got to do the best we can."

"With them little ones to worry about, I cain't rest."

"Seems to me we're all quarrelin' too much, Pa."

"I s'pose you're right. But when you're danged mad, it's bound to show."

"It doesn't do you any good to show it. It doesn't get us there any sooner. Save it till we get to California. When you're upset, Ma gets upset and she can't nurse the baby."

"I wish we'd of never come now. I wish't we'd of follered along the Fort Hall way instead of chasin' down the road after this passel of fools."

"No use wishin' for things you can't have." It was hard work, trying to cheer Pa. John was just as bad. One night when he started off to his bed, without even a word or a nod to her, she stopped him.

"What's the matter, John. Have I hurt your feelin's someway?"

"Nope." He looked at her, half angry. "Why don't you say we can get married? Didn't think I'd have to wait all summer for you to make up your mind."

"I told you I'm thinkin' about it, John."

"What's the trouble? You lookin' for somebody better? They's plenty of girls I could ask ...."

"I know that John. But when I marry, I want it to be something special. What's the hurry?"

"Don't you know?"

No, she didn't, and yes, she did. John was handsome, about the best-looking man she'd ever seen, tall and light haired, his skin dark from the sun. She knew very well why he wished they were married, when he hugged her, held her, kissed her. Yet she resisted him. It was hard to do. But this bleak journey was no place to start married life. Her sister had married Jay just before they left, but what kind of a honey moon was this? No place of their own, nowhere to be by themselves. Children everywhere, like flies, everyone sleeping together in wagons.

John had been good to Pa, who was getting along in years. John kept them all laughing, and it had been fun, real romantic, having him along ... up till now when they'd joined this Donner bunch. Pa said John would make her a good husband. Mary guessed that he would, but she didn't want to be rushed. It wouldn't be long now before they'd be in California. Then Mary would decide.

She didn't like John the way he was now, a cross old married man, scolding her for things he thought she'd done ... like the other day when she stopped to talk to Will Eddy ... or the time she helped Milt Elliott with his harness. His black face. His ordering her around. "If you've no more than that to do, you might think of helping me." Why, he even acted jealous of little Charlie Stanton, half her size, and fifteen years older, she guessed. What was eatin' at John about her talkin' to Charlie? He was only tellin' her he was going on ahead for help, to bring back enough food so they could make it to Califorina.

"Why, Charlie? If you left us all and went on ahead, why would you come back for us family-people? You'd never think of us again."

"You don't really believe that, do you, Miss Mary?"

"I don't think that many single men would bother to come back to save a passel of strangers ... not when they'd reached California. Why should they?"

"I have deep ties with all of you." Those strange, serious deep eyes of his!

"You haven't got a girl here, have you Charlie?" she teased.

He didn't speak for a while. His eyes met hers and turned away. "No, I haven't any girl."

"You ever have a girl?"

"Not before now."

"You gave yourself away, Charlie!" she cried in feminine triumph. You *do* have a girl. You just said so yourself."

He didn't answer. His hand shook as he raised it to his half-averted face. His voice was choked and tight when he finally tried to answer.

"There! Charlie, I didn't mean to tease you. It was mean of me, and not very ladylike. I never guessed you were in love, Charlie. I didn't mean to pry."

John's voice broke in like a rifle shot. "Hey, you Mary Graves, you git back to the wagon and help your Ma. She's been lookin' for you ... you can't just stand there gabbin' when there's so much to do." Oh, my, John sounded as mad as a wet hen.

"I'll be there in a moment, John." She turned back to Charlie. "Do you forgive me, Charlie? Please? I'll never say another word about it."

His eyes were brighter than usual.

"Don't feel bad, Miss Mary. It's all right. It's just that ...."

"Just that what?"

"Just that my girl ... I call her that ... is in love with someone else."

John grabbed her by the arm. "You're no young filly, Mary Graves, to be making eyes at Charlie. I told you to git back to your ma. Now, you git going, and git going fast."

Mary turned to him angrily. "Listen here, John Snyder," she said, flinging off his arm. "What makes you think you can talk to me like that, I'd like to know? I don't belong to you yet!" They stared at each other, both faces flushed. Then she turned to walk away. Mary heard John saying to Charlie, "You can't let women get ahead of you, can you, Stanton? If I was married, there'd be another story, for sure. She's a sassy one and needs a bit of tamin'."

What in goodness name had got into John's head? He'd never treated her like this before, ordering her around as if he owned her. What was eating at him anyway? It must be all the bad luck they'd had lately. Come to think of it, she'd never seen John Snyder when things weren't going his way. He always had his say about everything. Free as a bird to do whatever he wanted, that was John Snyder. Well, so was she free as a bird, to talk with anyone she wanted, so long as she didn't do anything disgraceful. Mary was as used to having any man she wanted to beau her around as John was at sparking any girl he fancied. Never had to face hard times before, she suspected.

None of the single men were as light-hearted as they'd been at the start. Come to think about it, they were farther down in the dumps, even though the married men worried about their families and gettin' through. The bachelors looked so hopeless, as if they didn't know what to do, or why they were there. All except that Patrick Dolan who joked and teased and kept people's spirits up with his tomfoolery. And Charlie Stanton, with his dark eyes that seemed to see right inside a person. You'd think he was kin to all the train ... just think, a man who could go on, leave them all and make it safe by himself, plannin' on going ahead and promisin' to bring back help.

Strange that he had a girl here in the group. Mary hadn't noticed a thing. Who was she? Leanna Donner? She was old enough to marry, but probably Tamsen Donner wouldn't have it. Virginia Reed wasn't old enough, but she was lighthearted ... just the kind Charlie needed ... and she was daring, too, full of fun and laughter. Right now she was just beginning to feel her oats with the men, sparking a little with the young boys, and keeping her eyes on the handsomest. Hardly anyone along good enough for her, perhaps, but she didn't look like the kind who cared. Too young for marriage and babies, still old enough to flirt in that half-grown-up way she had, and her still a child. She was a girl to make men look twice, that long hair flying when she rode that pony of hers, cheeks rosy, whooping like an Indian. Probably it wasn't Virginia ... Charlie was too serious for her.

Someone had caught Charlie Stanton's eye, though. She'd watch him from now on, she'd find out what girl he was after. It didn't work out quite that way, though, because she always caught his eyes on her and she had to turn away for fear he'd think she was prying.

Later, peeling potatoes, some of the last they had left, she thought about it some more. There weren't enough girls he could be interested in at his age ... certainly not Leanna Donner. Her hands stopped on the knife. It couldn't be .... Oh, *no,* it couldn't be ... he was already in his thirties ... he never offered to take her by the hand, even, always called her Miss Mary, as if there was a gulf between them, as if she was a thousand years old or an old maid school teacher. "You're a puffed-up woman, Mary Ann Graves," she scolded herself, dropping the potatoes into the pot of water. Forward, vain, thinking bad thoughts ... pride goeth before a fall, Mary Graves.

Maybe she had asked for attention. Had she? It all came from being too loving, perhaps too helpful, too willing to try to cheer them up, to give them some of her strength and good spirits. Helpin' Will Eddy with his harness wasn't what a modest woman would do, was it? It just came natural to her to reach out and give a hand. Was she too free-and-easy-like? She had always enjoyed helping Billy with his work ... Sarah'd been the one to stay inside and help Ma. She loved being outside, much better'n sewing and washing up and fancywork. She sort of liked it when men looked surprised that she was almost as strong as they were. She just purely liked to help, no offense intended. Had she given Charlie a wrong idea about her? That bitty fellow ... she could easily open her heart to him, but maybe she better not talk to him quite so much. No use givin' him wrong ideas about her. Everyone talked as if she was promised to John. Tall, handome, big as almost any man along, her intended. Poor Charlie, small, almost as old as Margaret Reed ... why, she didn't even know what he was going to California for.

Her mind told her that age didn't matter. George and Tamsen were years apart, so were James Reed and Margaret ... they both were happy.

It was purely natural that John, who was the handsomest fellow would like her, Mary Graves, who was the prettiest — they said, anyway. A match made in heaven. Pat Dolan said once, "Why do you wait? Why are you teasing that John Snyder so?" Even then, Mary hadn't been able to answer except with a laugh. God had given her a pretty face and a love of smiling and a heart that warmed to everyone; she couldn't help it if people liked to be with her. Oh, shame, Mary Graves ... how fluttery you are! She lifted the pot to the fire, and thought with a bitter-sweetness of both John and funny little Charlie Stanton, with his sober eyes.

The next time she encountered Charlie, her face reddened in spite of her inner scolding.

"May I talk to you, Miss Mary?"

Mary knew that he had volunteered to go ahead to Sutter's place in California for extra supplies. James Reed guaranteed payment from his own purse. Big Mac McCutchen also had agreed to go. That made the women feel better, for they were afraid that a single man would feel no need to return, once he got to the promised land. The expedition was almost ready to leave.

"Please listen, Miss Mary, to what I have to say. Some of the people don't believe that I'll return, that I'll run out on them. I want to make a solemn oath that I will, God willing. Unless God cuts me down, Miss Mary, I will be back with supplies for the train. On my honor I want you to remember me with kindness, and say a prayer for me."

He added, almost as if it was a wedding, "Give me your hand to hold while I promise you I will come back."

What had she answered? What had her eyes said to him? For now she knew what she had suspected was true. His vow to her was as sacred as any he could make, whether he mentioned love or not. "Pray for me, Mary Graves, and wish me luck."

"I will pray for you. I'll wish you luck. Every day till I see you again." It was the least she could say.

She stood in the early morning under the lightening sky, the clouds pink and blue all at once, the air clear and cool, the mountains outlined by the rising sun. Big Mac was clowning as usual, shouting in his great voice. "Give me another horse! Bind up my wounds! A horse, a horse, my kingdom for a horse!", and James Reed, smiling for the first time in weeks, came back at him with " 'Beggars mounted run their horse to death.' Mac, remember that and don't gallop off and leave poor Charlie behind on his mule — you're the short and long of it, and that's the truth!" Everyone had put on a good face except that sour German, Keseberg. "God Bless and Godspeed!" Tamsen Donner reached up and handed them a package of food for the nooning, and shook their hands. Then they mounted, Charlie on the mule, and Big Mac on a horse. Everyone cheered. Mary saw Charlie looking toward her with his steady gaze. She would cherish that look, and she would remember him, and pray for him, poor man, who had no one else.

The two men left. Space lengthened between them and those behind, farther and farther along the ragged ill-marked trail into the sage brush and sand until they were only vague movements in the bleak distance, until only a plume of dust in the air marked their passage.

The Donner Party started out later that same morning, a week into September. Each day's drive brought its own adjustment. People buried possessions in the desert with the faint hope that they could return some time to claim them, if Indians didn't discover them first. Some merely dropped beloved furniture and heavy chests by the side of the road and drove on without looking back. There were fewer wagons remaining ... five or perhaps six stood desolately alone, but not so alone as Reed's Palace wagon cached in the salt desert. The next week was hard going, but there was almost always water as they rounded one of the strange mountains that made no rhyme nor reason to them. There were antelope and sheep meat left. Will Eddy, hunting every day, kept people supplied with whatever game he could find.

They came to a high range crossing their path. James and Eddy and the Donners stood looking at the tracks of the lead party, scratching their heads in puzzlement. Hastings had gone north first, but the scouts they sent ahead reported that they went only a short way and turned back. Well, that meant that they had gained a day or so on the party ahead, but it also meant that Hastings was groping his way west. Why else would he change his route? There was nothing to to but follow, but it was with no confidence at all that they turned south, a way they were loath to go.

The trail was weeks old; the cattle dung accounted for that. Where was the man going? It worried them to follow after, but they were afraid to break away; no one dared to mention a short cut again. For three days they traveled south, then turned west through a gap in the mountains, and then north again, on the other side of the range. Good God, they were paralleling the last week's trail with only the mountains between! After three more days, they reached a point only a few miles farther west than they had been before they made the great costly loop. Hastings now had another mistake to answer for, when they found him.

It was a weary monotonous march now, with only the rotation of the wagons each day, the leader falling to the rear, as they had done all across the prairie.

Whether by agreement or some other reason, the Donner brothers drove on ahead taking their five wagons, their own teamsters, plus some of Reed's since he didn't need them now. The others, twelve wagons in all, followed behind and the distance between the two sections lengthened into several days' journey. No historian has explained this behavior. Was it because their oxen were in better condition, or was it the lack of cohesion in the party that led them to separate themselves in a country which began to take its toll in a more disastrous way? This division gave both sections far more exposure to the Nevada Indians ... a far poorer sort than the plains Indians. A ragged, dirty naked group, without horses nor guns, they were at first taken lightly as no threat at all.

Low spirited and muttering, they lumbered on, crowded into too few wagons, impinging on each other's lives, hearing the same criticisms, suggestions, doubts, fears repeating themselves like echoes in a cave ... and so they were, although in open desert country, people in a cave with no light visible in the end.

The desert dotted with grey-green bushes seemed to go on forever. If they looked west, they could see only pale blue mountains through the autumn haze; if they looked back, they saw only a wavering mountain-line ... the peaks that they had passed weeks ago, that seemed to be scattered willy-nilly on the broad land. Each day they hoped that they would come to the joining of the Fort Hall trail, each night they camped without reaching it. They were making better time now than they had ever made, even back on the flat prairie, but it was small comfort. They prided themselves when they could stretch their day's travel a little farther than Hastings' group had done. The few signs of the lead group were small: burnt fires, discarded equipment, bits of half-burnt wood, feathers of eaten birds, hooves from game that had been killed or eaten ... once in a while, the remains of an ox that had not been able to go on.

I, MARGARET

I felt the tightness in James; he had dismissed his losses with a sort of wry philosophy, he had tightened his mouth in bitterness at the demands made by people for their shares of his food ... food they were only glad to be given; this last stupidity of Hastings' brought James almost to despair. When we turned south, driving for three days in the wrong direction, only to turn north on the other side of bare red-brown mountains, with a monstrous waste of time and the strength of the animals, his impatience grew again. I wondered how he could keep from breaking into rage. Taking inventory of the food each family carried made him feel better; sending Charlie Stanton and Big Mac McCutchen ahead helped too. When they left, he sighed deeply. "I've done all I can do now ... all that is left is to keep the train moving. Surely we have seen enough trouble. If only I could forget that it was my stubbornness in not listening to James Clyman ...."

"You must forget, James. Here we are. Make the best of it."

"I don't mind making my own mistakes; I hate making them for others."

"How long will it take Stanton and Mr. McCutchen to return with supplies?"

"They will travel fast. They've got good animals. It's hard to guess. They can make thirty-five miles to our eighteen or twenty ...."

I thought to myself, poor Charlie Stanton, if he is in love with Mary, as Will Eddy says he is. John so big and strong and handsome. James likes John ... says he cheers people up and teases the women folk out of their doldrums. He does his allowance of work and more. Gets a lot out of the animals, though James says he's rougher with them than need be. Mary's too light-hearted for Charlie Stanton, anyway. All gossip, probably. People need to have something to talk about. No use worrying about John and Charlie and Mary. I'd better be keeping my mind on my own youngsters getting to California. I must keep my eye on Eliza so she won't waste a mite of food.

If only James isn't pushed any farther. All of us Reeds have kept silent about losing things ... our furniture, carpets, clothes, family pictures, seeds, bulbs, linens, books, silver, wines, gew-gaws for the Indian trade, and silks for the Spanish, all buried back in the salt flat with the Palace car. I can see that amazing wagon yet, James calling us down to the factory to admire it and the conveniences he'd installed for our comfort. People said it was the finest wagon ever to set out on the emigrant trail. When we had to leave it back in the desert, I couldn't ask him to bring the oil paintings, the chest that was my mother's ... not with our lives in the balance. Tamsen says she's known times when you'd trade anything you had in this world for the lives of those you hold dear, and I know, I know. Perhaps we have lost a fortune in memories and in possessions, but oh, my dear God, you have spared me and my four children and my dear troubled husband.

Now we turn north to cancel the days we drove south. How fidgety James is! The fear I have in my heart comes from living with a man, loving him, knowing his changes of moods, knowing when he's about at his limit. The Donners are now far ahead of us, following Hastings' stupid meandering wagon wheels. I wonder what Tamsen and George think now of the great adventure: journeying by schooner to a climate that is peaceful and warm all year long, where winter does not exist, where there are no aches and fevers and no snow, a second honey moon, George said.

I wonder, to myself of course, why the Donners have left us all behind. Is it because George can't face making any more decisions? George said it is to spread the little feed left on the trail so that there will be more for all. I wonder. People grumble, "He's getting the best pasturage, the best water." That isn't like the Donners. Maybe they see that James would have made the best leader, and they want to give him a chance ... but it's not much of a chance with a group as shattered as we have become.

Thank goodness for Milt and good Will Eddy. Last night, when Patrick Breen brought out his fiddle, I saw Milt watching James, who was watching the dancing with a smouldering, impatient look on his face. James rose and left the fire, and Milt followed him. They paced together back and forth, for hours in the deep dark behind the circle. There were stars out, but no moon. I could hear their voices, low and urgent, rising sometimes, but not in anger at each other, more in rage at the bad luck that had been following us. How hard it is to be a man and be responsible for a whole family, day in and day out. I wonder if it wouldn't have been better for James to have made this trip ahead, and come back for us later. No, James would want us with him. No one knew all this would happen. James can stand hardship as well as any man, but he flares up and loses his temper at stupidity. Surely the Donners knew what they were doing, going on ahead. Surely they didn't mean to abandon us without a leader. Tamsen had a strange look on her face when they left. If they had just brought us all together and made some public admission ... or called for a vote so we wouldn't be here with the leadership dangling as it is. "It won't be for long, Margaret," Tamsen said to me. "George thinks it will urge people on if he sets a faster pace." I hope so.

If there were any spot where I could be with James alone! I can ... I know I can soothe and relax him, ease his impatience. Two families in a wagon ... there's no way to have any times alone.

James did not come to the wagon to sleep last night. He wasn't with us for breakfast. I looked questioningly at Milt. He said in his slow way, "Ma, I sent Mr. Reed hunting. He needed to get away."

"Good," I said briefly. Hunting would drain some of the violence and impatience out of him. Milt smiled a half-smile.

In a sort of desperation, I said, "Oh, Milt, Milt, what is to become of us?"

"That's Mr. Reed's question too, Ma," he said to me, kindly as always. "He sees no way out. He likes choices, and there ain't no choice but to foller along on a trail of a man he don't trust."

It was a long speech for Milt. "I know you're sorry you came with us, Milt. I pray every night no harm will come to you."

He rolled his hat between his fingers and smiled sheepishly. "Ma, I pray for you and the children, same as you. The girls is like my sisters, and you're the only family I have."

"That's a big trust, Milt. We'll try to deserve it."

"When he comes back from huntin' he'll feel he's been some use to us all. He hates having his hands tied."

I looked at his big broad, trusting face. How Milt grieved because he'd lost the oxen!

I'm glad that James hadn't been as hard on him as some felt he should. Milt, I think, would put down his life for us. "Thank you, Milt. I guess all we can do is stick together."

"Mr. Reed will get us there somehow. But it's eatin' out his heart how slow we're moving."

Something made me recollect a day back somewhere on the trail ... I'm not rightly sure just when. Some stupidity had made James angry ... was it when Keseberg beat his wife, or before that when he robbed the Indian grave? He was red in the face with rage, and I tried to quiet him down. "I've got to work it out of my system," he said irritably for him. "Don't try to pacify me."

"I hate to see you so worked up over a trifle ... it isn't your fault ..." I said as calmly as I could, though I had never heard him speak to me so. He took my arm roughly, as rough a touch as I have ever had from him, and said, "Don't you know how riled a man gets, Margaret, when wrong's been done? That man's a jinx, a hex on us all, and a bad man." And I said, to placate him if I could, "Perhaps it's because he doesn't speak the language. Perhaps he doesn't understand our ways ... " and suddenly he looked at me in utter rage, and for a terrible moment, I thought he would hit me. Because I had crossed him? I don't think so ... just because he wanted to hit something, someone, and I was there. My face must have shown the horror I felt, for he let go my arm and the hand raised against me fell to his side and he almost wept, if a man as strong as James would weep, and he said in a shaking voice, "My dear, dear Margaret, my pet ... I was about to strike at *you* ... only becaue I was angry about what a stupid stranger did today ... my dearest dear. I would cut off my arm before I would hurt you."

And he did weep. I said nothing, just stroked his head and rubbed his tense neck, and soon he was himself again. I wanted to say, "Don't care so much, dear," but I was afraid he might become angry again. That night we slept in the other wagon and Eliza stayed with the children. That was what he had needed, to be alone with me, and that's what he needs now, to be with me so I can love him and cherish him. But there's no being alone ... not now.

"I'm glad you thought of sending him hunting, Milt," I repeated, and patting his hand as I would one of the children's, I turned and walked away. Oh, but now I hurt for my strong, proud James!

We have reached Mary's River at last! We are now on the main trail to California after our long wanderings. I pray this will change our luck. Already we have seen Indians staring at us from a distance, without a single stitch of clothing on them. Thank goodness they have not come closer for the sake of the young girls. James seems happier now that we have rejoined the main emigration road, but when he looks back and sees how little farther west we are than a week ago, his jaw tightens. Every chance he gets he goes hunting with Will Eddy. They are increasing our supply of food, in case Stanton and McCutchen don't come as soon as we expect. People don't save. They gobble up everything as if every day more will come.

This beautiful, beautiful trail along the Mary's River. Our friends have long since passed by on it, but we feel their presence just the same. We are not so alone. I saw Virginia staring down it toward California, looking so hopeful ... and with something else on her face ... a sweetness. "Remember that nice boy that danced with me at the Fourth of July picnic? Do you suppose he went down this trail, Ma?"

"No, Virginia. He was going to Oregon, remember?"

"Don't always be thinking of boys. You're young yet, Virginia." "I was only thinking of good times we had, Ma." Poor child, she hasn't complained. I patted her on the shoulder. "Time enough for good times when we get there. You're still young." Just now I said this *beautiful* trail. It is beautiful only because it has been well traveled, and it is, for the first time in so long, the right road, a road we can trust. It's ugly, if you think of the places we have been. A thin, shallow meandering stream, not deep enough for any large pools, lined with scraggling willows, edged with wiry grass that has been cropped low by those ahead of us. We must be the last on the trail now. At least we have a real road, almost like a pike at home.

Some people called it Mary's River, some Ogden's River, and yet others, the Humboldt. It was a brackish miserable example of a stream, intermittent, thin and muddy. At the end of 1846, the emigrations ahead had left spoor along its shallow banks; human waste, blackened campfires, cattle dung, broken fragments of dishes, rusted pans, discarded things too heavy to carry. The willows along its edge were grey with dust, the grassy meadows were trampled. But there was water, even if it had "wrigglers" in it. Sage brush and chamise tinted the grey-brown soil with faint green, the soil was rocky and thin.

The party would have liked to rest their animals, but there was no rest for them now. Another danger confronted them.

The book, Fatal Decision *written in 1950 by Dr. Walter Stookey, furnishes pertinent background for the incidents that followed along Mary's River. A longtime student of the Donner Party activities, Stookey was particularly interested in the Utah and Nevada crossing.*

Captain Benjamin Eulalie de Bonneville of the United States Army, a graduate of West Point Military Academy in 1815, was assigned to duty on the western frontier. Bonneville's first visit to the West was in 1832, during which time he became familiar with the mountain men and the Indians along his western passage. Intelligent, determined and brave, Bonneville spent three years in the Rocky Mountains without the loss of a man. After a misguided attempt to start a fort at Green River, he established a fort at the Salmon River in Idaho, where his usual popularity with both natives and trappers made this a gathering spot. He spent more years in the west, during which he gained the experience he needed. His dream was to explore and map the region of the Great Salt Lake, discovered by Jim Bridger earlier.

"This important task he assigned to his trusted lieutenant, Joseph Walker. No pains nor expense was spared in fitting out this expedition. Forty picked men with supplies for a year and otherwise well equipped, were to assume this important undertaking under instructions to meet the captain the following summer on the Bear River.

Walker was told to keep accurate notes and records of his journey; to make maps and charts as well as notes on his route and the country he explored.

The Walker Party began its westward journey in July 1833 ... pursuing its journey westward passed to the north of the Great Salt Lake. It found scant beaver country and little else of interest — just the barren flat stretches of salty waste lands bordering the lake shores, which was almost devoid of vegetation of any description.

Walker seemed to forget or disregard the instructions of the captain as to exploring and mapping the country. The party continued its course westward, found no beaver, but at length crossed the Sierra Range, and finally arrived in Monterey in California ....

With the advent of spring, 1834, the party began its return journey ... Walker and his men brought upon themselves a lasting disgrace by the ruthless slaughter of poor helpless Indians they encountered in the valley of the Humboldt. According to reports, several hundred were killed just for sport. For this he was severely reprimanded by Bonneville. These infamous barbarities and the failure of the expedition of its purpose so deeply grieved the captain that he considered it a personal disgrace, and turned away in indignant disgust and horror. This wanton massacre generated in the Indians passion for revenge which later immigrant companies, including the Donner Party were to suffer. The failure of the expedition was a blow to his (Bonneville's) pride and his honor, as well as to his purse. The captain was most kindly, hospitable and friendly to all the natives with whom he came in contact, even down to the poorest and most inferior tribes such as the Root Diggers, otherwise known as "So-Shokoes" .... Finally the Donner Party, already in a weakened, perilous condition, presented an opportunity for the poor Digger Indians partially to balance the score for what they had suffered at the hands of the Walker Party. Stookey, *Fatal Decision* p. 45 ff.

From here on the party was attended by these Indians. Some came into camp and were allowed to stay, although Reed disapproved. After their departure one of Franklin Graves' yoke of oxen had gone with them as well as some clothing. Almost every night following brought a loss ... a horse one night, small items of kitchenware, food. Oxen were shot with arrows; apparently the Indians had found cattle more interesting than their usual diet of roots. Although some of the party advocated revenge and strong measures against these depredations, the rest of the party, firm in their Christian upbringing, would not hear of murder. Instead they set up heavier guard duty, which did not stop the raids that came almost invisibly. It was one more frustration in the seemingly endless trip across the broad Nevada desert. Making at least twenty miles a day was hard enough on man and beast in their cramped and irritated condition, but long wakeful nights must have further worn their spirits.

With the grueling speed they were making, they knew they were gaining on Hastings, but he was still far ahead. With their trail-knowledge firmer now, they could gauge fairly accurately the days they were behind by the state of the burnt-out camp fires and the appearance of the dung-crust.

Eddy and Reed spent days hunting. Indian arrows came far too close; they knew they were in constant danger. No one knew how many Indians were following them, for they kept themselves hidden, appearing unexpectedly when any watch was relaxed. Their losses, so far, were only in animals, but how long would they remain that way? All those able to walk were following the wagons to save the worn oxen. No one was allowed to wander from the trail as they had earlier on the prairie. Breathing the dust that whorled up from the wagon wheels, drinking the water with its live wrigglers, having no privacy for any kind of function wore on the women, who were naturally on edge because their men were. Closing their small number of wagons into the nightly corral made nearness even more oppressive. It was hard, dirty and noisy when the cattle, at dusk, were driven into the small circle. Whenever the teamsters drove the animals farther afield for grass, Indians were sure to appear from over a hillock or from behind the poor dusty willows. Try as hard as they could to be reasonable people, they were nagged by worry and fear, and irritation grew. They should have been in California by now. They were far too late, and too far out on the trail.

It was inevitable that an explosion of some sort would happen.

MARY GRAVES

Mary Graves was resting in the shadow of the family wagon at the top of a sandy hill, waiting for John to bring up the last of their three wagons. How hot it was! John must be on fire! The smaller children were with her, and she was singing to keep them amused. A yoke had been driven down to help John ... whatever was taking him such a long time? After their wagons, there were only two more, the Eddy-Reed one and the Murphy's. Goodness, men accused women of talking, but it seemed lately men were doing all the gabbing, every time there was some decision to be made, with some sort of argument. My! it was dusty and tiresome! John had asked her to wait for him for the nooning. She hoped he was in a better mood than he'd been last night. He'd had a double-watch; even so, Indian arrows had wounded several animals. "I'm goin' to git one of them savages," John had said. "I'm about fed up with them ... 'bout time someone taught 'em a lesson." He'd been mad clear through.

If she herself weren't so glad for the few minutes rest, she'd go down to see what was holding them up. Such shouting! Whatever was going on? One of the Murphy clan, climbing the steep yet soft rise, turned and yelled. A woman screamed. Men, coming from behind her started running back down the slope. Mary stood and absently brushed the dust off her skirt, listening.

"Where you goin', Mary?"

"I don't know ... something's happening ... I'll go see. You-all wait right here for me ... maybe one of the oxen's got loose."

Mary walked quickly to the brow of the hill and looked over. Sally Foster was running up toward her. Below, there was a clump of people at the bottom. Someone must be hurt.

"Stay back, Mary, stay back ....."

Sick fear ran through her, and her hands turned cold. "What's the matter?"

"There's been an accident ..." Sally had her arms around her. "Don't go down there, Mary ... there's nothing you can do."

"Let me go, Sally! I'm not afraid. Whatever is it?" She tried to pull away, but Sally held her firmly. Her sister Harriet, panting from the the climb, reached them both.

She was crying, "Don't let her go, Sally. Don't. It's too late!"

"What are you talking about, what is it?" Mary demanded. "It can't be Pa ... he's here with Mama ... who is it?"

Sally patted her back softly, and held her head to her bosom. "It's all over now, Mary. It's all over."

Mary wanted to scream but she was choking, and could hardly speak. "What's ... all ... over?" she began, then she slumped slightly, not trying to push Sally away any more. "Is it John?" she asked in a voice that sounded to her like a child's. "Has John been hurt?"

Harriet said, "John's dead, Mary. John was stabbed to death."

"Oh, my God, my God! You're lying to me, Harriet. Tell me you're lying."

After a moment, when Harriet didn't answer, Mary said in a thin incredulous voice, "Who would stab John? Let me go to him. He can't be dead ... I only just spoke to him, minutes ago ...."

The two Murphy sisters watched her as she flung herself headlong, down the steep sandy hill. Her long dress blew out behind her, her hair tumbled down, her arms stretched forward.

They let her inside the circle of men, where John lay motionless, blood running from his chest. She took one look, then her eyes traveled around the circle of men, one by one asking, without words. No one wanted to answer. Nearby, James Reed was on his knees, his head bloody, his hands over his face. Mary knelt by John's body and put her hand on his pulse.

Will Eddy said, "It was an accident, Mary ...."

Louis Keseberg's gutteral voice yelled. "An accident vas it? It vas murder!"

"But why ... what ...? No one spoke, and the men edged between her and John.

"Come on now men, all together. Heave him up. Careful, now, careful!" and they began carrying him up the hill. As they passed Mary, John's hand slid limply and almost caught on her dress before someone snatched at it and put it over his chest.

"He'll swing for this!" someone said near her ear. She looked around. Reinhardt was shaking his fist at Reed. Were they blaming poor Jim Reed for this, too?

"I don't understand. I don't understand ...." She saw Milt Elliot, beside James Reed. "Milt, tell me what happened ... for the love of God, tell me."

"Miss Mary, I don't rightly know. There was a fight. It started with me. My wheels got tangled with John's and the harnesses were twisted ...."

"Did you do it, Milt?"

"No, ma'am." Tears ran down her face. "No ma'am, I didn't ...."

"What's the matter with Mr. Reed? Isn't anyone taking care of him?" Mary looked around as Eleanor Eddy came to her side. "Mary, I'm sorry."

"I'm so confused ...." Virginia and Margaret Reed were now kneeling over James Reed. "Pa, Pa, speak to us!" Virginia had a cloth and she was wiping blood from his head. Margaret looked up just then and saw Mary. Her face was white, her brown eyes like blank, burned things. "It's Mary, Mary Graves," she said quietly as if she was talking in a trance. "James, it's Mary Graves."

"Oh, Mary, Mary, forgive me. Forgive me ... I didn't mean ...."

He flung a knife from his hand and she saw it make a long arc and splash into Mary's River ... her river. Virginia led her father away, and Margaret, bent as an old woman, followed, looking back at Mary once with her face shattered by grief.

Eleanor Eddy pushed back Mary's hair. In a toneless voice, Mary said, "Never mind, Eleanor ... help me up the hill. I must go to John ... perhaps he's not ... Oh I'm so afraid, so afraid. I've been so afraid ..." she kept repeating the word. She recognized her father coming down the hill to her. She ran to him as she had done as a child.

"Papa! Oh, Papa. They say John's dead. Is he dead?"

"Yes, Mary." His arms were around her. "He was murdered."

"Who would murder John?"

"Jim Reed. He drew a knife on John. That's the talk."

"Jim Reed? No! Jim and John were friends. Why would Jim Reed kill John?" In her mind flashed the memory of their conversation together beside the fire last night; they had been friends last night. "No, Pa, it must have been an accident."

"John's dead and Jim Reed killed him in a fit of anger."

"I don't believe ...."

He held her close. "I'm sorry, daughter."

"Yes." She would feel for herself, tomorrow, maybe. Right now nothing could touch her. "Wasn't there anybody to stop them?"

People gathered around. Voices. Comments. "There was reason for Jim to do it." "It was either John or Jim." "Self defense." "By the loving God, no. Deliberate murder." "Murther it was." That was Patrick Breen. "John jumped Milt, then turned on Jim Reed." "Reed's got a nasty temper." "Mad dog, and oughta be treated like one." Shootin' ain't good enough. "Reed's been the Jonah all along." "Listen here, you can't let a man beat you and your wife and not hit back! John hit Mrs. Reed too." "Who says he hit

Mrs. Reed?" "How'd she get into it?" "He was hittin' her husband with a whip stock, and blood was coming out like a waterfall." "Mizz Reed ran in to stop it." "The fact is, men, it was murder." "Pure and simple murder." "Murther!" "It vas murder."

The voices mocked, battered her ears. Would she ever know what happened, first to last? She wanted to tell them to be silent in the presence of death, to stop yelling. In the excitement, she walked away and began to climb the sandhill. Only an hour ago she had climbed this same hill, holding the youngsters by the hand, singing funny songs to keep them going. Now, a little later, everything was changed, like a terrible storm hitting in the prairie. Before she reached the top, Pike's wagon double-teamed past her, and the dust rose between her and everything else. Now, only Eddy's wagon hadn't come up. They had the Reeds inside, she supposed. Someone yelled, "Soon's you get that wagon up the hill, Reed, you'll answer to us!"

Mary reached the top and went to the place where they had laid John. Her sisters and brothers were watching, holding on to her mother's skirts. Mary walked to the center of the group around the body, pushing the men aside, and the women too.

"This is rightly my work," she said simply. "You all get back. I'll do the laying out."

Suddenly silent, the family groups stared at her uneasily.

"Go on. Git. Ma, you take those children to the wagon. Billy, you help me. The rest ... you go on about your business. This belongs to me."

"Go on," her brother said to them. "There's no arguin' with Mary when she's a mind to take over. She's laid out the dead before. I'll help."

One by one they detached themselves and moved away as if they were under a spell.

Kneeling beside John Snyder, Mary looked at him steadily. Then with the corner of her petticoat, she wiped his face free of dust. "You got some water, Billy?" He gave her a basin and a cloth, and she said quietly,

"Now Billy, you tell me what happened, true as you can."

MARGARET

I have wept until there are no tears left, only an emptiness. My God, tell me this is a strange dream, that I will wake and it hasn't happened. I pray to you, God, and you do not hear. Are we to be punished again ... why are we guilty, what have we done? I cannot bear any more. This cannot have happened. James will come to me in a minute and laugh at me, saying, "You've had a nightmare, Margaret. Everything is all right."

But the children too are crying. Patty, Virginia, come here. Stay with me. Your father has done no wrong. He is a good man. He would not harm anyone.

Virginia looks sadly at me, puts a damp cloth to my head. "Mama, don't have one of your headaches ...." Her eyes are red and swollen, and Patty's face is streaked with tears and dirt. She says, over and over, "Never mind, Ma, it will be all right, never mind, never mind." But her eyes are large and dark and she looks like a little old woman. Virginia washes my face. "Does your cut hurt, Mama? Poor, poor Ma, it's been an awful day."

"When is Papa coming to us?"

"I washed his cuts, Mama," Virginia said. "There was blood all over, but he didn't seem to notice ... what are they going to do to Papa?"

"I don't know, I don't know." I hadn't the courage to be strong for them. My James, oh my dear James, what have you done?

"The cuts will heal, won't they Mama? Papa will get well?"

"He'll recover from the cuts, Patty. He will never recover from what has happened.

He wants to give his life for the one that ... died."

"Ma, I was sick to my stomach. Everything got black, and I thought I couldn't take care of Papa. Pa said, so quietly, 'Keep on, Puss, I can stand it.' Oh, Ma, there was so much blood!" Virginia gags as blood from my wound stains the bandage.

"Here, Puss, I'll do that for a while," Patty takes the washcloth, her face pitifully stern.

"Virginia, am I asleep? Am I dreaming?"

Patty says calmly, "I wish we was all asleep. I wish it was a dream. But it isn't. So maybe we all better start thinking how we can help Pa."

"I have to lie down for a while ... watch out for Papa. I have to think."

How had it happened? I went back in my mind. That hill. Most of the wagons had made it up by double-teaming. All the women were walking: most had reached the top. James was out hunting ... he'd gone early with Will Eddy. John Snyder's wagon was waiting for the extra yoke to start him up the hill, and Milt was ready to start Eddy's wagon, with Pike's oxen to double-team. Everybody was irritable. There'd been a lot of impatient talking, swearing. Dust was all over, and sand scratched our eyes. Milt had been waiting for John's second yoke to come up. Finally he started up ahead, since John wasn't ready. At the same time, John Snyder whipped his oxen, saying he'd get the wagon up by himself.

Nobody was mad at anyone else until the two wagons, starting at the same time, tangled their chains. Then John Snyder yelled and began beating his animals, and Milt's lead team got out of hand, and there was dust and dirt and yelling and whips flying out. Milt dodged and John swore. I've never seen Milt angry before, and I didn't know there were words like those John said. Even hardened Peggy Breen put her hands over her ears. Eleanor Eddy ran away and started to cry. The Murphys were scattered all around, people started running, a woman screamed. All that yelling and roaring got the animals excited. Then John Snyder started beating his beasts unmercifully, first with the whip, then with the butt end and swearing. "Damn you, git up that hill!" "Wait a minute, John," I heard Milt say. "Don't beat them, it ain't their fault!" My swift thought was I'm glad James isn't here to see this, then all of a sudden, out of nowhere, there he came running as fast as he could. He yelled at John to calm down ... and from then on ... oh, I don't know what rightly happened ... it was all too fast. James said, "Damn you, John, stop abusing those animals!" Then John turned on him, and forgot Milt. "It's none of your damned business, I'll whip any critter I choose, I'll use the whip on you, too!" I've never seen a man so angry, so red, so much in a fury. "You and your damned fool driver."

Women were running. Men were yelling. Was Mary Graves there, or did I see her later? Where was Virginia? Oh, yes, I had the little boys, and we were all waiting for Milt to get the wagon up the hill ....

I did hear James say, "Let the chain drop, John, the cattle will untangle themselves ... let's settle this after we get to the top of the hill." He reached for the chain, and John bellowed and jumped down, his whip butt over his head.

"Don't you touch my team, you black-hearted devil! We'll settle things now. This here's as good a place as any." And then dear God, oh dear God, the butt came down on James' head ... I could hear it hit ... how many times? Oh, why did you come back early, James? This wouldn't have happened. You were keeping your temper till then, James. I can't blame you, I can't, I can't. Blood was all over James' face. I ran to him. Patty says I said, "For shame, John, for shame!" I don't remember. It's all so mixed up. People say I ran between them and John hit me too. I know I have a cut on my head, I know I was bleeding. Was it James' blood or my own? I can't remember ... maybe Will Eddy will tell me what I did ... I don't know. I can depend on Will to tell me the truth. All I know is that I was running to James, trying to stop what was happening, and that the next thing I knew we were both covered with blood and John Snyder fell. People say James drew his knife, and killed John Snyder. It can't be true. They were *friends* ... How can this have happened? I remember hearing Virginia scream. I remember someone leading me away. I remember James kneeling. I remember someone saying John Snyder is dead and James Reed killed him. Mary Graves was there, I remember seeing her, poor thing, her empty hurt face ....

There is nothing but an aching hole where my heart used to be. Oh, what is to become of us all? Lord, Lord, have mercy on me and my children. God, tell me this isn't true! Tell me I have dreamed it all! Only now I can hear the children crying. I can hear James' voice, and Will Eddy's and Milt Elliot's and they are the voices that say yes, it has happened ... this horrible thing has happened.

"Mama," Patty says, "Pa's here ... Papa's back." I take a deep breath. I must help him as much as I can.

MARY

While they sponged the body, Billy told Mary how John Snyder had died in his arms. "I am dead," he said to Patrick Breen. James Reed, blinded by the blood streaming from his cut, rose from where he fell and came to where John lay. "People say that John said it was his fault," Billy said bitterly. "I didn't hear that," he told his sister.

"What did you hear, Billy?"

"Only the cussin' and the yellin' and the screamin' and the cattle bellowin' ... John was hittin' them pretty hard ... and Reed sayin' something about settlin' this later and then the sound of the whip butt ... I didn't see anything ... I just heard, and I ran ...."

"Why was John angry?"

"Don't rightly know, Mary. He'd been waitin' a long time for the extra yoke, and Milt Elliot was ready to go, and they just started at the same time and got tangled up and then all hell broke loose and John's dead. They ain't no reason for it, Mary. No reason at all, and it all comes from everybody bein' so wore out and irritated in the heat and ... well, it's been this way ever since we joined this consarned party, hasn't it? That damned Reed ...."

Reed again. Mary thought oh, John, John, didn't you know about Reed and his temper? How he hated to have animals beaten? But probably John didn't think. Nobody had been thinking since she could remember when ... just acting, just trying to get places as fast as they could, just being scared to death of what a mess they were in ....

"Did John hit Margaret Reed?"

Billy hesitated. "I didn't see that ... I did see a knife flash out ... I heard Mrs. Reed scream ... or somebody scream. Harriet and Sally said John hit Mrs. Reed when she ran between the men, trying to stop them. She had blood on her, — his or hers."

Mary said, "So someone tried to stop them ... why didn't a man try to stop them?"

"It happened too fast, Mary. It was all over before anyone knew it wasn't more than a squabble between the teamsters ... we've been havin' squabbles every day over something."

"Why would John hit a woman? I can't believe it of John, I can't."

"Well, anyways, then Reed pulled the knife, and John was done for. People's mighty mad. James Reed's gone too far this time. Tryin' to shove us around, tryin' to make us hurry, fussin' about wasted food, nervous as a cat, thinkin' he knows more about everything than the rest of us ... serves him right. They're plannin' to hang him."

"That won't bring John back," Mary said dully. "Nothing will bring John back. And it's my fault." Suddenly she began to cry, and words came tumbling out as if she couldn't stop them. "There's no one to blame but me. John wanted us to get married in California and I wouldn't say yes or no. I've been afraid, so afraid somethin' was going to happen, but not this. Not *this!* Oh, Billy ... not that he'd *die!"*

"Go on, Mary, get your cry out. It'll do you good!"

"I'm not much for cryin', you know that Billy." She sobbed softly between her broken words. "I can't help ... feelin' ... this ... was some ... of my fault."

She was smoothing John's hair back. She pulled the lids down over his blank eyes. "He never did harm to anyone before this, Billy. He was always laughin', until lately. He's been mad ... at me, even ... because of all the bad luck. Maybe I didn't stand by him like I should ... you know I hate complainin' when there's nothing you can do about it ... he didn't like me to help the men, either ... I shouldn't have acted so independent ...." Her hands continued to work swiftly, making John look presentable. "Maybe I was too ...."

"That's woman talk, Mary. This wasn't none of your business. It had nothin' to do with women ...."

She went on as if she didn't hear him. "Maybe if I'd smoothed his ruffled feathers some, maybe if I'd listened to him more ... maybe even if I'd ...."

They both heard the racket as the last wagon came up the sandhill. Milt Elliot walked beside it, his white face stern and intent. Straight through the clustered wagons he went, stopping finally in a spot distant from the others. Mary looked hard at the wagon ... where was James Reed? Had he been downed by his head wounds? She wished she could talk to him simply, ask him to tell her the truth. Would he tell her? She believed he would. She should hate him, and perhaps she would when she was ready to hate. Now she was too numb with loss.

The body was laid out on a board, and Milt Elliot came to offer his and Mr. Reed's help; would they accept the tailgate of their wagon for a coffin for John? Mary looked at Milt, standing there with his hat in his hands, his head bare in respect. He was trying to speak. "I ain't one for words, Miss Mary. John wasn't our enemy. We liked him. All of us is sorrier than you can know. Mr. Reed in particular."

"That doesn't change a thing, Milt," Mary heard herself say in a leaden voice. "Thank Mr. Reed and tell him we'll take care of our own." She looked up at Milt, and saw that his mouth was moving as if he wanted to say more, but couldn't. Tears were running down his face. "I wish I was dead instead of John."

"That wouldn't help a bit." Mary didn't know what to say to this poor tongue-tied man. She turned to Billy, "Get Pa. Tell him John's all ready now."

With a broken face, Milt looked at the body that was ready for burial, tried to catch Billy's eyes, and then twisting his hat between his fingers, walked away. Mary stood, bracing her feet stiffly one at a time on the ground; she would go to the Graves' family wagon.

Many of the women had gathered there. There was a meeting going on nearby and they were listening to what the men were deciding to do with James Reed. When Mary climbed into the wagon, their faces turned toward her, curious to see how she was taking the tragedy.

"He's all ready, Ma. Tell the men to come fetch him any time." The children ran to her and put their arms around her skirts. They weren't trying to comfort her; they couldn't know how she was feeling. They were asking for her comfort ... she had always brought comfort to them when things got difficult. She patted them softly on their heads, thinking of John's voice, "She's a sassy one, needs some tamin'." Well, John had his wish. She was tamed down considerable now. Then she thought of her answer: "John, I don't belong to you yet!" and wondered if she'd smiled at him would he have forgotten his evil mood, would he have been alive now? Did he think Charlie was in love with her? Oh, that was foolishness. Stanton was gone now, and men's promises being what they were, he'd probably never be back. Oh, but why hadn't she been kinder to John?

No use crying over spilt milk, Mary Ann Graves, you know that. It never did anybody any good. The women and their sad looks and their curiosity stifled her. They wanted her to bawl and scream and make a scene. She couldn't stand their prying eyes. She had to get away. What was the use putting blame on either James Reed or John? There had been ugly anger in John; James Reed had been wound as tight as a clock. All she wanted was to have this day over. Maybe tomorrow she would be able to hate. Get this all over with, bury John, go ahead ....

"There a safe place around here to be alone?"

"All the men is down to the meetin'." She walked away alone.

"Like someone to go with you?" Sally said. Mary shook her head.

"No thanks. I'll be back soon's I ...." Mary's voice trailed off.

Outside she could hear the men at the meeting. "Hang him! Hang him!" It was the German's hateful voice. And Will Eddy's answer, "He acted in self defense, remember that, Keseberg." She didn't want to hear any more. No one cared what she thought, anyway. She wandered on past the wagons, trying to keep out of sight, trying to think. One day she'd know what happened, one day it would make sense to her. "One day ... one day," as she always did, she made the phrase into a quiet little song ... not happy, to keep children walking, but sad, just for herself, to keep herself going. One day, one day ... it fit into her slow steps. One day ....

McGlashan, the meticulous investigator, wrote in his 1877 edition of "The History of the Donner Party" these words: "No other portion of the history of the Donner Party, as contributed by the survivors, has been so variously stated as this Reed-Snyder affair. Five members of the party, now living, claim to have been eye witnesses. The version of two of these, Mrs. J.M. Murphy (Virginia Reed) and Mrs. Frank Lewis (Patty Reed) is the one here published. In the theory of self defense they are corroborated by all the early published accounts. This theory was first advanced in Judge J. Quinn Thornton's work in 1849, and has never been disputed until within the last two or three years. Due deference to the valuable assistance rendered by Wm. G. Murphy of Marysville and W.C. Graves (Billy Graves) of Calistoga, demands mention of the fact that their accounts differ in important respects from the one given above. This is not surprising in view of the thirty-three years which have elapsed since the occurence." (George Stewart arrived at the same conclusion.) Charles McGlashan *The Donner Party* p. 45-46

MARGARET

Eleanor Eddy came back to the wagon where Margaret waited. Margaret noted how thin and peaked Eleanor looked.

"They still are arguing, Margaret."

Margaret put her hands to her head. Pressure was growing.

"Will says to tell you that any delay is good news. He says once they get their bile out, they may settle down and be sensible. The trouble is that there's only Milt and Will to stand by Jim."

Margaret sighed. "If the Donners were here ... and our teamsters, we'd have a better chance, wouldn't we? Wouldn't they have some influence?"

"I'll ride ahead and tell them," Virginia said.

Margaret cringed, thinking of a girl alone with the Indians about.

"Dear Virginia, thank you ... but you must not go. It's too dangerous, far too dangerous, we don't even know how far ahead they are."

"I'd go with her, Ma. I could sit on back of Billy and watch for Indians!" Patty said. Margaret wanted to weep. Her two beloved daughters ... how they loved their father ... as I do. As I always will do, no matter what happens.

"Your father would never let you go, nor would my Will," Eleanor said.

Margaret's head was aching. Was she going to have a bad spell? She hadn't had one for many weeks now ... no, she must not. She must be ready to help James.

"Keseberg's the worst. He keeps people stirred up. And of course the Graveses, because of Mary ...."

Margaret thought of Mary, beautiful laughing Mary.

"She's walking by herself, all alone ... I just saw her."

"Children, I'm going to go to her," Margaret said suddenly.

"Can I go, Ma?"

"No. I want to go by myself."

I walk toward the distant figure, alone, bereaved, so young to have lost her man. Who would know better than I? But will she face me in hate? I call her name and she turns toward me. At first her face is blank, then something flashes over it ... I don't know what ... recognition of me, and something else ... resignation? I felt that way too when I finally realized Lloyd was dead, those years ago when I was her age. I go toward her, blind to everything but her eyes upon me ... eyes that had lost their shine. "Mary," I said. "Mary ...."

She waited.

"Mary ... this happened to me too, once ...."

"I know," she answered simply. "Virginia's father ...."

She looks at me as if to ask what does that matter? That is life, these things happen to women.

I hold out my arms. "Please ... I want to say so much, Mary. I know that nothing I say will help the hurt ...." In spite of myself, I begin to cry.

For a moment she stands looking at me, her face twisting in many emotions: hopelessness, pity, sorrow. She puts her hands to her face as if to hide what she feels. Then she comes to me, and we weep together, our hands linked so hard that our knuckles are white. "I thought I couldn't feel anything," she said once in a broken voice. "Now I feel again."

"One has to feel. One can't" ... I was going to say bury, but I stopped. "One has to cry, Mary. I'm sorry, I'm sorry, I'm sorry ..." I say over and over. She answered, "I know," in a choked voice. "One day it will be better." I say, too, "One day ...." She puts her head on my shoulder for a second, and then turns and walks away without saying goodbye, only, "One day ... one day ...."

When I return to the wagon I see the children have been watching me. Perhaps it is good to let childen see you cry. I do not think it is bad for them to know how much I care ... and that enemies can love each other ... and that one day, one day, things might be better.

Will and James come back after a while. The verdict has been made. James is not to die, and for this I lift my heart in thanksgiving. At one time, Will says, Keseberg had raised his wagon tongue to serve as a gallows. Milt and Will had taken their guns to the meeting. They would have fought this, even if it meant more senseless deaths, but luckily, some good will prevailed ... perhaps someone had remembered the food James had distributed so freely a time ago.

James is to be banished. He can take nothing with him.

"That's putting me to sure death. I will not leave my family ... they may kill me now, but I will not go."

Milt and Will are adamant. "You must go, and go quickly. We'll try to get you food and a gun ... if you can reach the Donners, they can help you. If you refuse to leave, the worst may happen."

"But my family? How can I leave them alone?"

Both men swear to help us. I try to look unafraid. "Hush, James, you must go. We will be all right. It's much better that you go." I had forgotten the children. The girls are crying and Jimmy's face is screwed up in an attempt not to cry, too. "I can help Pa. I'll gather wood for Ma."

Virginia says passionately, "Those awful, awful people to do this to you, Papa. I hate them, I hate them ... after all the food you gave them."

James looks at her sadly, "I never want to hear the word hate again, Virginia."

"You can trust me," Milt says. "I'll do my best."

James puts his head in his hands for a minute, then straightens with a jerk of pain. "This wound has made me think badly. Perhaps you are right, Margaret dear. Do you think you can make it alone?"

With all the assurance I can muster I manage to say, "Yes, James. I can. I will bring the children through to you!" Then I add in the silence that has fallen, "and James ... this may be a blessing in a way ...."

"A pretty grim blessing ...."

"But if you get ahead to the Donners and meet Stanton and McCutchen coming back with supplies, you can return with them. You are taking one appetite from us."

I think perhaps it was that remark, coming from I know not where in my troubled mind, that decided James finally to go.

"Then they'll be sorry they were so mean," Virginia says.

"Shh, Virginia ... yes, Margaret. Yes. If I get a horse from the Donners I can travel much faster. If I only knew how far ahead they are. Jake manages to travel faster than George ... but you do give me reason to go ...."

I back up my argument with as many reasons as I can summon in my terror.

"Nothing could be worse, James, than to have the children see you come to harm before their eyes! Instead, you may be the one to save them! James, I beg of you, in all you hold dear and sacred ...." Now, spurred by his change of heart, I wish him away as fast as he can go. But he insists on remaining till morning when John Snyder is buried.

In the end, they allowed James to take his beloved mare.

"In the morning, Reed sorrowfully assisted at the burial of Snyder. No coffin had been made, and the poor fellow was laid away merely wrapped in a shroud with a board below for decency, and a board above to keep off the coyotes. When the grave had been filled in, Reed, amid the tears of his wife and children, took his leave, mounted upon Glaucus. They were a sorry pair, the man haggard and worn, and swathed in bandages, and the once proudly stepping steed now so gaunt with hard fare that she could scarcely carry a rider."

Stewart, *Ordeal by Hunger* p. 65

MARGARET

I sit here beside the wagon watching the trail ahead where James has disappeared, and I think suddenly of how old I am, and about to be widowed for the second time, perhaps, left here alone ... I who have always had someone to lean on ... my father, my brothers, my sister, my mother. I wish we Reeds could all have gone ahead with James, left this train with its hate, its vengeance, its fear. They hate my husband; they say bad things about him to my children.

I will not weep. There have been too many tears already. I must pretend I do not care what people say. I will not let them see how much this cruelty has hurt me. There is nothing for me to do but go on as if nothing had happened. I must see that the children do not brood nor be poisoned by their hate. They must be proud of their father, and live for the day that we will be together again. I will not acknowledge their hate. It will wear off, one day, when this will be far in the past. I remember Mary's repeated phrase, "one day, one day." What crosses we two women bear! One day it will be forgotten. One day, one day.

VIRGINIA

"Milt, you have Papa's gun, haven't you?"

"Yes, sister."

"Where's Billy?"

"What you planning to do, Puss?"

"Never you mind. You get Papa's gun and some stuff to make it shoot and I'll get some food, and you harness Billy. When it's dark and no one can see, I'm going after Papa. He can't go alone."

"You mustn't do that, Virginia," Uncle Will Eddy said. "Your Pa will get along all right."

"I'm almost the head of the family now, Uncle Eddy. "I'm going. If Papa will let me stay with him, I will. But if he hasn't got a gun he can't make it to California. We can't depend on him finding the Donners."

"But sister, I promised your Pa ...."

"Now don't you try to stop me, Milt Elliot. My mind's made up. I'm not a bit afraid." She faced the men defiantly.

Unexpectedly, Uncle Eddy said, "You'd better go with her, Milt. She's right. Every hand is against him here ... I'll go, if you won't."

"You'd better not tell anyone, especially Mama, till tomorrow."

The two, Milt Elliot and Virginia, sneaked out as soon as it was dark. Since their wagon was far from the others, it wasn't hard to slip away, even though the watch was out for Indians. Milt had persuaded her to go behind him on his horse instead of taking Billy. One horse would be easier to control: a snort or the sounds of hooves would put an end to everything.

"Your father couldn't have gone far; Glaucus was worn down, and your father's wounds must slow him up."

As soon as they were free of the encampment, she was glad Milt was with her. It was scarier than she'd thought to be out on the trail, with only stars above and nothing to help her find the way. What if the horse stepped on a snake, and spooked? Snakes came out at night. What if she heard Indians coming? Or an arrow whish past her? She peered through the darkness. What if one was hiding right now, behind that bunch of willows? She and Milt had decided to keep silence until they were far from the wagons. She clung to his broad shape and felt grateful that he'd come. But she would have come anyway. No one was going to stop her from doing that.

She looked at the stars ... the same stars that came out every night, the same stars that were over Mama's head, and Patty's and the little brothers ... the same stars Papa would see, if he were lying down waiting to get to sleep. The same stars were above Grandma, back on the Little Blue, and the same ones she'd seen when she was a little girl in Illinois ... the stars didn't change, but she had. She shifted the packet of food from one arm to the other and watched the gun ride on Milt's shoulder, glinting just a little.

The next morning, when they'd returned to camp, and everything was the same as ever, that night became a strange dream, or something in a story-book. They'd found Papa. How lonely he looked, sitting beside the trail in the dark. Glaucus snorted long before they reached Papa. As soon as she was sure it was Papa's horse, Virginia called gently so he wouldn't think they were Indians.

It was hard to see his expression in the dark. "Virginia!"

"We've come, Papa."

There was something like a sob in Papa's voice. "My dear daughter ... Milt."

"We've brought you all kinds of things, Papa, matches and a gun and some bullets and I've some food for you in this package, and a water flask." The words rushed out. Oh, how glad she was they'd found him! Milt had warned her that they might not.

"Bless you both."

"It was Sis's idea, Mr. Reed."

"I wanted to come alone, but Milt wouldn't let me."

She didn't realize that Papa was crying until she felt tears dropping on her hair and cheeks. "Can I go on with you, Papa?"

"No, daughter, you must go back to your mother and the children. They need you ...."

"But Milt will take care of them, and Will Eddy. I could see after your cuts ...."

"I'll have Aunt Tamsen change the bandages when I catch up to her. So far I haven't come to any of their camp sites yet. It's hard to tell in the dark."

"Please, Papa?"

"No."

"But I love you and I want to help you ...."

"Thank you, Puss. I love you too ... I love you all. But you must help your mother ... she needs you more than I."

When she started to cry, he said, "I'll tell you what ... I'll leave little signs for you along the trail. Letters."

"But you have no paper and pencil, Papa."

"Aunt Tamsen will give me some."

She had clung to him until he pulled her arms away from his neck. "See she is safely back, Milt." The two of them shook hands out there in the desert as solemnly as if it had been a wedding or a funeral. Then each put his other hand on the arm of the other.

"Watch out for Indians, Papa. Come back to us soon!" Virginia said, and she and Milt turned back. Milt let her cry all she wanted on the way home. He didn't tell her to be quiet or be brave or anything else silly. She cried until she was empty of tears. A swift hurt came every time she remembered how pitiful Papa had looked in the dark, all alone, with not even a fire, only dear old Glaucus, looking so old and tired, to snort if Indians came. Papa, who was always so proud and straight and fussy about his clothes and being clean and shaved around his beard, she could not imagine his not being at the head of the table when they ate ... with that horrible old bandage on his head. How could people be so cruel to him? Were they like wolves and rattlesnakes and bad Indians? She didn't think even Indians would be as awful as that old man Keseberg yelling, "Kill him! Kill him!" with that wild sound in his voice. Was Papa worse than Keseberg? She bet even John Snyder, if he was alive again, wouldn't have been that mean. John Snyder hadn't been hateful except that one time. That one moment of time when everything had changed.

She sighed a deep sigh, the last shuddering end of tears, and thought that now Papa had a chance, he could kill things to eat, and Glaucus was with him, and there were matches and some bread. He wasn't hanging on the end of the wagon tongue with that crazy German yelling.

They arrived at the encampment in time to hear the first yell of "Chain up!, Chain up!"

"Let's get the hell out of here," a man's angry voice shouted in the pre-dawn.

"Stop your god-damned noise. We'll start when we damn well please." Another voice answered. "It's every man for himself, from now on."

"God will get us through. Put yourselves in his hands. Pray."

"Shut your blatherin' mouth, Patrick Breen." Peggy Breen's voice was loud and definite. "We'd best be gettin' where we're goin' this fine day."

"There's ice on the water-bucket!" a child's voice cried.

"Git yourself back here for your breakfast, y'hear?"

Milt went right to work helping Uncle Eddy with the oxen. It was just like any other day. The Eddy wagon with the Reeds was the last to leave.

Mama seemed to know what she had done without her having to confess, hugging her tightly, almost tightly enough to stop Virginia's breathing. She whispered in her ear, "Bless you dear. You're a good brave girl. Mama's very proud of you. I'll try to be brave too, and we'll all be with Papa soon."

"The sad parting between Reed and his family and the second parting with the devoted Virginia, we pass over in silence. James F. Reed, Jr., only five years old, declared that he would go with his father, and assist him in obtaining food during the long journey. Even the baby, only two-and-a-half years old, would fret and worry every time the family sat down to their meals, lest father should find nothing to eat on his difficult way. Every day the mother and daughters would eagerly search for the letter Mr. Reed was sure to leave on the top of some bush, or in a split stick by the wayside. When he succeeded in killing geese or ducks, as he frequently did along the Humboldt and Truckee, he would scatter the feathers about his camping ground, that his family might see that he was supplied with food. It is hardly necessary to mention that Mrs. Reed and the children regarded the father's camping places as hallowed ground, and as often as possible kindled their evening fires in the same spot where his had been kindled.

But a day came when they found no more letters ... no further traces of the father. Was he dead? Had he starved by the way? Had the Indians killed him?

History of the Donner Party, C.F. McGlashan, p. 50

VIRGINIA

"Time for bed," Mama said. The campfire had burned down to a soft glow.

"In a minute." She couldn't face the nightly crowded scramble and hurly-burly of the wagon. There was no space to think. Outside, the sky was wide and dark, with stars everywhere, every one an angel, people said. Auntie Eleanor's baby whimpering, the children pushing and shoving, and finally settling down when Patty made up a story to tell them ... Mama holding Tommie till he drifted off, then sitting in the front of the wagon with Auntie Eleanor, talking softly ... it was all too much. She needed to be away from them all.

"I'm going to sit by the fire for a while."

"Be careful, dear. Don't stay up too long. Don't wander away ...."

"I won't." What was the danger? The wagons were in their tight circle, the men outside were standing guard, hunched over small fires of their own. Uncle Will Eddy had gone into his tent early, for he was to take the second watch. She sat by the fire in the same place Papa might have been a few nights ago. She imagined him here. She was both sad and happy.

She leaned far back on her elbows and looked up. They said there was a star in the sky for everyone who died. Which one was Grandma's? Luke's? Which one was for John Snyder? Three deaths now.

First Grandma ... long ago, it seemed to her. When she was a child. But Grandma had been old; she hadn't been afraid to die. Then Luke. Poor Luke ... there was still a halo of sweet sadness about Luke. All alone, as she was. As she felt now, anyway.

Then John. The name dropped like a stone in a pond. John. The stone made ripples which grew and grew, touching everything she loved. What had happened to make John die? Not old age, nor sickness, but something else ... something strange in her life. Something she would never forget, certainly. Would she ever understand?

What had Papa thought, sitting here? Did he understand? Perhaps she could ask him someday, the someday when they would all be together and happy again.

Willows rustled in the slight breeze, and she saw the men start up, hold their guns firmly. Indians? Had Indians crept up on Papa sitting alone by a fire in this same spot?

Why had people who liked each other come to such a terrible point, so that anger and rage and something beyond all her understanding had made them angry, had made them fight each other? Now John lay dead underground on that pitiful board, Papa was far away, all alone, Mary walked so slowly, hardly paying attention to her sisters and brothers she'd laughed with so often. Mama crying at night when she thought no one would hear. Uncle Milt and Will whispering together, worrying. The world's a mixed up place. The trip had been so much fun, and now, it wasn't any more. Anger and hate and selfishness and suspicion and ugliness were everywhere.

Nothing would ever make her believe it was Papa's fault. He'd had things that were too much, suddenly, too much to stand ... the animals being beaten, the whip butt coming down ... not just on him ... Papa was brave, he could have stood that ... but on Mama. Mama, whom he loved.

She remembered again Grandma's fascinating stories ... about how Papa married Mama when she was an invalid, "to take care of her" after Virginia's real father had died. How he'd been in love with Mama's sister and was to marry her, and how she had died before the wedding. How good he was always to Mama. He called her "Pet." And how, when he'd heard her asking Grandma about her real father, he'd said, "Puss, I never want you to forget your father. But I do want you to think of me as the next best ...."

"See, child, what a good man your second father is?" Grandma had said, with a tremble in her voice. Gram had smiled at Papa, and patted his hand. They loved each other.

How was it then that people could hate Papa? He hadn't changed. He was always gentle and loving. Oh, he had a temper ... she'd known that. There were times ... but storms flared up and went away like thunder and lightning.

The flames blazed for a second, as if to remind her. But they died away into the bed of coals.

The night sounds of the camp: the cattle moving, the willows blowing, the soft conversation of Auntie and Mama at the other end of the wagon, the far off cry of coyotes or sometimes the swish of a bird, an owl, probably ... she let herself drift into a fugue of hearing ....

A stick cracked. There were soft footsteps — someone was moving quietly along the edge of the wagons. An Indian? For a moment, her skin chilled and her ears were wide open pits.

The guards had not noticed. One threw a log on the coals and sparks flew up. Hardly breathing, Virginia watched the figure ... oh, it was a lady ... someone maybe going outside for a while ... then she recognized Mary. Mary, alone, as she was, drifting toward her.

She must have startled Mary as much as she'd been frightened. For a moment, she saw Mary's hand go to her heart, and then she heard her quiet voice.

"Oh, Virginia, it's you."

"I couldn't go to bed, it's so pretty out here ...." What a silly thing to say! Mary probably didn't think anything was pretty any more.

Mary sat down beside her quietly, and looked into the dying fire. "I couldn't sleep either. I thought perhaps a little walk ...."

What could she say to Mary? It was the first time since all that happened that she'd seen Mary alone. Virginia's mouth was dry. She reached out her hand.

Mary took it quietly, held it. Virginia felt her own hand quiver like a frightened bird.

She wanted to say she was sorry ... but the words were too silly. Mama had already said that. She pressed her lips together, then blurted out, "Oh, why did it have to happen? To you and us? Because we all love you so much ... everyone does ... it's all wrong, Mary. I'll never understand. Papa loves people ... he wouldn't hurt anyone ...."

Mary didn't answer at first. She patted Virginia's hand quietly. Then she said, "I don't rightly understand, either, Virginia ... why things have to be this way. All I hope is ..." she paused, and Virginia prayed hard that she wouldn't say anything against Papa and their family. "All I hope is that ... people ... won't hate each other any more."

A great sob rose in Virginia's throat.

"And that whatever happens, we keep on loving everyone, and trying to understand ...."

The tears in Virginia's eyes made the stars blur together, made the firelight bloom with a rosy glow.

"Then ... we can be friends?"

"Yes. We will always be friends."

There was silence again between them, warm as the fire on their feet. They sat together, looking at the flames, which flickered softly on their faces. Mary rose to leave.

"Goodnight, Virginia. Don't worry any more."

Virginia stood and moved toward the wagon. Now she could sleep.

The reduced number of emigrants started the day after Snyder's improvised coffin had been covered. Then was completed what Bernard De Voto called the "atomization of the party." In part, De Voto said, "They had ceased to be a group long since. Some of them now ceased to acknowledge membership in the human race. Obeying the law of averages, the daily disasters grew worse."

"Hardcoop, who was more than sixty years old, had been traveling with Keseberg and had suffered badly from the desert. One morning he could walk no more, Keseberg, with the limpid logic of the German mind, would not take him in a wagon, condemning the unfit for the preservation of the strong. Eddy was at the end of the caravan that

day — it was of course no longer a caravan but only an irregular line."

Bernard De Voto, *The Year of Decision* p. 339

"... a scout sent out on horseback found Hardcoop about five miles back on the trail. He said Keseberg had put him out of the wagon to walk or die. (On the next morning) Eddy ... was probably the last to leave camp. When he had been on the road only a half an hour and was working to get his wagon through some sand, Old Hardcoop approached him, and saying that Keseberg had again put him out, asked Eddy to take him into the wagon. Eddy promised to do what he could, if only the oxen could get to the other side of the sandy stretch. In the toil of the day, hard-pressed by his own troubles, Eddy neglected to find out what had happened to the old man ... at night he was missing again.

"Eddy, conscience stricken, built a large fire on the side of a hill ... and kept it burning as a signal, hoping that with the aid of the full moon the old man might find his way in. The night was bitter cold.

"In the morning, Mrs. Reed, Eddy and Milt went to Keseberg and urged him to return .... Of the emigrants in the second section, only Breen and Graves still had saddle horses. Both of these refused to lend them. Elliott, Pike and Eddy offered to go back on foot, but the others refused even to wait ... the company plodded on. Upon this section of the trail, the passing wheels of many wagons had pulverized the light alkali soil; it rose in clouds of dust upon them as they walked. It settled upon the men's beards like gray powder; the oxen were chalky specters; the faces of the whole company looked pale .... The emigrants were no longer a 'company' they were only a number of family groups each for itself, some of them ready to cooperate only when manifest good was to be gained for themselves. Hatred and inhumanity walked beside the wagons. The country was getting worse all the time now, drier and less hospitable. Pasturage was scanty. Almost daily, as they followed it down, the river by a strange perversion grew smaller instead of larger as a proper river should." Ibid p. 66-69

Hardcoop died alone, unable to walk on his swollen, splitting feet. He had started to California to "see the world" before returning to his family in Belgium.

Soon after his abandonment, the second section of the train caught up with the Donners at four in the morning after a forced march. Another danger signal awaited them here. A member of the Hastings-led, Harlan-Young contingent had been buried there, after dying from the effects of an arrow wound. They found his grave uncovered by Indians, who had taken his clothes and left his body for the coyotes.

Nothing was joyous about the reunion. Reed's crime and punishment had once more to be discussed and argued by both sides. The loss of Hardcoop must be reported bitterly. Loud talk, accusatory statements, alibis and explanations were made and fought over; in the morning, Indians had stolen the rest of Graves' horses, and people said, "I told you so!" because he had refused to lend them for the search for Hardcoop. Graves would never forget this.

Losses piled up without mercy. The night after the horses were stolen, Indians ran off eighteen oxen and a cow. The third night, they shot twenty-one oxen: many died, and all became useless. With no oxen left, the Donner men were forced to yoke up cows. Will Eddy was left with a single ox.

But for the Reed family there was a modicum of joy. They learned that James Reed had reached the Donners and had proceeded with one of his own teamsters, Walter

Herron. They had food and guns with which they hoped to kill enough game to survive their forced march. Herron had no horse. However, he could easily keep up with Reed who often led his thin and stumbling mare.

The disasters that struck day after miserable day left the party so shattered that they could not muster enough spirit to mourn their bad fate. They went west mile after mile, heads down, their necks bent for the next blow. Most of the party was now on foot, with each day animals killed, wounded, and wagons cached. At the dreaded sink of the Mary's River, where they knew another bleak dry desert stretched before them, they stopped to rest. It was midnight. A guard was set up to prevent the Indian attacks that came with such suddeness and irregularity. When morning came, the cattle were allowed out of the corral to graze while the guard went in for breakfast. The Indians pounced, and twenty-one more animals were shot. Those that didn't die immediately were too injured to travel. There was nothing to do but cut and dry as much of the meat as was possible. With so few animals remaining, most of the wagons had be left beside the trail, and dearly loved possessions hidden as best they could, in case some day far in the future, they might return to repossess them. There, Wolfinger, who had started the crossing like Reed, wealthy, his wife dressed in silk and brocade, was left to hide his belongings. The party refused to wait, but two of his countrymen, Reinhardt and Spitzer, stayed with him to help, while his wife, her fine clothes tattered, dusty and worn, walked ahead with the other women. Days were to pass before two of the three men rejoined the train.

By this time, the clothes of all the women, many simple linsey-woolsey dresses they would have scorned at home, were worn and ragged. Some pinned or sewed their wide skirts in a semblance of men's trousers, but these were bulky and unmanageable. The trail itself took care of skirt lengths; briars and brush and rocks and sand had shredded the hems so they didn't reach the tops of their pathetically worn shoes. Washing clothes was almost impossible now, even if they had had the energy after the long marches of twenty miles or more a day. There was little water, besides, and it was brackish, warm, and swimming with living creatures. Margaret Reed and Tamsen and some of the others still insisted on boiling the drinking water; the rest shut their eyes and drank it as it was.

Meals had long since ceased to be regular. There was no time to be spared setting a table or washing dishes, though the pans were scoured in sand as often as possible. Bits of bread were parceled out, and pieces of dried beef from the dead cattle, with sometimes a taste of loaf sugar or the luxury of coffee. Everyone walked. Sometimes, to save the strength of the animals, Margaret and Eliza or Virginia carried the boys ahead, returned for blankets and the bundles of food they carried, making each stretch three times. Will Eddy had no animals left to pull his wagon. The little that was left of Margaret Reed's once ample provisions was stashed in the Breen wagon, and the Reeds moved up to walk with the Donners. Margaret Reed was offered two horses from the Donners upon which her small boys could ride. The Eddy family had no choice but to leave everything. Each parent carried a child. Their food was completely gone, Will's provident gun broken and discarded. He still carried powder, bullets and a little loaf sugar; that was all. No one offered to take even his year-old daughter into a wagon. When Eleanor thought back to the hours Will had spent hunting for others, mending wagons, lending his hand to one and all, her thoughts must have been bitter indeed. Will was proud. He would not let people see how he felt.

There was nothing to to now but plod, one struggling step at a time, across the forbiding sink of the Mary's River toward the west that seemed every day to be farther away.

MARY

Mary Graves walked doggedly beside the family wagon, listlessly holding the hands of the smaller Graves children, sometimes rousing herself enough to sing a little tune of her own making. What would she have done without those small hands in hers? They were all that kept her from disappearing like a disembodied ghost. She was alone in heart. Every step took her farther from the crude grave where John lay in the gray-green sagebrush ... or did he lie there? Perhaps he had been uprooted as the Indians had done with the man killed in the Harlan-Young Party? She didn't want to think of that. California was as distant as the certainty of death. At night around the fire, when she missed John's laughter the most, her sister Sarah was her great comfort, brushing her long dark hair into order and braiding it into a long rope and tying it with a string. It would be easier to care for, and with luck, wouldn't have to be done so often.

Mary was vaguely aware of the privations they were all enduring, but she seemed incapable of caring. It was enough to rise, eat her small portion of breakfast, and set out with the children to walk. Jay Fosdick drove the wagon, and Sarah walked beside him. Once Sarah had said, "Mary, if you'd married John you would be a widow now, perhaps with a baby on the way." And Mary had answered in a far-away voice, "Yes, I suppose so." Sarah added, "I'm glad I haven't one coming ... I guess everything's dried up in me." "Me, too," Mary said. She had lost trace of days. Sometimes she took comfort in the thought that this wasn't real, that she would wake and be herself again. She didn't want to remember the joyous days when they started out, when spring had made the prairie brilliant with flowers, when there was singing and laughing and hopes like the great rainbows that seemed to span the entire prairie, one end to the other when a sudden storm was over. Her only duty was to hold on to the damp tiny hands that clung so dutifully to hers as she walked, to heed the small voices saying, "Mary, I have to go pee-pee," and see that they did, or to tend their other needs. She didn't care about Mama and Papa ... they could take care of themselves. They had each other. Sarah had Jay. Once in a while she would gather enough heart to sing out, "One-two, buckle my shoe, three-four, shut the door ..." so that the children could walk in time, but after a few stanzas her voice would trail off and she would stare into the west, seeing the impossibly far dry mountains gray-white against a pale faded sky, seeing a dust-devil swirl somewhere ahead, absently counting wagons lurching along, the white dust rising over them like a veil; the half-obscured figures of women walking, walking, walking as she was walking, one step at a time. There was no plan in their progress, only the disorder of a rout. They were fleeing forward because they could not go back. Oh, if they could go back, back to the mythic sometime before everything started to go wrong. Were all the women as lost as she, a lost soul in a bleak, dusty desert?

Was she mourning? She wasn't sure. She had never mourned before. Had she loved John? True, he was everything she had expected out of life: handsome, jolly, hardworking, and in love with her. That he was also ready for a fight anytime she had known too, but that hadn't mattered ... men were made to fight. She would always regret him. She would always carry him with her as a weight, and a turning point, as a warning, too ... a warning against pride and vain-glory. But if she had really loved him, wouldn't she have given in to him? Wouldn't they have been married long before this? Everyone said what beautiful children they would have; she mourned the children that would never be born. Would she have loved him always? The ache was deep. Sarah had said, "If you'd have married him, Mary, it would have been even harder." "Why?" she had asked. "Because he would have really belonged to you ... you would have had a life together ... this way it's like it never was, like a dream. Jay and I haven't had an easy time, but we've got something together that you haven't had." "You mean because we never ... because I didn't ...." Even with her sister it was hard to say they hadn't gone to bed together. Sarah understood though. She said, "That, and other things too. You didn't ever really belong to John. You were still making up your mind ... and you'll never know if you would have married him in California when you got there ...." That conversation haunted her. There was some truth in it that she didn't understand about herself.

It couldn't have hurt any more than it did, no matter what Sarah thought. Sarah was only trying to help her, to make her mend. She was not ready to mend yet. She was in a deep hole of loss, and she carried a weight of something with her that she couldn't drop. Time and time again, she would see his sun-bleached hair shining. Just because she wasn't quite ready to surrender to any man didn't mean she didn't love John. And the fact that she had waited, had teased him, had loved the feeling that he loved her, perhaps added to the weight.

Their soft little hands. "Mary, what's the matter? Why don't you make up songs any more?" brought her back to the thing she was doing, doggedly walking west, guarding her young sisters and brothers .... "Come on, then, let's count together. One, two, three, what do I see? By the time we get to that patch of bushes, how many steps will we take? Come on, guess!" Before she had counted past twenty, she would have forgotten the game. "It took forty-three, Mary Ann!" they would yell, and she hadn't even heard their counting. Maybe she was drifting ... maybe she could keep drifting toward California. Because she was strong and young, she was never quite tired enough to sleep at night. If she were tired, she would lie down and sleep and by morning another day would have come and she would feel some relief from the inner weight she carried. Her "one day, one day, one day" carried her over many miles, many miles when she hardly knew that her feet hurt or that her legs were tired ... miles when she only endured the pain that wouldn't disappear, but was there every morning to pick up and carry again. California was like the paradise Hastings described ... and no more obtainable.

There came a night sometime in the long desert crossing when everyone put down animosities, irritations and inner focus, when Pat Dolan started singing and Uncle Patrick took out his fiddle, and, for the first time since the killing, the teamsters joined in and the party, or at least some of them, gathered around a fire in the bitter cold of the night and they sang some of the old songs from back home. Not the jolly ones they'd sung on the prairie, but the soft, sentimental ones, with a hymn tucked in now and then. Mary caught Milt Elliot looking at her, and for the first time in her mourning, wondered if she had washed her face and whether her hair was combed. The fire seemed to lick at their faces, exposing the endurance in them, the hard lines. For the first time, Mary begun to wonder how much her sadness was shared, how the struggle to survive had been etched in their faces. The music, soft and sweet, was good to hear. How she had missed it. It hurt ... oh yes, it hurt! especially when they played a song that John had loved, but it drained away some of the weight. For a time, everyone seemed to be able to put aside the worry of the diminishing, thin, ugly Mary's River, the sage and the sand that sucked at them all during the day, and sing.

Mary felt her feet tapping time with the music, and as if Pat Dolan had caught the signal, the tempo increased to that of a jig. Although she had no desire to dance quite yet, she found herself singing and clapping.

Milt said, "It's good to see you smile again, Miss Mary .." and Pat Dolan, the old tease, said, "There! Mary Ann Graves, you look like an Irish colleen again when your eyes sparkle!"

John Denton said, "You'll not make her an Irish lass, Pat, when I'm around. She's an

English lady to me."

And someone else, from the back of the fire-circle said, "When we get to California, Mary Graves, can I have the first dance with ye?"

That hurt for a minute, but how was the man to know? And it was the first time anyone had said for some time, 'when we get to California' instead of '*if* we get to California.'

Mary looked around her, and brushed her hair back with her hands. Oh, she must look a fright, like an old scarecrow! "I'll dance with you all, if you ask me. Right now my shoes are too worn out for a dance with anybody."

Hope had stirred, and she knew, bad as it was, that tomorrow might be better. John was lying in the past. She had begun to live again.

MARGARET REED

For Margaret Reed, the days were as long and hard as Mary's, but she knew that every step carried her closer to James. She wondered that she cared so little for the valuable things she had lost: fine furniture, dresses, silver pieces, paintings, silks they were to trade for land in California. They were nothing. Only the tall, handsome fugitive who was her husband and the children mattered. Sometimes as she struggled to keep them all going she imagined that she was holding to a strong rope and that he was holding fast for her somewhere ahead.

Sometimes she looked at other women and wondered if she looked as bedraggled as they. The mirror that her friends had brought for the Palace wagon was an eon away, back on the desert. If those at home could see her now! Margaret Reed, her frivolous leghorn bonnet, fashioned in a Shaker style but trimmed with rosebuds, reduced to a sunbonnet plain as any other. She brushed her hair and kept it as smooth as she could in braids looped over her ears, and she carefully cut her shredded skirt straight so she wouldn't look so tatterdemalion. Had she appeared on any street in Springfield, she would not have been recognized as the Mrs. James Reed who had left so stylishly in the Palace car.

It served to amuse her, worried though she was often. What, after all, was the worth of silver and silks when life was in the other scale? And would she give up the strength within her, growing and flourishing to be the pale-ailing woman that left home so long ago? What had made her strong? She remembered her mother's words when Lloyd had died less than a year after their marriage. "Now therefore keep thy sorrow to thyself, and bear with a good courage that which hath befallen thee." She was no more that old Margaret Reed; she had no desire ever to be that Margaret Reed again. When she and James and the children were reunited, as they surely would be, they would bring up a hardy group, a family that nothing could daunt, that no tragedy could break. That she had learned to turn off the gossip of the women, the hateful remarks about James, the blame and the shame, and walk forward, head high and eyes toward the far horizon gave her a strength she had had no idea lay within her. That other Margaret Reed was far in the past; another had come to take her place.

It had been good to see Tamsen again, to be with her and hear her calm logical mind working, to tell her the story of what happened at that sandy hill and have no look of blame come into Tamsen's eyes, only the firm touch of her hand, and the remark, "These things, like so many others, Margaret, will pass and be forgotten."

Margaret had hoped that Tamsen would explain why George had felt it was for the good of all that he and his brother had gone so far ahead; she expected Tamsen to say, "Oh, Margaret, if only we had been there to support you in your agony!" But

Tamsen didn't comment. Somehow, this created a barrier between them, though neither mentioned it. Was Tamsen ashamed because they hadn't been with the rest when the need for a leader was strongest? There was a remoteness in Tamsen that Margaret couldn't fathom, though on the surface, Tamsen was the same. It was as if Tamsen were reading a book about herself, and wouldn't know the answer until the last page.

But they were still friends and allies. They worried about keeping the children clean, they tried to bring order into their lives. Tamsen's wagon was as tidy as ever, her children brushed and neat; she wrote in her diary and once in a while mentioned a bit of bush or a dried flower wilting beside the trail. They walked together much of the time, but Margaret noticed that Tamsen looked away quickly when she saw Margaret's worn, broken shoes, and she avoided commenting on the one dusty, torn dress that Margaret had left, even though Margaret herself made a joke of it.

But the rift, if rift it was, was only a wisp of cloud on their friendship. Margaret knew Tamsen would treat the Reed children as her own, that she was as generous as always. Perhaps, Margaret concluded, Tamsen had not yet learned what Margaret had learned: that wealth meant nothing, that fine clothes were a joke, that bad luck came to the good as well as to the bad.

TAMSEN

Tamsen too was glad that Margaret had caught up with her. During the weeks when they were separated Tamsen had become more confused than she liked to admit. George's sudden decision to hurry ahead had puzzled her; when she asked George why they left the others so far behind, he made no definite answer. There must be a good reason. George was no coward, no one to shirk responsibility. His brother's obviously failing health was not enough cause to leave the others; they had, now that James Reed had no use for them, more teamsters than they needed. Tamsen worried about it constantly. If George was the leader, then why had he gone ahead? She tried to talk to Betsy about it, but Betsy, busy with her children, kind, sweet, loving and loyal and unquestioning of the actions of her beloved Jake, had no answers. Sometimes Betsy, friendly as she always had been to Tamsen, (who after all had taken the place of Betsy's own sister as George's wife) grew slightly impatient at Tamsen's questioning of men's motives and actions. "George and Jake know what they are doing," was likely to be her response.

When James Reed and his broken-down mare reached the Donners and told his tragic story, Tamsen knew immediately that had the Donners been with the divided party, some of the bitterness might have been avoided. She waited to see if James Reed would comment on their absence, but he did not, and for that she admired the man. He was no one to reach for an alibi. George, open-handed as usual, offered him what help he had, released Walt Herron to accomany Reed, and augmented their little ammunition. She herself redressed James' wounds. She gasped when she saw them. No wonder James Reed had drawn a knife; these were deep cuts that would leave scars as long as Reed lived.

"Was Margaret badly hurt?" she asked.

"She has one cut. Fortunately, not so deep as mine. Virginia washed and dressed my wounds, for Margaret, with her own, was not able."

"Virginia! Bless the child, I had no idea she had such courage."

"It was hard for her," Reed said simply, "but she is a loving child and she behaved like the soldier she is." Her told her of Milt and Virginia's visit to him on his first night out, and her wish to go with him, and Tamsen felt tears rise in her eyes.

"You see, only Will Eddy and Milt stood up for us. They were ready to defend me with their guns had the rest decided to hang me, as Keseberg demanded."

Still no mention from Reed of the lack of George's leadership. The shame of it caused Tamsen to blush; yet she was loyal. It was not fit for her to apologize for the absence of the Donner brothers. She still must believe there was a good reason.

"Shouldn't Mr. Herron take a mount also?" she asked.

"George mentioned it. My poor horse is about done for ... I will not be riding him a great deal, and Walt is strong enough to walk ... we will keep up with each other. And when the rest catch up with you, perhaps one of the children can ride. There are few horses left in our section."

She watched him leave the next morning, leading his horse, carrying his gun and a small food pack, and sent her prayers with him and Walt Herron.

Tamsen wondered, who is the leader now of the group behind? Reed had suggested that Eddy was the strongest of the men following. But Eddy had taken Reed's side in the fatal fight. Surely now George would slow his pace so the others could come up. But he did not.

So Tamsen sat in the wagon when they stopped to rest, and, to keep her anxiety in some sort of control, knit. Idleness had become an enemy she could not bear to face. Scant desert flowers, unending artemisia, sand and sage were not enough. She was afraid to write in her diary, afraid to trust her feelings to paper. So she knit. She was coming to the end of her supply of yarn. What would she do when it was gone? She had always been proud of her quick even knitting ... she knit "german style" without throwing the thread. Perhaps she should reknit one of the shawls she had made for her girls. It had a mistake in it she regretted. She would do it over and make it right.

She could not shake her feeling that somehow their mistakes had been ones that could have been avoided, if they had thought beforehand. The first mistake was trusting Hastings' book. When she knit, her mind went back, as it often did, to the day the school officials had come to visit her classes ... that had been before she had met George Donner. Someone (she had never known whom) had complained that she knit in class when she should be teaching, and that the children were not getting her full attention. How silly and apologetic the trustees, men all, had looked that morning as they rapped at her door, hats in their hands, trying to explain in their bumbling masculine way, their unannounced visit. She listened politely, without a change in her pleasant expression, thinking how inadequate her small, five foot size looked next to these tall men. She nodded kindly, asked the boys to double up and give the visitors their benches, and then continued the lessons as if nothing were out of the way. She passed books to the visitors, pointing to the passage where the class was working sums, called on one of the pupils to recite, picked up her knitting as if nothing had happened.

"Very good, Matthew," she said, dismissing the first pupil, and calling on another. The knitting didn't stop, nor did her eyes leave the pupil while he recited. When she came to the end of a row, she felt it with her fingers and neatly reversed, continuing with no perceptible pause. She could see that the visitors were watching her rather than the lesson. Little wonder. Their wives probably knit the slow way, looking down at each stitch. Inside, she was smiling to herself. Someone had told the trustees that no one could knit and teach at the same time. It was a triumph, though she showed no more surprise when the men finally left than when they came. She kindly invited them to visit any time they wished. "It is splendid knowing that you gentlemen are interested in what our children are learning."

It was soon after that that she met George Donner. That day, she was taking some of the children on a nature walk, teaching them about things they were seeing and listening to them tell her which herbs their mothers used in the kitchen. George loved to remember how tiny she looked, half-hidden in the grass, "little and spunky and no bigger than a button, with all those big words in her little head."

Her smallness, she knew, was deceiving, for she was strong and healthy and resilient. And, she knew, because of her stepmother's careful training, she had a great many ideas in her "bitty" little mind. Sometimes she wished she could be more like Betsy. She knew she was as loving, as generous and kind, but she also had questions to ask, and Betsy had not.

A few days ago, she had had to leave many of her books beside the trail. She'd boxed and covered them as best as she could, had George disguise their hiding place under the artemisia, but she knew in her heart they were gone forever. Books weren't silver; they mildewed and went to pieces. She had left her birthright behind.

Most of the day, however, was spent in walking, now that the animals were so worn. Mrs. Wolfinger had joined the Donners when her husband stayed behind to hide his goods. She didn't talk a great deal, for her knowledge of English was small. She stopped often and shaded her face with her hand (she rarely wore the sunbonnets that most of the women had adopted) and looked back down the trail they had come. When she saw no one she turned and plodded on, tears in her eyes. She was a quiet thing, no nuisance at all.

Tamsen admired her for her containment of emotion. What good was emotion when it didn't change things? People were acting as if civilization was a set of clothing that one discarded as not being useful. In her mind, there was no doubt that the party would finally reach California, if not in the condition they had expected, at least able to start again. From experience, she knew that starting again was not impossible ... she had done it; others could. It helped to go on if you kept your standards high. If there was not enough food; one could still keep one's hair brushed. Buttons fell off, they could be sewed on again. If the water was dirty, boil it and let it stand till it cleared. On the rare occasions when there was enough water, one could wash. If you couldn't wash dusty blankets you could at least shake them out and air them in the sun. It was up to the women to keep order.

Poor Margaret Reed. Tamsen had heard many versions of the tragedy ... there were things to be believed in many of them. James' temper, of course, was known to her from the beginning; in a way, she understood it better than George's complacence. Had she been in either George's or James Reed's shoes, there would have been times when it would have been hard to control her irritation. Stupidity, repeated again and again, made her seethe. John Snyder, now, that handsome young man who looked like a statue of one of the young Greek gods ... she had not seen him in any but his happy moods, glad to joke with the company, loving to sing and dance and tease the rest of the company ... what had actually happened? Margaret wouldn't lie; she knew Margaret believed John had been at fault. Even the most genial of men lost control when things were impossibly bad. Could anyone have seen this boil forming ... the boil that broke and poisoned the party? That James Reed had been forced to leave his wife and children seemed as senseless as the crime; what good had it been to lose a man of Reed's caliber? A little thought would have made them all see that Reed was of value ... his crime, if it was a crime instead of a matter of self defense, could have been delayed until they reached California. If George, with his slow, reasonable way of thinking had been with the party could he have influenced them to a less devastating punishment? Who had received the punishment for James' misdeed? His family, his wife, who walked so silently, so steadfastly, herding her four half-orphans across this desert, with that silly Eliza more of a hindrance than a help. Oh, why must she worry that phase of their trouble ... no matter how hard she knit, she returned to dig it up as a dog does a bone.

She was sorry she had not been able to do much about Virginia's spelling, back on the prairie, but the girl was always out on that pony of hers ... Billy, wasn't it? .... "I'll go to school when I reach California, Aunt Tamsen. Right now, I'll only get to cross the plains once in my life, like as not, and I want to see everything!"

Well, those poor Reed children were seeing everything on foot now. Billy had been left behind long ago. Oh, it was embarrassing to be so much better off than her old friends! Margaret Reed's bad luck offended Tamsen in some hidden way. Shouldn't people be more in control of circumstances than that? Why should Margaret be punished for what had happened? She hadn't wanted to come in the first place. It was James who had made the mistakes. In her heart, Tamsen knew that James wasn't to blame, either. His position had been ambiguous when it should have been clearly defined. Whose fault was that? Tamsen took up her knitting; there were thoughts she must avoid.

At last they were at the sink of the river, where water disappeared into sand, and another dry drive lay before them. Only, now, all but the babies must walk; there were few animals left to pull.

According to George Stewart:

"Ahead lay the long desert reach between the Humboldt and the Truckee. Most emigrants counted this stretch as the worst of their experiences, but for the members of the Donner Party who had suffered so much worse things before, and were to suffer still more terrible ones in the future, this was merely an incident.

It was a sorry-looking train that led out from the sink that morning of October 13. Only about fifteen wagons were left, hauled by scrawny teams of mixed oxen and cows, all half-starved. The emigrants themselves were tattered and disheveled. To lighten the wagons, they were even carrying odds and ends of household goods, like people escaping from a fire. One of the Murphy boys walked with a copper camp-kettle held upon his head. Each family group was fending for itself as best it could. Daily, the journey seemed more of a rout ....

That day was sheer horror. Across the heat-stricken sand of the sink naked mountains of rock, luridly sinister in brown, red, yellow and poisonous green, leered out at the straggling train like devil-haunted hills in a dream. The road was the mere scratching of wheel tracks. The ash-like surface of the desert showed only the thinnest scattering of sage. The sand and dust were in places so light that horses sank almost to their knees. In other places the trail crossed ridges of jagged volcanic rock, the sharp edges of which cut through moccasins. Hunger and thirst, heat, dust, exhaustion and fear for the future combined to torture the emigrants." Ordeal by Hunger, p 72-73

The suffering of the Eddy family was worse than any other. They had nothing except what they could carry; a little sugar to offer when the children cried for food, a bundle of ammunition for a non-existent gun, a canteen of water, a child for each, and only Indian moccasins to wear on their feet. They plodded on, one step at a time, barely speaking, for talk took strength. The sky was beginning to lighten in the east when they finally caught up to the rest of the party, who were resting temporarily near a spring of boiling water. Betsy or Tamsen, they hardly knew which, gave them coffee, which Eddy brewed in the hot water. When it was cool enough to drink, he refused any for himself; it was enough to see his wife and children rouse from stupor.

The next day was no better. The Eddy children suffered from thirst. Will Eddy, almost beaten beyond endurance, threatened Breen with death, and forcibly took water from his casks to revive his family. Again, he took none for himself. The desperate march continued all that day and the following night. More animals died. Toward dawn, the vanguard saw trees ahead. A river! At last, they had reached the Truckee with its fast running, clear water. Pasture, trees! They waded into the stream, splashed it on their faces, drank deeply. Heaven could be no better than this. After what they had been through, it was no wonder that they stayed one day to rest and restore themselves, to become human again, to wash their stinking clothes, to feed the famished cattle. Even with the halt of John Snyder's death and burial, they had come down the Humboldt, or the Mary's River, in twelve days. They had averaged more miles per day in this forced march than they had done in any other part of the long trip. They were to know the agony of wishing they had extended their stay all through the coming winter.

Food supplies were dangerously low. Will Eddy's family had eaten nothing but coffee and a few bits of sugar since leaving the sink. Eddy himself had had nothing for forty-eight hours. Borrowing a gun with the promise of some of his kill to the owner, Eddy shot nine fine geese, which he shared with those who had refused his family food or assistance. The irony was lost.

Now that they had reached it, nothing would make them leave the Truckee. No matter that it ran through canyons almost as precipitous as those in the Wahsatch, they clung to its banks. Reinhardt and Spitzer, the men who had stayed to help Wolfinger, here caught up with them, reporting that Wolfinger, ambushed by Indians, had been killed and robbed, and the wagons burned.

Few people believed the story. For the weeping Mrs. Wolfinger, it was just as well that they pretended to believe. Any more murder could wait until they reached California for a solution. Meanwhile, the widow, as destitute as the rest, moved in with the ever-generous Donners. The wagons went on. There was barely any flour left; people chewed upon the poor jerked meat from cattle that had died from arrow wounds.

If they rose early before the haze of autumn hid the landscape in heat waves, they could see the pale blue mountains ahead ... the last barrier.

There was not enough food to get them over the mountains, still they had no choice but to move ahead, step by terrible step. Move they did, as fast as they could go in their broken-down, creaking, dried-out wagons pulled by famished animals so thin that their hip bones were pitifully visible. Men and women, even the animals had only the choice to lie down or move toward some fate that they carefully avoided contemplating.

ELEANOR EDDY

Trudging with the women along the Truckee River, Eleanor Eddy wondered each tired morning what was keeping her moving at all. Always slender, she was worn to a network of bones that stayed together only because skin covered it. Never brave, she was encompassed by terror, the kind of frozen fear she had felt when she had seen her first rattlesnake on the prairie, coiled and ready to strike.

She wanted to forget the hell-filled days last week when she and Will had struggled alone across waterless land, the wagons ahead disappearing into the distance. The immensity of their loneliness was so great, the depth of her disillusionment in her fellow creature so depressing that she felt she was smothering. Only the sight of Will's determined back, the little hands of their son clinging to his sun-burned neck, was all that kept her putting her feet, one step at a time, ahead of her.

Shifting the weight of their baby Margaret from one arm to the other, she thought only of the blissful time that she might put down her burden and rest. Will ahead, with Jimmy, had denied himself everything to bring them across. She must not fail him. Still, the dog-eat-dog evil that had crept among them all, making them behave like animals instead of humans, tore at her fragile courage. She knew how poor old Hardcoop had felt when he had refused to go another step. The world had become something she didn't want to live in any more.

How she wished she had the courage to give up. If it were just she, herself, Eleanor

Eddy, she would refuse to move. Following the river, glinting with shards of light that pierced her eyes, a dangerous river that could pick her up and toss her like a log until she died, she remembered a time when she was a youngster. Caught in a current and unable to swim, she had been tossed and turned and beaten under the water; she had no breath, nor the strength to refrain from taking a deadly breath. Someone she loved ... was it her father, her older brother? which brother? had come after her, grabbed at her, held her head out of water until she could breathe again ... "You've got to help, Nellie!" a blurred voice demanded. "I can't save you by myself!" She didn't want to help. She was too tired. She wanted to let go, sink quietly under water and be carried anywhere ... downstream, to death. Anything but fight any longer. It was an eerie feeling she was to remember with mixed horror and a kind of fascination: the letting go, the giving up, sweet and tempting, the release, the floating, the falling.

She did try harder and they had reached shore. Crawling on her hands and knees when at last the current released its hold on her, she had lain in the sun, exhausted.

She had lived to love, to marry Will, to have her two exquisite children, delicately beautiful. Beautiful? Yes ... they had been beautiful once, as she had been. Had Will known what he had asked of her? Did he think she was as strong as he was?

Now, walking, she would look forward to a certain spot ... a patch of grass, a willow tree, a boulder beside the river and say, "I'll walk that far before I give up." It gave her something to work for. Without that she would fail. Or she would count steps, allowing herself twenty-five, sometimes fifty, before she would let herself stop to catch her breath, shift the baby. Poor little tyke, she looked as if she didn't weigh anything, yet she was heavy on her arm. She slept most of the time now. When Eleanor moved her from one arm to the other, she would whimper softly, barely open her eyes, and go back to sleep. Sometimes Eleanor would rouse her, wondering if she was really asleep or had she already stopped breathing entirely. Once death had nearly taken the baby, but the sips of coffee had brought her back. Another time, a bit of sugar was forced in her mouth. They were rewarded by a slight movement, and minutes later, her wide blue eyes, so much like Eleanor's, opened. The sweet taste had reached some spark left in her wasted body.

Eleanor remembered the wild geese Will had brought in a few days ago. How good they tasted! The children had revived! Why had Will given so many away? He *had* to give Will Foster some, because he had borrowed his gun, but Will needn't have given any to that selfish Peggy and crabby Lizzie Graves, who refused to share anything. What was there in Will that made him do such things? "Pouring coals of fire on their heads," he called it.

"They don't care about coals of fire if they've got the geese to eat," she had responded with the little spunk she had left.

"Maybe they'll realize how selfish they have been. I don't want to be like their kind."

"You won't be alive to be like them if you don't stop helping people who spit in your face!" The hurt look on his face was rebuke enough for her bitterness.

"We'll get through, Eleanor. Don't you trust me?"

Repentant, she said in a rush, "Of course, Will. We'll make it." She didn't believe it, yet she wanted to, when she looked at his anxious face. How could they make California with no food, no gun, no shoes, nothing? How could she walk another step? Didn't he see how thin she was?

Perhaps he saw her as she saw her children, beautiful as they had been once. Slender, like a wild iris, he had said once when they were courting. She'd seen wild iris ... blossoms trampled and broken. Didn't Will know how nearly broken she was?

She *would* try harder. She would shut her fears out of her mind. She wouldn't think of the day ahead nor those behind, or how they were such a proud family, starting out. She would only think of the next step, and then the next until she reached that bush, or that stunted tree, or until she had counted to twenty-five, and then, when that failed she would lie down and let them all go on.

At least this affair of the geese had made people realize how necessary he was to them. Families were kinder now, lending him guns and ammunition for their share of what he could shoot. They forgot that he had tried to teach them a lesson about Hardcoop. They forgot that he had been on Reed's side. Why, people had even forgotten that Reed had been banished! She heard them speculating sometimes about when Reed or Stanton or McCutchen would return with supplies. Now the men were thinking only of speed and getting across the mountains before the snows came. They argued about how many miles they had made in a day. They knew they had gained on Hastings' party, although it was still far ahead. They reached for every straw ... as she had reached for whichever brother had come to save her from drowning.

Let them worry. All she cared about was the next twenty-five steps. And after that, twenty-five more. And then another twenty-five, before she could sit down and quit moving anymore. When she finally reached a place to rest, she was almost afraid to close her eyes for fear she would "die before I wake," as the little child's prayer went. Will's figure, striding ahead with Jimmy on his shoulder sent an invisible current toward her, and she had to follow until she fell ... she hoped he would turn and notice that she was gone.

Let everything wash over me. Stop being afraid. Just lift a heavy tired foot and put it down a little farther ahead. Comfort the baby when she cried. Take another step. Take one more. Please. Please, please, God, please, let me take one more step.

What was the shouting about? She didn't care. Only another fight among the men, probably. It didn't involve Will just ahead. Then he started to run. Another ox fallen? Someone hurt? One more step. The shouts seemed different ... there was an emotion in them she had almost forgotten ... something stirred her heart. Fifty more steps and she would know what it was. People were gathering. People passed her. Take ten steps more, Eleanor. Don't think, don't waste energy. Just catch up to Will, then sit down and rest and rest and rest.

Someone rushed past her, throwing back words.

"They're here! It's Stanton and Big Mac! They've come back!"

It was like that strong breath of air when she had been caught in the water and someone had pulled her out. She was coming up, she was breathing again.

The world rushed over her in a great enveloping wave. She fell to her knees, careful to protect the baby, and then lay down and let unconsciousnes take her. She wouldn't take the next steps. She would let this great overwhelming peace float her downstream.

MARGARET

James was safe! A cry of joy escaped her. She hugged Jimmy. "Papa is safe, Papa is safe!" Oh my dear God, how happy I am! Tears ran down her face, and she felt as if she could fly ... fly all the rest of the way to California. "Girls, have you heard?" Of course they had ... their faces were brighter than the sun, their smiles dazzlingly happy. Patty was jumping up and down, clapping her hands. Milt came toward her in a blur, and he too was cheering. Could any women be more thankful than she was right now? Stanton had talked to James. He would be following in a few days! Virginia, long legs flying, ran toward her and they squeezed each other, and Virginia said, "Don't cry, silly Ma, Papa's safe and well!"

We are saved! Joy rolled over her like a warm comforting breeze. Was she dizzy, was she going to faint? Oh, but she couldn't, she couldn't waste this bliss.

But where was Big Will McCutchen? After all the talk of the bachelor not coming back, and sending a married man with him to keep him steady, it was Will McCutchen who had not returned. Poor Amanda.

Ah, but Big Mac was with James. McCutchen had been too ill to return with Charlie Stanton ... he would come with James.

Charlie was saying, "Now, if only the snows don't come. There was a flurry in the mountains one night, but it melted by morning ...." Always some barrier to happiness. Ah, but she would not let him worry her.

Amanda was trying not to cry. Margaret saw her walk away, carrying her baby. Poor thing.

Someone said Eleanor had fainted at the news ... now she sat quietly smiling, rocking the baby in her arms, feeding it a little of the bread that Charlie had given her. Poor Eleanor. Margaret remembered the words she had said last week when they left their wagon and walked: "Goodbye, Margaret, don't worry about us, we'll see you tonight." Their trudging figures, so far behind, finally fading out of sight. She had sat by the fire watching the waning moon rise and daylight come, too exhausted to sleep. She had even thought of asking Milt to go back for them, but the sight of him sleeping nearby on the hard ground, made her change her mind. No, Milt had done enough. She had only neck-jerking snatches of sleep, before she waked again, listening for the Eddys to come.

It had been almost sunrise before they dragged in. Margaret ran to Eleanor and took the baby from her. Will said hoarsely, "Is there water here?" "Yes," she had answered. "Countless holes of water, but it's all boiling. Here's a bucket that has cooled."

Will Eddy turned down the coffee Betsy Donner gave them.

Eleanor, her eyes large with exhaustion, begged, "Will, take some of mine." She was so frail that Margaret wondered what was keeping her on her feet.

"No, my dear. I will not take anything until we are across this desert. I am not hungry nor thirsty. I am stronger when I am driven."

Margaret had looked at him thinking, you lie, Will Eddy, bless you." He was like James in many ways.

That was all over now, thank God. James was alive. McCutchen was alive, Stanton had returned with two Indians to help him. There was food for all. He had brought mules loaded with food, flour, dried meat, bacon, and rice.

After the excitement quieted a little, Margaret went to find Amanda. "They will both be back, and together. How glad I am that your husband is with mine! They are both so strong! Don't worry, my dear."

Amanda smiled wanly. "If he had to stay back, I'm glad he's with Mr. Reed," she said, but she could not control the quivering of her lips. "I'm glad for us both." They put their arms around each other silently. Margaret was praying for both men; she hoped Amanda was too.

Stanton was already dividing the supplies evenly among the families. Margaret said nothing, but it seemed wrong. If someone could explain to Stanton what had happened since he left the party, perhaps he would see that some families had much more than others. The Breens were known to be well stocked. The Donners were not so desperate as the rest. But he couldn't know those things, he had been away from the train so long. He couldn't know the horrors of the last weeks when they had dragged themselves over the desert, after the Mary's River had sunk into the ground, nor could he know how many cattle had been killed by Indians, nor about the thefts. If James had come, she could have explained, and James would have seen justice done ... then she cringed. James was an outlaw. Much of the nastiness, the cruelty of one family to another, the selfishness had come after he left. Charlie Stanton was too good to see it or believe it if she'd told him. Who would tell him? Not Will Eddy, who had been treated so shabbily; his sense of pride would never let him beg for more than anyone else. The selfish were the first to opportune Stanton for their "rightful share." It was James who had guaranteed payment to Sutter, didn't they remember? She was grateful for the amount she received. She would hoard it. Charlie told her that James and Walter Herron had been ready to kill Glaucus when miraculously they had found some beans on the trail, dropped from the party ahead ... beans, five beans! Just those few beans had given them the strength to push on to a train ahead. An abandoned wagon had some dirty lard in its tar bucket. Herron had been able to keep it down, but James couldn't stomach it. What James had said before he was banished was, "Don't waste anything, Margaret, not a single thing. The least little crumb can save your life. Save what they throw away ... it may come in handy." She listened to him, she obeyed.

Stanton also brought news of the successful arrival in California of the party Hastings had been leading, the Harlan-Young contingent they had been trying desperately to overtake. Scoundrel though he may have been, Hastings had profited from an experience two years before, when he had crossed the Sierra just before Christmastime and the late snows of that year. To give the man credit, a two-month earlier snowfall could not be prophesied. Surely, had he thought of it, he would not have wished to have the notoriety the tragedy of his blind followers gave him. He was never known to have taken any blame.

After all, he had been the single-minded leader, whether for his own neck or the necks of others, and it took a leader to get a large party through without a major disaster, as he had come close to finding out years before.

TAMSEN

Tamsen was alone in the Donner wagon when Charlie Stanton came with the Donner supplies.

"I wish there could have been more, Mrs. Donner ... I had no idea there was such need."

"Thank you, Mr. Stanton ... yes, some of the families are really destitute ... the Reeds, the Eddys ...."

"I heard ... I heard of the tragedy when I returned. Mr. Reed did not tell me he had been banished ... only that he had come ahead for supplies."

"I suppose it is natural. He told us what had happened, but I imagine he wishes to forget ...."

"I can't believe how the party has changed since I left! Such hardships and losses ... Mr. Reed mentioned some ...."

"Most occurred after he left, I think. So Mr. Reed is planning to return presently?"

"As soon as he possibly can, but not as soon as he would like to. I hesitated to tell Mrs. Reed how exhausted, thin and worn he looked, and McCutchen has been very ill, very ill. Mr. Reed and Herron almost starved before they reached Captain Sutter's."

"They are safe now, however?"

"They're safe. Both Reed and Big Mac are strong men, eager to return to their families. I have seen George, Mrs. Donner, but tell me, how is Uncle Jake?"

"Poorly. He coughs nearly all the time, and suffers ... but seems resigned."

"The trip has been hard on him." Charles Stanton looked into the distance that sepaarated them from the great mountains he had just crossed. "There is still far to go. I hope you'll urge Mr. Donner to hurry the party on as fast as they can. I hope the Captain ...."

"Captain Donner? They do not listen to him now."

Stanton looked at her questioningly.

"There is no leader any more. Everyone has lost all sense of discipline. People start in the morning whenever they are ready. It's everyone for himself. We string across this barren land as best as we can. No one waits for anyone else. We're just a group caught up in a sort of panic, all going in the same direction. Some walk, some ride, no one waits for laggards ...."

"I heard of old Hardcoop's trouble ... can those who walk keep up with those who have wagons?"

"They catch up, sometimes after nightfall. We keep fires burning for them. No one seems to care when people don't come in at all ... we left Mr. Wolfinger far back on the trail with two of his men. They returned. He did not."

Charlie Stanton shook his head sadly. "Perhaps I can make them realize what they are facing. How does Uncle George feel about what has happened?"

"He doesn't know what to think. Oh, there are some who listen to him, as in the old days, but most do as they please. We even went ahead, thinking to force them to follow faster .... Tell me, was there snow, much snow?"

"Only little flurries that melted as soon as they fell. Captain Sutter says we are fairly safe. The heavy snows don't start until the middle of November."

"And by that time our travailles will be over ... we'll be there, at Thanksgiving with Sutter ...."

Stanton opened his lips as if to speak, then closed them. After a moment he said, "I certainly pray so, Mrs. Donner. Well, it has been good talking to you ... I must be on my way. Others are waiting .... Tell me, doesn't anyone call our 'Chain Up' and 'Roll!' as we did before?"

"They are all animals now, Mr. Stanton, fighting each other. We don't bother even to rotate the order of wagons. Somehow we manage to camp together at night, mostly for our own protection ...."

Charlie sighed deeply.

"The strange thing is that in these weeks when we've been under such agonizing strain, quarreling and angry with each other, we've made better time than we did 'way back."

Tamsen watched him as he walked back to the others. He too looked tired and travel-worn, yet he had the same steady gaze, the same courteous manner. He still called her Mrs. Donner, though he called her husband "Uncle George." He was as reserved as she. Too bad he wasn't as tall as McCutchen or George or James Reed ... he would have made a good captain. Leadership was puzzling. She, now, was small, but she had maintained discipline with those taller, even though she was a woman. It was a puzzle to know why some people managed and others didn't.

George hadn't seemed to care much that people ignored his position as captain. Once he had said, "Tamsen, my dear, perhaps we made a mistake going ahead of the rest ...."

In a sudden spurt of anger, she had replied, "The whole thing has been one huge mistake, ever since we took that fatal turn left." She stopped herself before she said she had been right. Her feelings that day had reason behind them.

Since then, George had never mentioned mistakes. People still liked, even loved him, clapped him on the back in friendship. Yet they didn't pay the least bit of attention to his orders.

MARY

After seeing Charlie and his mule train arrive, Mary returned to the Graves' wagon to wait. He would come to the Graves' wagon first or he would come last. She had seen him search through the crowd; when he saw her, his face brightened.

Ma was cross. "If he'd bring some flour, I could get some bread to baking. Where's your father?"

"Down with the men helpin' Charlie unpack and pass things out."

"I hope he isn't such a fool as to take less'n the others. You tell him that, Mary? Your father's a silly old fool sometimes."

"You told him already, Ma. We'll get our share."

"He'd better. I never knew your Pa to be so wishy-washy before, so half-scared, so beholden to people when there's no cause to be ...."

"Ma, you know why. He feels bad about not lendin' that horse to Will Eddy. He wants to make it up."

"Well, time to make it up after he gits the family across the mountains."

Mary sighed. The children were with the men, begging, she supposed, like the others.

Charlie had come back as he'd promised. They'd given him up. They'd expected Big Mac, but not Charlie. She wondered if he'd heard about John. Oh, of course he had, he'd run into James Reed. She wanted a little time to order up her feelings.

Later, her father, not Charlie, came up with the Graves' allotment.

"That all we git?" Ma said to him.

"It's divided fair and square, Lizzie. We got the same's anyone else, and that's quite a bit because there's so many of us. Only the Breens got more."

"Well, let me git at the flour and we'll have bread," she said grudgingly.

Mary bit her lips. Couldn't Ma ever be satisfied? Didn't she realize what good shape the Graves family was in compared to the others? She was willing to wager that some of the party would make the ones walking share some of their portion in payment for carrying it in their wagons.

She walked slowly down to the place where the mules and the packs were. She hoped he knew about John. It wasn't her place to tell him. Probably though, people were so fired up about food that they'd forget everything else. People didn't want to admit that those two Germans had killed Wolfinger. Two murders, if you didn't count old Hardcoop ... all the cattle shot and stolen or arrows stuck into their sides so they could hardly move ... steady bad luck ever since the day the Graves family had joined this crazy bunch.

There the little children were, following the Pied Piper like in that book. Shy ones with their fingers in their mouths, probably imagining how good the food would taste ... the smarty ones up front pulling at each other so they could get a better look.

Oh ... there he was! Just the way she'd remembered him. What was the matter with her? Her heart was spinning around and thumping. Funny how she hadn't forgotten how he held his head, his hands, how quiet he was, as if wrapped in thoughts of his own. She stood still, heart beating fast, watching good little spunky Charlie Stanton ... just the same as ever ... oh, would she seem the same to him, would he be glad to see her?

The children spied her and little Johnny yelled, "Hey, Mary, come see all the grub Charlie's brought! Come quick!"

She saw his head turn as if he'd been shot, saw him look at her frozen almost, saw the smile start and spread on his face.

"Miss Mary ..." he left the group and came toward her. His hands reached out and she took them. "Miss Mary. I came back. I said I would." He paused, "You're a sight for sore eyes!"

She couldn't speak for a moment, and when she did get her voice back it sounded far away. "I knew you'd come, Charlie ... you promised me."

"You're thinner, Mary. Just as pretty as ever, though."

"You look fine." What a silly thing to be saying. Sillier words were never said. Why couldn't she think of something special to say?

He was still holding both her hands.

"It's been a long time, Charlie ...."

"A million years."

"I say thank you, Charlie, for all of us."

Why did he stare at her so? Maybe he didn't know what to say, either.

"You make it worth it, Miss Mary ...."

Had he heard about John? "So many things have happened ...."

"I know."

Her hands in his began to shake. She saw that his lips were moving, but he wasn't saying anything out loud. His eyes were talking, though. His eyes were looking at her as if he'd like to eat her up. Slowly he lifted one of her hands to his lips and kissed it.

"I'm glad I'm back ...."

She whispered, very low, "I'm glad you're back too, Charlie ...." They stood just looking at each other as if the world had stopped and they were in the center of it.

In spite of Charlie Stanton's urgings, the party rested for four days at Truckee meadows. The cattle were so worn that all doubted they could make the final pull over the dark barrier ahead without a stop to recruit their strength. Women washed clothes, cooked bread, dried meat from the fallen oxen, and talked among themselves. There was no one eager to make this last step, yet there was not one who didn't want to start as soon as possible.

MARGARET

Margaret and Tamsen found themselves washing clothes together at the river-edge, Tamsen put her arm affectionately around Margaret. "I'm so happy for you, so glad about James and Mr. McCutchen."

"James will be coming soon. I watch for him any day now. Charlie said he was almost ready to go when he left."

Tamsen looked toward the barrier that swept up from the desert to what seemed unbelievable heights. Already the trees, aspen, she supposed, were gold, running down the creases of the mountains like spilled paint. "Margaret, do you remember when we talked about this trip ... more than a year ago? Tell me, do you wish as I do, that we had not come?"

"Many times, Tamsen ... more times than I can count. Now, of course, with most of what we brought gone, I find myself in a new mood ... since we *did* come I am happy we have lost none of our own."

"I sometimes wonder that if we had been more firm, I might have persuaded George not to take this step. Perhaps I should have paid more attention to what seemed to be silly women's fears .... Certainly we knew far less than we should have. Certainly Hastings' book was not the one we should have read."

"And now, Hastings is in California, and we aren't. James' mind was so firmly set on coming; he had all those letters and recommendations. I doubt that I could have changed his mind."

"I've thought, thousands of times, that we, as women, should have had more to say. We should not have given in so willingly ... after all, the children belong to us as much as to the men. George too is determined ... sometimes almost stubborn ... and he is older than I ... almost as old as my father was, I think. One doesn't lightly question a man who has made several treks before. He was so sure of himself."

"But who was to know it would turn out as it has?"

"I think of the letter I wrote back to Allen Francis in Illinois. Oh, it is on my conscience too, Margaret. I said the trip was easy ... that we were well prepared ... how many people have I, like Hastings, influenced by my optimistic, ignorant words?"

"You mustn't think of that, Tamsen. You were telling the truth, then. If we hadn't turned off on the short cut ...."

"I was down-hearted that day, Margaret ...."

"We were sure we had all contingencies covered."

"How could we have guessed the pitfalls? Hastings' book was a lie. You've had it harder than anyone else ... yet your face is cheerful ...."

"That's because I know James is safe and well and on his way here."

"And that makes the difference, doesn't it? I had lost all hope of making it to California until Mr. Stanton returned. I am better now ...." She hesitated. "I have never told you ...." She straightened her blouse and then looked up into Margaret's eyes. "I have never told you how sorry I was for you these last awful weeks ... I even hated seeing you in your misery. I avoided you ... I had everything, you had nothing. Your shoes, for instance...." She looked down at the almost colorless, scratched and worn boots that had once been shining black leather. "I felt guilty. I admire you, Margaret, for everything ... I hope we will always be friends...."

Tamsen's voice had broken, and she turned her face away.

"Of course we will, Tamsen. Of course. Thank you for speaking. I've felt there was something that had come between us ... or that you blamed James." She put her arm around Tamsen and they hugged each other and kissed. "We will always be friends." Then they both took a deep breath that was close to tears, and laughed at the same time.

"And we will both forget the horrors, someday."

The two stood a minute more together. Then Tamsen said, "Oh, dear, there goes George's shirt downstream! Heavens!" She ran to retrieve it. Tamsen's hair is beginning to gray a little, Margaret thought. And Tamsen, coming back with the dripping shirt thought, Margaret's hair is as black as it always was. I thought worry made the hair turn.

As Homer Croy has said in his novel about James Reed, the Donner Party trek was riddled with "ifs." George Stewart has also conjectured what would have happened had certain decisions not been made. The story tempts an imaginative mind. Probably this is why the tragedy refuses to die in the minds of man.

As intelligent as he was, Stanton must have been horrified at the party on his return. He had left a distressed, irritable group of people who were beginning to feel the cold breath of death, but one that still believed they could get through as a group, by helping each other. The people he found on his return were completely undisciplined. Every man was for himself, his family alone. Those outside family groups were stragglers, broken in spirits, worn, tired, unable to do anything but walk or ride. It was a disastrous route. They had had no leadership since Reed had left. The one man who might have brought order to this chaos, Will Eddy, had been, for all intents and purposes, abandoned to survive or die.

Perhaps if Stanton had been taller and more forceful, he might have drawn the party into a whole, but he was hardly a figure of authority. They listened to him; they were grateful for his return; they wanted to believe his comment that Sutter said the heavy snows did not come until a month later, and they shrugged. It was as if they were saying, "God, you have brought us this far, surely you will not abandon us now." Few people are willing to believe that the unbelievable will happen to them.

One cannot blame Stanton. If, Reed first, then Eddy had not been able to unite the party, how could Stanton? Eddy could not lead because he had taken Reed's part in the tragedy, and they would not forget that. In some ways, the bedraggled remnants of what had been known as the Donner Party were no better than a group of tired children, frightened, desperate, and completely out of control.

While they waited, Stanton went forward to the pass, reporting on his return no snow on the summit.

At this point, there were still options. The comparatively low, fertile valley around the Reno area would have sustained them all winter, had they chosen to make that decision. They could have built themselves shelters, slaughtered the animals against the winter, and waited till the following spring. They would have had to divide supplies equally, according to need, not numbers. A winter spent thus would have been uncomfortable, but with Will Eddy's hunting ability, they would not have had to endure what they did. Did anyone suggest this alternative?

The second choice was to push forward immediately, with the firm plan to take the wagons as far as they could go, pack all the food they could carry, and cross the Sierra on foot before the deadly snows hit. But with the burden of babies and children too small to walk that far, few would have agreed to that choice.

The third choice was to do what they did do, equivocate for lack of a forceful leader, rest for four days, start forward with no plan in mind if the worst did happen, and let the devil take the hindmost. The four days they spent in the meadows may have strengthened the cattle a bit, but they were in the long list of rest-stops the most critical. Hit or miss, they started up the Truckee River, following the dim tracks of the party ahead, crossing the river more than forty times, staying together in units of speed and panic rather than in organized progression.

The Donners, ahead at first, fell behind. Easy-going George didn't seem to worry. Tamsen Donner's lost diaries might have clarified a great many of the happenings. Accidents continued. They were, ironically, the only thing they could count on. While handling his gun, Will Foster shot his brother-in-law Will Pike to death, leaving still another single mother to go ahead with her baby. While the Donner brothers were chopping a log, one of their axes slipped, and George was wounded severely, a wound that festered and refused to heal. Sometime during these final days, Lewis Keseberg stepped on a sharp stick, part of which broke off in his foot and lodged there; he became lamed and in constant pain. Ten men, all but two able-bodied and strong, Keseberg, Reed, Herron, McCutchen, Snyder, Hardcoop, Halloran, Wolfinger, Pike and George Donner were now lost to the ordeal of taking the women and children over the pass. Jake Donner was unwell. This was a fearful loss of manpower.

So they advanced slowly to what is now called Donner Pass, in disordered sections of panic-stricken, hungry, ragged, miserable people with no plan of action. By guess and by golly they would make it over the summit, when they got there, each in his own time. That any made it at all is the miracle.

Margaret Reed and her family were now in the advance group. Stanton, brave and loyal, had taken them under his protection, as possibly he had promised Reed to do. Her children rode the pack mules. Following in a random way after Stanton were the others. Mrs. Wolfinger remained with the Donners.

Great black clouds whorled about the summit as they approached. Charlie Stanton shook his head.

One by one, the wagons and the families started up the final barrier to California. Stanton knew the trail, but alas, snow had fallen since his earlier scouting trip. It was not deep enough to hold them back, but it was enough to hide the faint wagon tracks. Once over the seemingly perpendicular granite wall, they would be comparatively safe, Stanton assured them. He didn't tell them how many miles more of mountains were beyond that, but he knew the trail was roughly downhill from there on, and would be freer from the deceptive snow. If they would just keep climbing!

There was an evil feeling to the day. Wind whistled through pine trees, making those who had seen and heard the ocean remember its roar. Hurry was as strong as the wind. Everything was at stake. Hurry. Hurry. Hurry before those ominous clouds started to smother the earth in snow!

MARGARET

Single-minded and determined, Margaret Reed climbed up and over the steep rocks as best she could. Patty and Virginia, ahead on the sure-footed mules, each with a little brother held on behind, were with Stanton. Margaret had begged them not to slow for her; she would make it. "Just get the children over the top, Charlie. I'll come. Don't worry." Her lack of possessions ... the few she had kept were stowed somewhere in the wagons behind ... were now an asset. The little she carried: food, blankets, were not enough to stop her.

Oh, it was steep! There seemed at times to be no breath left in her body. Did altitude do that to a person, she wondered? She gulped cold air in hungry agony. After all the walking these last months, she ought not to be so out of breath. There simply was not enough air to fill her lungs. If she took a deep breath, everything turned dark for a space of time and she felt dizzy. No matter. She would go as far as she could, and God willing, it would be over the pass, the top of which was out of sight. It was like a memory of Pilgrim's Progress, one last trial, one Herculean task.

She felt something on her face: cold and wet. Frightening. Snow.

Looking up, she glimpsed Stanton, waving his arms at her. He cupped his hands around his mouth. "Keep on! Keep going! We're at the top." She was pushing with every bit of spirit she had. Get them over, get them over. She didn't waste breath to speak. She dare not waste anything. Stopping for a few seconds to ease the ache in her chest, she looked back and down. The others were following. She could see one of the wagons, lurching dangerously, but moving. They'll never get that thing up. They should leave it, she thought. She must start climbing again.

The wagons below had stopped. She heard people yelling. At this distance, the shrill voices of the women came to her better than the deep tones of the men, although she could plainly hear shouts. For the love of God, they weren't stopping to argue again now, to fight? "Climb!" she commanded them to herself. She started upward once more.

With the top only a little bit ahead, she saw Charlie Stanton coming back down. Why? Snow was falling faster now with the soft, quiet finality that at home meant winter had come. Individual flakes seemed soft and harmless, like babies' kisses, but these were the kisses of death.

She could still see Charles' dark blurred figure. Climbing behind Margaret was Mary Graves, as usual with the smaller sisters and brothers she herded so faithfully. Eleanor and Will and their children were next. Eleanor stumbled, then rose again. Keseberg had brought his wagon up part way. The Murphy clan was strung out and walking, but the Breens were in a clump, their wagon moving heavily behind them. Men were shouting and pushing and yelling, sometimes by sheer force holding the wagons upright.

Charlie appeared. "Your children are waiting up ahead with one of the Indians, Margaret. I'm going down to see what's keeping the others ...."

"I'll go on up with the children."

"Good! We're almost over the worst!"

When she reached the place where the children were waiting, Margaret collapsed. Her chest burned from the cold air. She was gasping.

"Ma! We're almost there!"

Margaret could only nod. She managed a smile.

"Charlie will be back with the rest," Patty said. "Don't we all look funny with our eyelashes and our heads all over snow? Mama, you look like you have gray hair!"

They waited there in the snow for a long time. The snow thickened. They could hear shouting below, but they could see nothing now. The Indian stood near a tree silently.

No one came.

MARY

Mary Graves looked down to see the wagons halted at the bottom of this last climb. "Why don't they come?" she wondered. There was Pa, standing beside their wagon, waving his arms. Did he want her back down there? That would be cruel ... to have to climb this stony trail once more. Trail? There were only scrapings of rocks to show anyone had ever been over it before. She wouldn't go down. She would wait here, till the rest came. When the snow started, the children shouted with glee ... poor tykes, they didn't realize what snow meant.

That crazy Keseberg was yelling his head off. What was the matter with the man, anyway? She'd seen him, tied to a horse, his foot bandaged. Did he think he was Napoleon, to be bossing people around like that?

She didn't see Charlie until she heard his voice behind her.

"What's the matter? You were almost at the top."

"Those people haven't a chance in Hades to get wagons over. I can barely see. Look at the snow! In an hour or so you won't be able to find a trail at all! They've got to walk!"

"How can we live if we don't have our things?"

"We've got to forget things and think of life ... I *told* them they'd have to walk ...."

The distress in his voice made the children's eyes large with fear. Johnny started to cry. "I wanta go home!"

"Take us back, Mary. Take us back to Ma and Pa!"

"Hush. We're going to be all right," Mary said, but her eyes belied what she said. "Charlie, you watch out for yourself, hear me? Please don't ...."

"You keep those children going. I'll get the others started. Then I'll be right back."

His slight figure almost ran down the steep granite. She saw him slip, then catch his balance and go on. "God bless you, Charlie Stanton."

Johnnie was waiting now. "I don't want to go up any more. I'm scared. I want go back to Ma."

"Ma's going to catch up to us, pet. We'll just keep right on and pretty soon we'll be all through!" For the first time, she didn't believe what she was saying.

Will Eddy, struggling along with Eleanor and the children caught up with them. "What's happened down there, Will? What's all the yelling about?"

"It's a mess. They are quarreling like a pack of hungry dogs over bones. They've got to leave the wagons and they can't decide what to take and what to leave."

Will snorted. "Maybe they'll get a taste of what it means to have nothing but what's on their backs." Eleanor swayed, and he put his arm out to steady her. "Honey, keep going. Keep going."

"You've ... been ... saying ... that ... for ...." Eleanor could hardly gasp out the words.

"Do you think I should go back to help?" Mary asked.

"Don't waste your strength, Mary. Your mother is one of the worst. She wants to take something she's got hidden somewhere, and she won't go without it. Your Pa can't do a thing with her, so I don't think you could either. They've been packing stuff on the oxen, but it's not working. Oxen don't seem to realize they're pack animals." Turning to his wife, "You feel ready to go a little farther, honey?"

Eleanor looked at him with eyes as tortured and patient as those of a dying animal. "I'll try ... a ... little ... longer."

A mule went floundering past. Mary ran to catch his rope, but missed. "One of Charlie's mules spooked. I hope he sees it in time to catch it."

A half-hour later, the children gave up and refused to climb anymore. "You said Ma and Pa was going to catch up, Mary!"

Johnnie said suddenly, "I'm going down to find them!" and started running down the slope, now almost blotted by the snow.

"Come back, Johnnie, hear me? Come back this minute!" Mary screamed at the boy vanishing into the whiteness.

"I'm going too," said Frankie.

"So'm I," Nancy yelled, following after. Mary looked at Lovina, "What'll we do?"

"I spose we'd better all stay together. They might get lost going down."

Mary wanted to cry in her discouragement. "But we've climbed so far! We'll have it all to do over again. Let's wait ... the Eddys and the Reeds are up there almost at the top!"

Lovina's nose was running and tears washed down her face. She looked like a waif from a story ... a lost waif in snowy woods. Now the children had gone out of sight, Mary was of two minds. Who would make the children walk up again, when the family was ready to climb with their packs? She took a deep breath that exhaled in a white fog, and ended in a sigh. Her shoulders drooped.

"All right, 'Vina. We'll go down and see."

It was chaos where the wagons had stalled. Everyone was yelling, running, walking, arguing. One of the cows, a bundle tied on its back, was bucking like a steer. An ox, unused to the freedom from the yoke and the strange new burden on his back scraped it against a tree; another was on the ground, rolling over his unusual load. Men were holding the animals with ropes, swearing and bellowing almost as loudly as the animals. One of the packs broke open, and Mary couldn't help laughing. Out popped pots and pans and a sack of flour, and on top of it was a vase her mother had bought at a fair back home and cherished. It wasn't funny at all, but she couldn't stop her laughter. That vase, brought so far, and so ugly to begin with, lay unbroken. Ma's luck, sure enough! She scrambled to save the sack of flour before the animals crushed it.

"Hey, you kids, help out," she called. Just then, the vase rolled over and broke. "Good riddance," she thought. "That ought to put some sense into Ma."

Everywhere women were screaming and children crying. It was like the Tower of Babel or that crazy house in England ... Bedlam.

Peggy Breen was sitting on a rock, legs spread to hold something wrapped in a cloth in her lap. "I ain't goin' to California without my silver dish, and that's that, Patrick Breen. You put down your Bible and I'll leave the dish."

"All right then, Mrs. Breen," Patrick said, "we'll stay right here and let the Good Lord

provide for us. That Stanton can't have no more idea what he's sayin' than I do, and I say the Almighty is on our side."

Peggy yelled back, "You'd be better doin' something besides dependin' on the Lord. He's got his hands full this day, I'm telling you!"

The Murphys, as much a clan as they could be under the circumstances, had their animals only half under control. They started to climb, everyone of them carrying something ... flour or a pot or a baby. Will Foster was ahead yelling, "Stop my ox, up there ... he's runnin' mad!"

Keseberg's voice began to dominate everything. He'd never spoken up like this before, only that time when he wanted to lynch Reed. His thick German accent broke the air around him. "Come along! Ve must get to the top now." His arms flailed wildly. "Don't shtop now, ve must leave tings behind! It's death or life!"

"Well look who's givin' orders now ... the kraut!" Even under the stress people laughed The laughter started, first slowly, then hysterically ... that dumb German, hadn't said much all the way across, now was telling them what to do!

Stanton continued to urge people on. "It's not too far, now. The Reeds are already there ... others too. Let me help you with that rope. Slow, now, slow, fellow, don't get so excited! This is only a little old pack on your back. Mrs. Graves, forget whatever it is and come. Fosdick, help her with this bunch of stuff she's taking ... she'll never get it over ... those trinkets won't help you now. Easy, easy there. My God, was that one of my mules stampeding? Hold the animals, men ... don't let them panic!"

The sounds clashed in Mary's head. Intent on gathering her sisters and brothers, trying to help Billy with the packing, trying to make Pa make up his mind to leave the seeds he'd brought so far ... above it all she was aware of Charlie's voice, and Keseberg's, both suddenly imploring, both trying to be leaders, both attempting to bring some order into the mindless people. "'Vina, you stay right here and mind Nancy while I find Johnnie. I think Ma and Pa are about ready. That's it, Sarah, you make Ma behave will you, while I bring the rest? Billy's got the animals ready to go. Ma, can't you help Pa for once? Come children, one two three, up we go, up we go, up we go!"

Somehow they got as far as the Eddys. Eleanor had sprained her ankle and lay stretched in the snow in pain. "I've hurt something. I can't go any farther today, Will.

"Let's all take a breath!" someone gasped.

"Nein, Nein! Later you can rest. Come up, dumbkopfts!" Keseberg yelled, his voice edged with terror.

But the motion upward had halted. Someone had started a fire in a dry spot under a large fir, where the snow was not so thick.

"Aaaah," *people said, drawn to the warmth. They held out their hands to the blaze.*

"Fires of hell! Fires of hell!" screamed Keseberg. "Come on!"

It was no use. The warmth tempted. One by one the emigrants gatherd around the blaze, which suddenly, with sharp snaps and crackles, jumped into the low dry branches. Warmth ... like home. Flaming limbs of the trees dropped among them, but they merely pushed them aside and gratefully drank in the heat.

"Aaaaah, a fire. We'll wait awhile and rest ... till morning."

The Reed family walked down slowly. Margaret was crying. They sat down among the others, who had grown quiet and calm.

The fire made the dusk deeper. How could they find their way in the dark? Tomorrow ... aah, tomorrow.

There was no talking now. Silence. Snow was everywhere, falling fast, hissing as it hit embers. Aah! Tomorrow.

They were utterly defeated.

PART TWO: THE MOVING VILLAGE

TAMSEN

ON A MAY MORNING in 1846, ten days out of Independence, Missouri, Tamsen Donner decided that the weather was fair enough for wild flowers and sketching. The wagon train was halted for the day, probably for some masculine reason or other, a sick ox or a broken axle. Since leaving the Missouri River, this was the first free time Tamsen had known. The trail leading west, across the prairie toward California, surprised her once again by land that undulated far and away, grass rippling in the wind, making the scene more like a green sea of New England than the prairie she had expected to be flat and dull.

For once, there were only a few clouds in the wide sky. Flowers bloomed everywhere. Her sketch pad under her arm, paints and a pencil tucked in a basket, she wandered away from the train, glad to be free for a little while of the constant companionship of people. Although she was not afraid, she would stay within sight of the wagons, for fear of Indians, although those the company had seen so far seemed friendly in a rather watchful way.

She passed other wagons, greeting Peggy Breen, her large red, freckled arms deep in a bucket of washing. Poor woman, still with a baby girl at her breast, and six sons, none old enough to be of much use. Thank God, Tamsen thought those days were over for her. Her baby, Eliza was three, and could be left at home with her sisters and step-sisters.

After the fording of the Missouri, every day had been occupied with new routines of the trail. Now, to be free on a May morning, not a cloud in sight, to paint, to be by herself! She would savor every moment.

The dire thoughts that had hung over her for the last eight months had almost disappeared. Ordinary wagon travel had become routine ever since they left Springfield over the old Berlin Road. There had been no hurry; they were free to stop over if someone was ill, or if clothes needed to be washed. Now, after the frenzy of Independence, they were part of a group whose ideas differed. Speed! hurry! hurry! the order of the day. They even were talking of traveling on Sunday, a day that until now had been kept for rest and worship. Their new-made friends from Independence had left before them, but they were traveling slowly so the Springfield party could catch up.

Ex-Governor Boggs, Captain Russell, Nancy and Jessy Thornton ... it would be good to see new faces. She had begun to tire of some of the women in their small party. Among the large party ahead she knew were people of some education, and with the same interest in botany as she herself had. Her closest friend in the party was Margaret Reed, certainly a superior person and of some education, but Margaret was so frequently unwell, and also taken up with her aged and sick mother.

Tamsen thought of the conversations the two had had before leaving home. Neither of them were anxious to leave Illinois. Both were well established there, with fine comfortable homes. How she and Margaret had dreaded the move! She almost smiled remembering. Now she wondered why she had worried so much. She had expected so much worse of the California trail. So far, if she excepted the inconvenience of cooking over an open fire, rain or shine, washing clothes any which day or way, the trip had been much easier than she had fancied it would be. George insisted that the teamsters help with the wood gathering and some of the clean-up work. She directed the preparation of the food, with her five girls to help in any way they could. Some women were expected to do everything, even drive the wagon if necessary. Poor things, their backs ached and their faces were drawn already.

She had counted on the fact that George's days of wandering were over. The last trip, to Texas that had ended so abruptly with his return to Illinois was to have been his last. She and George had been in Illinois long enough to have their own three girls ... she should have recognized his restlessness cropping out again. He had fretted to go, for he was tired of the climate in Illinois, with its ague and fever, and he wanted to spend his declining years in a warmer place.

"Oh, but George!" she had said, when he first brought Lansford Hastings' book home for her to read. "We're so comfortable here. Your children are all around you ... just like ..." and she had almost said like Jacob, with his many wives, or like Job, which would have been worse ... for weren't Job's trials unendurable and unfair? She had always thought so, no matter what the preachers said.

"We won't sell out completely, Tamsen, my dear. We'll leave the farms here for my older children to care for. If California isn't all that Hastings says it is, I promise you that we'll come back. You've never traveled in a wagon, as I have. You don't know what you have missed, dear one. Why, we'll take everything you can possibly need, any furniture you've a hankering for, your books and your paints. There will be room for any gew-gaw you fancy. You may help me with a list of things you'll need, and when we get to Independence, there will be time to find any little things we've forgotten. The men will do the heavy work. You'll see, it will be like a honey moon all over again."

George could persuade her of anything. That was why she had taken to him ... he knew what he wanted. He usually got it, too ... look at the way he'd courted her, she almost twenty years younger than he. There was no saying nay to George Donner, even if she'd been of that mind. She admired his ability to get things done, to persuade her, to make up her mind for her, she who had been so independent for years ... not a mean thing to accomplish when she'd been a teacher used to being obeyed. But this last whim of his ... she could not bring herself to call it anything else, frightened her. Was George at only sixty-two, hardly a gray hair to his head getting to be in his dotage?

Well, here they were, and that was that.

Across the green prairie grass, flowers were like a palette of mixed paint, pink verbena, larkspur blue, wild-geranium red. Tamsen broke off a piece of strange weed and smelled the odor of turpentine. She took up her notebook and wrote in it and sketched the plant with closely observed detail. Lupins had not begun to bloom yet, but their foliage made a flower-like pattern on the heavy loam.

She found a prairie pea. Someone said that they made a fine pickle, as well as a delicious variation as a fresh vegetable. Tamsen hadn't tasted them yet. Let the others try, if they were so bold. She knew too much about poisonous plants to make the experiment. Oh, what fine soil this was! A good land for farming, George said. The whole landscape like a garden of waving grasses, with no trees, except along the streams. Nothing stopped her view except the horizon ... there was no end to it. Truly the prairie was a garden of Eden, with the Donners wanderers in it, just as George had said. How could she have been so fearful? There could be nothing to frighten her here. She laughed to herself at her fancy. She and George, old married people with their five girls, wanderers in a garden of Eden? They were not exactly innocents, were they?

Well, they were on their way. George didn't turn back, once started, so she might just as well enjoy as much as she could, and study the flowers and plants. When a man like George made up his mind ....

She remembered the long discussions, all winter long, ever since that Hastings' book had come into the house. The Reeds had been to their house many a time, the men with their heads together, making lists, reading passages from the book, while she and Margaret sat before the fire embroidering or knitting ... and talking, talking, in quiet tones, of their husbands' decision to make the trek to California.

Margaret Reed had remarked, "There's no stopping James when he's in the company of George Donner. The two of them set fire to each other ...."

"They do. Your James is the daring one ...."

"George is brave too, and has had experience ...."

It had been hard for Tamsen to learn to call James Reed by his given name; hard also to hear Margaret call George by his. But one evening, they had decided to accept the informality, "since we'll be together all across the continent," Margaret said with a smile. Tamsen had agreed with this lack of decorum, but she preferred not to let rules down with anyone else.

She had become fond of James, admired him, and now considered him part of the family. It was not so unseemly.

"James is fearless," Margaret went on. "Sometimes I wish he were more cautious. People say the Mormons are waiting out there on the trail to massacre us all because of Nauvoo. He just laughs."

"I should think, Margaret, that you'd worry more about Indians. The stories your mother tells about some of the terrible things that happened to her family ...."

"Oh, that was thirty years ago! I think she likes to tell the children those stories just to watch their eyes grow big."

Tamsen said comfortably, "I hear prairie Indians are mild, quite friendly souls, really. I don't propose to let them frighten me."

Margaret laughed. "Tamsen, you're so little! You delight me with your courage! I'd be frightened of them, I think, if they caught me alone ... I've heard so many awful tales!"

Tamsen said nothing. That was a topic she wouldn't think about nor discuss. After a little silence, she said, "Well, our two husbands make a fine pair. They're just like school boys inciting, almost daring, each other into some mischief. Though I suppose this is more serious than boyish mischief, isn't it? Our whole way of life will change. Tell me, Margaret, do you mind leaving Springfield very much?"

"I hate it. I hate having mother going with us when she isn't well, even if she's so determined to see my brother once more ... my sick headaches ... what will I do away from any help? James knows how I suffer. I love my home here, Tamsen. No, I *don't* want to go." Then she looked up from her embroidery. "But I must. I am married to James."

Tamsen let her eyes wander around her parlor while she continued to knit. In her mind, she was saying goodbye to everything she had done to make this her own home. She loved every part ... the large rooms, drafty as they were, the fireplace with its big glowing log, splendid furniture she'd inherited from those others.

When they were married, George had offered to buy her new things, but she had refused. Deep inside, she sometimes minded that his other two wives had chosen much of it, but she forbade herself to dwell on that. They were gone, and this house was George's, and therefore hers. She brought much of herself into it, paintings she had done herself, her beloved books, her arrangement of the furniture, comfortable and welcoming. She had asked only that George put his ... and those others' ... bed into the guest chamber and buy a new one for her. She felt color rise in her face even thinking about it. It had been immodest, daring, to ask. George had only laughed in his fatherly way. "You women! Of course I will, my sweet silly girl."

Finally, Tamsen answered Margaret's question. "Yes. I will hate to leave this home I have made. My three girls were born here ... it has been so secure ... I have moved so often ... from New England to Virginia, back to my home in Newburyport, after my loss ... then out here to my brother's home in Illinois. When I moved into this home I thought it would be forever ...."

"If you asked, would George give up his plan?"

Tamsen hesitated. "I don't know. Perhaps, perhaps not. George is a very determined man." With a downcast glance she added quietly, "I don't know that I would like to ask ... I should be testing my husband's authority ...."

"I think James would stay if I begged him, but I'm too proud to beg," Margaret said. "He would resent it, when he saw all of you rolling off west. He'd come to hate me for holding him back, I think. I couldn't bear that ... I can't fetter James, although he has always asked me my opinion ... he does, you know, Tamsen. He's so determined, headstrong ... he wouldn't mean to blame me, but he might. No. My mind is made up to go, though I weep sometimes thinking of it."

Margaret hadn't mentioned James Reeds' temper which flared and subsided easily. Margaret was a good Southern woman, she could soothe and smooth his fiery spirit. He was always kind and gentle with her ... he called her "Pet" ... that amused Tamsen as much as George's calling her his little girl.

"The two of us, both with our second husbands ... you just into your thirties, I should imagine, and my George over sixty and still wild for travel and changes ...."

At the moment, the women heard George's hearty laugh as he and James Reed entered the room. "Come next April, we'll be the best prepared train starting over the prairie!" he said in a voice that matched his size. "That wagon you're making at the shop will scare the wits out of every Indian on the plains!"

Tamsen compared the two men. Both were over six feet. George was even taller than James, and almost as straight, though James Reed was nearly twenty years his junior. George looks no more sixty-two than James looks forty-six, she thought. Hardly a gray hair in his head ... why should I worry about his age and the foolishness of this idea of his? He came to her. She felt his strong hand on the back of her chair, touching her neck. Quiet, loving, tender with her, almost as if she would break ... when she was as strong as iron! Oh, she was torn, though, with this decision!

"Well, ladies, it's all settled. We're off to California in the spring!"

Tamsen heard Margaret's sharp intake of breath, and knew that she minded much more than she admitted. "You've made up your mind James?"

"It's decided. Now we must work to be ready for this jaunt." He took Margaret's hand and added, "It's time we left these good people to their rest."

Jaunt. Tamsen looked at the fire in the grate, bright, glowing coals. She saw the paintings on the wall, imagined the light place in the wallpaper when they would be taken down. She ran her hands over the new mohair sofa, chosen with such care two months ago. She smelled the faint odor of the roast they'd had for dinner. She listened to the old clock on the mantle, ticking on regularly, like hours and days, faster, faster, faster ....

A strange sound broke into the thread of memory. Her fingers gripped her sketching pencil, and she held her breath. She was back on the prairie, and it wasn't the clock she was hearing ... it was racing too fast for a clock. Something was warning her. What was wrong?

She saw the wide sweep of prairie, her box of paints and her notebook, then looked down toward her feet. She fought her instinct to scream and run. A rattlesnake was coiled nearby, his ugly flat head weaving in her direction. It was his low-pitched whirr of warning that she heard. Don't move, she begged herself, her hands clenched and wet

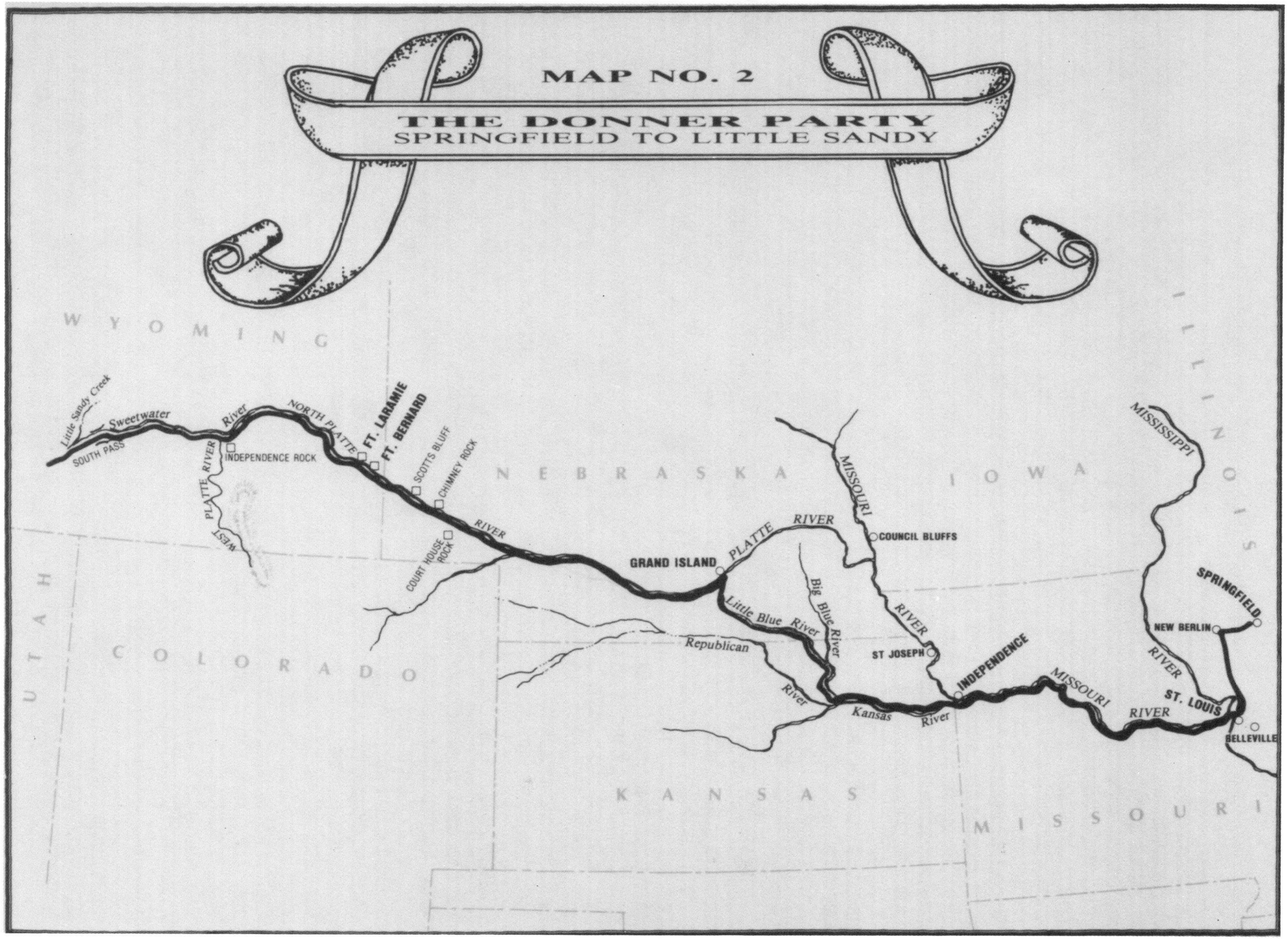
MAP NO. 2
THE DONNER PARTY
SPRINGFIELD TO LITTLE SANDY
WYOMING
NEBRASKA
IOWA
ILLINOIS
UTAH
COLORADO
KANSAS
MISSOURI
Little Sandy Creek
Sweetwater
River
SOUTH PASS
INDEPENDENCE ROCK
WEST PLATTE RIVER
NORTH PLATTE
FT. LARAMIE
FT. BERNARD
SCOTTS BLUFF
CHIMNEY ROCK
COURT HOUSE ROCK
RIVER
GRAND ISLAND
PLATTE RIVER
MISSOURI
COUNCIL BLUFFS
RIVER
Little Blue River
Big Blue River
Republican
River
Kansas
River
ST JOSEPH
INDEPENDENCE
MISSOURI
RIVER
ST. LOUIS
BELLEVILLE
MISSISSIPPI
RIVER
NEW BERLIN
SPRINGFIELD

with fear.

She waited, hardly daring to take a breath. Slowly the snake uncoiled and slid away like a stream of oil. Tamsen took a deep breath and stood, her legs stiff. This was the closest she had come to a rattlesnake ... they were everywhere. She had been warned, and she must remember to be careful. There were many snakes in this garden of Eden, she thought. Always there was evil everywhere. She must never forget that.

Some days later, when they had caught up with the Boggs party, Tamsen, remembering the snake, was only too glad when young Mr. Bryant asked to accompany her on one of her walks. He too was a botanizer, and he made notes of everything. It was said that he kept a diary listing everything along the way: streams, flowers, trees, weather, incidents of the trip. He was writing a book for people who would follow. Well, she hoped it was better than Hastings' over-wrought writing. Mr. Bryant was an intelligent man, young though he was.

She accepted. "I was to go with Mrs. Reed, but her mother is not well today. I'll appreciate your company."

"You're taking painting materials, I see."

"Yes. I would like to write a little book on wild flowers ...."

"Perhaps you could do some illustrations for my book," Mr. Bryant said.

Tamsen smiled. "That would be a delight!"

"This morning, for instance, I found what appeared to be a wild honeysuckle. Imagine my surprise when it had no odor at all! I'll bring you a spray on our return. I have absolutely no talent for drawing. Mrs. Donner, do stop whenever you will. I'll be within call, so you need not fear when you're drawing. Aren't you afraid of Indians?"

"Young man, you haven't come along to protect me from the savages, have you?" Tamsen asked in mock severity. "I think such dangers are exaggerated. And I keep a few gew-gaws in my packet to offer any Indians." She noticed that Mr. Bryant suppressed a smile. "You think I am foolhardy?"

"No, Mrs. Donner. But you're very much the teacher I have heard you were. I imagine you could face any Indian down."

Tamsen laughed suddenly. "Oh, dear, do I sound so severe? Well, I am not very tall nor very strong, but I make up for it by pretending I am. Strangely it works."

"It does, Mrs. D, it does." She did not correct his presumptous use of her initial but she thought of doing so.

Tamsen chose a small rise on the prairie, and took out her sketch book. Edwin Bryant moved onward, stopping to pick a few rocks and an occasional piece of flint. Tamsen watched him for a moment before becoming engrossed in her drawing. She let her mind roam as it would, feeling secure in his presence. There was a small twinge of guilt also, as she drew, thinking that perhaps she should be superintending the washing. Lavina Murphy had her fire and her kettles going early, her first load of clothes in the tubs before anyone else this morning, with her young son helping her. On the trail, boys must help as they could; everyone must do what was asked of him, or the party would fall apart. Some women took turns in the driving of wagons. So far she had not. This was a new society. And she? Botanizing. That Margaret Reed and she were the two most favored women on this trek she well knew, but Margaret had those headaches and her mother's age as an excuse not to work as hard as other women. Well, she must not let that spoil her day. It was not her fault that James Reed, George, and his brother Jake were the wealthiest men in the Springfield group. Sometimes she sensed resentment in other women. She must ignore that. George had said she was to be spared hard physical work. Such a large group of people ... there had been almost one hundred wagons, by the time they had caught up with Governor Boggs and Captain Russell. With the departure of the party from Kentucky, there were still almost ninety. Col. Russell said the party was too large and was proceeding too slowly. Impatient men! Why should they hurry when days as pleasant as this one could be enjoyed along the way?

"Mrs. Donner! Mrs. Donner! We should start back, if we're not to be drenched!"

Tamsen looked up. A black cloud had built up behind her. "Oh dear me! I was so busy with my thoughts I didn't watch!"

"Let me help you with your equipment. It's not a good idea to be in the open in case of lightning ... we must hurry."

They started toward the line of wagons, Tamsen walking as fast as she could to keep up with the young man.

"This will make the stream rise higher than ever! I am afraid we should have forded the stream yesterday ... we will have yet another delay!"

Tamsen stopped to catch her breath. "But so much needed to be done ...."

"California is not just around the corner. I wonder if any of us realize just how far it is!"

"But it is only May, Mr. Bryant!"

"The size of this company makes slow going. We must never forget that the last half of the journey is the worst. The snows make the California mountains impassable."

They started on.

"Remember," Edwin Bryant continued as they went, "the Kentucky people left the train to go on ahead. These delays, one after the other, mustn't continue!"

"You *are* concerned! But Mr. Russell seems a fine leader."

"Fine or not fine, there are too many of us ..." he interrupted himself, "Who's that riding toward us?"

Tamsen peered ahead. "Oh, that's Virginia Reed. How she loves to canter that pony of hers!"

"How well she rides! Her father must be proud ...."

"Mr. Reed is her step-father. Virginia's name is Backenstoe. Mr. Reed seems as fond of her as if she were his own."

Virginia was close now, she reined her pony. "Aunt Tamsen! Aunt Tamsen!" Her gray-blue eyes were wide, her brown locks flying.

"What is it, my dear?"

"Mama begs you to come. Grandma is worse ... Mama is afraid she is dying!"

"Tell her I am coming."

Mr. Bryant took her packet from her. "Go on, Mrs. Donner. I will see that this is put in your wagon."

"No, you come with me ... you have a knowledge of medicine, please come!"

As they reached the train, rain began to fall. "This cursed storm — another two days lost!" Bryant remarked.

"We are in the presence of death. Hurry has no place ...."

"This is not a village at home, Mrs. Donner. Delays will cost us dearly, I'm afraid. Even more than the expected death of an old woman ...."

Tamsen shuddered, as she had done when she saw the rattlesnake. Was it old Mrs. Keyes' death that made her afraid, or was it Edwin Bryant's worry?

That night, after her return from the Reed wagon, Tamsen asked George, "Are we going fast enough, George? That young man, Edwin Bryant thinks we shouldn't be stopping so often."

"Let him go ahead then. We must wait for a funeral, certainly. So you have been botanizing with a young man, Tamsen? What will the neighbors think of you!" His eyes were twinkling.

"Now, George, don't you tease! He's a very intelligent person." Her school-teacher voice suddenly vanished in a laugh, as if she had been a little girl caught playing grown-up. "You know I enjoy young minds."

"That's how I caught you, isn't it?"

"Yes, it was, so you oughtn't to make fun. And I like people who make up their minds and are good, as you are, George!"

"Ah, don't be cross, Tamsen. You're a high spirited little girl, no older than my daughters back home."

"To tell the truth, I'm *not* much older than they, am I, George?"

As a matter-of-fact, she liked being called his little girl. Strange, when she was such a reserved person, disciplined as a teacher must be. No one had ever thought of her as a little girl for such a long time. It went back to her mother's death and her father's remarriage. Her very dear new stepmother had encouraged her in her learning and her love of study and books. At the time, it had been good to feel grown and independent. She left home soon to attend the academy where she met Tully Dozier. He didn't think of her as his little girl, ever. He thought of her as his beloved. They were in love, interested in the same things, involved with dreams and plans. Tully wasn't rich, but he was well-placed, and they were married. Those years would never cease to catch her in unguarded moments ... those beautiful years; their two little girls, their plans for the future. The school they were going to start when they were able ... all that love, all those dreams snatched away as if they never were in two months that were as long as eternity in her mind. How many times had she wished that she too had been snatched away with them when the disease had struck! How many times had she called on God, asking him, as Christ had done, why must she drink this cup, had prayed that it could be taken from her? She had returned to the town of her childhood, broken, to mourn, weeping often, like Niobe. Had she, like Niobe, caused the Gods, the pagan gods, to scorn her hubris? Had she deserved this punishment? It was as hard to understand as the sufferings of Job. For, like Job, she had tried to go on ... and she had. She had met George, had three more little girls. They had never taken the place of those other two. No, she would never forget them nor those weeks of their suffering when they cried in pain. Was that fair of God? She had always been troubled by the story of Job. God so easily disposed of his wives, children, and handmaidens as if they were chattels ... what of them? Were wives and children just naughts in his great scheme? He rewarded Job's faith with new wives and children casually as if they were new sheets for his bed. All that she would allow herself was the small consolation that the minister had proffered her: "They have been taken from you to the arms of your Heavenly Father where they will never know unhappiness again." But hadn't they *been* happy? Hadn't they been good, kind, loving? What had those two baby girls done to offend God? She would never understand, never. Perhaps ... just perhaps, she had paid for her hubris, the hubris of being proud and happy. Now, maybe God had finished punishing her. Perhaps she would never feel loss or fear and unhappiness again. Perhaps; there was no logic to it. It called only for faith. Oh, that was where she must have failed .... George had faith. He must have enough for two. He could believe. She could doubt, always, in her inner soul. Why? The eternal questioning of a questioning mind.

George broke into her thoughts. "Your face is sad, Tamsen. You've that faraway look again ... be my laughing wife ...."

Tamsen smiled. "I was just thinking ... how much younger I must seem to you! Yet look at you ... hardly a gray hair to give away your age. Why, I have more gray hair than you!"

"Is that what is making you sad?"

"Of course. I'm plain jealous! ... but George, you haven't said a thing about what Mr. Bryant said ... that we're traveling too slowly ...."

"Now don't trouble yourself over men's concerns. You tend to your sketching and your flowers and teaching your children the ways of the Lord. I'll see to it that we get to California in time."

VIRGINIA REED

After finding her Aunt Tamsen on the plains, Virginia put her horse to a gallop and rode back to the Reed Palace wagon, easily identified because it was much larger than any of the others. Wind blew her fine dark hair into a tangle and made her cheeks pink. The clouds were beginning an ominous stirring. It would rain again tonight. Papa would be unhappy. He had hoped to start crossing the river tomorrow ....

But tomorrow ... Virginia must not forget their grandma was dying. Mama said so. Grandma had known she might die on this trip ... the doctors had told her so before she came. But she had so wanted to see Virginia's beloved uncle Cadden, Grandma's son who had gone to Oregon last year and was on his way to take her back to Oregon with him.

Dying! Virginia had no memory of her own father's death. She had been a baby. It was strange sometimes to think her father was not the man she had grown to call father. Pa had always been Pa or Papa. Father was a word she saved for the man she didn't remember.

Now Grandma was going to die. In a way, Grandmother Keyes was her only tie to her past and her real father. Mama didn't like to talk about him. "Someday, Puss, I'll tell you all about him," she said, turning away. But Grandma would tell her stories about father if they were alone ... how young and handsome he'd been, how he had died, how sad Mama had been.

"That's when your mother's headaches started, I think, my dear," Grandma said once. "Your mother isn't one to let people see her cry. She was very young, she married again, and a fine man James Reed is. Remember, Virginia, every bit as fine a man as your father was. Look how he has treated you. You have a pony, nice clothes, a loving home and sisters and brothers ... everything, and he loves you very much. Many girls could envy you."

Grandma would be gone forever. There would be no more talks, no more scary stories about the Indians that had almost captured Grandma's sister, no more tea parties when she and Patty had cambric tea and pretended they were grown up ladies come to call. No more tales about Mama when she was a young girl and so pretty, and her beaux and how she had almost married a man named Mitchell, till she met Lloyd Backenstoe, Virginia's real father, and fell in love with him at first sight. Or about Mama's sister, who was engaged to marry James Reed, but died before they could be married. And how her real father had died of cholera less than a year after he and Mama were married, when Virginia was a tiny baby and how Papa came and asked Mama to marry him. Mama had been sick after her real father died, but Papa didn't mind ... he wanted to nurse her and make her well ... and they were married anyway and now, Mama almost was well ... just those headaches. Grandma was the only one who could tell her how her real father looked ... Grannie said that Virginia took after him. The funny part was that her real father and Papa Reed knew each other. It was all so romantic! Mama was prettier than anyone else when she was young. Grandma thought Mama was still young, but she was an old married lady ... thirty-two, Grannie said.

"I know, Grandma. I love him too. I'm not unhappy when I ask about my father. I wouldn't trade Papa, never in the world! I'm just curious. Wouldn't you be if you had a father you couldn't remember?"

No matter how she loved Mama and Papa, she could talk to Grannie better, say things to her that she couldn't say to anyone else ... that one of the Breen boys had asked her for a kiss for instance. And when she started having her monthlies. "Now you are a woman, Virginia," was all Mama said. Virginia hadn't really understood till she told Grandma.

"Poor child ... it's such a bother for a woman ... and on the trail, too. It will be hard to hide from the other children, I suppose. Oh dear, there are compensations for being old," Grannie had said in a matter-of-fact voice as if there wasn't a thing to be ashamed of. Virginia hadn't been quite as surprised as some girls were, because she'd listened to talk and knew what was supposed to happen. Mother had tried to explain once, too, but she'd seemed so upset, and her face was bright pink and embarrassed. Mama called it her "courses" ... at first she'd been sort of proud she was grown up. It wasn't all that bad, just messy, and then Mama didn't want her to ride Billy on the days she was "sick." Mama called it being sick ... why? she wondered. She wasn't sick at all, just messy.

"Why do girls have to have all this bother?" she asked Grannie once.

Grandma smiled. "It's the curse of Eve," she said. Whatever did Eve do to deserve this! Virginia wondered. Was it one of those things she would understand when she was older? Then Grandma added, "I *must* tell you this. You listen to me, Puss. Kissing boys is all right, once in a while, but be careful. Too much kissing ...."

Even Grannie had hesitated then. Virginia waited to see what she would say. She'd already heard some pretty strange stories from her best friends, but she'd like Grandma's version.

"Too much kissing, what?'

"Too much kissing sometimes leads to more than kissing, child. It leads to making babies. And girls must not have babies before they are married, you hear me, Puss? This trip, now ... there's so much more freedom than Mama allowed at home ... could lead to too much kissing. I wasn't born yesterday, child. It's all right to flirt a little. You're only young once, but remember to stop before anything else happens ...."

There it was. Anything else happens ... that was about what Mama had tried to say, and what the girls at home said their mamas said. Well, she thought she knew what they were trying to say. She didn't know *exactly,* but she knew it had to do with taking clothes off and she wasn't going to do *that.* It was a comfort to know that much at least.

She'd have to remember all the things Grandma had told her, for Grandma was going to die. Grannie didn't want to die till she saw her son, but she was going to die, all the same. Grannie didn't mind talking about dying, either. It didn't seem to bother her one bit. "I will go willingly if I could see dear Cadden once more. I've said farewell to the rest."

Virginia's uncles had ridden two or three days with them on the way from Springfield to Independence, and Grandma *had* said goodbye to them, as if it was to be her last time.

"If you do die before you see Uncle Cadden, Grannie, what shall I say when I meet him?"

Grandma's eyes looked glazed and far away for a moment. She was seeing what was there, and what wasn't.

"Tell him that I love him. Just tell him that. That's all."

"Of course I'll tell him that."

"Tell him, dear child, that you ... and your mother ... and your sister and brothers ... and your Papa ... have given me great joy."

The next day, when Grandma did die, Virginia wondered how she could have been so casual about it when she called to Auntie Tamsen that Grandma was dying. Now, suddenly, she knew that it was forever, until she died herself. Forever and forever ... always and always ... like the marriage ceremony.

There was a fine funeral. The men stopped building the raft they were going to use to cross the Little Blue. They built a box out of cottonwood tree and Grandma was put in it in her very best dress, and they dug a hole and put her in it and everyone in the whole wagon train followed behind as they took the box and carefully lowered it into the hole and covered it with dirt, and Reverend Mr. Cornwall said a long prayer and people sang. Papa had asked her to be strong and brave so the smaller children wouldn't cry, and she watched everything and held her tears inside. Papa stroked Mama's hand; Mama was shaking all over. She would have another sick headache when this was done, Virginia thought. How would she herself feel when her Mama died? Thinking of that almost did make her cry. They put green sod all over the grave, so Indians wouldn't find it. Even when that was done, Virginia didn't weep, and Patty, who was such a cute little black-eyed copy-cat, looked up at her and didn't cry either. Eliza was taking care of the little brothers. They were too young to understand, Papa said.

"There goes Grannie," Patty said. "We're going to have to do without her."

Virginia knew that was Patty's way of consoling her. She squeezed her sister's hand, and they walked together back to the wagon, where the women had put away all the things that would make them sad ... Grannie's Bible and her sewing basket. They'd moved the comfortable chair where they always expected to see her, and had hidden her pillows.

There was a big moon that night. A whipoorwill and an owl made their strange sad noises in the trees by the river.

The next day, everyone seemed to have forgotten. The men went back to making the raft ... they called it the Blue River Rover ... and nine wagons crossed to the other side. Some of them almost tipped over. Everyone cheered as each wagon made it safely.

Will ours tip over? Virginia wondered. Then she realized with a hollow in her heart that when they crossed the river, Grandma would be left on this side all alone. After dusk had fallen, she went back to Grandma's grave. She must say goodbye. Now she could have her cry.

She heard someone behind her, moving quietly.

"Don't be frightened, Puss." It was Patty's quiet voice. "I guessed you'd be here."

"Oh, Patty, Patty! I didn't want you to see me cry ...." She tried to choke back her sobs.

"Don't worry. I cried too."

"I can't bear to leave Grandma here all alone ...."

Now that Patty had found out she wasn't brave any more, Virginia let the tears come as fast as they could, until it hurt clear down to her toes almost, and there weren't any more. There was a big hole where the sorrow had been. Patty sat beside her, stroking her shoulders, smoothing her hair, saying nothing. After a while, tired and empty, Virginia sat up. "I guess that's all. I can't cry anymore."

Patty said softly, "Look, Puss. Look what I have." She reached inside her chemise and brought out a piece of lace, part of a collar Grandma had often worn. Wrapped inside it was a lock of gray hair.

"It's Grandma's. I cut it off when nobody was watching. I'm going to give it to Uncle Cadden when we meet him."

"You funny little girl," her sister said, hugging her hard, "You're so grown up you make me feel like a baby."

They walked back to the Reed wagon, hand in hand, without talking any more.

The next day, the Reed wagons were finally ferried across the Little Blue. The children watched from dawn until late at night, fascinated by the shouting men, the bellowing oxen, and the weeping or praying women. Some were angry. The children laughed because things tipped over in their wagons.

In the afternoon a cold wind began to blow, and another thunder storm brought torrents of rain. It was hard to remember this was May. Supper had to be served cold, for fires went out. The men were too busy with the wagons to keep them going. Some of them had been in water up to their waists most of the day.

Just after the Reed wagons were taken across, a fight broke out between two men ... best of friends. The Reed children watched from the shelter of their wagon.

"Look out, he's got a knife!" A man's voice shouted and then there was a horrible mass of legs and arms and yelling and grunting. Men ran past to stop the fight.

"Come away, children. Don't watch!" Margaret Reed commanded. "They're all just tired and worn out and hungry, and no telling what will happen!"

Virginia and Patty still peeked. After a while, the voices subsided, and the two men who had been fighting stood up and backed off from each other. "No use making a bad day worse!" someone said in a level voice. Then the men began to go slowly back to their wagons, muttering, sounding almost like thunder in the distance. A the group of men passed the Reed wagon, Patty leaned out and said in a clear, firm voice, "For shame, you bad men, with my grandmother dead only two days ago!"

"She's a smart one, that little brat. I'd like to give her a hiding."

"Aw, she's just a kid. Let her be. She misses her Grannie."

When they had gone, Virginia said, "You mustn't make them mad at you, Patty. People think we're uppity enough as it is."

MARGARET REED

The day after they completed the crossing of the Little Blue, the company progressed only a mile. If she looked back, Margaret Reed could see the trees lining the river: oaks, walnuts, elms, the inevitable cottonwoods, dogwood and haw beginning to bloom. She tried to locate the tree under which her mother had been buried, but it was impossible to discern. Such empty lonesome land!

Her mother's death made her sensitive to the other graves that she saw with painful regularity along the trail. One, that of a child, bore the date of May 28, the day before her mother had died. In spite of herself, Margaret could not help putting herself inside the other woman who had had to leave her child in this lonely wilderness. Could she, Margaret, have done it? It had been hard to lose her mother, yet her death had been anticipated. Her mother had not rebeled against its coming, but had accepted it as a danger of the trip. She so wanted to see her other son, Cadden, before she died. But to lay one's baby in a grave, and callously go ahead, hoping the Indians would not uproot it ... oh, it was unbearable.

What kind of an adventure were they on, she wondered? Why were there so many graves? She began to count them. Little children, some from accidents, from falling under the wheels of the wagons, or from the vague illnesses people grouped under cholera ... James had not told her of this.

Men thought only of the adventure, the daring, the challenge, the achievement. They forgot the illnesses, the deaths. James was going to California because the weather would be better, because there would be more opportunity, because ... well, because of all the reasons men used when they wanted to do things to make them seem logical. She herself would have been happy where she was ... in her lovely home, with her neighbors and friends in Springfield, and her standing there. There was sickness in Illinois. Why had they thought there would be none on the long trail? Not a day passed that someone in their party wasn't sick. Jacob Donner hadn't been entirely well since that chilling rain storm the day before mother died. Poor children, they had to wear their heavy winter clothes and keep running sometimes in order to stay warm. They'd expected warm weather. It was "unseasonably cool."

Colds, coughs, runny noses, insect bites, skinned knees. Edwin Bryant told her of the boy who had died in the train ahead, after his leg had been amputated. They had sent for Mr. Bryant, but he had refused to cut the leg off, knowing the poor child couldn't survive, hoping to spare him the terrible pain. Someone else volunteered to perform the operation; the child died screaming, the parents unable to sooth his agony. That night, in the same party, everything happened that might happen in a village at home: a birth, a wedding, and a funeral.

Margaret looked at her two boys. Could she have stood that loss? Would all her children make it to California? Oh, those sad little graves, cold and lonely in the rain, frightened her, made her want to turn back. Suddenly a vision of her Springfield home overwhelmed her: warm, well-built, a fire burning in the stove, the cat curled behind it, the delightful odors of dinner cooking, the sounds of children laughing, clomping noisily down the stairs for supper, James' footfall on the porch, the squeaking of the pump as he stopped to wash his hands, the neighing of a horse in the stable, the supper table covered with a white cloth, their napkin rings lying beside each place, the painting of fruit and grapes on the wall ... the Bible on the side table ... all the things she loved. Margaret felt her forehead pounding ... one of her sick headaches was coming on. Oh, how *could* a mother force herself to walk away from a little grave, knowing she would never in her lifetime look at it again, nor place flowers there nor would ever feel the softness of baby hair under her hands .... The strain of the last days suddenly enveloped her. She began to cry. Mother had never reproached her for that earlier marriage, had taken her home when her young husband died, leaving her with Virginia to bring up. Mother knew about death. She had not been afraid. Why then should Margaret cry? Oh, when would this trial end, when would they be in California, making a new home? They were going so slowly. She had never dreamed the days would drag on like this. All she wanted was to have this dreadful trip over and done with and to be in her own home, no matter where it was, California, Illinois, anywhere.

Tamsen, in spite of her early worries, seemed to be enjoying herself. She found happiness in a new flower, joy in the rolling land, and she loved walking out in the endless grass, where any minute a snake might appear, or an Indian or goodness knew what.

Then think of that poor woman, Phillipine Keseberg, baby girl in her arms, another about ready to be born, being dumped in the middle of the stream the other day! All her precious belongings scattered and drenched in the rain. She had stood, big with child, eyes downcast, covered with shame while her husband scolded her as if it had been her fault the wagon tipped over. He hadn't a thought for her condition. Poor thing, pretty too, unable to talk with other women, alone with that tall blond husband of hers, whose handsomeness (if it could be called that ... Margaret wasn't one to take to fair-haired men) marred by his sullen face, his arrogance. He seemed to have it in for the other men. He didn't mix, and he wouldn't let her mingle either. They'd all have to keep an eye out for the day her time came, so there would be women around to help. So many German men in the party, and only two women, neither of whom could speak English. Mrs. Wolfinger didn't even try. Why ever did they want to go to California, and why in heaven's name had they joined this party? Was it because George Donner had a German background? Supposing Mrs. Keseberg's little baby-to-be would die? She'd have to leave it here, alone ... that was far worse than leaving Mother. Margaret's thoughts raced in all directions as they usually did before one of her attacks. Oh, why must we take so long to get to California? She resented every delay. Oh now, her head *was* aching! Now all her thoughts were jumbled like a tangle of yarn. Now she could think of nothing, nothing ... only the pounding and pressing against her brain. She dipped a cloth into a pan of cold water, and placed it over her eyes.

"Eliza!, Eliza!" she called. "You are going to have get the supper tonight. My head is bursting."

Thank goodness for James ... bringing this strange girl with them ... she had stood there so defiantly beside the road, her pitiful pack of clothing in her arms, her sunbonnet pushed back. "Baylis is going. Take me too." Baylis's albino eyes also had a pleading look. Dull though Eliza was, Margaret could not have made this trip without her. "Could you make me some tea?" she started to ask, but of course Eliza couldn't, even if she could have heard what Margaret asked. There would be no hot water for tea until they stopped tonight. She said slowly, forming each word carefully with her mouth, "Call Virginia for me. My head is breaking in two."

Headaches were vile! They came on, lasted an interminable time, then receded .... This one was a nightmare of all the things that had been happening ... the bouncing and jerking rides over this wibble-wabble land, the miles you walked in clouds of dust because your back ached from so much jolting, cooking over a wood fire, smoke burning your eyes, searing your face worse than the prairie sun! Burned pans, overturned skillets, stacks of dishes scraped of their food, washed in water that looked none too clean. Eliza must always boil the water, Mother said so. Eliza must sit by the pot of beans and see that they came to a bubble, and were hot all through. Eliza's disgusted face, sometimes, and those uncomprehending eyes, as if she didn't quite know what the world was doing to her. Still Eliza obeyed. Eliza would sit beside the fire on a three-legged stool, stirring and stirring until the steam came up around her absent-looking face. Margaret knew that many women were giving their husbands and families cold food at night ... not she. No wonder so many children were sick and ailing, throwing up, or having a running off of their poor bowels. The trail ... now you could see where the people had been, just like the animals ... dropping their dung behind them. Oh, and wishing you could have the old privy at home, where you could sit without people staring at you. Or worse, pretending that they didn't notice you. She used the pot inside the wagon, but it had to be emptied, all the same. To think she would ever become as brazen as she was ... to think she would dream of the privy as something of a luxury ... the lurching and continual jouncing of the wagons ... the pain in her poor exhausted head ... if she could just forget all that was happening, would the headache ease?

Yesterday when she asked James just why they had come, where were they going ... how far was it, why did he think it would be so much better than the lovely home they had in Illinois? he said with a flare of impatience that he rarely used with her, "Maybe there are more reasons than you know, Margaret ... a man doesn't leave a good home for adventure alone. There may be happenings there that we can only guess at .... You have to trust me."

"You would go for adventure, though, James. You've always loved adventure."

"Especially when there's a goal. Perhaps, with the war with Mexico started at last ...."

"At last? You were expecting it?"

"There were rumors when I went to the State capitol building. But Governor Boggs is with this party too. Remember, this isn't your ordinary kind of drifter. None of us, excepting a few, were so poor we had to go ...."

"What are you saying, James?"

"More than I should. You'll understand, someday, Margaret. California may probably belong to us ... you'll be at home in your own country ... the opportunities are great ... the chance of a lifetime. They say opportunity doesn't knock twice. I think this is my knock."

"You should have told me this before ...."

"I haven't told you anything ... you are assuming ...."

"I hope the game is worth the candle ...."

"You take care of the children, Margaret. You are a born mother. You'll have to trust me for the adventure, as you call it. You'll see, you'll see. Try to be patient. It will soon be over."

Soon be over. Soon be over. The words went through her spinning head. The way was hard. The way of the transgressor is hard. But she had not transgressed ... maybe she should not have let Mother come. But Mother wanted to come. She had not put Mother's Bible in her grave with her ... what would Mother do without it? Twenty-nine graves since Mother had died ... most without names. Some of them opened. Walt Herron and Milt had covered them over, stamping the ground level, removing the topsy-turvy marker. All the wagons had rolled over the reburied man, so that no one would see there had been a grave at all. Had Mother's grave been desecrated already, her wedding ring taken from her finger? It was torture to think about it, but the thought would not leave her mind. The Promised Land ... the long walk through the desert, the manna that saved them ... did those people leave graves like pathetic road markers along their trail? They had arrived at last ... would she and her beloved family arrive too, in the promised land?

The caravan had stopped. The rocking and jolting had ended. Oh, but it was peaceful to be still. Someone was chopping wood. She smelled the smoke through her pain, and then Eliza ... no, it was her dear Puss, brought tea. Delicious, warming tea.

"Rest, Mama. It'll stop now." It was Patty's voice. Her dear children. Caring for her. She was the luckiest of women ... James was good, he loved her. He loved their children ... even the one they had not had together. James ... so little like other men ... he, who loved his mother-in-law, his step-daughter ... his own. Everything he did was for them. Sometimes, in deep sleep, she thought of Virginia's father. Dear too, in his own way. Dear first love ... I must not put him out of my mind, even though he has died, even though my love for James is greater ... oh, I will go where you lead me, James. I will not complain any more ... I will not rebel. I will be as strong as you, as strong as Puss and Patty ... I will sleep awhile and I will wake and take up my burden, because of you, James.

From far off, she heard Virginia's voice. "She's asleep. When she wakes up, her headache will be gone." Beloved children ... I will be brave ....

Because of heavy rains and muddy roads, most of the four hundred, more or less, wagons that started in the spring of 1846 gathered at one of the several crossing places of the Missouri River, replenishing stores and repairing equipment. Emigrants with lighter wagons, or those going by horse and pack mules, could start earlier than the others. By the time the weather was favorable, the family wagons were lined up at the ferrying places, ready to go.

Because of the fairly simultaneous beginning of the trip, the wagons were strung along the trail in a great white line. It took only a short time for emigrants to realize that large parties traveling together could not do so with any kind of efficiency or speed.

Soon the emigration was broken up into smaller parties, each with its own captain, but even this was not a permanent arrangement. There was continual re-grouping; smaller parties with light wagons and determined leadership easily made better time than the family-oriented segments concentrated in larger numbers. At first, the groups united for safety; Indians, still greatly feared, were one hazard; the Mormons were more dreaded. Rumors were as thick as blackbirds on newly plowed ground: A large emigration of Mormons was on the trail with the avowed intention of killing any "gentile" in sight.

When it was seen that generally most plains Indians were more involved with their own wars than killing emigrants, and could be pacified with small gifts, and that the Mormons were taking a more northernly route and when encountered were actually kind and helpful for the most part, the great unbroken flood of wagons began dividing into more manageable numbers.

Those bound for Oregon were more likely to travel together, as were those bound for California. When deaths or illnesses and accidents held up families, they fell back and joined a following party. When differences and quarrels arose families either went ahead or waited for another party, and made application to join. Young men, unencumbered by family or domestic details, discouraged by the frequent delays, sometimes for nothing more than a woman's wish to wash clothes, spurred their animals and light wagons ahead.

Still there was not more than a day or two's ride between the parties. Impatient young men rode back after a day's drive to rendezvous with "the girl they left behind." Others sometimes rode ahead to share a supper with new-met friends.

During these first weeks of travel, adjustments to the new mode of living were all-absorbing, both for the men and the women. The children were the only ones who seemed unworried. It didn't matter to them if they stopped often, where they were going, or why. They dashed between the wagons, playing tag, ran with the men astride their horses, learned how to jump out of moving wagons without falling under the wheels (though some didn't learn soon enough to prevent broken legs and death). They got lost, had runny noses, threw up, fell down, skinned their knees, picked themselves up again and flew on like a flock of birds. Freedom they had never known before was heady stuff. Some of the older children had horses or ponies of their own and they galloped ahead or across the prairie, scattering dust and frightening the prairie dogs back into their holes. Snakes were everywhere; they learned to avoid them as they had learned not to fall into the spring-swollen streams and drown, fall under the wheels or fool with their father's guns, by having those mishaps happen to others. Some women thought that there was a providence that watched over their children; others learned sadly that children were as vulnerable and mortal as anyone else.

Nothing was quite what they had imagined it. The great expanse of sinuous prairie with its waving knee-high grasses surprised them with its spring beauty. Farmers picked up fistfuls of soil, running it through their fingers thoughtfully. This would make fine farm land some day. California would have to go some to better this kind of soil. The frequent spring thunder storms they were used to, but to endure them in the open, wearing wet clothes from morning till night was another thing. Every river and creek was brimming with water, and each stream meant a crossing that could take several days. For men, nighttime did not always mean a rest; a watch was needed for Indians or Mormons. Sick animals, squeaking axles, broken wagon tongues, mired wheels, unreliable leaders, arguments, frequent fisticuffs over some slight difference of opinion ... all these were faced by the men.

For women, the hardships were no less difficult to accept. After a day of bumping spines on rough roads or driving the teams when their husbands were ill or too busy, keeping their children from falling under the wheels, drying out clothes or attempting to clean diapers when there was no water, they must at the end of a day, cook over an open fire, eat food out of hand in the rain. Dresses became dustier from the road, and shoes caked with cattle dung must be scraped. They attended to their toilet needs and those of their children, prepared food that would keep for the next day's noon meal, washed dishes in water they would have scorned at home. When this was all done they were worn enough to sleep at night, once the dishes were washed and stored for the next day.

Before dawn came the call to rise. The encampment stirred like a great coiled snake. Quiet voices were soon augmented by the sound of crying babies, the screaming of children, the rattling of pans, the snap of fire igniting. Most women had tried to have wood ready for the morning fire, but there were always those who had forgotten, and the sound of chopping added to morning confusion ... that is, if they had camped near a stream lined with trees. By six o'clock, breakfasts had been prepared and eaten, and a simple lunch made for the noon stop. Then dishes must be washed, children dressed and sent to run off some of the energy that would be cooped inside them during the day's drive. Their hair was brushed and pinned back severely, their faces washed of syrup from the slam-johns they had eaten with side pork for breakfast. Now women were free to rinse out a few things and hang them to dry, either on the outside of the wagon where they would be caked with dust before nightfall, or inside on a makeshift line stretched across the narrow wagon bed. This left little time for primitive functions, but they were attended to as discreetly as possible.

Women tried to hurry, tried not to rebel when starting time came. When was there time to go outside the ring of wagons, unless they had slop-jar hidden inside (which, of course, must then be emptied somewhere, surreptitiously and certainly unhygienically.) At night, going outside the circle was terrifying; they feared Indians, but most of all they feared snakes. It was comfortable to go in pairs. They learned to laugh about this. "I never thought I could be so shameless!" or "These pesky dresses are hard to manage ... aren't men lucky! They have only to turn the other way!" "Yes, but if we wore pantaloons like men, we'd have to drop them clear down!" These were moments of intimacy and understanding between them, once they became used to having their private necessities exposed. They began to use common words instead of usual delicate evasive ones. Some of them wondered if they were becoming coarse and hardened.

Yet, to a group of women who were used to a chamber pot under the bed, these were public but not unendurable hardships. That women of that era did not speak of such functions is not strange. There are many accounts of diarrhea and constipation, or caustiveness, but seldom a mention of the facts of childbirth.

As they became used to the new routines, they thought less and less of these things, accepting them as naturally as they accepted the five-hole outhouse back home, and they went about such functions as matter-of-factly as they did eating and sleeping.

In a busy hour-and-a-half after breakfasts of bread, fried bacon or hominy, the westward roll was on its way, women stowed in the wagons with their knitting or mending, babies tucked down for a nap after their nursing, little children sitting wide-eyed and restless next to their mothers in the bow-frame of the wagon.

The lead wagon of the day before was at its place in the rear, and its occupants prepared to eat dust until they again worked up to the front.

At twelve o'clock, or thereabouts, depending on the reports of scouts sent ahead, the train stopped for the nooning, mainly to rest and water the oxen. It was a pleasant respite from the jolting, and gave the children time to run and play. Some of the older ones walked along side, with the bull-whackers, and a few rode horses. After perhaps an hour of rest, the trek began again, ending at about an hour before dusk, so there would be daylight for wood gathering and cooking.

When the evening camp site had been chosen, they watched with never-failing fascination for the grand sweep of the wagons into a circle, or corral. How the men shouted, the horses nickered, bucked and snorted, how the whips flew out like the tongues of snakes, and the dust rose in great whorls that hid everything while the train coiled into its circle of security! It was like a parade every night!

When the camp was made in buffalo country, children were sent with sacks to pick up buffalo chips, or "bois de vache" as some of the more delicate women preferred to call them. On wooded river-banks, there were twigs and some sizeable wood to collect also, but the bulk of the emigration gone ahead made such prize scarce. Use of buffalo chips seemed disgusting at first, but as with snakes and other perils, the people learned to take them for granted.

Tents were set up, camps made, food boxes opened, tables and chairs improvised for eating by the fire (unless it was raining) and women went to work again, cooking. Children wandered about, looking for fuel and playing tag and teasing each other.

After the supper dishes had been scraped into pans for the dogs and the spoons and forks and plates washed, the oxen brought in from their grazing outside the corral, there was a little time for gossip or discussion, and the designation of the lead wagon for tomorrow. Men sat around the fire, using its light to mend harnesses. Women nursed their babies or told old stories to the children.

Sometimes, if they had stopped early enough, there would be a time for a little singing or dancing after the evening meal. Men brought out their banjos, guitars or fiddles and played the old songs: hymns, Yankee Doodle, My Bonnie, The Bear Went Over the Mountain, Money Musk. Feet tapped and young people gathered to dance. A girl didn't need to be much more than ten years old for someone to scoop her up and start a reel or a jig. Older women felt their feet beating to remembered rhythms, and their dusty shoes beneath their long skirts moved like little wild animals to the tunes. Oh, those were merry evenings! A full moon, the day over, music making you feel as if you were home again under the elms ... just a few bars of music could do this to you: bring back a past you'd thought gone forever. Even the most watchful of mothers smiled indulgently when their daughters and sons started a little sky-larking to the sound of the scraping fiddle and an old tune, and their eyes blurred at the sad, sentimental songs.

Then the migration seemed not so dangerous. It was more like a moving village, a small town oozing across wide, undulating prairies, sweet with spring grasses. That bulky wagon, looming so patiently behind them in its circle was all the home they had. Not until the music finally faded did the women shudder again at the constant howling of wolves, the shuffling of cattle's feet, the lowing of a discontented cow, the whisper of feet returning from a trip outside the wagon circle, the soft talk of the night guards, then the silence that stretched already two hundred, four hundred miles back, like the vanishing streak of a falling star.

It was about this time they heard of the Mexican War from a newspaper left by a passing train. James Reed and his friend George Donner were not surprised, and when they caught up and were admitted to the large party of about one hundred wagons, they found that many of them also had been expecting the outbreak. Edwin Bryant the young newspaper editor from Kentucky, had seen it coming and had felt it was inevitable. He felt this would be an opportune time to be in California, and see it all first-hand. There was great interest in the States in the possible new territory to be acquired, either by war or by purchase. James Reed also was prepared: he had papers from the governor of his state, recommending him as a man of honor and leadership. George Donner had provided himself with bolts of beautiful silks and satins, with which he proposed to buy land from the luxury-loving Mexicans in California.

Traveling now in this light-colored river of wagons were those in the Bryant party, the Harlan-Young Party, the Boggs, Aram, Russell, and many other parties. The interchange between them was constant; indeed, many changed parties as often as captains were elected and deposed ... from whim, from delay, from minor irritations, or from an urgent sense of time passing ... time passing, while they made sometimes only ten or twelve miles a day ... like patient snails carrying their houses with them. Slowly this moving village crawled across the plains to the meeting with the Platte River.

TAMSEN

The women weren't sure when it was that they had started noticing Louis Keseberg, the German with the pretty young wife. Certainly, when the wagon tipped over and his Phillipine was drenched in muddy water, her fine clothes ruined, the women were outraged at his seeming indifference to his wife who was bulging with her second child. He seemed only to care for their little girl. Although he spoke several languages, he was not fluent in English, and they may have distorted what he was shouting in his harsh voice. Tamsen chose to believe that he was misunderstood, although he seemed to avoid the other members of the party, and often stood apart even from the other Germans on the trail, arrogant, tall, handsome in his Teutonic way. What a pity. His wife was pretty even in her condition. Phillipine ... what an exotic name compard to the Marys, Peggys, Lavinas. She was small except for the baby she carried. Her eyes darted from face to face, as if searching for something or someone, but she too kept herself alone ... or her husband saw to it that she did. Her clothes were far too fine for the prairie trip, as were Mrs. Wolfinger's, and they both wore jewelry.

The other women made attempts to include the two German women, but neither spoke English well, and when they did accept, they were silent.

Once, when Tamsen had tried to engage Mrs. Keseberg in conversation, she had been startled to see the woman's eyes widen and her face pale as they spoke brokenly to each other. Tamsen turned to see what the matter was, and behind her stood that tall blond husband of hers. He said something to his wife in German. The color came back to Mrs. Keseberg's face and she bit her lips.

"Vill you blease oxcuse me? My little kindchen ..." her hesitant voice trailed off into silence.

"Of course, my dear. We can talk later."

With difficulty, the German woman pulled herself into the Keseberg wagon.

Louis Keseberg made a perfunctory bow. "My vife is unvell today," he said shortly, and followed her into the wagon. Shrugging her shoulders, Tamsen continued on the path of her original destination. As she moved away, she was sure she heard sobbing from the wagon. "Well, I tried. I meant no harm," she thought. "Poor thing, she looks so lonesome, somehow. Her time must be coming soon; she's carrying the baby low ... probably a boy." She could not help thinking how she would hate to be anticipating a child to be born on the trail, especially, as like Mrs. Keseberg, with no friends to help her. Why had the Kesebergs started this year? They were young enough to wait to go to California when their children would be easier to handle. "I must watch, and alert the others to be ready to help, when her time comes," she thought. But would that distant, cold, sneering man allow anyone to help his poor wife? Maybe she could make friends with her later on. She'd like to hear of Germany, and perhaps learn a little of the language and the country ... it was George's country too, if you went back a few generations. It was so odd that people just over from Germany would wish to go to California or Oregon. Obviously, they knew nothing of the trail, or they would have dressed more suitably.

PATTY

Patty and Virginia had developed an intense dislike to Mr. Keseberg. Margaret overheard Patty say, "He's mean. We didn't do anything!"

"Who's mean, Patty?"

"That German man ... the tall one with yellow hair."

"Why do you say that, Patty?"

"He won't let us anywhere near his wagons, Ma," Virginia said. "He chases us away. He acts like he thinks we'd steal something ... and he yells at us."

"He chased us away again today," Patty said.

"He makes his wife cry. I've seen her cry."

"Well, you know dear, she's expecting ... maybe she doesn't feel well ..." Margaret said.

"Oh, we all know that, Ma. That's why she's so fat. Will she be thin again when she's had it?"

"Well, you know I was fat before I had Jimmy and Tommie, and I'm not fat now, am I?"

"Well, I can't for the life of me see how a baby's going to get out of that little lady, all the same."

Oh, dear, Margaret thought. More questions. "Didn't Grandma explain, Puss? God takes good care of us and makes it happen."

"Well, when I have babies I hope God's on my side," Virginia said irreverently. "And I hope I don't marry a mean man like that Mr. Keseberg, either."

"Me neither, Ma, if I ever get married." Patty didn't like Mr. Keseberg any more than Virginia did. The boys made fun of him behind his back. Patty tried to remember which had happened first. Had the boys teased him about the way he talked before or after they had decided they didn't like him? She remembered one afternoon when they were playing tag near his wagon and he came out yelling at them and shaking his fist.

"You yust get away now, you bad kinder!" Once she'd seen him with a gun in his hands, but then, all men owned guns. Maybe she had imagined that he looked as if he was going to shoot them. Maybe he didn't know what fun it was to tease him because he got so mad. Maybe she should try to like him. Maybe he was ashamed of his funny way of talking? But then, Mr. Wolfinger and Mr. Hardcoop talked funny too, and they didn't get mad, and the young ones didn't tease them. Mrs. Keseberg wasn't mean. She looked frightened though, and always took her little girl away when they were around. She was as pretty as Virginia's best doll. Maybe her mama didn't know they wanted to play with her. Her mama probably was scared to death of everything in America ... the snakes and the yelling around the wagons, and the cows and oxen and horses and dogs. Sister was right. It wouldn't be any fun at all to be married to a man who never smiled ....

In a series of reminiscences related by Patty Reed, then Mrs. Frank Lewis, 89 years of age, to Evelyn Wells, the arrangement of the Reed wagon is described. That some memories may have dimmed or altered in her mind must temper our acceptance of some details. For instance, Patty says that her father took 52 hounds with him. This could be a printer's error, for the usual number was reported as closer to five. Fifty-two baying hounds would certainly have made their noisy impression on many a member of the party. However, that aside, Patty says that in the Reed wagon there were two wooden chests in the front of the wagon interior. One was for daily food, the other for medicines. There were other chests, which could be used also for seats. One contained toys, for instance. Since James Reed was a cabinet maker, there were possibly more special storage places than in other wagons.

In this high wagon, there were two large spring beds, a wood stove, books, boxes of silks and trinkets, the former for land purchase in California, and the latter for Indians along the way. Another chest held a supply of fine wine and brandy. Others were for guns, kitchen equipment, stores of dried food and sea biscuit, to be used when the fresh food was exhausted, stores of clothing, paintings, and a comfortable chair for Grandma Keyes. The Reed cabin also had a large looking glass that had been presented to Margaret Reed by the members of her Springfield reading club on the day of their departure, so "she would remember to keep herself looking as pretty as she was ...." guns, "looking glasses," or a telescope, seeds, all those things that James Reed and George Donner had listed on the cold winter nights in Illinois.

A delightful description of the clothing worn by women and little girls is also given by Patty Reed. All of the women wore "Shaker Bonnets," either of straw or cloth. The bonnet Margaret Reed wore was of this style, but it was made of fine quality leghorn, lined with gauze, and trimmed with ribbons and French rosebuds. All the feminine members wore shoes laced to the ankle, with no heels. At nine years of age, Patty wore dresses that hung to the tops of her shoes.

THE WOMEN

Whenever there was a wait on the trail, the women came to the Reed wagon, the Palace car, as Puss called it, bringing their knitting or mending or a quilt they were piecing, and she "entertained" them in the room her mother had occupied. The cushions, the rug, the one comfortable chair, brought an illusion of home to the traveling women. Eliza served lemonade and it was exactly as if Margaret were back in her home on a summer afternoon with friends. Often Tamsen came in later, after a walk on the plains, bringing a gift of flowers. Another group had broken off and gone ahead toward Oregon. Women spoke of the departed ones, wondering if they should ever see them again, wondering what life in Oregon might be like, and speculating on what would happen in California when they reached it. They gossiped about the young men who were still mooning over a girl gone ahead, and of the young girls who were pining over a "lost love" that had departed. They would learn, the women said, nodding their heads over their handwork. They would learn that there would be others to take their place. The word was that any young girl could find herself a husband as soon as she arrived. Better to wait. A honey moon on a trip like this ... well, life was hard enough without starting it too soon.

"Look at that poor little woman, the German's wife ... for instance ...."

"Phillipine?" Eleanor Eddy asked.

"Yes, the wretched thing. Her time will come, and who's to help her? That man she's married to doesn't look like much of a mid-wife ..." Lavina Murphy went on.

"And morning sickness to boot," Harriet Pike said. "My baby was born before we left the States, thank goodness!"

"Morning sicknesss, you say Harriet? Maybe. But there's more than morning sickness to make that woman look the way she does." Lavinia Murphy bit off a thread. "Morning sickness doesn't make you cry out like she does."

The women exchanged glances. All had heard the cries that came from the Keseberg wagon, and had heard her husband's harsh, accusing voice. "I'd like to see a man lay a hand on me, more'n once," Lavina said, "I'd send him packing."

Betsy Donner's face was pink. "Are you sure, Lavina? Maybe she's just homesick ... poor thing, so far away from home ...."

"Well, beatin' a woman ain't after makin' her no less homesick," Peggy Breen said. "Gettin' up with the baby yelling, your husband's tongue lashin' ye, washing dishes and packin' a lunch and morning sickness besides."

"We must all help when her time comes ...." Betsy said, and all the women agreed. "It's hard enough at home, with a doctor nearby if you need one ... but out here ... well, it's no place to have somethin' in the oven ...."

"And the Good Lord sends children, shure as fate ...." Peggy Breen was not one to dodge the facts.

"Your youngest is one-year-old, Peggy Breen. You'll be expecting soon."

"May the Lord be praised! But I'm still nursing. They say if you've got a child at the breast ...."

Eleanor Eddy said, "I intend to keep on nursing all the way, then I can't chance another baby this soon. The doctor said last time I should be careful ... I'm not terribly strong."

"And now, may I ask, are you going to be careful? Men are men, and women are women," Lavina said. "I'm the only one who needn't be careful, since my dear husband lies back in the churchyard in Missouri, God bless him."

Lavina was a strong woman, to be sure, with five little ones of her own to start out for California, even if she did have two married daughters and their families with her.

"You must be thankful that your sons-in-law treat you so well."

"They should. It's my wagon and my savings," Lavina said. "I'd be willing enough to marry again. If anyone would ask me, I'd say yes quicker'n scat. Not likely at my age I'd have any more children .... It's not good to be alone. I like men about the house."

Betsy Donner said, "I'm forty-seven, with a baby a year old, just when I thought I was through with having young'uns."

"If God wants us to have young'uns, young'uns we'll have," Peggy Breen said, making the sign of the cross. "I hope me guardian angel helps me. I say a prayer to the blessed Virgin Mary every day."

With a smile and a twinkle in her eye, Margaret said, "I don't think prayer is quite enough, Peggy. God helps those who help themselves ...."

"Don't be sayin' a thing against prayer, me lady. We say our prayers every blessed evenin' and every blessed mornin'," Lavina said. Peggy was such a huge woman, with a face as broad and rough as a washboard. She held her youngest on her vast lap, her legs spread wide so that her skirt made a cradle.

Eleanor said softly to Margaret, so the others wouldn't hear, "But what do you do? When you love someone so much ...?"

Margaret Reed looked at her with compassion. Eleanor was such a tiny, frail, wide-eyed girl, looking much younger than her twenty-four years. While the others were talking, she whispered, "There are ways, Eleanor ...."

"I wish I knew ...."

Margaret whispered in her ear. Eleanor's eyes widened. "Oh, no! I couldn't ...."

"Oh yes you can. It's better than having a child who might die on this trip ...."

Impulsively, Eleanor picked her little baby girl from the carpet at her feet and hugged her. "I love children, Margaret. I'd be glad to have as many as Will wants me to ... but they take every scrap of strength I have. Will's so strong, so willing and so hardworking ... nothing's too much for him. I don't think he realizes that I'm not as strong as he is ..." she shuddered. "Those graves along the trail — how frightful they are."

"And you love him very much ... there's nothing wrong in loving a man ... any way you can ... he'll love you just the same ...."

"You're sure?"

"I'm sure."

Eleanor swallowed hard and looked worried. "Oh, dear me, dear me ...."

Margaret patted her arm. "Don't fret so ...."

"What are you two whispering about?" Betsy Donner asked.

"Oh, just woman-talk," Margaret answered quickly. Eleanor's face was bright red.

Betsy started folding up her mending. "I hate to have this afternoon end, Margaret ... thank you so much. But I should be out washing this very minute, when I have a chance ... no telling when we'll get a day off and be near water at the same time."

"Your children washed all morning, Betsy. You just sit and rest."

"I couldn't let them do my mother-cloths, and I'll be needing them soon. I can't help feeling ashamed when I set them out to dry ... at my age! I know the men notice."

Margaret said, "Mother used to say that the happiest time of a woman's life was when all that mess was over ...."

Betsy said with a rueful laugh, "But you'd better be really sure it's over ... and how is one to tell?"

Lavina Murphy said, "Well, as I always say, there's only one way to be sure, but it's a hard way, with a husband lying dead under the sod."

"The Lord be praised, but that's a wicked thought, Missus Murphy." Peggy Breen crossed herself again. "The Lord decides these things for you. Bend your necks to it, me ladies."

Eleanor opened her waist and put her baby to nurse. Her face was open and tender.

Harriet Pike, married with two children under three and one less than a year, who had said nothing up until now, said, "At least once a month I wish I was a man!"

Eleanor said, "Harriet! With that dear baby of yours?"

"I was just teasing, Eleanor. I no more want to be a man than you do. You think I want to drive cattle, sit up all night on Indian watch, get up and chase all over after every maverick cow or mule that strays, mend harness, hammer the wagons that come apart, make ferry boats so we can be tipped over in the middle of a river? I'm not crazy. But I think it would be a lot easier if we were rid of our courses."

"The curse of Eve," Peggy said. "God made us that way ...."

There was a voice from somewhere close above them. "Grandma Keyes said that God must be ...."

"Virginia Elizabeth Backenstoe Reed! Whatever are you doing in your cot this time of day?"

"Listening to you ladies talk, Ma ...."

Betsy Donner exploded, "You should be ashamed of yourself. You're just a child. You're bad to be eavesdropping. Wait till you're older to listen to woman-talk. You just forget everything you heard. My lands, child! You're too young."

"I'm not a child. I'm a woman just like you. I know what mother-rags are. I'm grown and old enough to be married!"

"Don't you be saucy to your Aunt Betsy, Virginia. You apologize, hear me?" Margaret's voice was firm, but she wanted to laugh. "Time enough later to listen to women talking when you're married."

"I'm sorry, Aunt Betsy." Virginia climbed down from her perch.

With some resignation, Margaret thought perhaps it was just as well Virginia had heard women-talk. Mother had told her she'd given Virginia some of the facts, or as much as she thought fit, and for Margaret it was hard to mention such things. Maybe what she heard would help her, when her time came.

"It's not at all polite to listen to people when they don't know you're there, Puss. Now you run and find Eliza and ask her to make some more lemonade."

"I was asleep when you all started talking. I didn't mean to pry."

Virginia took the pitcher and jumped from the wagon.

"Thank goodness she was asleep," Betsy Donner said. "If she knew all we knew would she be so quick to say she's ready to get married, I wonder?"

"Best to keep young'uns innocent," Peggy Breen said. "The Lord will take care of what they need to know."

Margaret thought, "But she isn't so innocent. Why, a few years and she'll be the age I was when I married Lloyd ... I'd better keep my eyes open ...."

Just then they heard Virginia's voice outside, "Auntie Tamsen, come on over ... all the ladies are at Mama's."

Short, quick steps, and Tamsen Donner, her arms full of flowers and leaves, tapped up the steps.

"Look here! See what I've found today!"

Women put down their knitting and mending. Harriet's baby stirred, and fell asleep again at her breast.

"Have any of you ever seen anything like this before?" Tamsen extended a pure white flower. For a moment no one spoke.

"Is that what you're after bringin' home today from yer galivantin'?"

"Specimens ... things I've never seen before, some of them first rate. Some I can classify, but some I can't. Maybe some of you ...."

"I'm afraid I don't know much about wild flowers," Eleanor Eddy said kindly. "Only the common garden kind. Could that be a wild rose ...?"

"No, it's not in that family, Eleanor."

"A hollyhock?" Harriet ventured.

"I've never been much for posies," Lavina Murphy said complacently."I've always had too much to do raising young'uns."

To soften the remark, Margaret said quickly, "Will you have some lemonade, Tamsen, dear? Virginia's just brought another pitcher. We've been mending and knitting a while, and talking of our homes ...."

"And women-talk," Virginia said, smiling mischievously.

"That's enough, Puss. You run and find your sister ... and thank you for bringing the lemonade."

Virginia made a short little bobbing motion, more a bow than a curtsy. "Goodbye, ladies."

Tamsen still stood with the plants and flowers in her hands. She was counting the petals of the flower. "Five. Now what has five petals and a leaf like this?"

"Do sit down. Here's a glass for you."

"Just for a minute. I want to sketch these and press them before they wilt. I've had the most glorious afternoon, away from the wagons and the dust."

"Aren't you afraid of Indians and snakes?" Eleanor asked. "A man told me yesterday about a girl who was almost captured by Indians, even when she was close to camp ... if it hadn't been that her brother had his gun no telling what might have happened ...."

"Gracious sakes! Was any harm done?"

"I don't think so."

"What kind of woman was she, a red-head? Indians seem to like red-heads."

"An unmarried girl ... Mary Ann Graves was her name. Nineteen years old."

"She's better be after gettin' herself married, then. She must be ugly as sin or she'd be spoken for long afore this," Peggy said.

"They say she's real pretty ... black hair and tall. And she's spoken for ... one of her Pa's teamsters ...."

"Well, I'm not afraid. You hear exaggerated stories like that every day, Eleanor. Most of them are rumors, I think. A girl like that probably wouldn't look at a hired man. I've wandered almost wherever I please and I've seen no savages except those that come begging every night."

Lavina said, "Some women think every man is about to run off with her, and some wishes they would too."

Harriet spoke up. "Well, it's news and we get precious little, true or not. It picks up our day just to hear about it." She laughed. "I bet that girl has a lot of explaining to do."

"Poor girl. She won't live that down for a while."

"It would scare me to death," Eleanor said.

"Likely it's only talk. Like that the Mormons was about to kill us all. When we came on this crazy business, Eleanor, we knew it wasn't as safe as sitting at home in our own houses ...", Betsy said.

The women were quiet. Home seemed farther away than California, even though they were only one third of the way.

"Sometimes I wish I was back in my own house, cooking in my own kitchen, sleeping in my own bed ... but there's no use thinking about it," Eleanor said at last.

Tamsen's voice was surprisingly soft. "When I started, I felt the same as you do, Eleanor. I thought George was out of his mind. But since I've been on a trip everything seems to go smoothly, and I've relaxed to it."

Peggy Breen snorted aloud. "It's easy for you to talk, me lady. You've after havin' girls to help you, whatever you do, and men to help them while you go scallywaggin' around pickin' flowers. I've got only me boys, six of them, and this baby, here."

"Young'uns dying and people hurt, and cattle lost ...", Eleanor continued softly.

Tamsen spoke quietly, "Those sadnesses go on at home, too. Death is always with us. Children die, and people steal and wagons lose wheels at home, just as they do here. If you keep your mind busy ...."

Again silence. The women knew Tamsen's sad story. Peggy Breen looked down where her baby was stirring and making sucking sounds.

Margaret Reed thought the little graves are here, just as they are at home. Only at home we visit the graves and honor the dead ... here they are little lost graves with no tombstones nor names. At home there are four walls and pictures and a fireplace, and an upstairs where you can run to when you have a headache. Then, looking around at the comfortable room where she now sat, that James had made for her mother, and for Margaret herself, who wasn't strong like other women, she pondered. Her mother would have died at home, just the same. James had even tried to make an upstairs or sorts, where she could hide herself. Had she failed him, with her fears and worries and disappointments? She looked at Tamsen, neat and trim in her black skirt and shirt waist, no linsey-woolsey for her, her face rosy from the fresh air, her eyes bright with unshed tears ... excited about a silly flower with five petals. Tamsen wouldn't sit still for a headache. Tamsen made the best of things. It was easy to be Margaret Reed, pretty and helpless and half-ill, as she'd been at home. James was fighting so hard to make things right for her. Was she afraid of the effort it took to be strong and healthy? Had she no gumption? That was Tamsen's term. Must she always think about the dead, her first husband, her mother? Tamsen had lost her husband too, and two little girls besides, and she had gumption enough to stand up to life and enjoy it. They were on the trail now. No turning back. All right, since there was no turning back she was going on, going to California as James desired, where they would make a home as pretty as the one in Illinois. She'd have gumption, like Peggy; she'd help frightened ones like Eleanor, who were pure love. She would admit to herself that she loved James deeply and dearly, without feeling guilty for those who were lost and gone.

PATTY AND VIRGINIA

Puss was harnessing Billy. She yelled, "Hey Patty, want to ride on back?"

Walt Herron was holding the reins, and when Puss got on Billy, he handed them to her, and lifted Patty behind. Good old Milt was driving the wagon.

"Where you goin' sister?" he asked Puss.

"Me'n Patty're going on a good old gallop, that's what!"

"Mind you hold on tight, Patty. Sister, don't you go as hard and fast as you usually do. There's prairie dog holes all over and I don't want to have to tell your Pa that you fell off and busted in your head or lamed Billy."

"I'll be careful. Billy's smart. He sees holes quicker'n I do."

"Stay in sight!"

Virginia looked off into the green rolling distance. "Auntie Tamsen's way out there ... ain't you sceered for her Milt? We'll go rescue her from the Indians."

"Mind you watch for snakes!"

Walt and Milt stood, watching the two girls, hair tossing, riding off. Virginia's voice came like a flag flying, "Snakes are sceered of Billy!" Walt said, "They're a pair. Pretty lucky girls, not a care in the world, and their Pa with all that money ...."

Tamsen's tiny figure in its dark dress was barely visible above the high grass. Auntie Tamsen did mostly what she wanted to do, Virginia thought. She minded Uncle George when she had to, but she always teased him about bossing her. "Just as you say, George," she would say with that little girl look on her face. She wasn't as tall as Virginia, even. Mama and Papa weren't like Uncle George and Auntie Tamsen. Papa and Mama talked lots when the children were put away in their bunks for the night. Papa would listen to what Mama said, very seriously, and then he'd say what he thought, which was what they usually did, even if he'd asked Mama about it. Uncle George just teased Auntie as if she were a little girl. Well, she wasn't much bigger than a little girl. Auntie Tamsen seemed to love to have Uncle George tease her. With other people she was pretty bossy sometimes. Mama said it was because she was a schoolteacher back home before she married Uncle George, and she was used to telling people what to do. But she was awful good to people when something went wrong. Gracious, she'd brought cooked food and a cake when Grandma died, and had made Mama lie down and she put cold towels on her head. She had hugged and kissed Patty. "You're young to be knowing death and loss," she said, "but this is in the nature of things ... it isn't like having young people die who haven't lived ...." Auntie Tamsen looked so sad that Patty almost started to cry, but then Auntie said, "There, there, child, I didn't mean to make you feel bad. Say your prayers and Grannie will be taken care of by God."

Virginia could feel Patty's strong little arms around her waist. "This is fun, Puss! Go faster!"

What a funny little sister she had! She was like Auntie Tamsen ... she never seemed to get upset about things like Virginia did. She kept Tommie and little Jimmy in sight a whole lot better than Eliza, who was absent-minded sometimes, likely off talking to Milt or Walt, poor dumb-bunny, thinking Milt would marry her someday. Patty taught

Jimmy numbers and she saw that Tommie didn't mess his pants any more ... all those things, just like she was their mother. Once Virginia had said to Mama, "I guess I'm about the luckiest girl in Illinois, Mama. Just think, Papa isn't really my Papa, and he's just as good to me as he is to Patty. That's not like in the fairy stories where the step-fathers and step-mothers hate the children. And I have Patty and Jimmy and Tommie for sisters and brothers. I can't remember long ago, when I was an only child."

Auntie Tamsen was putting wild flowers in a flower press, she called it. She looked neat and all starchy. How did Auntie manage to look like she was wearing Sunday-go-to-meeting clothes all the time? Mama's hair fell down unless she braided it in big loops around her ears, and sometimes her skirts got dirty on the hems, and her shoes needed rubbing with grease, but not Aunt Tamsen ... here she was out on the grass, looking just as if she was going to town.

She was glad to see them, though. "Sit down, girls. Let's have a little bit of refreshment. I brought bread and pickles."

"What are you doing, Auntie?" Patty looked at Tamsen's flower book. "Read this to me, Puss. I don't know all the words."

"How would you like me to help you with lessons, girls? Virginia, I've noticed that your spelling is poor. You're a grown girl, and you ought to learn to write better ... your mother says you write letters back home to your cousins ... I could help you with them."

Virginia felt her face redden. Goodness sakes, had Mama shown her her letters? She didn't want Mama to read everything she wrote ... some of the things she told about Eliza ... well, Mama wouldn't like that.

Patty was saying, "Puss and I missed school a lot last year, and now we're going to lose another year, going to California ... do they have schools there? I'm good at numbers, even if I don't read fast."

"I'd love to tutor you ...."

"What's tutoring?" Patty asked suspiciously.

"Teaching, child. You know, I've even taught grown men to survey, and I've helped Milt with the letters he's sent home. Virginia, you could have me look over the letters you send back and I could correct the spelling errors before you send them off."

"When we meet someone going back, I just hurry and write," Virginia said, red in the face. Then she added politely, "But we'd like to have you teach us when we have time."

"When *you* have time? You're out of school, riding your pony, teasing poor Milt Elliott, flirting with the little Breen youngster ...."

"And taking care of Mama when she doesn't feel good, and looking after Jimmy and Tommie and me," Patty said practically.

Auntie Tamsen said, "You're a loyal little sister, Patty, and a joy."

After they left Auntie, Patty said, "She's a little bossy, isn't she, Puss?"

"So're you, funny-face. Auntie can't help it. But I don't see why I need to spell when people can read what I write already."

By word of mouth, travelers anticipated certain things: the first buffalo, the first sight of the Platte River, and the strangely shaped rock formations that were milestones on the montonous journey. For some time since leaving the Little Blue the trail had slowly ascended a plateau that culminated in bluffs overlooking the wide bed of the shallow Platte. Their road took them to the river at approximately the spot where Grand Island divided it. The banks were sparsely lined with cottonwoods, the soil poor and sandy. Now they felt they were on the main highway going west to the Great Divide.

Instead of on gentle waves of blowing grass over an oceanic prairie, the way took them along a wide river-bed, sometimes as much as two miles wide. The river was so shallow that it could sometimes be waded by rolling trousers above the knees, but there was always the danger of quicksand. Imaginations ran wild at the shapes of sandstone ... Chimney Rock, Courthouse Rock, formations that spurred their memories of towns back home. The reflection of the trees and shrubs in the water intensified the shapes until, at camp fires each night, they concocted new names for places that reminded them of home.

After the novelty of having at last reached the Platte, the character of the trip had new facets. Some emigrants traveled on one side of the splayed river, some on the other. Crossings were sometimes easy, sometimes dangerous or fatal for men and animals. Then came buffalo in quantities, their meat enhancing their diet of sow-belly, salt pork and beans by broils of only the choicest parts. The remainder of the animal was skinned and left for the wolves who howled so mournfully through the night, or for coyotes with their weird up-turned scream at the end of their bark.

It was as if they were on a well-marked pike at home. Messages were many along the trail, written on buffalo skulls as well as on paper waved from forked sticks. Sometimes now there were returning wagons bound east, who stopped to explain their reasons: the death of the father of a family, or a wife who left children, discouragement at hardships, illnesses, or loss of animals. Some of the women going west stared hard, lips trembling with regret or envy as these home-bound wagons whipped up their oxen and left in a cloud of dust that caked under their wet eyes. Often with them went letters to relatives at home, hastily written, with news of their health and welfare.

Some only shouted at the returnees, "Where are ye bound for?," and hearing that the destination was somewhere near their former homes, called out, "Let my people know you saw me on the trail and that we're doing fine! .... Name's Barker, from down in Fayette County, Illinois!"

Young men venturing forth to climb the rocks after a hard day's travel felt as they reached the high spots that they could almost see the ridges of the Rocky Mountains ahead. Still, at Scott's Bluff they were haunted by the story of the solitary sick man who had been left to die alone, and isolation crept in on them once more. Now, ahead were Independence Rock, Devil's Gate, the South Pass.

Experienced travelers now, they easily fell into new routines. Oh, wagons broke down, axle-trees broke, animals fell (Poor things, the women thought, watching them blend into the eastern distance ... they had come so far for this). Quicksand, dry grass, heavily cropped, bitter water, the lack of wood for wagon repairs, flares of temper, petty disagreements ... all these became part of daily routine. Somehow things were righted, and most went on, helped by big-hearted people who always appear to help in a crisis.

Illnesses continued; women worried more about those than broken wheels. When they reached a spring, who wanted to be the first to try the water? Some of the clearest tasted the worst. Ed Bryant found a sulphur spring and advised them all to take a supply on ahead; it was healthful. They came to depend on his suggestions. He was always ready to advise them, and he reinforced their native distrust of the frequent "dosings" the men were taking in the belief that if a little was good, a lot would be better. When a child "came down" women went to Bryant, but they kept their peace about their own health. It was hard to describe their own troubles to a man half their own age, but all right to talk of diarrhea of children. If their ills became unbearable, they sent their husbands to him to explain.

It wasn't easy to keep well when the routine was stringent. Didn't men realize that they had so many things to do keeping the children regular and "flushed out" that the "Catch up!" in the morning came far too early for them to attend to their own needs?

Was getting started on time the only thing that mattered? It was a stern life in a bare country, and few women had the hardness in them to discuss the simple facts of daily comfort. They coped as well as they could. With a kind silent thank you for Bryant's thoughtfulness, they filled a canteen with sulphur water. The longer they were on the trail, the easier it became, and the less they thought of modesty. But how they longed for the comfort of the outhouse back home behind the barn!

They tried to hurry, tried not to rebel when starting time came. They needed time for everything, washing, baking, cooking, straightening wagons cluttered with things they regretted having brought. They rarely met the 20 miles a day they had aimed for.

Tamsen Donner's letter to the *Springfield Journal,* printed July 23, 1846 was penned near the junction of the North and South Platte, June 16, 1846: Directed to "My Old Friend" the editor, "We are now on the Platte, two hundred miles from Fort Laramie.

"Our journey so far has been pleasant, the roads have been good and food plentiful. The water for part of the way has been indifferent, but at no time have our cattle suffered for it. Wood is now very scarce, but 'buffalo chips' are excellent; they kindle quickly and retain heat surprisingly. We had this morning buffalo steaks broiled upon them that had the same flavor they would have had upon hickory coals.

"We feel no fear of Indians, our cattle graze quietly around our encampment unmolested.

"Two or three men will go hunting twenty miles from camp; and last night two of our men lay out in the wilderness rather than ride their horses after a hard chase.

"Indeed, if I do not experience something far worse than I have yet done, I shall say the trouble is all in getting started. Our wagons have not needed much repair, and I can not yet tell in what respects they could be improved. Certain it is, they cannot be too strong. Our preparations for the journey might have been in some respects bettered.

"Bread has been the principal article of food in our camp. We laid in 150 pounds of flour and 75 pounds of meat for each individual, and I fear bread will be scarce. Meat is abundant. Rice and beans are good articles on the road; cornmeal, too, is acceptable. Linsey dresses are the most suitable for children. Indeed, if I had one, it would be acceptable. There is so cool a breeze at all times on the plains that the sun does not feel so hot as one would suppose.

"We are now four hundred and fifty miles from Independence. Our route at first was rough, and through a timbered country, which appeared to be fertile. After striking the prairie we found a first-rate road, and the only difficulty we have had, has been in crossing the creeks. In that, however, there has been no danger."

Tamsen's letter continued:

"I never could have believed we could have traveled so far with so little difficulty. The prairie between the Blue and the Platte River is beautiful beyond description. Never have I seen so varied a country, so suitable for cultivation. Everything was new and pleasing; the Indians frequently come to see us and the chiefs of a tribe breakfasted at our tent this morning. All are so friendly that I cannot help feeling sympathy and friendship for them. But on one sheet, what can I say?

"Since we have been on the Platte, we have had the river on one side and the ever varying mounds on the other, and have traveled through the bottom lands from one to two miles wide, with little or no timber. The soil is sandy, and last year, on account of the dry season, the emigrants found grass here scarce. Our cattle are in good order, and when proper care has been taken, none have been lost. Our milk cows have been of great service, indeed. They have been of more advantage than our meat. We have plenty of butter and milk.

"We are commanded by Captain Russell, an amiable man. George Donner is himself yet. He crows in the morning and shouts out 'Chain up, boys — chain up' with as much authority as though he was 'something in particular.' John Denton is still with us. We find him useful in the camp. Hiram Miller and Noah James are in good health and doing well. We have of the best people in our company, and some too, that are not so good.

"Buffaloes show themselves frequently.

"We have found the wild tulip, the primrose, the lupine, the eardrop, the larkspur, and creeping hollyhock, and a beautiful flower resembling the bloom of the beech tree, but in bunches as large as a small sugar-loaf, and of every variety of shade, to red and green.

"I botanize, and read some, but cook 'heaps' more. There are four hundred and twenty wagons, as far as we have heard, on the road between here and Oregon and California.

"Give our love to all inquiring friends. God Bless them. Yours truly, Mrs. George Donner."

Tamsen put down her pen, and rubbed her stiff fingers. She had sent back information that was needed, hadn't she? Should she have signed her name Tamsen Eustis Donner? She could have asked Mr. Bryant ... he would know. Others could use their first names without a quiver, but she was unable to ... asking Edwin Bryant might have bridged the formality that lay between them. She confessed that she would have liked to call him Ed or Edwin, as everyone else did.

Still pondering what she had so carefully written, she folded the letter into a packet, and sat back.

Later, when George came back from delivering her missive to those who were to take it east, he had additional news for her. Several men had just arrived bound east. They had counted 478 wagons on the trail, adding those in their party, this brought the total to 518. Talk in the camp was that there were twenty more behind. That would have been an interesting statistic for her letter, and she quickly sat down to write a second one ... this time much shorter, ending the new information with the note, "Tomorrow we cross the river, and by reckoning will be over 200 miles from Fort Laramie, where we intend to stop and repair our wagon wheels."

"Take this, George, and see if it can be sent with the other," she asked her husband, handing him the second note.

"That party has started, my dear, but the young men have not, and I think they will carry this on ... they're going faster than the others, and the second may arrive first. Such a conscientious little woman you are, my dear," and he smiled in his genial way and left the wagon.

That evening, sitting by the side of the wagon, looking at the evening star bright in the sky, Tamsen wondered again about her letter to her old friend. Had she been too familiar with him? The remark she had made about George came to mind. "Chain up, boys ...." Would he think that she was making fun of George? Well, the sentence, now on its way east, would have to stand. No use to think about it any more. They were such good friends ... he would undoubtedly understand. It had been only a little suggestion of humor in a letter devoted to facts that would help the next year's emigration.

She had wanted, most of all, to be honest. She didn't want to discourage people as she had been discouraged before she left. In these weeks on the trail, she had felt a surge of new beginnings, of hope, and of the prosperity that lay ahead. Oh, there had been people going back who had no use for California ... they must not have been made of very sturdy stuff.

518 wagons had been met by these men coming east. They had made a game of counting them, she was sure. Certainly there were more than that ahead ... twenty yet behind. She looked at the sky, where color was draining off. Soon someone would start a fiddle or a banjo. It was a peaceful evening, with the rather exciting prospect of something new tomorrow, crossing the Platte ....

Something nagged at her ... some other piece of news she had reported ... oh yes, the men had told George that the advance wagons were 150 miles west of Laramie. That would make approximately 350 miles between their party and the vanguard. Quickly her teacher's mind divided the 350 by the 20 miles they tried to make every day ... they were more than 17 days behind the leaders. And the 17 days would stretch into many more ... they rarely made 20 miles, and there would be stops ... crossing the river tomorrow would take all day, for instance ... and after such a strenuous day she was sure they would rest over ... and only twenty wagons were behind them.

A streak of golden cloud had crossed the horizon. Tamsen stirred uneasily. They certainly *were* far behind in their crossing, if only 20 wagons were later than they. Probably only talk. But the thought would not leave her. No wonder Mr. Bryant talked about selling his wagon at Fort Laramie and going ahead on mules. If they made Fort Laramie in twenty days, that was two-thirds of a month. Why, that would make it well into July and they would be less than halfway across, according to most estimates. July, August, September — Good heavens! less than half the projected days remained! The elation she had felt when she sent the letter off was gone now, and she thought about her comments in it.

She had wanted to be honest. But had she? Her old friend, the editor, had been so pessimistic when they left; she hadn't wanted to worry him. She didn't want her friends to read a letter full of complaints and irritations ... had she made things look too good? "Certain it is, the wagons cannot be too strong ..." she recalled. That would be a hint. "Our preparations for the journey might have been in some respects bettered ...." Her cheerful words now sounded ominous to her. *How* could they have been bettered? "We may be short of bread," she had written .... So they would need more flour, if they read between the lines. Why had she made this trip sound so idyllic? Of course, she wanted to reassure those at home, waiting for the news ....

"Four hundred fifty miles from Independence ...." May twelfth to June 16. Thirty-five days out of Independence ... a little over thirteen miles a day .... The force of the numbers hit her. Oh, gracious heavens!

It was her nature, she knew, to be cheerful. Had she told lies? No, but she had seen everything with the clear eyes of the optimist George was ... where had the doubts gone she had earlier? Or was she just making the best of a bad bargain?

No danger crossing creeks, when wagons turned over and people were thrown into the water! The grass is scarce ... when proper care has been taken of them, none have been lost ... "proper care" ... what did most people know of the proper care of the animals? The thieving Indians that came every night ... "I cannot help feeling sympathy and friendship ...."

Captain Russell ... an amiable man. A slave to the bottle. Given to making endless, rambling speeches. "Full of sound and fury, signifying nothing ...." Was Owl Russell, as they called him ... (Captain, indeed!) a man to lead them speedily through the rest of the journey? Her face turning hot in her secret embarrassment, she remembered another sentence ... "Indeed I never could have believed we could have traveled so far with so little difficulty ...." Just because she had become so used to the daily troubles and inconveniences, and the frequent quarrels, arguments, she should not expect that others would adjust as she had ... she was among the best cared for women of the trip ... what about the Breens, with their wagons crowded with children? What about Lavina Murphy with her large group, on a desperate trip to join friends in California ... no money left ... only the hard work of her sons-in-law? Of the pathetic Phillipine Keseberg, of frail Eleanor Eddy and her not-too-strong babies? Of that Mrs. Wolfinger, unsuitably dressed, unable to understand anyone? Of that poor lad Luke Halloran, coughing his way across in a search for good health? She was ashamed. If she had the power, she would have brought that letter back and amended it. But then people at home would worry about us all, would be able to do nothing, would dream bad dreams ....

Tamsen stood up. The camp fires were burning down. There was singing far off, and laughter, but when there was a pause she heard the long terrifying sound of the wolves who always seemed to be waiting for disaster. Oh, Tamsen, Tamsen, Tamsen, she said to herself. What are you, Tamsen, a believer or a non-believer ... an optimist or a pessimist ... a thinker or a listener to wild tales, both of good and bad?

And she had ended the letter ominously, though at the time she had meant it to be only realistically. "We have of the best people in our company, and some too that are not so good ...."

When was it, back on the prairie, that Lewis Keseberg had stolen the buffalo robe from the Indian grave? Grave was not the word. Indians laid their dead on a platform constructed high above ground, and covered them with a buffalo robe. The German had come into camp, carrying one of these, before they were in buffalo country, perhaps? That was why they had gathered around him to gape at it. He had tried to explain where it came from ... and they had not thought much about it until James Reed joined them. She'd had a chance to see James in one of his flares of temper.

"You've stolen this from an Indian grave!"

The sullennes of the man. "I steal nodding. It was there!"

"Damn it man, you've put us all in danger. The Indians will be after us. The robe is sacred to them."

She knew how stubborn Germans can be. Furthermore, Mr. Keseberg was as arrogant in his way as James Reed. Indeed, both were said to have noble blood in them, undoubtedly a fiction. In a way, it was conflict between two men, both of whom felt themselves better than the others ....

The people gathered around became instantly frightened. An Indian attack was one of their greatest fears. They took up what James Reed had insinuated. "Take it back. Take it back, robber! Grave Robber!"

She would not forget how the handsome, sullen blond German giant stood, like an animal at bay. James Reed insisted. James was right, of course. The party had been warned about desecrating graves. Had this man Keseberg understood? He pretended to a good knowledge of English and French ... but how good was it, after all? He spoke with a thick accent ... was his understanding as thick?

Finally, looking at all eyes accusing him, the German had said, with contempt as heavy as his accent, that he would return the robe to the place he had found it. Whether he had or not, it was not seen again. Mr. Keseberg had been banished from the

Springfield party. Without asking permission he merely transferred his wagons to the end of a nearby party when it rolled in the morning ... in a few days, perhaps a week, he had rejoined Owl Russell's group with no acknowledgement or refusal ... and it was loosely taken for granted that he had learned his lesson. Tamsen would not soon forget the face that stared back at James Reed over the stolen buffalo robe. It was pure hatred. Cold, insolent hatred of someone who had humiliated him.

James was "one of the best people" and she had been thinking of Mr. Keseberg when she wrote, "And some too, that are not so good."

However, there could have been a better way of handling the poor man, Tamsen thought, though she could not fault James for having said that such actions would endanger the whole group. He could have explained more deliberately why it was wrong ... tribal customs, their need to respect them. He needn't have been so forceful in his idea of right and wrong. He needn't have frightened all the party with his alarm at what the Indian tribes might do to retaliate. For retaliate they would have done, if they had found a grave violated. No matter that Indians themselves violated the graves of emigrants ... after all, Indians were the hosts in this country. Which came first, the violation of an Indian grave or the violation of an emigrant grave? Justice was a hard quality to explain. Justice was so often accompanied by a sense of pride in being right.

The calm of the evening had been spoiled for Tamsen. The music, far off only made her sad. She wished she had the letters back. The first she had thought out carefully for days, because Mr. Francis had so kindly asked her to send back reports of the journey. The second, of course, was no more than a postscript. She had intended to write cheerfully, but she had dropped hints of trouble all along, without explaining them. And she had given false impressions, without meaning to, and she had disguised the truth in rosy language.

Everything was a lack of understanding and communication. Oh, the written word was so irrevocable! The hatred that James Reed had planted might grow and grow ... all because Keseberg understood little. Still and all, no gentleman would have robbed a grave. The dead must not be desecrated.

She went into the wagon silently. George, who had taken the girls to the fire to sing with the others, returned soon, and all were put to bed. Little Eliza, her baby, was already asleep, her thumb in her mouth. Tamsen softly removed the thumb, and undressed quietly. All night long she had frightful dreams. Dreams that would have made her cry out, had she not thought of the children.

Afterwards, none of the women recalled exactly when the weeping that came from the Keseberg wagon had turned to screams. All of them had tried to help poor little Mrs. Keseberg. At night, when the wagons were gathered into their circle, her neighbors often heard her crying, yet since she did not seem to wish to confide, they only closed their ears and tried to forget. James Reed brought up the subject, some said, to her husband, but his interference only angered the tall, contemptuous German.

Those nearby recognized the sudden scream, and the groans that followed. News circulated fast. Phillipine Keseberg was in labor. One by one, they gathered to do what they could. No woman ought to be left alone in childbirth without another woman to help.

Standing outside, they discussed who should offer first. Then they heard Lewis talking in German to his wife. His tones were angry, impatient; somehow they sounded obscene. The women were silent; none moved toward the wagon.

"I'll go," Tamsen Donner said finally. "I have talked with her a little, and I think she understands me."

"I'll go with you," Margaret Reed said. Then others offered to go.

"Perhaps one at a time ... wait here, and I'll call for you," Tamsen said in determination. Women watched as she approached the Keseberg wagon. Eleanor Eddy had her hands over her ears. "Poor thing, poor thing," she said over and over.

"It's just push, push and it's over," Peggy said.

"She hasn't looked well. Not since the wagon tipped with her."

"She looks bad because that man beats her. I'm sure of that," Lavina said. "He's a cruel, cruel man."

The cries and groans increased, and as Tamsen knocked, all heard Mr. Keseberg yell.

Tamsen knocked again and called out, "Phillipine, this is Tamsen Donner. May I come to help you?"

The wagon flap opened abruptly and Lewis Keseberg stood like some tall avenging spirit. "Vat is it? Vat you want?"

"I've come to help your wife."

He glowered. "She needs no help from you."

"This is a time for women ..." Tamsen began.

"Nein. Nein."

The women heard Phillipine say something in a low tone, and her husband turned. "She does not vish you to help."

"You do not tell the truth," Tamsen answered.

"Go away. It is nodding of your business."

"Phillipine! Phillipine!" Tamsen called out. "Tell your husband to let us come in to help you."

"Ja, ja," was the faint answer, and then another groan, animal-like in intensity.

"She has had kinder before ... there is no trouble ...."

Tamsen hesitated, stepped forward, but Keseberg blocked her way. "Nein. Nein! No vun vill come in."

"I will only hold her hands, help her in her travaille ...." Tamsen was begging now, but the man dropped the flap over the door. Tamsen waited. The curtain did not open again.

They heard screams and groans all night. In the morning, the noise stopped. Mrs. Wolfinger told by signs that Spitzer had told her the baby was a boy, named for his father. George Donner suggested that the wagon wait over a day so Phillipine could rest, but was refused, as Tamsen had been the night before.

"Go on, go on!" Keseberg shouted at him. "Too many days haff gone by. My vife will be all right. Go on!"

When the women saw the new son, they shook their heads ... such a thin little thing! It would not be long for this world, they predicted. Phillipine said nothing. Her eyes were "burnt holes in a blanket," poor woman.

On June 27, Lillburn Boggs, ex-governor of Missouri, who had replaced "Owl" Russell as the elected leader of the party, led his group into their first settlement since leaving the United States, a little ahead of the schedule Tamsen had predicted. The stopping place was not Laramie, but a half-finished trading post, Fort Bernard, located on the junction of Laramie Creek and the Platte, six miles below Fort Laramie. The word was that the Sioux Indians were gathered in war dress at the latter, larger post, and that grass at that location was cropped to the ground by the Indian ponies. It was a decision of the entire group to stop here to repair wagons and trade tired animals for fresh ones.

Here James Reed met his old fighting companion from the Black Hawk War, James Clyman. Yes, Abe Lincoln, a fellow Black Hawk soldier, was doing fine back in Springfield. Why, his wife and family had come down the street to bid them goodbye and godspeed the night before they left town! As a matter of fact, she was one of a group of home towners who had given them a bottle of brandy which they were saving for the Fourth of July. Well, no, they hadn't quite decided to go west by Fort Hall. They were behind time, a little, and Hastings' new cut-off would save them as much as two hundred miles .... You've just come that way with Hastings himself? Well, what first rate luck! You can give us some advice.

TAMSEN

Tamsen, standing nearby, overheard. With unaccustomed lack of ceremony, she broke into the conversation. "Oh, Mr. Clyman, you'd be such a boon to us all if you would describe the road to us truthfully ...."

"It ain't much of a road, Madam. If it was me, I'd avoid it like the collery. Hastings took that road with me just now for the first time hisself."

"Why, he describes it in his book as if it were a good pike, as if he knew it like the back of his hand."

Tamsen looked at this man, dusty in his buckskins, hair long and uncombed, his hat battered and engrained with dirt and his fingernails black.

"Do you tell me the truth, Mr. Clyman, or are you joking with me?"

"I'm afraid, ma'am, that I tell you the truth. Mr. Hastings is no mountain man; he pictures things a lot more rosy than they are. Maybe someday that route will be passable for wagons, but now it's only a faint trail made by mules ... ours just now, and Fremont's some time back .... We barely made it through."

"But you did make it," James Reed said. "If you made it I don't see why we can't."

Oh dear, I hope James Reed hasn't made up his mind before he even listens to this man, Tamsen thought.

"Tell you what, Clyman. You come down to our camp tonight and we'll open a bottle of my wine, and you can talk to the top men of our party," James Reed said. "We'll smoke the peace pipe, and think of old friends, and talk things over," James added genially, slapping Clyman on the back.

Tamsen sighed in relief. "Oh yes, do come down and have supper with Mr. Donner and the rest of our group," Tamsen said.

"I'd be honored, ma'am," James Clyman said with a certain awkward grace. "I'd purely like to talk to you afore you set your minds to going that cursed way. I've got to be on my way east tomorrow."

"We'll expect you any time you can come ...."

Tamsen thought, "I'd best have biscuit tonight, and some of the dried apples in a pie ... poor man, all that way with no one to cook for him." James Clyman, rude as he looked, had touched her in some strange way ... it was his eyes ... eyes that looked so directly at you, eyes that had nothing to hide.

Lavina Murphy said as Tamsen passed, "Who's that old tramp you were talking to?" And Peggy Breen added, "Well, I never! Mrs. Donner, without a speck of dirt on her shoes, after making friends with the likes of that bum!"

"He's just been over the road Mr. Donner is thinking of taking," Tamsen replied and with some spirit she added, "I don't judge a man by his clothes. Anyone wanting to know what the man has to say is invited to hear him out."

When she had left them the two looked at each other, shaking their heads and smiling. "Don't she know George Donner had his mind made up to take that road weeks ago? And that smart James Reed too? Might as well talk to a pair of mules. She's a great one, thinkin' she can change her man's mind."

Lavina Murphy laughed. "Here I am, payin' for the whole bunch o' them, and do you think those two sons-in-law pay a bit of attention to what I think? Not on your life, though I have nothin' but good to say of them otherwise. Men is men, and they're going to do whatever they have a hankerin' for."

"Well, I'm for gettin' another sack of flour, no matter what it costs. Praise the Lord, we'll make it, whichever road we take," Peggy Breen said, hefting a sack of beans on her man-sized shoulders.

That night, after Tamsen's supper, James Clyman met with the Donners, James Reed, Governor Boggs, Jessy Thornton, Owl Russell, Edwin Bryant, all the top men of the large party. The meeting lasted long into the night, until the fires had burned down and the cattle and children were sleeping, the dogs were lying under the wagons, quiet at last.

James Clyman had nothing good to say of the cut-off. "It's up and down, to hell and gone. I doubt that wagons could make it through. We had trouble enough with horses and mules. Ed Bryant here, who's trading in a wagon for mules probably will do all right, since our trail is fairly fresh. Even if Hastings says he'll lead you through hisself, I'd think hard about it afore I'd go. He ain't got the know-how. It's a rough go, no matter what he says about them 200 miles."

After a few such speeches, most of the leaders were persuaded by Mr. Clyman. Some were Oregon-bound. The short cut would do them no good. They thanked Clyman and drifted off toward their wagons.

James Reed and the Donner brothers were adamant. Jake was feeling so exhausted and sick that a short cut seemed the only way he could possibly reach California before he gave out. George nodded his head in agreement. James Reed said stubbornly, "It's right there in the book: '200 miles shorter. The most direct route, for the California emigrants, would be to leave the Oregon route about two hundred miles east from Fort Hall; thence bearing west southwest to the Salt Lake; and then continuing down to the bay of St. Francisco.' Why, we can't afford not to take it!"

James Clyman snorted. "Sounds so god-damned easy don't it? Sounds like a Sunday School picnic. Y'ever been in real mountains afore, Jim Reed? You know what a salt desert looks like? You're a good fighter and a good man to have around, but ye ain't seen nothin' yet. You're late as it is. Take my word, Reed, Hastings is a tenderfoot, no better'n you, and a man none too careful of the truth .... Why, man, we barely made it, and we was alone, not takin' kith and kin and young'uns and that hulk of a wagon!"

There was silence. "I'll say only one thing more. Y're late. If ye take the Fort Hall road, there's a chance, if nothing happens ... y' got no chance this new way. Think it over hard before ye make that turn south."

James Reed smiled. "Thanks, Jim," he said, and held out his hand. They parted friends, slapping each other's backs in a comradely way.

"I'm afeared for ye, Jim Reed. Take care."

"Don't worry about me. We'll make it, one way or the other." Jim Clyman shook his head. He was dead tired from arguing and he looked down-hearted. He pushed his old hat down over his eyes. "Thanks for the brandy, and the good eats afore ...."

"See you, next time you're in California."

Jim Clyman didn't answer. He walked into the darkness. They heard his horse snort, and the sound of its hoofs going off into the night.

Reed turned to George and Jake, whose eyes were almost closed.

"Still game to try?"

"Why, sure, I am," George said. "Way I see it, there's no choice."

Tamsen was still awake when George returned from the meeting. "What did he say, George?" she asked anxiously.

"Talk, talk, talk. I'm surprised you wanted me to listen to an old broken-down has-been like that, Tamsen. Hasn't had a bath for a year, I bet. Ed Bryant's going our way ... he's got more sense than to listen to an old fool."

"Our way? You mean you're still taking the Hastings' route?"

"Started with that in mind, my girl. Nothing that man said did much to change things. He's gone down hill since James and Abe knew him in the war ... look what he's made of himself."

Tamsen turned her face into the pillow.

The Boggs Party stayed at Fort Bernard until the third of July. The Sioux, gathered at Fort Laramie, were reported to be restless, the grazing for cattle almost depleted. Six days passed before the train started west again. However, the wagons were now in good order, the cattle refreshed, new animals traded for old, wheels tightened and oiled, clothes washed, supplies sorted and counted. The group was short of staples, but at Laramie there would be one last chance to replenish them.

When they reached Laramie it was a lonesome sight. Edwin Bryant had described it as teeming with Indians, but most had departed leaving the grass chopped and trampled. Still, since leaving Independence, they had not seen anything this grand. Standing on land high above the prairie Fort Laramie was a stark enclosure, built for utility. Two blockhouses for defense against raiding Indians dominated the yard, a square area surrounded by a series of small rooms in which the employees of the fort and their squaws lived.

Boggs stopped at Fort Laramie only a half-day. That morning, many of the emigrant women put on their cleanest clothes and clustered inside the fort, fingering goods there, looking over what was to be purchased as if they were in the finest emporium back home. Grand were the prices they paid: flour was sold at fifty cents a pint; sugar, coffee and tobacco were one dollar a pound. Had they known, the women would have been aghast at the money being laid out for whiskey ... a dollar a pint!

However, now that they realized that this fort was almost the last civilized spot before they reached California, money that had seemed important for the journey seemed far less important than the goods it could buy.

Emigrant women looked curiously at the Sioux women that remained, as curiously as their feminine counterparts looked at them. For some, contempt was the emotion the emigrants felt at seeing pagan women dressed in white leather clothes, some as sodden with whiskey as their braves were. For others of the American women, there was a faint touch of envy at the simplicity of their dress, so different from their own long cumbersome skirts. Still others thought, there for the grace of God go I, and pondered how it would feel to be that other woman, to live as she did, to make do, work and carry their men's baggage, to be slaves of a primitive man with no consideration of their sex. Very few women realized that they were alike in many respects; each was doing what she had been brought up and trained to do.

For Margaret Reed and her family, there was disappointment that her brother was not waiting for them here, as they had expected, even though a rumor had reached her that he had gone to California. She left a note for him, just in case the news was in error and he did come to meet his sister and mother, neither of whom would be there.

For Tamsen there was also disappointment. She had heard of the two young Harvard men who were studying the Indians, living and traveling with them as friends. How she longed to speak to them. She would be touch with her own people, her own background! Although she had spoken without introduction to James Clyman at Fort Bernard, the two young men looked remote, as if they saw the emigrants as a class by themselves. "Owl" Russell had made a fool of himself, as everyone knew, and

Tamsen hesitated to be put in a category with him and his disgusting intoxication. Well, the young men were probably far more interested in Indian women than emigrants with their Shaker bonnets shading their sun-darkened faces. She held her head high, somehow wishing that she was not to be classified as an ignorant, misguided middle-class farmer's wife; yet as she thought she wished mightily she could speak to them in the accents of her youth, to change their opinion, and to defend all the fine women who had come so far without complaint and with courage.

After only this half-day at Fort Laramie, the Boggs party moved on a few miles to a grove next to a stream where they were to meet many of those who had crossed the plains with them. A real Fourth of July celebration was being planned. It would be as much like home as they could make it. The seventieth year of their nation, all Americans would be in a festival mood. For the people from Springfield, this meant even more, for their friends at home would be toasting them as they looked west; they in turn would look east and raise their glasses. For this reason, the anticipated visit at Fort Laramie was cut short.

As soon as camp was established women started cooking for the holiday. The high jinks at Fort Bernard had made the women wary of a celebration at Laramie itself ... the "spirits" had been high that night when Owl Russell had made such a fool of himself. It wasn't a good example for the young'uns ... the carousing, with Indian women in their white leather robes dancing in a "quite unacceptable manner," as some of them put it.

All the teenage children had begged to go to that dance, but none had been allowed to venture out of the watchful eyes of their mothers, though some of the boys who thought of themselves as young men, sneaked out from under the wagons where they slept to join the debauchery. The noise of drums, the screaming and shouting and laughter had lasted all night.

Some women objected to their men's desire to join the crowd of drunken emigrants and Indians, but what could they do about it? Others remarked that the men needed a little recreation after the trials of the march to Fort Bernard. A few of the younger women whispered as they nursed their babies that it would be jolly to join the men in some of the dancing, just for a while.

Well, tomorrow they would have a celebration of their own ... not rowdy, like that at Fort Bernard, but one worthy of patriots. A collation would follow, the best they could provide.

Some had dried peaches or apples for pies, others made pots of beans. Those with enough flour left to be prodigal made bread or cake. There would be buffalo steaks aplenty and lemonade for the ladies and children. That it was made with vinegar and sugar instead of lemons would make it taste no less refreshing. James Reed had saved wines for this very occasion, in addition to the brandy that was to be sipped at high noon as they rememberd their friends back in Springfield.

The fires glowed until late at night as the women prepared their dishes. Not until after midnight did the last woman fold her apron, wash her hands, and climb into her wagon for a sleep.

PATTY AND VIRGINIA

Patty tapped softly on her sister's shoulder until she sighed sleepily and said, "Wha's a matter?"

"Shhh. It's the Fourth of July."

Virginia sat up. "Already? I was having such a funny dream ...."

"Come on. We don't want to miss anything!"

Virginia was awake at once. She began to pull on her clothes under her nightgown.

"Don't make any noise, Mama might say we can't go."

The two girls slipped down from their bunks, shoes in their hands, and tiptoed across the room they still called Grandma's, down the steps into the fresh mountain air smelling of pines. "Look! There's frost on the canvas!" Patty whispered.

"We never had frost on the Fourth before, have we, Patty?"

When they were far enough from the wagon to dare to talk naturally, Virginia asked, "Now what are we going to do, Patty? No one's up. The guns aren't going off till nine o'clock, Ma said."

"You just wait. Someone always shoots one off early. Let's just wander around and see if they won't."

The Fourth of July! They had been anticipating the glorious celebration for days. It was almost the best day of the year, if you didn't count Christmas and Easter. Both were remembering the Fourths they had known ... flags everywhere, parades, picncs in the Courthouse park, gun shooting and salutes and hip-hip-hooraying, and someone reading the Declaration of Independence and then the long speeches in the park when you sat and listened to your stomach growling because you'd been too excited to eat much breakfast and the big tables spread with white tablecloths on the grass, cakes and pies and sandwiches and melons and potato salad and pickles of every kind imaginable and puddings and sometimes home-made ice cream and ham and fried chicken or big platters of everything in the world that was good to eat, and lemonade and root beer and jelly and jam and biscuits .... Then just lying there on the grass, your stomach hurting from all the goodies while mothers cleaned up and put things away so the flies wouldn't get at them. Later on, there were music and singing and dancing sometimes, and everyone free to run around and do almost anything since it was such a special day. Virginia reels and Paul Joneses and all the old tunes, and clapping to the music and then, late at night, that bugle call that made you want to cry, it was so beautiful, with its long last note pulling at your heart.

Patty said seriously, as they peered here and there among the wagons, "It's sort of scary, isn't it, Puss, when you think how far away we are. We're not even in the United States any more. We're not even Americans any more, are we?"

"Pa says we will be again, when California belongs to the United States."

"Is that really true?"

"He says so. There's a war right now and when it's over, we'll be right back being Americans again."

Patty smiled. "That makes me feel better, Puss. It seems sort of funny, being this far away and still a part of home ... hey, Puss, here come the boys! See, I *told* you!"

A couple of the Breens, Lem Murphy and Solomon and Billy Hook and boys from the other companies were up. She looked to see if that nice boy (he was sixteen years old, people said) from Missouri was with them, but he wasn't. Oh dear! But there were others old enough to be sort of fun ... Will Yum somebody ... he pronounced it as if it were two names, just behind the rest and Peter and Zeke, and that little skinny boy, Jake ... they were outside the wagons and one of the boys, was it Will Yum? had a gun. Suddenly shy, she stopped. There weren't any other girls out this early.

Patty asked Will Yum what he was going to do with the gun and he said, "We're going to shoot it, that's what. It'll make a heap of noise and wake up the whole camp!"

Patty looked at him with respect. It took courage to borrow a gun from your Pa. She'd never dare touch Papa's. Will Yum said some more guys were going to bring guns and they'd start the celebration right.

Patty asked, "You know how to shoot, Will Yum? Don't you dare aim it at anybody!"
"Huh. You think I'm crazy? I been handling guns since I was a baby, scaredy-cat!"
A couple more boys came out with guns too, and some bigger girls followed, and they were all standing around, ready to count one-two-three - go! when here came Charlie Stanton. "Cripes," Solomon Hook said, "a grown-up!"
But Charlie came among them and helped them all aim up in the sky and he even counted, and made the girls stand back. One, two, three GO! and Bang! Bang! Bang! went the guns and one of the boys fell over backwards from the kick of the gun and they were all laughing their heads off at him lying there on the ground, his hands over his ears, and people running out of tents half-dressed, and pulling on their pants and acting as if a bear was after them. Then Milt Elliott arrived, and he said, very quietly, so no one would hear and make fun, "You Reed girls skeedaddle right back to the wagon 'fore your Paw finds out you were here," and she and Patty ran like rabbits around the back of the wagons and got back fast, breathless and still laughing in spite of their fear that Pa might see them and guess they'd been where boys had been shooting guns.
Eliza was standing with her apron over her head, scared at the racket "I guess she hears something, even if she doesn't think very good," Patty said. Ma came out with the boys and said, "Don't be a silly, Eliza, it's just the Fourth of July. Take that apron off your head and help beat up some slam-johns."
Pa said a longer prayer than usual before breakfast, and wished the Nation could be blessed as well as all the family, and all his good men who had come with him, and Eliza and Baylis, for what they were all to receive, and Jimmy added, "Don't forget Cash, Papa. He's walked a lot of the way."
"Shh," Ma said. "Just think, children, our country is 70 years old today."
Patty said thoughtfully, "Grandma was 72 when she died ... that makes her two years older than the United States."
"That makes me feel funny," Virginia said. "We have someone in our family older than our country."
"We *had*," Patty corrected. "Papa, how did you feel when you came from Ireland?"
"I'll tell you girls, nothing ever looked better to me and my mother, too, than that shoreline. After Ireland, and before that Poland. You children must always realize how fine it is to be in a country where you can make a good living and you can say almost anything you want to ... you've always been free."
Patty nodded, and Virginia thought how serious he looked all of a sudden. When she looked at Mama, she had tears in her eyes. "Don't forget, James, it was a good day when you came here ... for me. For us all." Then, her face as red as the tar bucket, she ran off to the wagon.
Patty had been counting on her fingers. "Pa, our country was only 24 years old when you were born."
"That's right, Patty child. Good thinking."
Patty said, "Pooh. It's easy when your birthday was in 1800."
Eliza said, "You girls hurry up and eat them johnny cakes so's I can get the dishes washed up before the doin's." All the children watched to see what Papa would say to such impertinence.
"That's right, children. You wouldn't want Mama and Eliza to miss anything this great day, would you?"
Virginia thought, "My, but the Fourth of July makes that Eliza pretty uppity. If Ma were here she wouldn't talk so. Oh, well, poor thing ... I wouldn't want to miss anything either."
The real celebration started at nine o'clock. There was a grove of trees nearby that

looked a little like the parks at home, and people from all the companies gathered there, all in their Sunday clothes. Then the men shot their pistols all at once, to start things off. After that, all those who could walk lined up, mothers carrying their babies, around the whole corral, with someone shouting one, two, one, two, march, hup, hup, hup, to keep them walking in time. A few had flags, but there was no bunting nor any flowers to carry. They marched around once again and up to the group of trees. One of the men from another party read the Declaration of Independence slowly and clearly, so there was time to think what it really meant.

There were some foreigners along, too, glad to be in on any celebration, no matter what. Some, like Pat Dolan, who had just become a citizen before he started, already knew the words by heart. Virginia watched that Mr. Keseberg, curious to know what he would do. He always looked at her angrily. He was sitting apart, keeping his eyes on everything. He looked puzzled as if he didn't quite understand, though his pretty wife, with her new baby, was trying to mouth the words. That poor old man, Mr. Hardcoop, who wasn't a German, but a Belgian, Papa said, was smiling happily, and nodding his head.

Colonel Owl Russell was up in front, as usual. He was going to give the Oration. You might know ... he'd been giving speeches all along the way, every chance he got. Some of the women looked at each other, nodding critically. They called him the "old toper." The men said he wasn't such a bad lot, and he'd been pretty good about losing the election to Lillburn Boggs, and it was only polite that he give the Oration.

Today he looked grand: his whiskers combed, hair brushed, clothes neat and the dust whisked off, and a red rosette in his lapel. Butter wouldn't melt in his mouth. Virginia'd peeked out, back there at Fort Bernard when they were trying to get him back to camp. He'd fallen down twice, his hair was a tangle, and he was singing words you couldn't believe at the top of his voice. My, he surely looked different today! And he was full of long words and elegant sayings and dignified poems said in a voice that rang over the gathering as loud as the wake-up trumpet. Such big words made her sleepy, with their rising and falling. Sometimes he looked as if he were about to cry, and once he took out his big handkerchief and put it to his eyes. Sometimes he looked like a bird about to fly away, when he waved his arms. Sometimes his voice sunk down to a whisper you had to strain your ears to hear, and he sounded holier than the preacher back home. It went on a long time.

Virginia yawned, and got a nudge from Mama. Then she glanced around, looking for that boy from Missouri, Jackson Strong was his name. He was the best-looking young man in the whole encampment. He made Sol Hook and the Breen boys look like babies. Why wasn't he in their party? All there were in their company were boys eleven or twelve and fourteen. Nobody as handsome and grown-up as Jackson Strong. That was a real nice name, too, about the prettiest she'd ever heard. She'd run into him once or twice back on the prairie when the companies were closer, and she'd never expected to see him again. He hadn't noticed her much till last week, when his bunch of people came into Fort Bernard.

"Hey, you again!" he'd said with a big smile. She thought the words 'Hey, you again' were just right. She'd come right back at him. "Hey, you again, yourself," and they'd stood, smiling at each other. His eyes were simply beautiful, soft brown and laughing.

"Where you been since I seen you last?"

"Following along. The same places you been, I s'pose."

"How long you stayin' here?"

"Till the wheels get fixed ... two days more, prob'ly."

"Still got that pony, Billy?"

How'd he remembered Billy's name, she wondered? "Yes."

"Still ridin' like some sort of a windstorm?"

"When Ma'll let me." That sounded babyish. "Ma's careful about Indians these days. There's so many." He didn't answer, just looked at her, so she helped him out. "Which way are you going?"

"Oregon."

"We're going to California." She said it proudly, but her heart lurched.

"I wish we was goin' there, but Pa's got his mind made up for Oregon."

"I wish you was, too." As she said this, Virginia felt her face warm.

"You do, honest?"

"Sure."

She tried to remember what else they'd said. Ma wouldn't let her go down to the Fort; there was too much drinking, she said. (She didn't say Mama had said she was much too young, that she was just a child and that it was simply out of the question ... that would sound babyish). "I s'pose you got to go. You're a boy and too big to be bossed much any more."

"I s'pose my Ma wouldn't be too cut-up if I'd went. I'm sixteen. How old are you?"

Almost fourteen sounded better than thirteen. It still must sound babyish to him. She felt grown up ... she was the oldest girl in their party. Leanna and Elitha Donner were almost as old, and Auntie Tamsen would no more let them go to the doings at the Fort than Mama would her. Why did she have to be so pesky young? There would be so many things to see. It would be as lively as Independence was, like a big country fair at home, everyone in the world there, crowding around. She wouldn't have got mixed up in the drinking or the carousing, as Papa called it. She just wanted to dance a little and watch all the excitement. She was glad today wasn't like Fort Bernard. Everyone was in a mood almost like Sunday at home, like this day was sort of holy, but after all the talking (would that Owl Russell ever stop?) they'd let down a little, as they'd always done back home. She hoped she'd get a chance to talk to that Jackson again today. They'd seen each other and smiled already, from a distance. Patty had caught her smiling at him. "There you go, Puss, making eyes at boys again. You'd better watch out Mama doesn't catch you."

"I wasn't making eyes. I was just smiling."

"Ho! That isn't the way you usually smile."

That was Patty ... you could never hide anything from her.

The Oration was still going on. Patty was squirming. She poked her elbow in Puss's ribs and made a funny face at her. Virginia stifled a laugh. Patty looked just like old Owl Russell ... she could imitate anyone.

"I hope it ends soon, Puss. I can't wait."

"Hold on, Patty. He's got to stop sometime." Mama shushed her again, but Virginia saw her pat her sister comfortingly.

Suddenly it was over. "I thought it would never end. Never, never. *Never!*" Patty said, and under the cover of the clapping and stamping and cheering, she ran, following the other little girls as fast as she could, into a clump of trees. By some sort of unconscious arrangement, the little boys were running into a different part of the grove. Did grown-ups ever remember how hard it was to wait?

Virginia didn't run. She walked slowly with Mama, her eyes searching every group for Jackson. She couldn't find him for a long time, and she felt like crying. Then, once more, she caught sight of that blond head, taller than any of the rest, in a group of older boys, and it was all right, after all. Maybe he might sit near her at the big dinner. Maybe they would talk again ... oh, the day was going to be perfectly lovely, after all.

The food was grand. The mothers kept saying they could have done better at home, but everyone sat down and ate as if it were a real picnic. "No cakes," Mama said. "You can't make good cakes in the camp oven. It's too hot." But the pies were wonderful. Patty thought how funny mothers were, always making food sound as if it wasn't fit to eat, when everything tasted so good she could hardly stand it. If she'd had a bigger stomach she could have eaten all day. After the food was eaten and the left-overs were put away in baskets, there was some more talking, and some singing. Lots of the men got up and said a few words about the United States, and someone would shoot off his gun, and people cheered. Then another man would get up and say his piece and there would be more clapping and shooting. Lying on the ground, stuffed with the food, Patty let the sounds blend together, louder and softer and louder and softer, and each time the guns went off, she'd jerk into life again, and then let sleep take over. It was hard to stay awake.

Then her Papa got up and called for attention. "Friends from Springfield," he said in his nice definite voice. "The time is here to honor our promise to our friends back home. Will you all gather with me to fulfill a pledge made on the night we began this great journey into the wilderness?" Goodness, Papa sounded real important. "I will pass this jug of brandy among us and we will all stand and look east, and remember our country and our good friends, who at this moment are facing west and toasting us with a similar libation." He moved among them, pouring brandy into each cup. "I'm sorry this toast must be made in tinware, but it is none-the-less honorable. Yes, you ladies, too. A tot for each of you, a moderate one. This event merits taking a taste of the grape ...."

Virginia wondered if she'd be considered old enough to toast. Her cousins at home would be thinking of her. Papa put a little in her lemonade cup, and a mere drop in Patty's. "Now, will the Springfield people stand, look toward the east, pledge their allegiance to our fine country and to our loved ones back in that finest of towns: Springfield, Illinois!"

What grand words! The group looked very important as they stood, lifted their cups together and drank.

It tasted hot, sort of, Virginia thought, hoping Jackson could see her with the grown-ups, as experienced as they.

Mama's eyes were shining, almost as if she wanted to weep. Virginia looked around. Auntie Tamsen too, and Aunt Betsy ... all the women had tears in their eyes. Papa took out his handkerchief and blew his nose, Uncle George wiped his eyes, and Uncle Jake just let the tears run down his cheeks shamelessly. Virginia looked at Patty, and without warning, both of them started to cry ... not out loud, but silently, and it hurt down deep when she remembered her cousins and the big trees in the park at home, and her uncles and aunts, her best friends, her teacher, and the preacher, and the newspaper man and the classmates from school. She didn't care if people thought she was a baby; she just had to, it was so sad and beautiful, all at once.

Papa had brought some wine too, and now some of the other people made toasts, and thought of their friends and declared they lived in the best country in the world, and where you would go to find more opportunity, and some God blessed everything they could think of. Uncle Breen made a speech and praised the good Lord for such a happy day. Old Mr. Hardcoop was smiling and bowing to everyone in his funny way. Poor Luke Halloran looked cheerful, though the brandy made him cough harder than ever.

What a wonderful day! Now the mothers began picking up the dishes and carrying them back to the wagons to be washed. They said, some of them, that they were "feeling" the brandy already, and many said it was the first they ever tasted. Mama looked at Eliza, who had begun to stack up the dishes, and said, "Miss, you just carry those dishes to the wagon, and I'll do them up myself. You take the afternoon off." Patty said, "Oh, Ma! you're not going to make me wash the dishes on a holiday, are you?" And Mama said, "No, silly girl. You each bring me a pail of clean water and you're free to enjoy the rest of the day."

When the girls returned, the men were still making toasts, but they didn't sound dignified anymore. The wine was 'most gone, but someone had brought out a jug of whiskey, and Owl Russell was singing. They had started with hymns — now the songs were livelier. Auntie Tamsen was saying goodbye to Edwin Bryant, who, with his party of men, were starting on this afternoon. Charlie Stanton was shaking his hand, and Auntie Tamsen had a piece of apple pie wrapped up to give him. The mules were all packed, and off they went, with people yelling goodbye and good luck and "We'll see you in California!" "Maybe before that," he yelled back, and off they went west.

"He's going to leave letters for us along the way, Auntie Tamsen said. "That is, if we take that Hastings' road." She looked sad when she walked back to the rest.

Patty ran off with her friends, and Virginia stood alone. The lump was still in her throat from thinking about home, but it was getting better. Oh, how Grandma would love this celebration ... she could have said she was older than the United States! She bet no one else would have been able to say that. How lucky they were ... and then she wondered suddenly if they'd been so lucky in the United States why were they on their way someplace else?

Pat Dolan started some dancing, Uncle Patrick had his violin out, and other men went to find whatever instruments they'd brought, and people started lining up for a reel. Someone tapped her on the arm, tentatively. She turned and looked into Jackson Strong's blue, blue eyes.

"Like to have a whirl?"

She could only nod yes.

"Well, off we go, then!"

She had never felt so happy in her whole life. She loved to dance, and she was dancing with Jackson Strong. Her skirts whirled around her ankles like sheaves of wheat in the wind ... faster and faster. She never missed a step, and she knew every call. Ladies right and do-si-do! Every time she met Jackson in the hands across, he smiled at her. Oh, wasn't it fun to be grown-up!

"Hey, you're a mighty purty girl," he said once as they spun around together.

"I'm not either!" she said in mock annoyance, but her feet flew faster than ever.

Even Pat Dolan, when he crossed hands in the reel said, "Looks like a mighty sweet lass has a man makin' eyes at her."

"Oh, Pat, you're an old blarney stone!"

Milt had a turn, too. "Sis, you're getting grown-up mighty fast on this trip. Tell me when you're ready to go home ... I'll take you."

"Don't worry about me! I'm never going to get tired!"

Right and left and bow to your partner, chicken in the bread pan, pickin' out the dough ... she hoped it would never end.

When the music stopped she was facing Jackson again, as she should be. "You want some lemonade? I'm purely parched."

Suddenly she was parched too. They went toward the pitchers. He held her hand as they walked. "We're rollin' out real early tomorrow."

Virginia stopped. "Oh, Jackson! I wish you were going with us."

"You mean that, Virginia?" It was the first time he'd said her name. It sounded lovely.

"Yes. I do. I'm just getting to know you."

"I wish you was goin' with us to Oregon. I wish ..." he hesitated, and she waited. "I wish you was my girl."

What should she say? "You really do?"

"Would you be my girl if you knew me better?"

"I ... guess so." Tomorrow ... tomorrow, he was going to roll out early. "Maybe I'll see you on the way, before we turn off for California ...." Her hands were shaking; she held them together to make them stop.

"Maybe," he was saying, "after I get to Oregon I'll come to see you in California .... Could I? I might even like it better there."

She smiled radiantly. "Oh, Jackson! Would you?"

"If you'll give me a kiss ...."

It was the most wonderful day of her life, she thought later. Could anyone in the whole world be happier? Oh, life was beautiful, beautiful, beautiful!

TAMSEN

As the wagon lumbered along, Tamsen sat in the bow with her knitting, waiting for the first sight of Independence Rock. That some trains ahead had spent their Fourth of July holiday there made her uneasy; yet, since Laramie, the company was making far better time than they had. People estimated the distance as a little over 100 miles. At the pace they'd been going, they should arrive in seven days, give or take a little.

Greasewood intermingled with the artemisia on the exposed slopes; cottonwoods lined grassy places, sunflowers and lavender daisies were still in bloom, as if it were spring. Yet, away from damp spots, the land was parched, soil packed and hard, and trees browning. At Laramie they had said this was a dry year. She hoped that meant a long autumn, which would give them the additional time they needed so desperately.

How good it had been to meet Edwin Bryant again! She had only a few moments to exchange words with him. He had told her, however, that unencumbered by families and wagons, their party with its mule-drawn cart and horses easily made thirty to forty miles a day. At that rate, they would probably not see him again. He must be far ahead by now.

Tamsen was surprised at the gradual ascent to the summit of the Rocky Mountains. She had expected a harder climb! In the blue distance, she could see mountains capped with snow, and she shivered, but not from cold. It was only July. She wondered why they had called these mountains the Sweetwaters? The streams, delightful to look at, clear and seemingly pure, often had water that tasted so disgusting that they were unable to drink. When they reached the river of that name, she hoped that its water would be as sweet as its title.

There was something ominous and sobering ahead ... the Continental Divide. They would be going through the South Pass right after Independence Rock. Try as she might, she could not dismiss the thought of that woman who refused to go farther. When she saw the place where the waters began to flow westward she started back on foot. They had to tie her to the wagon.

Hastings' cut-off loomed even larger in her mind. Oh, why was George so stubborn? Often in the past he had accepted suggestions from her, but this time was hard-headed. Somehow, taking the cut-off was a challenge to him, as if he'd be a coward if he didn't take it. Hadn't James Clyman pictured a bad enough picture? Hadn't he said, over and over, that there was only one chance they could make California before the snows, and that was if they took the Fort Hall road? Couldn't George understand plain English? He reminded her time and time again, that this wasn't the only trip he'd made by wagon, as if she could forget it. She had retorted, rather acidly, she supposed, that those trips had been only the matter of a few weeks, and that this was of months ... months that slipped by as silently and speedily as the trees did when you took a river-boat. Somehow George had established the reputation of being an experienced traveler. Was his mind slipping, or was he showing off in front of the younger men? Drat, yes, *drat* that James Reed ... he was every bit as bad. Two stubborn mules, that's what they were.

Whenever the subject of leaving the main trail came into the conversation, her heart took a downward lurch.

"What's making that face sad, my dear?" George asked, and she wondered if he had read her mind.

"I needn't tell you again, need I?" she said mildly, continuing with her knitting.

"Still worried about that rag-tail Jim Clyman and his stories, aren't you?"

"I trust what he said. He's been there."

"So has Hastings."

She sighed in exasperation. "When Hastings wrote that book, he'd never been over that route. He is a liar, and that's that."

"I thought you set store by books."

"I set more store by people who tell the truth."

"Now, now, don't fret so. Have I done badly by you since we were married? Why don't you trust me now? You forget it. You're much prettier when you don't have a long face. Why don't you write in your notebooks, as you used to ... or sketch?"

"I guess I could ask you why you don't pay a bit of heed to what I say, but it wouldn't do a speck of good."

He laughed indulgently. "It's just those mountains ahead. You're not used to their size ... they can't help scaring you. We're almost to Independence Rock, and right after that, the Pass, and then, you'll see how easy it is."

"Late. We're late. You've got to take that into consideration." She was knitting faster and faster. It helped her to keep from crying or speaking out cruelly. Knit stitch after stitch and don't scream. Don't weep, don't worry ... as if she could keep from worrying. He said she was a good mother ... a good mother could not help worrying.

On and on climbing up and over the Great Divide. She had taught geography to children; she had never visualized it like this. It was dry and parched and not even dramatic ... it was purgatory. Sometimes she wondered why they hadn't stayed the rest of the year at Fort Laramie, and waited till next spring to go on. Then she remembered those hordes of Indians with their war dress, their paint and their dancing and yelling ... oh no! No matter where she looked she was trapped.

Never in her life had she felt this way, even when Tully had died. Lost, frightened, despairing. Then she had been young, a home to go back to, no fear, only heartbreak. Was it the turn of life, she wondered? It was about time for that. Some people took it hard; she had always meant to be strong. She felt like a dried up old woman, and George was a silly old man in his dotage. She must get hold of her wobbling self. "Take yourself in hand," her father had said when she was little. "Make the best of a bad bargain." Silly adages.

Well, there was still time. Perhaps George would change his mind. Her place was with George and the girls. Whither thou goest was written in the Bible George believed in so much. No one would have to tie her in the wagon when they came to the South Pass.

The Reeds could do as they pleased. Let James Reed call George a traitor. Let the people think George was a turn-coat and a coward. It took courage to change one's course. The hand to the plow, indeed! Oh, there was a verse in the Bible for everything!

"I will lift up mine eyes unto the hills, from whence cometh my help." That gave her a kind of courage, a sense of inevitability. She looked off to the horizon where the mountains were white, "from whence cometh my help," ....

There was a lone rider coming toward them, far off. She shuddered. Someone alone in this wilderness? Frightened and instantly distrustful, she watched as he grew larger and near, and came into focus. He wasn't an Indian, thank goodness. The stranger had his arm in the air, like an avenging angel. A fluttering paper in his upraised hand. What news was he bringing? Strange, ominous. She finished her row of knitting, neatly folded her work. Whatever the news he was bringing, she knew it wouldn't be good.

From Tamsen's point of view, the news couldn't have been worse. The name of the strange unknown horseman was Mr. Bonney. He was from Oregon, returning to the states to fetch his family. Most of the time, he said, he traveled by night, hiding himself in the daytimes. When he had seen the large train approaching, he had come forward with this letter, waving it like a signal of truce.

AT THE HEADWATERS OF THE SWEETWATER: To all California Emigrants now on the road: it began. The text of the message was concerned as usual with the new route south of the Salt Lake but it also informed the emigrants that the war with Mexico made travel dangerous for small parties, and it added that Hastings himself would be at Fort Bridger to take any party over the trail to California.

TAMSEN

That dratted Hastings again. What was the man up to? Why was he urging people to take a road James Clyman had described as being impassible? The lone horseman moved on before dawn, but he had strengthened the case for the cut-off. Surely Hastings wouldn't wait to take them across a route he didn't know well? The horseman hadn't known the route, either ... he was taking the paper as a favor. It was some comfort to the doubters that Hastings himself would conduct the trip. James Clyman said that most of the tender-feet on this journey were apt to hire an experienced mountain man, say Caleb Greenwood or his son Brit, when they took this section of the trail. Why hadn't this occurred to the men before? Probably because they were following an established path. Hastings must be telling the truth. He wouldn't jeopardize his own life, now would he? If it were just she and George taking this risk, she would not mind so much. But her family ... and almost resentfully she thought to herself ... I have had nothing but girls. Five of my own, and three of George's ....

What was she thinking of? What would George's God say to that? Would she be judged by George's interpretation of the word of God, or her own? She must cling to him, for better or worse, as she had promised. Hard rebellious thoughts swarmed and tangled in her mind, like yarn that the cats had played with. She began to knit furiously, her face troubled, her heart as black as the thunderclouds that boiled up ahead. She herself felt as angry as the cloud seemed committed to harm.

A few days later they reached the Great Divide, so innocuous-looking after the expectations of these many months. It was more a great level plain than the sharp arete she had expected. Wild currants grew in moist places, their taste sharpening their appetites used to hominy, sow belly and beans. Purple thistles caught at skirts; they were the only flowers now. The crickets were as bad as the mosquitoes. The mountains were bare and treeless. Independence Rock came and went; they drove through Devil's Gate, and impressive it was, too, far more impressive than the South Pass. The Wind River Mountains, visible here, were like stiffly starched white jabots inverted against the sky. Innumerable creeks edged with willows were shallow and made easy crossings this late

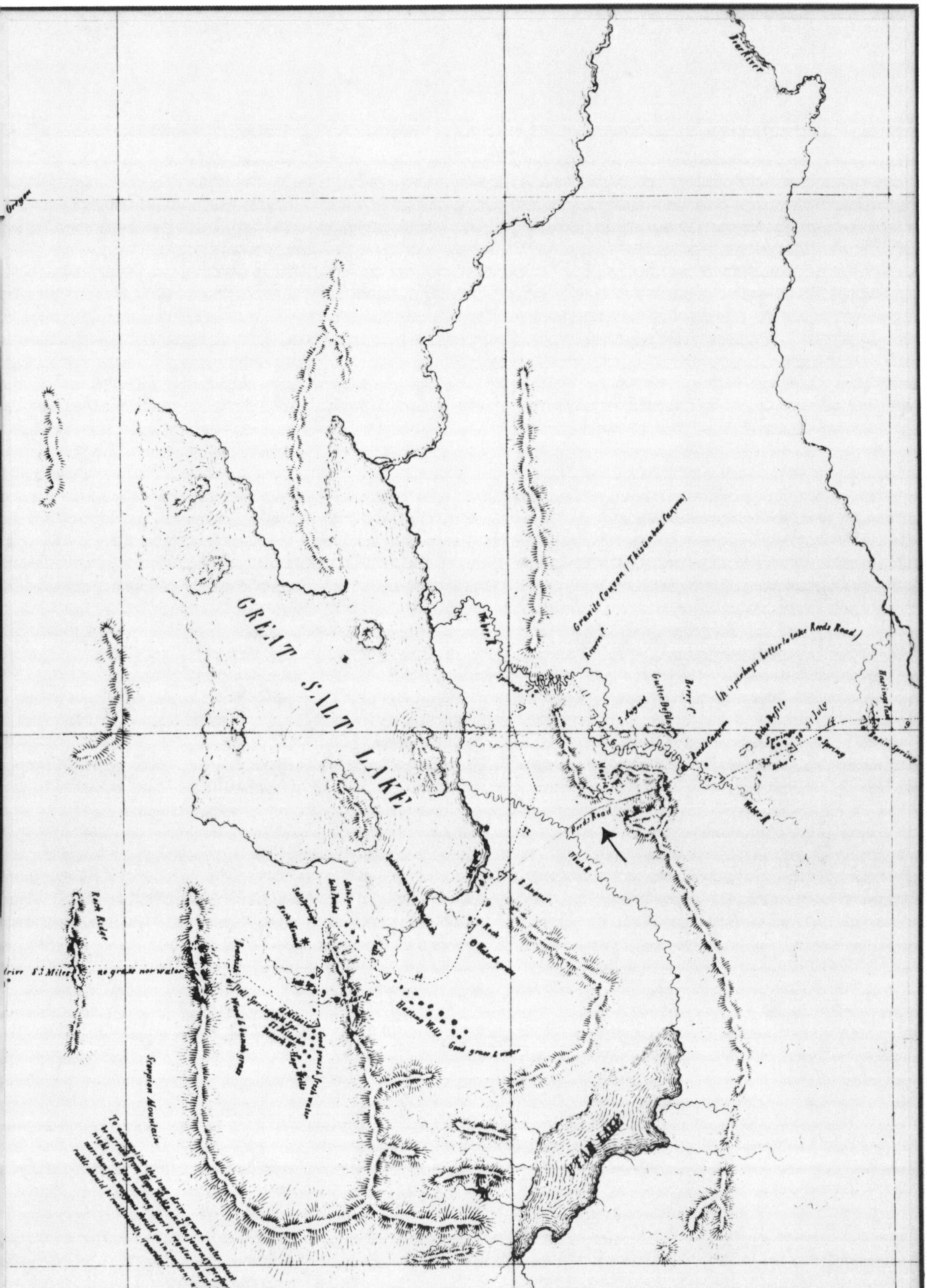

Map of the Emigrant Road By T. H. Jefferson, Part III. Jefferson was in the Harlan-Young party just ahead of the Donners. Reed's Road is shown in a rudimentary fashion. On the map Jefferson recommends, "It is perhaps better to take Reed's Road." Jefferson Maps courtesy of the Bancroft Library.

in the year. The lupin appeared again, blue as the sky. But alas, the sight of bones of oxen were constant curbs of pleasure. Savage, unfriendly country, beautiful and treacherous.

Tamsen shuddered as they passed near the fallen and partially eaten animals. The odor of rotting flesh was enough to make her gag in disgust, but the meaning, which was far worse than the smell, made her angry. Poor lonesome beasts, left behind to defend themselves against wolves as well as they could ... ill, tired animals brought so far across this wide land, up these great slopes. Tamsen's common sense told her the animals should have been shot, and the carcasses been dried for the little meat in them, rather than to have been abandoned to the cruelty of the wolves, who seemed to follow them night and day ....

And at last, that day that everyone had waited for; the Sweetwater left behind, Pacific Springs ahead, flowing west. The final commitment had arrived. They were West. In a few days they would reach the Little Sandy, their Rubicon. There the road divided: the right hand trail, heavily traveled that summer, led off northwesterly to Fort Hall; the faint trail on the left headed toward the Wahsatch Range and the Great Salt Lake and its shimmering, blinding white sands.

In The Year of Decision, *Bernard De Voto wrote an omimous comment in connection with the choice the Reed-Donner contingent made to take the left hand turn:*

"In (the summer of) 1846, no map ever drawn had filled in the country between Fort Bridger and Great Salt Lake — no map showed what the Wasatch Mountains were like. And no map filled in the country between Great Salt Lake and the north bend of the Humboldt River — which included the Salt Desert ...."

There was nothing but a faint trail turning left into a black hole of almost total ignorance, away from the Fort Hall road to the short cut to the Mary's River.

PART III · SNOW PLANTS

Preface

IN HER BOOK *Wild Flowers of California,* Mary Alice Parsons wrote: "I shall never forget finding my first snow-plant. Following the course of a little rill which wound among mosses and ferns through the open forest where noble fir shafts rose on every hand, I came expectedly upon this scarlet miracle, standing in a sheltered nook in the woods. A single ray of strong sunlight shone upon it, leaving the wood around it dark, so that it stood out like a single figure in a *tableau vivant.* There was something so personal, so glowing, and so lifelike about it, that I almost fancied I could see the warm life-blood pulsing and quivering through it ....

"I had heard that the plant was a root parasite; so it was with much interest and great care I dug about it .... But I failed to find its root connected with any other. I have since learned that it is now considered one of those plants akin to the fungi, which in some mysterious way draw their nourishment from decaying or decomposing matter .... They gradually follow the receding snows up the heights; ... They often grow in clusters, and I have counted as many as fifteen springing up together."

When morning finally came on November 5, 1846, early winter snow covered the entire area around the summit. Pine boughs were bent with frozen weight, cliffs, crags and the trail itself were hidden under smooth coverings. Gray skies over the pass seemed to unite with the heavy fall of snow, making the landscape deceptively simple. The silence, after the confusion of the night before, was as ghostly as shrouds of white distorting everything familiar.

Slowly, as light came, mounds of snow began to tremble. From underneath whitened buffalo robes and thin blankets, small curious faces, like those of young foxes, peered out.

"Mama!" some of them called, rubbing snow from their hair and eyelashes. Others whimpered, then burrowed deep under covering again. A silent Indian, wrapped in his blanket stood unmoving against a pine. The fire had melted through the snow. Men crouched like aboriginals around the bed of coals. Occasionally one would rise slowly and look for branches to replenish the fire. A few oxen remained; their breathing made plumes on the air.

Little by little, people stirred and looked about them, their eyes weary and dull. Babies cried, and mothers sat up, their hair undone and wet against their cheeks, and nursed their infants under their shawls. A few older children rose to run behind a tree to urinate.

MARGARET REED

Margaret moved stiffly in first light, easing her body slowly from the cramped position she had held all night to protect her children. Her immediate feeling was despair; then came a yearning fancy: this life she was caught in was a dream, a mere imagining of a mind.

Tommie moaned in his sleep, and Margaret took a deep breath and faced the day. Without shelter, her few possessions stowed in one of the wagons down the hill, her small pack of clothes and food rubbed off and scattered in the storm now heaped beside her, a shawl or two and thin blankets to keep her warm ... how was she to survive?

This was the end, then ... the end of the long journey. They had failed. They could not go on. Charlie had said that if the snow stopped, they could make it to Bear Valley. It had snowed all night. Clouds hung low, threatening more snow. Margaret reached into her pack ... the one that was to take them to California, selected four pieces of dried

I. Schrock

meat for the children. She would take none for herself just yet. She could wait.

She hadn't the energy to cry. What hurt her most was that she had failed James. He *must* be on the other side of this pass, waiting for her to bring the children to him. She thought desperately, "Oh, James, I *tried!* I didn't give up until there was nothing else to do, until everyone else had refused to go farther."

What was she to do? A lone woman, crossing the plains with only Milt to help ... Eliza and Baylis were only two more children. Baylis' eyes must be killing him in this snow-glare. Four children to save. Could she do it?

She looked down at the mound of snow that covered them. Jimmy's face peered out sleepily. He rubbed his eyes, shivered, and dived into the warm comfort the other children made. Virginia had stirred earlier, but Margaret whispered to her to stay to protect the others with the heat of her body. Her dear dear Puss complied with a sad encouraging smile.

The silence was eerie. Last night, the curses, shouts, crying, yelling, bellowing of frightened animals had been as confused as pictures of Dante's hell. This morning, men said nothing. They were stunned, broken at last. The whole beautiful dream of California had come to nothing. Their hats pulled down over their eyes, their beards, even their eyebrows and lashes whitened, they looked like dead men frozen into a portrait forever.

She took a deep breath and tried to move her feet. The pain almost made her cry out. From another mound, a baby started crying in the confident, demanding way babies had of wanting something and being given it immediately. It made her remember all her children at that age: demanding and being given. She too wished to cry out like that baby and be given warmth and food and security ... she would bawl at the top of her lungs if it would bring her what she wanted. She remembered times when she was a child, waking from a nightmare and her mother's soft voice saying, "There, there, dear, everything's all right." That was the way to wake from a nightmare. She longed for her mother to come, push the hair back from her face, to say, "There, there ... it's just a bad dream."

Wake up, Margaret Reed. You're not a child any more. You have four children of your own, one almost grown, and you've promised to get them over that pass to where James waits ... in bright sunshine, as the book said? He must be trying to reach her. He *must* be just over that barrier, deep in the snow.

Milt was slumped against a tree. Under his growth of beard, his face was nearly black with exhaustion. Good Milt. What would she have done without him!

But what of Milt himself? She had caught him looking at Mary Graves once, his face open, naked. Milt was a man. These weren't his own children he was bringing through. Perhaps, since he always called her Ma, he felt he was their big brother, always so kind, gentle, sensible, slow-spoken ... like a great loving dog who let puppies climb all over him, pull his tail, rumple his coat, tease him to death. He stood, as beaten as the other men. What had she done, insisting that he drive their wagon? She owed it to God to get him through too, if she could. How could she do that? Big Milt ... one of the few strong men left. No George or Jacob Donner, no James Reed, no John Snyder, no Bill Pike, only Milt and Will Eddy and Stanton and the teamsters ... what were they do do?

Last night she had felt James calling to her. "Margaret! Margaret, try! Try once more. Try to reach me, I am here!" She was dreaming again. It was hard not to dream. It was beginning to be hard to tell what was a nightmare and what was really happening.

Why hadn't she refused to come? If she had, they would all be safe back in Springfield, sitting at the big kitchen table, with a fire in the stove and one in the grate, eating hot oatmeal ... while snow speckled across the curtained windows. Safe. And James' face would be a hard mask as he turned toward her, hard and accusing because she had not let him come. *Let* him come? The very idea of her being able to prevent his doing something made a smile flicker across her cold face. James was not a man to wait on a woman's whim. She had said her piece. He listened politely, as always, saw no reason to change his mind, decided to go. *Let* him go?

Now she was here and he was not. She only knew what Charlie had told her when he returned from Captain Sutter's with the supplies. James had arrived in California, almost starved. He was rounding up men to follow Stanton. If James was trying, there would be no stopping him. She knew him that well. She could hear him echoing her words: "I'm doing my best, Margaret, have no fear ...." No fear?

Some of the men were building up the fire again. Mary Graves, her thick black hair tumbled, her dress hanging wetly around her tall body, joined them at the fire. She held out her hands and rubbed them. One of the men turned aside and peed on the snow, as if he didn't care if anyone saw him or not. Mary looked across at Margaret, smiled and shrugged, and returned to the place where the Graves family were huddled together. Her little brother reached out and grabbed her hand. She held him tight and smiled again.

Mary Graves loved everyone. Children followed her everywhere. Men did too. There was much more than a pretty face in Mary Graves. There was love and it shone like a lantern in the dark. How hard she had worked last night! Margaret would never forget. A brother in her arms, little Frankie, and a sister pulling at her skirt, she had kept chanting in that funny way she had "One more step to go! One more step, one more step!" She had almost coaxed them to the top ... following Stanton, some of the women would say.

Patty crawled from the den of animal robes. "Funny how you can pretend you're warm and it almost comes true, except for your feet," she said brightly. "Come on, Puss, it's time for breakfast. Mama's got it in her hands, ready."

The day was started now. They must face what they had to do ... go back down to the lake, find a better place to camp, wait, admit they had failed. Well, *she* hadn't, not yet. She wouldn't fail James.

MARY

As she reached out toward the fire, Mary saw that the heat had melted the new fallen snow leaving a ring of muddy earth around the coals. Trying to reach the warmth, she felt dampness through her shoes, almost worn through. Poor old thin-soled things ... how far they had walked, one step at a time!

All night long she had cuddled against the children, but she had not slept much herself. She could not forget Charlie Stanton's streaked, bruised face. Like intermittent lightning came memories of the night before: Keseberg's agonized yelling, Eleanor Eddy's faint whimpering, Margaret Reed's discouraged tears, Milt Elliott's grey, silent expression, her mother's scolding voice, the grunts of oxen. Her eyes burned with irritation from the heavy pine smoke and weariness.

Poor Charlie had not sat down until the last of the party had given up and refused to move. He had patted her hand gently as he passed, and his sad eyes had looked into hers with anguish and despair ....

"I can't make them climb and I can't carry them all ..." she had gasped.

He hadn't breath to answer her. He merely nodded. This morning, she saw him leave early, to look for his mules.

It was faint light now. Snow had begun to fall again, lightly, steadily. The mounds of snow covering huddled family groups stirred; they reminded her of the garden at home just before the earth broke for a seed to emerge. Oh it was cold! She had taken her shawl off to cover the children, and her dress was damp and sticky from the perspiration that had caked on it. She pushed her heavy hair back from her face. Would they try again this morning? She doubted it. Charlie had said this was the end, the last chance to make it over the pass. Looking up, she could see the summit faintly outlined through the misty snow. It looked impossibly steep and forbidding.

The hopelessness of their situation began to seep through to her. The final failure of failures ... it was November. Short days, snow, winter, when they had thought that by now they would be in endless sunshine. Why didn't Charlie come back and tell them what to do? She would do as he said.

Perhaps they were all dead under the snow. What if she were the only person left alive? She shivered.

No, the Indian still stood, his blanket wrapped around him. Did he sleep that way? Charlie was alive. The children were breathing. There were men moving stolidly here and there. She was not alone.

She blew on her fingers and clapped them together to warm them. Perhaps it would be better if everyone froze to death. Wasn't freezing better than starvation? All that seemed to be in the future was death. That was always true, wasn't it? One step at a time, all one's life, toward death. She knew about death. It didn't respect mothers having babies, or the babies themselves or men who were shot or thrown from horses or killed with a knife. Or old men walking across the desert on swollen, bursting feet, or brothers-in-law testing their guns together ... what was the use of worrying? She had made her peace with death; she had learned to be alive once more, perhaps to love again ... oh, don't give in to morbid thoughts, Mary Ann Graves.

One of the men threw down an armful of dead pine boughs. They cracked and snapped into fire. There were deep lines in the man's face, dark designs of dirt and soot and sweat. His eyes were red, his shoulders slumped in despair. Why, it was Milt Elliott! She looked at him, suddenly smiled. He nodded at her, but his eyes were brooding.

Little heads popped out, like spring crocus back home. Tousled little heads, like seeds in the cornfield. Like first flowers. It was November, not spring. "Go back, little heads, it's too soon for you to sprout, go back to sleep." She had said that to Pa once when a late snow had come. Pa had teased her. "They'll be all right, Mary. Nature will take care of them."

But this wasn't home. She wasn't a child. The little heads were not crocus ... they were the hungry faces of children.

By midmorning, drugged by despair, men began gathering themselves together for the job at hand: plunging and stumbling back down the slopes buried in snow, carrying everything with them back to the small cabin at the lake they had seen as they passed.

"Better butcher the oxen and cattle now, while there's time," someone said. Immediately conflicts surfaced.

"Maybe the snow will melt, maybe the sun will come out."

"If we butcher the critters today we haven't a chance to get out ...."

"You're goin' to have to foot it into California anyway. Better to have meat dried and ready."

"Dried meat ... that's a laugh. What would dry in weather like this?"

"It was the women's fault. Squabbling over whether to take some damned keepsake or not, instead of getting the kids over the hill."

"Hill, he says. This ain't no hill ... no hill a-tall."

"We'd of ought to stripped down to nothing and got ourselves over that pass ...."
"And left all our goods to them thieving Injuns? By God, no!"
"God damn it, men, can't we agree on *anything?"*
Keseberg sat silent, looking as if he could kill anyone who came close to him. For one moment on the long crossing, he had taken over leadership and was rejected, as Reed had been, as George Donner would have been, if he hadn't been somewhere back on the trail.

One by one, discouraged, heart-sick and weary, families gathered their belongings and made their way down the cliffs to the far end of Truckee Lake. Here a cabin had been built by emigrants the year before. The Breens, arriving first, took possession of this log building. Against one side, Lewis Keseberg threw up a rough lean-to for his family.

Some distance away, at the outlet of a stream, the Eddys and Murphys constructed a cabin against a huge, flat-faced boulder, and located their fire-hole against the stone.

On higher ground and perhaps a quarter of a mile upstream, the Graves and Reed families erected a double cabin. Amanda McCutchen and her baby stayed with the Graveses. In the other half were the Reeds, Eliza and Baylis, Charles Stanton, Milt Elliott and the other teamsters.

At Truckee Lake, there were sixty people; of these twenty-nine were infants.

The Donner families did not reach the lake that was to bear their name. Delayed by an accident with George Donner's wagon, which over-turned, nearly killing Georgia and Eliza, they were halted by the storm at Alder Creek. It was probably about this time George cut his hand while chopping wood with his brother Jake.

The two families raised crude shelters, hardly more than tents built around trees, covered with whatever was available: old coats, blankets, buffalo skins, secured by branches and poles cut from small trees. Their fireplace was a hole dug into the ground; their beds were raised on crude platforms to keep out moisture. The two shelters were not close together. Across the stream the teamsters built themselves a shelter patterned on Indian tepees.

In the Alder Creek encampment there were twenty-one people: six men, twelve children, three women — Tamsen and Betsy Donner and the widowed Mrs. Wolfinger. At both locations, eighty-one souls, grievously short of able-bodied men, snow-bound, low on supplies, were caught in the Sierra Nevada. It was early November. A long winter stretched ahead.

The storm continued for more than a week.

Both men and women now faced the fact that hunger, perhaps starvation were upon them. Stanton's relief supplies were almost exhausted, and only a little of their original foodstuffs remained: tea, coffee, sugar, a small amount of salt, and some rice, flour, and a little dried fruit ... certainly not enough to carry them through a winter. Their lives depended on the cattle that remained. Unable to crop grass because of the heavy snow, the animals were little more than bones and hides. Some had been slaughtered and frozen, but not all. Some of the emigrants had a lingering hope that a thaw might come; some hated to kill the animals for fear they would spoil.

Hunting and fishing were almost impossible. Will Eddy, the best shot in the company, succeeded with a borrowed gun only in killing a coyote and an owl in three days of hunting, nourishment they would have scorned on the prairie. Mice, appearing from nowhere, were not refused as food.

Of all the people at the lake, the Breen family was the best prepared. They had lost the fewest cattle on the Mary's River. Peggy Breen, her husband ill with the gravels, slaughtered their cattle, and with the help of her sons, stacked the meat like cord-wood next to their cabin.

The Reeds and the Eddys were almost destitute now. The Eddy family had one ox. Mrs. Reed had none at all.

After more than a week of continuous snowfall, there was a thaw that encouraged them all. Throughout the month of November, confused and disorganized as they were, several attempts were made to climb the summit. Each failure brought them to a deeper level of discouragement, and divided them further. Hardship had broken them; even the specter of death did not succeed in healing old wounds. There was no leader now who could bind them into a whole. Survival took all their time and energy. With George Donner back on the trail somewhere, Reed banished, only Will Eddy and Will Foster had any chance at all to make a concerted effort to save them. Fear of the future was as constant and real as the wolves howling. No one caught sight of them, but their terrible animal sound threaded through their dreams, as did their nightmares of starvation and death.

MARY

Mary Ann Graves shook her eighteen-year-old brother's shoulder.

"Come on, Billy-boy, we're going fishing."

"Aw, Mary. It's snowing. What's the use?"

"It's stopping. I've got a fishing pole tied up and we're going."

Lavina said, "I'll go with you, Mary."

Mary smiled. "Fine. I'll take 'Vina and Eleanor, if you're not goin' to go, Billy."

"I'll go, I guess." He rose, brushing dirt off his trousers.

"I'll stay with Mama and help with the little kids," Eleanor said. "Mama's so wore out with trying to nurse the baby...."

"Whatever," Mary said definitely. "It's about time we started agreeing with each other instead of fightin' like cats and dogs. You see the Breen family fightin' like we been doing? Their Pa keeps them in order ...."

"Aw, quit soundin' like a preacher, Mary. I'll go, but you better stop lecturin' me." Billy chafed his hands together and shivered. "I suppose I better get my blood up ...."

Amanda McCutchen was in her corner of the cabin, holding her baby, looking into the fire ... half asleep ... quiet, alone, waiting, dependent on others.

Mary stopped at her mother's bed. The little kids were huddled around her exactly like a passel of kittens, their eyes following every movement. Thank goodness Pa had seen to buildin' a fireplace at each end of their cabin.. At least they had that to be thankful for. Ma looked peaked this morning. After all, Ma was forty-seven years old, with a nursing baby to boot. She was purely downhearted, half-sick and worn out with having children, maybe. Jay, Sarah's husband was out looking for wood, and Sarah herself was washing out rags in a bucket. She'd tend to Ma. Thank goodness, Sarah didn't have a baby or one on the way. Sarah said her courses had stopped some time ago, when they were in the desert. "Maybe I lost the baby," she said. "I thought I'd swallowed a watermelon seed, but I guess I'm just dried up. Maybe all this struggle had somethin' to do with it."

Lots of the women talked that way. Mary herself had dried up. Ma said worry'd do it sometimes, and there wasn't any other reason. It surely made things easier ... none of those monthlies to bother with.

"All right, my friends. We're going to get ourselves a big fat fish for dinner!"

"Hip, hip, hooray for Mary," Nancy said, clapping.

Mary couldn't help stopping to take a big deep breath of fresh air as she crawled up and out of the cabin. The air got pretty bad inside, with so many people breathing it. In the brief shaft of sunshine that came through the pines the snow looked as if sugar had been dusted over it. It was pretty ... too bad they were so purely worried that they couldn't enjoy it. There was more snow bundled up in the clouds that hung over the pass, and the trees had white dresses on and the bushes were like little children in Sunday best.

"Let's get goin' Mary, since you're so all-fired up," Billy said. "That cloud'll be dumpin' snow on us soon enough."

"Well, lead the way then. You're the strongest. You plow on ahead and 'Vina'n I will follow. Straight down to the lake."

The water was not entirely frozen over, though it was iced farther out than when they'd come. Mary tried the edges for safety. She and Billy found a spot where a rock stood near a deep open place, and climbed on it warily. 'Vina followed after, carrying willowsticks with strong cord on them. Among the things Pa had brought they'd found some big hooks. If they did catch a fish, they wouldn't have a chance of the line breaking.

"What're you goin' to use for bait, Mary?"

"I'd like to use some meat, but we daren't. None to spare. I tried to dig worms, but I didn't find any. At first I'm just goin' to jig the hook up and down to see what happens."

"You'd better quit talkin' then, if you aim to ketch any fish," Billy said. "I've got a shiner on my line, and I brung a speck of meat if that don't work."

"Well, don't waste it, hear me? You try first."

The shiner brought fish all right. They flashed in groups, nosing around the lure, then darted away.

"Shucks. I missed 'em."

"They'll come back," Mary said confidently. "It just takes time. Try again, and when they come close, jerk the line."

"It didn't work," Billy said disgusted. "You try, Mary."

She lowered her line into the water, jigging it up and down just a little. Again the fish came close, their shining bodies looking like underwater lightning. One hit the string, and Mary caught her breath sharply. No, another miss.

They tried over and over, again and again. They changed to another rock. No luck there, either. 'Vina tried awkwardly, and gave up. Billy cast until his arm ached and his sister took his pole. They threw their lines in at the same time, trying to confuse the fish. Then, finally, the fish disappeared as silently as they had come.

Another hour went by. Mary's hands were so stiff that she could barely use them.

"I'm hungry," 'Vina said. "I'm going back."

"Be careful when you go over the slippery spots."

The black clouds that had hovered all day lowered until it seemed they would be engulfed. Still Billy and Mary fished, hardly speaking any more. Mary put her fingers in her mouth to warm them, and Billy stamped his feet on the mashed snow. Mary watched, fascinated, as a thin tissue of ice started to form on the water's edge. Snow began to fall. Mary had a rosy frozen grin on her face, and Billy laughed at her.

"I'm giving up," Billy said.

"It's getting near dark, isn't it? Goodness ... we've fished all day!"

A short figure, bundled against the cold, appeared from the trees, and approached the lake. "Hi, there, Charlie," Billy said to Stanton. "Tell this fool sister of mine to quit fishin'. We've been here all day and nary bite."

"Afternoon, Miss Mary. Afternoon, Billy. Let's see what you've got here ...." He took Mary's pole from her stiff hands and pulled the heavy, soaked line from the water. His brown eyes, so serious most of the time, lightened with a quiet merriment. "Good heavens, Mary Graves, did you expect to catch a whale with this big hook?"

"It was all we had, Charlie. Pa used it for catfish back home."

"Never been trout fishing, eh?"

"Never went any kind of fishin' before today, I reckon. I've watched the men."

"Nothin' ever stops her, Charlie, nothing, when she's a mind to do somethin', and she was a mind to catch a fish."

"Here," Mary said, half laughing. "Give me that bit of meat you had. I bet I catch somethin' after all ... the fish must eat sometime ....."

"I started to put it on the hook, Mary, and I et it up without thinkin'."

"Well, I hope it did you more good than it did the fish. You could've divided with 'Vina."

"Wasn't enough to bother with."

"We can't waste even the littlest bit, but I guess you needed it. Well, it'll be dark soon and we'd best get back to Ma." She turned to Charlie. "I'm goin' to try again tomorrow."

"I'll find you a better hook, Miss Mary."

By now the snow was falling thickly, silently. He put his hand on her arm. "Don't be discouraged, Mary. It's better to try than to sit around and worry ...." But when he saw her carefully twist the cord and fasten the large hook on the willow stick, he couldn't repress a smile.

"Don't you dare laugh at me, Charlie Stanton!"

"I'd never laugh at you, Mary ... you just looked so ... vulnerable, I guess. Like a funny little girl, just for a minute."

"Well, I'm a grown woman!" she said fiercely, smiling suddenly in spite of herself. "I was so sure we'd bring something home to eat! .... We're not entirely out ... we've enough for a couple of weeks yet, I guess. But there's so many of us .... How soon do you think the snow will melt?" She knew it was a silly remark, but she wanted him to say something, anything encouraging.

"If your Pa would see his way clear to lending Will Eddy his gun, Will might bring in some game. There must be some somewhere ... and he's far and away the best shot in the party."

"I think Will and Pa have made it up. Pa's mighty sorry about not lendin' that horse to Will when he wanted to go back for the old man ...." She paused. "He's got it in his head that God's punishin' him for not helpin' a man in trouble. Will Eddy wouldn't let him forget it. I think Pa'd be glad to lend Will his gun. I'll ask him tonight, shall I?"

They walked on through the snow. Mary's lashes were white. She pushed her thick hair under her hood. "My legs are about given out from standing so long today." They could see Billy ahead of them hurrying, almost blotted by falling snow.

Charlie said slowly, "There's talk of a party going on for another try at the pass ... strong ones who have a chance to make it ...."

"I heard. Pa was talking about it last night."

"They want me to lead them out, since I've been there before. The Indians may help us, too. We're going to make a try soon."

Neither one said anything for a moment. A branch near them let go of its load of snow in a great rush. Mary shivered.

"If you go, Charlie, I'm going too."

"You know what that means, Mary? We may not make it."

She shrugged. "If I go, there will be one less of us to feed. I hate sitting still waiting to freeze to death ... or starve ... waitin' for spring ... well, if you go, I'd purely like to go too."

It was almost dark now. Charlie Stanton's eyes were nearly swallowed up in the dusk. He put out his hand. "I'll watch over you, Mary, if you really want to come."

She put her hand in his. "I trust you, Charlie. I'd be pleased if you would."

"If we get out, Mary ..." he began, and hesitated.

"If we get out, what?"

"If we get out, I'll take care of you as long as you live, Mary."

She was silent for a moment. Then the ghost of a merry smile blossomed on her wind-rosy face. "That's a pretty big promise, Charlie Stanton, and I think I'll hold you to it ... if we get out."

He raised her cold hand to his lips and kissed it gently, solemnly, his brown eyes intent. "To the day we get out then. To that glorious day!"

MARGARET

As she and Virginia were arranging their end of the double cabin, Margaret wondered how they were to manage ... Eliza, Baylis, John Denton and Milt, and Stanton and his two Indian guides, herself and her four children, all in one small space, shut off with a flimsy partition from the large Graves clan! She was grateful to the Graveses for helping her. Part of the bitterness of that terrible day was dissipating. It was partly caused by Uncle Frank's guilt about leaving Hardcoop; perhaps too, there was an unspoken guilt about the harshness of James' banishment. Whatever it was, Margaret was glad. Thinking over the charges in her care, Margaret thought also that she had the best with her. John Denton, gentle, thoughtful, sensitive; Charles Stanton, a prince ... no, a male angel, if there were such things. He had put her children on his mules, brought her the good tidings of great joy that James was safe and coming. There wouldn't be trouble with the Indians, if Stanton were with her. Baylis and Eliza: two orphans, two mouths to feed, two burdens she had accepted when she had no knowledge of what was to happen. Baylis uncomplaining and Eliza uncomprehending. Milt Elliott, her strength. Ah, they would manage. One needn't point out delicacy to Milt, Charlie or John; they were gentlemen. What if she had some of the others as cabin mates? Keseberg, for instance, though her heart pained her, remembering Phillipine's hard birth on the prairie, and the thin, wasted baby boy as the result.

"Puss, do you think it would be better if our family stayed in one corner and the rest in the other? We can't divide between men and women ... there's too few of us, and the men must have more room ..." she said, as she arranged cooking pots near the fire-pit.

Virginia stopped folding shawls and buffalo robes. "Ma, whatever has made you so different?"

"What do you mean?"

"You're just about the best manager in the whole crowd. You used to let Pa do everything for you, or Grandma."

"I guess I did, didn't I?"

"Now you make me feel stronger, just because you are." Virginia grabbed her mother by the waist and hugged her. "I love you."

"Why, Puss!" Margaret could only say. She wasn't ashamed of the tears in her eyes.

From the back, where Patty was minding Tommie, came her voice, "Me, too, Ma. Milt said the same thing about you. He said he never would've thought you could manage us all ...."

"Well," Margaret said, when she could control her voice, "Don't let me be too bossy."

"If we're going to get through, someone's got to be bossy, and it might just as well be you, Ma. Aunt Peggy is bossy too, and she has all boys and they don't seem to mind."

"If your Pa was here, he'd have to direct things," Margaret said. "He isn't, so you'll have to make do with me." She brushed away the tears and the straying hair from her eyes. "If we all stay together, God will get us through to your father."

"He'd better," Patty said, "or I'll scold him pretty hard when I say my prayers."

"Huh, prayers!" Virginia sniffed. "All you do is talk to your doll." Margaret was glad that the scene ended with a burst of laughter from the girls. She couldn't have stood much more sentiment. "Well, then, I say, let the men have the larger side to sleep in, and our family and Eliza will sleep on this side of the blanket we'll hang up at night."

Virginia saluted. "Whatever you say, General Reed."

Margaret *was* stronger. She was glad the children had realized. Ever since Charles Stanton had returned with food and word of James, Margaret had felt her inner strength grow.

The news that James had made it ... the fantastic story of the five beans and the tar bucket had made her promise to herself that from then on nothing, *nothing* would be wasted. She wondered privately about the beans. Had they stopped to soak them and cook them? Or had they somehow dropped from the wagons ahead already swollen, perhaps cooked? Had the morning dew swollen them so they could be eaten? That was one thing she'd ask James when she joined him.

Meanwhile not the tiniest bit would be thrown away. She would obtain what she could by dealing with the gold in her money belt. She would promise to pay when that ran out. She must save every scrap of food with eight people as her charge. She was too much her Southern mother's daughter to discard servants when they were of no more use.

From then on, anything that anyone threw away, bones that had been skinned of their meat, bits of hide, any leavings at all she gathered and saved for the day when there would be nothing. No scrap went unnoticed. With a lurch in her stomach, she thought of Cash, the pet the children loved so much. No matter how the children felt, she would handle that problem when the need arose. After all, Virginia had watched, dry-eyed, when her pony Billy disappeared into the dusty distance making no sign of her grief. The other children would have to be brave too. If there was any way with her family intact, she would get through to James.

She thought of herself as a funny, busy little squirrel, running about the cabins, looking for crumbs ... or a bird swooping down to pick up every seed. She became quiet, self-contained, almost secretive. No use arguing with the Graveses over what had happened, no use shying away from Lewis Keseberg, gossiping with Lavina Murphy over Peggy Breen's store of food, nor worrying over Elizabeth Graves' complaints. No use wasting her strength over anything but survival.

She and Eleanor Eddy exchanged glances of understanding when they met, but they didn't speak of what was between them: the desire to bring their loved ones through this ordeal. Poor Eleanor. She was paper-thin and looked hardly able to walk. She seemed to be burning with a fire within, and Margaret knew what it was; love.

Strangely, some of the women she had secretly scorned while crossing the plains as crude and rude were the strongest. Lavina Murphy, for instance. Peggy Breen and her rough exterior. Peggy loved her girls ... perhaps because she was in a family of men. She had seen Peggy slip food to them when Uncle Patrick wasn't looking. Now she knew that everything they did, cruel as it might seem to others, only reflected their desire to keep their children alive. And Mary Graves ... poor girl! Though why Margaret should call her a poor girl she didn't know. She was most loved of all, always with a smile and a pat of encouragement. She had no little ones of her own to fight for, but she would fight, Margaret knew, for her beloved sisters and brothers. It was strange that she could give off such an aura of cheer and laughter when she too must know what might be in store for them all. She wasn't stupid like Eliza, whose thoughts never went beyond the present. Poor Eliza was the one to be pitied, really. Not entirely deaf, but combined with her slowness, she lived within a strange cave of silence, always watching, watching for someone to tell her what was happening. Peering out like a lost animal sometimes.

Strange too, Margaret herself, who had been so carefully brought up, so ingrained with modesty and decorum, had faced the lack of privacy with the same resigned resolution with which she had accepted their peril. What must be done must be done.

"Hate eats a body up," her mother had said once when she was a child. "Hate and fear and all those wrong things ...." Mama had had her finger in a place in the Bible when she said it. Why should those words come back now?

Well, she would waste no time or energy with hate. She could not afford to be destroyed, no part of her. If modesty was another hurdle, she would take it, and forget it.

Eliza giggled whenever the question of modesty came up, or when she overheard remarks from the other side of the blanket that shielded the men from the Reeds.

"Don't be a silly, Eliza. We are all human beings now. You must not hear nor see evil."

"All right, Mizz Reed." Eliza smirked just the same. "But I can't help listening ...."

"Well then, Eliza, don't talk about it," Patty said severely.

Virginia said, "They're probably thinking the same thing we are, Eliza. How we're going to get out of this snow and into California. You just do like Patty does. She talks to her doll."

"I ain't got a doll, Miss Puss Reed," Eliza said and giggled. There was no help for Eliza. Without impatience Margaret thought, she tries, she really does. Impatience was another of those things to keep crushed out of your behavior. Impatience made you think crookedly, and she must think in a straight line. Strength, food, surviving and being ready to go when the time came ... to go to James.

She would monitor the food herself. She hid food, so Eliza wouldn't find it and eat it. She didn't want even her children to know. She would divide it as fairly as she could among them all, the way her Mother did when she was growing up in Virginia, taking care of her servants as a woman should. She kept a kettle hanging near the fire, and into it went anything she could find to eat. She would manage some kind of stew. People ought to think before they tossed out bones. She made a soup, of sorts, but it was hot, which the men relished, thanking her, even though there was mighty little strength left in the thin broth.

Once, on one of the futile attempts to get over the pass, she had sat down in the snow, tired and breathless from the altitude, cold, empty inside, feeling she could never get up again. Milt, carrying little Tommie, was behind her. His face grey with weariness, he put the boy down beside his brother.

"You tuckered out, Ma?"

It was all she needed. She tuckered out? If she fell, all of them would fall with her: Virginia, Patty, Jimmy and Tommie, Eliza, maybe even Milt himself. That Baylis now, he wasn't even trying any more. She'd promised him a bonus if he'd carry Jimmy. He'd shaken his head no, covering his strange albino eyes from the light, and walked back to the lean-to. Snow was harder for him to bear; it seemed to scald his eyes. Eliza turned out to be stronger. "You'll see, Eliza, there will be plenty of husbands waiting for you when we finally get over," was all anyone had to say to Eliza. "Just you keep on walking."

"You promise, Mizz Reed?"

"I promise."

She would promise anything if it would keep them going. Tuckered out, was she? Not until she saw James. Her legs aching, she pulled herself to her feet, shook the snow from her dress, and started on. It was easy, once you made up your mind to it. You were like a strong stream, a river of strength. You just told yourself you could do it.

"No need wasting breath, Milt. Keep on going, one step at a time."

That attempt had failed, but they tried again. Each time they had to return to the lake camp it was harder, but each defeat fed her determination. Some day she would allow herself to be "tuckered out" as Milt called it, sometime she would rest in a soft bed, with warm milk and fresh bread on a tray beside her. Then she would rest as much as she wanted. Now she would just take one step at a time, take a step, take a step.

Virginia yelled. "Ma, I can't keep up with you. Wait a minute!"

"You want to see your Papa once more?" That's all she had to say to the children. Virginia was on her feet again.

Hours later, Margaret faced an immutable fact. With the children refusing to walk another foot, with Milt swaying ready to collapse, with the others who had started with them already black specks on the downward trail, she realized that no amount of inner determination and strength could force a group as large as hers to keep going. They made camp and rested that night around a miserable, sputtering campfire. Tommie was asleep in Virginia's arms; Patty was telling stories to Jimmy, his tears drying on his cheeks. Milt bought in an armful of wood for the fire, looking so miserably wet and weary that Margaret didn't have the heart to ask him to look for more.

They still hadn't reached the height they had on the fateful first try when the storm broke. Margaret had not realized how exhausted she was until she sat down for a rest. If Milt should fail, could she get her children and Eliza to safety by herself? The plain truth, she had to admit, was that she couldn't. Should she send the little ones back with Milt and go on with Eliza and the girls? Send her two baby boys, perhaps to die ... if Milt shouldn't make it?

Milt was worrying her. Always her strong protector, his eyes lately were dark, defeated, lost. Was great, dependable Milt losing his will?

As she sat there, thinking hard, a great rush of snow plummeted from a pine tree, extinguishing the fire. The enormity of the task she had set for herself seemed suddenly to be buried too. Starting out that morning, carrying everything they could, she had thought her act was a simple one of survival. She still felt James was there, just out of reach, that she would find signs of him as soon as she had passed this barrier. All her garnered strength was there. Was this a foolhardy way to waste it?

"Eenie, meenie, minie mo," she said in a sort of pagan prayer. "Tell me, God, the way to go."

It was not a question of giving up; she would never do that. It was a question of keeping her wits sharp, and not making foolish mistakes. Before they started back down to the lake at early dawn, she looked at the still dark western sky saying under her breath, "I tried, James. I tried hard."

TAMSEN

Six miles away at her makeshift tent under the pine tree by the frozen creek, Tamsen Donner also drew herself in for the long winter. George ill and disabled, Tamsen depended on the teamsters across the creek to help her with wood. With her five girls and Mrs. Wolfinger, she was surrounded by women. Elitha and Leanna were well able to help with chores. Frances was trying as hard as she could. Eliza and Georgia were little more than babies. Tamsen must be strong. This did not dismay her as it did Margaret, for Tamsen in many ways had always been left to her own resources; she was capable and calm. She must marshall all the strength she had. If she felt isolated in a world she had no power to change, think of poor Mrs. Wolfinger, her husband dead, she herself lost in an in comprehensible land whose language was only a Babel of tongues.

Matter-of-factly, Tamsen set the children to duties: straightening the tent, washing dishes in melted snow-water — not an easy task, for buckets of snow must be brought down the steps, only to become a small panful of water — spreading their makeshift beds, reading to George. Even little Georgia, only six, was to care for her baby sister, Eliza, and see that her hair was combed and her face washed.

The morale of the Donner Creek camp depended on having something definite to do every day. When Tamsen read to the girls, she was pleased to see that Mrs. Wolfinger listened too, sometimes trying to mouth the words. Tamsen taught the German woman how to knit. There were brief lessons in arithmetic and spelling. Being trapped in the mountains was no reason for their young minds to fallow.

Weather permitting, the children were bundled up and sent out every day for fresh air.

If George's hand would only heal! She poulticed the wound, dressed it in clean rags, but still it remained raw, oozing and ugly. Proud flesh, Tamsen called it. George didn't complain, but she knew his pain made the days cruelly long. The lessons and her reading distracted him at times, though he often lay with his eyes closed. Strange that he hardly mentioned what had happened to the rest. He only seemed to wonder when James Reed would return.

Tamsen kept a fire going, except when long-lasting snowfall made finding wood difficult. Tamsen tried to keep a supply ahead, when she could get scatter-brained Baptiste to gather and chop wood. The damp dirt floor was kept as clean as possible. "No refuse of any kind, hear me, Baptiste ... savez?" The odor inside was fetid, she knew, but she faced this as she must, climbing outside often for a breath of fresh air.

Tamsen wondered where the rest of the party was. Were they far ahead, over the pass in the mountains into California? Were the two Donner brothers left alone here in this vast open snowy country? Would the others remember they had fallen behind, or did they care at all, after what had happened?

Did they know the Donner wagon had tipped over, almost killing baby Eliza and Georgia? If George hadn't let his axe slip ... if, instead of trying to make a new axle, they had packed their food and gone on, as Mr. Stanton had urged them to do, might they be, right now, in the warmth of the fabulous California? Tamsen recalled parts of a sentence of Hastings' book, something that had worried her when she read it ... let's see; "the description ... of the mildness of the climate ... applies only to the valleys ...." Wasn't that what he had said? The quotation ended, "for the mountains present but one eternal winter." Mountains ... she must remember that mountains over a summit were only the beginning. Hadn't the Wahsatch mountains stretched like an ocean, when they had finally made the top?

The Jacob Donners were in a worse situation than she and George, Tamsen well knew. George had only that stubborn wound, but Jacob had been ailing for several months ... ever since that cold he took in the thunderstorm on the Blue ... the day old Mrs. Keyes had died. Betsy had her hands full, seven children, one a babe in arms.

Betsy was easier-going than Tamsen, and her children hadn't been trained to help, as Tamsen's had been. When Tamsen had suggested that Betsy's children join her girls for lessons, only Mary had made much effort. The Hook boys were unruly, and their noise bothered George. Tamsen tried to keep Mary's hair brushed and her face washed, but she couldn't seem to manage much more than that.

Tamsen kept her thoughts in order all during the day by sheer force of inner control. At night, when she was too cold to sleep, she saw the shadows wavering across the buffalo robes and heard George moaning in his sleep or the children whimpering. Mrs. Wolfinger's soft snoring. She would toss from side to side, feeling the depth of the snow smothering her, and the isolation stretching on forever. Then she would remember that by moving, she was losing the precious heat she had garnered, and she would force herself to lie still. Then the specters of what she didn't want to think about would creep insidiously into her mind: death, starvation, dying alone in this unknown wilderness. Involuntarily she would groan, and the sound of her own weakness would wake her again. She would clench her hands and pray to George's God, and to the God she'd prayed to in the past, whatever God there might be, the one she'd been brought up to trust. She would pray for strength to find a way out. Tamsen firmly believed that God helped those who helped themselves; when He failed, she felt the guilt as hers. She had always extricated herself from the agonies of her life, why couldn't she see the Way? "Thy rod and thy staff they comfort me, I will fear no evil," she said over and over, until she drifted again into troubled sleep.

She would endure. She would keep herself ready, she would find a way out. When the time came to leave, she would be ready.

MARY GRAVES

Mary took note of the date: November 12. It was the clearest day in some time, a good omen.

She and her sister Sarah, the only women, started with thirteen of the strongest men. When the women decided to go, there was much discussion; wouldn't they hold the men back? How could they keep up? Sarah stoutly declared that if Jay went she would go too. They had no children to leave behind; besides, Franklin Graves was going along. Mary said then that if her sister and her father were strong enough to go, so was she.

"What if every woman wanted to go? We'd never make it," someone said. Sarah didn't answer. She merely linked her arm in Jay's.

"I'll take care of Sarah, men," Jay said.

Then the men's eyes turned to Mary. She returned their glances, half-defiantly, half-pleading. "I'm as strong as any man," Mary said. "You men know that. If I can't keep up, you can send me back. No one needs to look after me."

Charlie Stanton said quickly, "I'll vouch-safe for her."

Will Eddy took her side too. "Mary's very strong."

"Thank you both."

Perhaps it was her smile that convinced them, but no one made any more objections. After all, if you were going to allow one woman to go, you might as well have two, and there was a cheerfulness about her that encouraged people.

This morning, each was given a small piece of beef. Each carried a blanket, some coffee, and no extra clothing. The men carried guns, an axe, and a hatchet and some tobacco. Mary tied a small pot on her belt to boil water in, and a bit of loaf sugar.

The party left among cheers and a fragile balance of sadness and hope. Three fathers were leaving families behind; the farewells were grimly cheerful. Mary and Sarah smiled and blew kisses at the children grouped around them. Billy who had wanted to go, was sullen; but he must stay to keep the fires going in the Graves cabin. In spite of the hopeful cheers, Mary felt tears running down her face as she saw her sisters and brothers clinging to Ma's skirts, crying. Will Eddy turned his face away as he left his petal-thin Eleanor, a baby in her arms and little Jimmy with his thumb in his mouth. All were close to emaciation already. Mary watched him pick up his burden and lead the group, his back rigid.

Only a few hours later, they discovered that the agony of parting had been endured for nothing, all the arguments and discussions come to naught. At the head of the lake, the party found banks of snow ten feet deep. There was no way they could go farther. Pushing through drifts higher than their heads, they foundered and finally gave up. It was a hopeless effort. Back they turned, the jauntiness of departure gone.

Twilight had come to the lake by the time they trudged back, not having been gone more than five hours. Sarah and Mary were silent, but the men were cursing. Mary couldn't bear to see Charlie's face, tense with struggle. Ringed with snow, his eyes looked like two black coals on children's snowmen, Mary thought.

"This is God's punishment to me for refusing you help to go back to get old Hardcoop," Mary's father said to Will Eddy. "I will die in these mountains, like the rat I am, because of His wrath."

"Forget it, Graves," Will said.

Mary would always remember the faces of those at the lake when her group returned. Disappointment, discouragement, disbelief washed over them, together with faint joy that loved ones were safe. Little Frankie Junior said, "Didn't you bring us anything to eat, Mary?", and cried when he heard there was no food.

"When will we try again, Charlie?" Mary managed to ask.

"As soon as we can, before our spirits break." He added thoughtfully, "Your father suggested snow shoes. If we had snow shoes, we could stay on top. We're going to try to make some."

The next day, to ease his frustration, Will Eddy borrowed Will Foster's gun and managed to kill a bear before it killed him. Spirits rose. Reed and McCutchen would be here soon now, they were sure. Days were clear, and the snow melted in the lake valley. With the snow gone, another party started out on November 21. Lavina Murphy and three of her young ones joined Mary and Sarah. Sixteen men made up the group, and taking Sutter's mules and Indians with them, started confidently up the pass once more.

This time the banked snow was frozen and they walked on its crust. Their determination was no match for their wasted bodies. Although they crossed the pass, they stopped in amazement at the sight of mountains heaped upon mountains ahead of them, snow, snow, snow, as far as they could see. They accused Stanton of lying. "When we got over, it was supposed to be easy ...." they said. Stanton told Mary, "If I'd told them that California wasn't just below the pass, would they have tried?"

They found a little valley and set about preparing camp. In the snow? How could you start a fire in the snow? How could a body sleep on top of snow?

Will Eddy and Charlie, exhausted, began to argue. The mules had not been able to stay on the crust as had the men and women.

"We've got to leave the mules."

"I promised Sutter I would return them."

"Sutter won't give a damn, when he hears our story."

"I promised, on my word."

"We'll pay for them, someway."

Luis and Salvador, the two Indians looked frightened. They shook their heads, and looped their fingers around their necks. "No! No!"

"They say Sutter will hang them if we lose the mules."

"You lie. Sutter won't hang them."

"I gave Sutter my word." Stanton was tired. Mary had never seen him stubborn before.

"Damn your word. We'll go on without them."

"How will you find your way? The Indians won't go without the mules. Nor will I."

Eddy picked up the gun and held it ominously, facing Stanton. Mary wanted to cry out. "I'll kill the damned mules, hear?"

"Will, you can't do that. Put down the gun."

"I say go. Go, and leave the mules."

"Never."

Mary had never seen Stanton angry, either. She too wanted to persuade Charlie to send the mules back, or kill them for food, so they could go on. But Charlie stood defiant.

These last weeks, Charlie had become dispirited. No wonder, the little he ate. He was ashamed to take food from the Reed family, and he was plain worn out. That was what was making him so stubborn and so angry ... his helplessness. He didn't have the strength Will Eddy had ... nobody left had Will's strength. But she thought of how he'd gone ahead to California and returned with all the food, alone. He had used his reserves. When people were tired and hungry, even good men didn't make sense — like back in the desert when Pa had refused to help Hardcoop.

"There's no way we can find the trail without you, Charlie," Will said, as one last try.

"I can't leave the mules. They aren't mine. Anyway, the Indians would run away ...."

Mrs. Murphy said in practical determination, "Let's make us a fire and stop arguin' for a while. No use lettin' dark come on us and no fire made."

Even that was no use. None of them knew how to make a fire on snow.

Mary went to Charlie. "Won't you change your mind? We've come this far ... we can't go back again."

Charlie turned an agonized face toward her. "Mary, I can't break my word. If you knew how earnestly I begged Sutter for these mules, promising on my honor I would bring them back ...."

"But, he didn't know ..." Mary began.

"Don't ask me, Mary. Don't ask me," he begged brokenly.

"You're not thinking straight, Charlie. You're tired and confused."

The party returned to the lake the next day, the mules struggling behind them, the Indians impassive, Charlie Stanton bent and worn.

As if to compensate for his stubborn behavior over the mules, Charlie Stanton helped Franklin Graves and Will Eddy in their attempt to fashion snow shoes, faintly remembered from Uncle Frank's boyhood in New England, from ox bows. When the wooden bows had been sawed into sections, they were strung with netting made of rawhide. Heavy and awkward, they might just manage to keep the men on top of the snow. Sitting side by side in this desperate last try for escape, the men forgot their differences, and planned how they could avoid the mistakes made in earlier efforts to cross the summit. If the next party failed, there would be no strength nor will to make further ventures. People were becoming visibly weaker as each day passed.

On Thanksgiving Day the snow turned to rain, and they debated starting at once, without finishing enough pairs of shoes for all that were to go. This plan was abandoned because another storm arrived with ice and sleet that cut their faces if they went outside. Three days, four days, five, six. Mary began to feel there were great evil giants in the black clouds bent on their destruction.

The few remaining cattle were lost in the storm, buried under drifts that were higher than the cabins. Charlie's sacred mules were gone, and of no use to anyone. Luckily, the week before, Patrick Breen, or rather Peggy, for Patrick was suffering once more with the gravels, went about the task of butchering and storing all their cattle. The provident Breens — big brawny Peggy was just in time.

"It serves Charlie right, him and his word of honor," Billy Graves said to Mary. "Stubborn fool!"

Mary flared, "Don't forget, it was his stubbornness that brought him back when we were starvin'. He saved us then."

"Saved us! Why didn't he hustle us up the hill? He let us take our own sweet time while the storms were building up!"

"Billy, he didn't! You're bein' unfair. He didn't know that the storms would come so early. Sutter told him they usually didn't start till later. We've no cause to place blame. None of us wanted to leave the valley. None of our cattle were strong enough ...."

"You say that because you're sweet on him. Will Eddy says he'd never come back at all if you hadn't been here ... little half-pint man."

"I won't hear any more, Billy Graves!" Mary cried out in anger. "Time and time again he did more than anyone else, and you know it! He went ahead in the Wahsatch. Did anyone do anythin' but blame him for that? He left us all and was safe in California and then he came back to help. Would you have done that, I wonder? McCutchen taken sick, no one to be with him but two Indians? You think he should have carried us over the pass, one by one?"

Billy looked at his sister and smiled. "I guess I'm runnin' off the mouth, Mary, but it's sure good to see your dander up. I was as glad as anybody to see them mules loaded with food. I guess I was just blamin' him because I feel so down and out and I hate to see Pa so worried and all. My, you look as mad as a wet hen, Mary, when anyone says a word against him."

"I didn't see you or Jay Fosdick or even John Snyder speakin' up to go ahead, nor any of the men lots bigger'n him. You just watch that tongue of yours! We're all getting pretty eager to put the blame on someone else, seems to me." She put her hand on Billy's arm. "Maybe we'll find the mules. We can get some long sticks and poke down through the snow ... and the meat will still be good. Don't take on so. They aren't your mules."

"I'd like a taste of them, for sure."

She scolded Billy, but underneath she was sorrowing. Others were saying the same kind of things ... that Charlie was a nincompoop. She often wondered herself what might have happened if Will Eddy had used his gun, there on the top of the pass. Where would they have been by now? Then she thought of the terrible storms they would have been caught in ... no, perhaps it was for the best. She knew people had to have someone to blame when a mistake had been made. They'd never admit they had any part in the wrong decisions. Look at how Reed was hated! How the chain of hate wound through everything, even as the chains of Milt's and John's teams had tangled. Didn't people learn from mistakes?

That afternoon when she left the crowded cabin, she saw Charlie leaning against a tree.

"What are you doing out in the dark and cold? You trying to catch your death?" She felt he had been waiting for her by the way his face changed when he saw her.

"Mary. I beg your forgiveness. I was wrong. I see it now. I should have butchered the mules ... at least they would have been some use."

"Now, Charlie, I don't set much store for feeling sorry for what's over and done. Everyone's made mistakes, this whole trip, ever since Laramie, when we decided to follow you people down to Bridger ... this whole thing has been a big mistake .... Don't think of it anymore."

He held her hands tightly. "I won't forget, but I'm glad you forgive me." He hesitated, then blurted out, "I think I'm losing my mind, sometimes, Mary. I can't seem to think things out anymore ...."

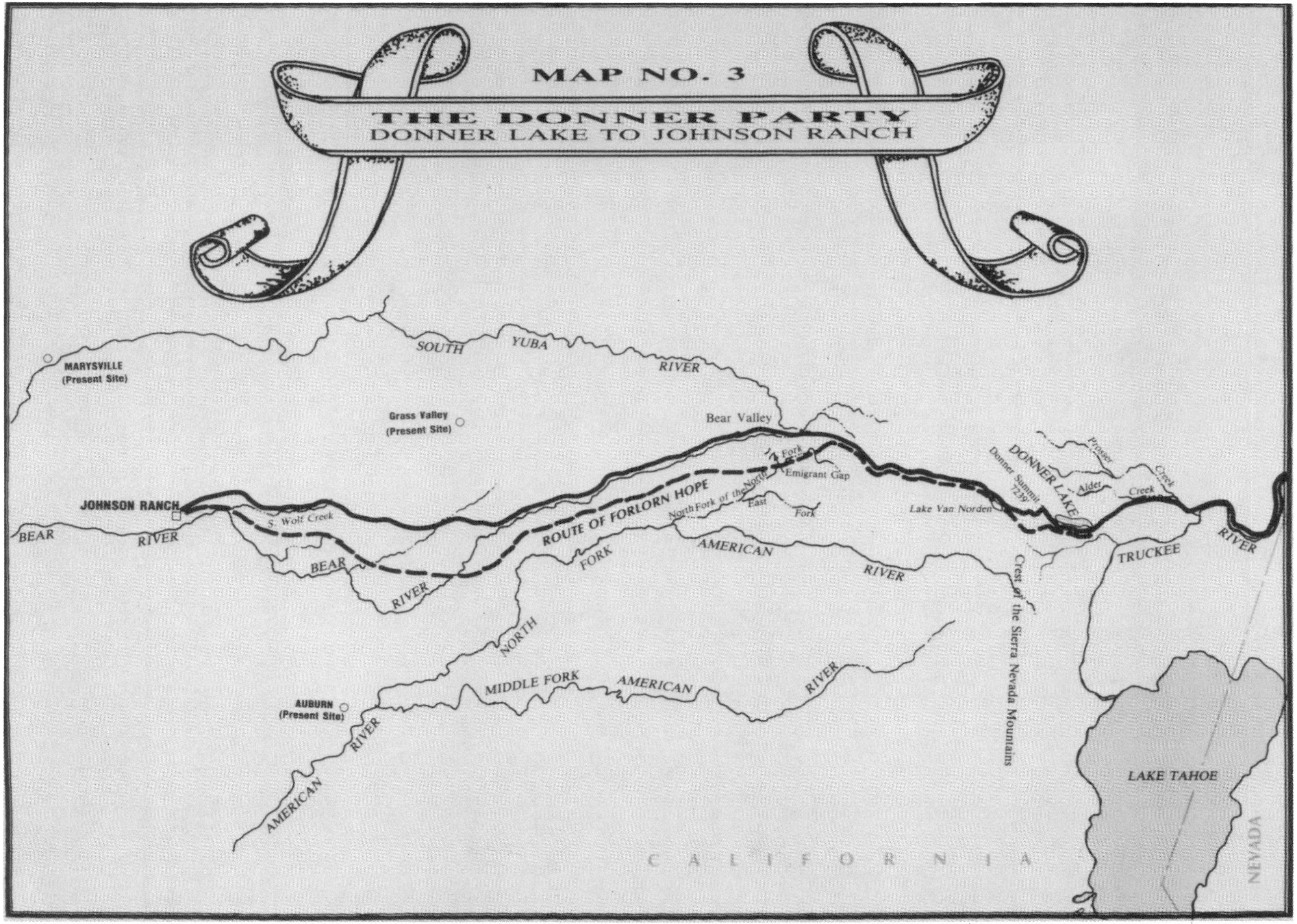
MAP NO. 3
THE DONNER PARTY
DONNER LAKE TO JOHNSON RANCH
SOUTH YUBA RIVER
MARYSVILLE (Present Site)
Grass Valley (Present Site)
Bear Valley
JOHNSON RANCH
BEAR RIVER
S. Wolf Creek
ROUTE OF FORLORN HOPE
North Fork of the North
East Fork
Emigrant Gap
Lake Van Norden
Donner Summit 7239'
DONNER LAKE
Prosser Creek
Alder Creek
TRUCKEE RIVER
AMERICAN RIVER
NORTH FORK
Crest of the Sierra Nevada Mountains
MIDDLE FORK AMERICAN RIVER
AUBURN (Present Site)
AMERICAN RIVER
LAKE TAHOE
CALIFORNIA
NEVADA

"You're tired, Charlie, and no wonder. You've been goin' mighty easy on food too. I've watched you. Nobody thinks straight when he's tired and hungry and plum wore out. Look here ..." she reached under her shawl for a small package wrapped in a paper .... "I've brought you somethin' I saved. I knew how you'd feel about those mules."

"I can't take it, Mary. You've robbed yourself ...."

She flared at him, her dark eyes flashing in the dusk, "You'll take it, Charlie Stanton, or I'll be purely mad at you. And you're to eat it yourself. You're not to give it to anyone else, hear? Not Margaret Reed nor Virginia or any of them. It's just for you."

"I can't ...."

"Listen, Charlie. You said once you'd like to take care of me, when we get through, didn't you? Well, this is my present to you. My gift. I saved it for you myself. Say it's thanks for what you've done for us all. Say it's a present ..." she hesitated, then rushed on, and put the package in his hand. "Say it's my promise to you ...."

"Oh, Mary ...."

"Because I love you."

She took his face between her two hands and kissed him. She felt his tears hot against her fingers. Then she turned and ran inside the Graves' cabin. "Mind, Charlie Stanton, it's for you!"

On Friday, November 20th, 1846, Patrick Breen started a diary. Fortunately, it was not lost. Laconic, unornamented, matter-of-fact and virtually emotionless, the comments always contained weather reports and wind direction. As the days wore by, many entries ended with prayer, the only overt indication of the writer's inner concern. Bowlderized versions of the diary appeared in many accounts, but it was not until the Bancroft Library at the University of California was given the original document did the diary appear exactly as written, with misspelled words, lack of punctuation and variations in spelling.

James Reed and Hiram Miller, his long-time friend, had earlier kept diaries which survived. These too were factual with only a hint of stress under the day-by-day accounts.

Tamsen's diary was lost, and what a valuable document it might have been! One can only surmise what she said, remembering the fine descriptive passages she had earlier sent to her friend, the editor of the Springfield newspaper.

The month of November brought nothing but delay and failure, except for the growing pile of snow-shoes. At the end of another persistent snow storm, fourteen pairs were ready, made by Eddy, Stanton, Foster, Graves and Fosdick. Sunshine broke through the pine trees. The signs were right. They would start. Milt Elliott and Noah James had gone back to see how the Donners were making out and had not been heard from since, but there were more than enough volunteers for this desperate effort, which most of them felt would be their last try. In the party were listed Stanton and the two Indians, Eddy, the tireless father, Harriet and Will Foster, leaving their two children, and Harriet's widowed sister Sally Pike who left her child Naomi. The children were to be cared for by Grandmother Lavina Murphy. The twelve-year-old Lemuel Murphy and his brother William were also of the group. From the Graves family, Mary, Sarah and Jay Fosdick and Franklin Graves. Amanda McCutchen was leaving her baby too. Silent and uncomplaining, Amanda had become fond of Mary, and been persuaded that by leaving there would be more food for her baby. Also with them was Antoine, a part-Mexican teamster picked up at Fort Laramie, "Dutch" Burger, the German, and smiling Pat Dolan, with no family to leave behind, but enough food to keep him through the winter, if necessary. None of the Breen family could be persuaded to go. The stack of frozen beef and hides outside their quarters were enough to see them through till spring.

MARGARET

Baylis Williams was almost dead. No one knew what was keeping him alive. Margaret's thin broth didn't tempt him, nor sugar passed between his clamped lips, Margaret was worried; was there more than illness or starvation in his refusal to eat?

"He's plumb wore out, Mizz Reed," Eliza said, wiping tears with her apron. "He don't want to eat. He don't want to be alive no more."

Perhaps that was it. Poor strange man, with his pale eyes, come so far to a place he no more felt was worth the effort. If Milt, gone to find the Donners, had been here, perhaps he could have persuaded Baylis to eat. He worshipped Milt.

"Please take a little broth." Baylis shook his head slowly, and closed his eyes. Eliza held her brother's hand, her tears falling on it, but he did not move.

"Patty, talk to him. He's always liked you best."

But when Patty tried to make him swallow the broth, she had no more success than the others.

Virginia burst into the lean-to. "Ma! the snow shoe people are starting. They want to know how Baylis is ... should they wait?"

"Tell them to start while they can."

VIRGINIA

Virginia ran back to the Murphy cabin, where the party was being fastened into their snow shoes. Mary and Sarah, from their former experiences, had advised the other women to remake their skirts into pants, splitting them and sewing them up again. They were all laughing at how funny they looked. What get-ups! Uncle Patrick had come over from his cabin and was God-blessing them all. Heavens knows, they needed it. It'd been better if he'd shared some of his beef with them instead of so many prayers, she thought practically. Still, maybe the prayers would help too. She didn't know much about religion, but they needed every bit of help, and maybe God would listen this time, though Uncle Patrick had God-blessed them before.

Amanda McCutchen fell over on her side when they tried to tie her snow shoes on. She came up with a mouthful of snow, laughing. The sunshine had made them all giddy ... sunshine and hope. A pretty forlorn hope they all looked, bunched up in their enormous bloomers. Funny, they'd seen women wearing them on the plains and they'd looked askance, as if there was something wicked about it. Now modesty was gone. Everyone knew they had legs. Some of the people laughed so hard they were crying at the same time. It was the way they'd felt whenever some dangerous thing had happened.

They each had a blanket, a shawl, provisions for the three-day trek to the next valley, where somehow they expected help. The men carried, as usual, a light hatchet and a gun and an axe. Will carried the gun ... it must be Foster's, the gun that had killed Will Pike. How bad that must make Harriet Pike feel, if she thought about it.

MARY

This time, Mary Graves was quiet and a little cynical in the face of departure. She had practiced on her shoes, with Charlie to help her, and she watched the others struggle with a smile on her face.

This had happened before — heart-break at leaving the children and Billy and Ma, then returning defeated. Charlie had said that no matter what, there would be no turning back this time ... even if they all died. The weeks since the last attempt had weakened the whole party; now people were dying. He was sure that Baylis couldn't last much longer. He was glad that Virginia had brought no sad news to dishearten them before they left. Poor Billy! He looked so bereft, watching them go, when he wanted so much to leave with them. Someone had to cut wood for Ma, though. She couldn't be left with no man at all. Lavina Murphy had sent her Billy. Only fourteen, he was the only one left to do for her. Maybe the Breens would send one of their boys to help with wood-cutting.

She'd told the younger girls what they must do to help Ma out. Ma had all she could do to keep the babies alive. Would it have been better if she had stayed? No ... she couldn't cut and drag wood, strong as she was. And she wanted to be with Pa. He had failed too ... he probably should have stayed behind, but he had made up his mind; there was no changing it. The worst thing was that Mary knew he felt he would die on the way.

The laughter had stopped. There was that awful moment of silence, just before something important was about to happen. Then Pat Dolan started a song ... not a sad song, just a funny little Irish song, and Will Eddy kissed Eleanor and said, "Well ... I guess it's time to start." Mary took a deep breath. Just having that jolly Pat Dolan with them made it easier. Why he was going, she couldn't imagine. He had plenty to keep him all winter. He tried to do a little quick-step with the snow shoes, which broke the sadness just when it seemed unbearable, and they were off.

Well, there were those who liked to wait for help, and there were those who went looking for it. Anything was better than staying cooped up in that crowded cabin with only four walls to look at, day after day, the smells and the snow building up and the supplies going down.

There. Amanda had tipped over again. Pat Dolan picked her up this time and Will Eddy came over to help. "You've got to spread your limbs more, Amanda," he said, and the men laughed. Amanda blushed.

"Don't be modest, honey," Sally Foster said. "Just remember, we're doing this for our children ..." and that made people laugh again.

"Which kind of meat do you want us to bring?" Pat Dolan called out, "I don't want any complaints when I come back with pork instead of beef!" That Pat Dolan! Light-hearted, as if life was a great big joke.

Still, as they single-filed along the lake shore, few left without tears running down their cheeks.

Mary turned back once. Dark figures were standing motionless near the opening of the Murphy tunnel.

"God be with you!" Peggy Breen bellowed through cupped hands.

"God be with you too," Mary tried to shout back, but the cold air caught the words in her throat. It took all a body's breath just to walk, they were all so thin and starved.

By the time they reached the end of the lake and started up the pass, they realized that the three without snow shoes were having a hard time. Those without, the Murphy boys, Lem and Billy and Dutch Burger, had thought they could follow along at the end of the line, putting their feet in the path the others had tramped down. Exhausted, Dutch and Billy turned back. That would make it a little easier for Lavina, poor thing. But little Lem Murphy, just 13, the youngest person in the group, was determined to continue. Someone found a pack saddle in one of the abandoned wagons and made him a pair of makeshift foot coverings, and he went doggedly on.

The crossing was not so easy as the last time. The crust was not quite hard enough to hold them at each step, encumbered by the heavy snow shoes. They sank at least a foot into the snow. They were weaker and in spite of Pat's jokes less certain of success.

Luckily, during the snow-bound work sessions, they had figured out a way to make a fire burn in the snow, by using green logs as a base for the dry wood. This held the foundation high enough to make them absorb its heat.

They did not go far that day. Only four miles. When they looked back toward the lake, they could see wisps of smoke, like Indian signal fires, rising from the makeshift homes which seemed, now they were without them, warm havens. They could not forget those they loved, existing miserably in fear. They wondered too, if those left behind would crawl up to the surface of the snow and see their fire ... and worry they had gone such a little distance. So near, yet so terrifyingly far. It was with a sort of perverse joy that, when morning came, they advanced into the pines where the cabins were invisible. Until they left them far behind, they would have accomplished nothing.

TAMSEN

Tamsen sat by George's bed, reading to him, the children grouped around her. The fire sputtered in its hole, the wood was damp, the earthen floor wet and the clothes the girls had worn yesterday during their walk were hanging behind the smoking logs. If Tamsen hadn't been quite familiar with the book she was reading, she would never have been able to decipher the words in the dim light. Lately it was hard to keep the fire going; water seeped in under the tent and hissed it out. While she was clearing snow off the tent covering, Tamen had noted another storm building up. Wind beat at the tops of the trees, sounding like an ocean in a strong blow. She hummed a tune to shut out the noise.

"Bless you, Tamsen, my dear. It helps to hear your sweet voice."

"Shhh, George, don't waste your strength ...."

"What day is it?"

"It's into December. The ninth."

"When can we expect James? Shouldn't he be here by now?"

Tamsen hesitated. Where was James Reed? If the rest had got over the mountains and were safe, would he come at all, no matter what good friends they had been? "Any day now, I suppose. Just you get yourself well enough to go with him when he arrives. All these storms have held him up, no doubt."

George's voice wandered, "There isn't snow in California. How far did we get, Tamsen, before the storm?"

"We're in the California mountains, George. Remember? Hastings said California sunshine didn't obtain in the mountainous regions ...."

"I'd like ...."

"What can I get you, George?"

"I'd like to get that Hastings and wring his neck the way I'd kill a chicken, that's what I would like." The long sentence exhausted him.

"Hush, George ...."

"And then I'd let him go, and I'd catch him again, and wring his neck once more for Jake's sake."

"Poor Uncle Jake," Georgia said.

"Poor Sam, and poor Mr. Smith, too," Frances added. "I hope God gives them lots to eat when they get to heaven," she went on. "Mashed potatoes and gravy and biscuits with butter and honey and ...."

"Milk toast with sugar on it," Georgia added. "Uncle Jake likes that."

"That's a nice thought, girls. Now put on your shawls and look for some dry sticks to make our fire burn better ... I'll have a treat for the one who brings the most."

Leanna said, "Ma, I'm too tired. Can't Baptiste find wood?"

"Honey, he can't do everything. We all must help. Besides, fresh air will make your cheeks as sweet as roses."

Finally they put on their wraps. "I'll come in a moment to help you, as soon as I change Papa's bandage."

When the girls had left, George said, "Mrs. Wolfinger didn't hear what Reinhardt told us, did she?"

Tamsen said, "Shh. I don't think so. I don't think she'd understand, anyway. I hope not. She sleeps most of the time ...."

George lifted his good hand. "Come here, my dear. Let me feel your soft skin. Stay with me a while. I don't want to think about what that man Reinhardt said before he died. Murder, Tamsen."

"I don't think she suspects. Or maybe she does, who knows? What could she do about it if she did? She just lies there so hopelessly on her bed. She has so little English ...."

"I'm going to report it when we get to Sacramento, Tamsen."

"You must, George. You must."

"If that Keseberg was in on it, we should make him pay her something ... if he has the money. Who else has it? Reinhardt didn't."

"Hush, George. You're working yourself up. Sleep my dear. When the time comes, we'll see that justice is done. Poor thing, she thinks he was killed by Indians, that's bad enough. And she hasn't got a copper with her ... only her rings and pins."

Tamsen tried not to think about what her sister-in-law Betsy had said a day or so ago. "Tamsen, you ought to be prepared. You're going to lose George, just as I lost Jake. He's not going to get well."

"Of course he is, Betsy," Tamsen had replied. "I won't give up. You oughtn't to suggest such things."

George *couldn't* die. Why the hand hadn't healed, she didn't know. People didn't die from such a clean, simple cut ... why, she'd done everything. The flesh was purply-red and ugly, and the wound was so deep she could see the bone sometimes. She wouldn't let George die ... it couldn't be blood poisoning. It mustn't be!

She heard shouting outside. What had happened? The girls! Danger! Oh God, don't let any more terrible things happen, she prayed as she ran to the tent entrance. The yelling was echoing over the snow. Forgetting her shawl, Tamsen climbed agilely the frozen steps into daylight. The sudden brilliance made her blind.

"What is it, children? What is it?"

"It's men! Men coming, Mama!" Elitha cried.

Were they saved? "Where do you see men?"

Frances was running over the snow, far ahead. "See, Mama, there they are ... maybe it's Uncle James with food!"

There was a halloo from the dark figures Tamsen could see emerging from the forest. "Mizz Donner, Mizz Donner! Is anyone here?"

It wasn't James Reed. Milt Elliott and Noah James ... where had they come from, what news did they bring? Forgetting how thinly dressed she was, she ran toward them, as excited as the girls. Betsy and her children came from their tent. Shouting and laughter rang over the snow. The first people they had seen in weeks!

Tamsen heard that they had come from the camp at the lake, and that they had brought no food. "Come in, come in, everybody," she said, trying not to show her disappointment. "George will want to hear the news too." As she went down the steps, she carried one of the few remaining pieces of wood.

"George! Here's Noah back, and Milt Elliott. They've been snowed in, as we are, at a lake ...."

"They didn't get to California?" George's voice, heard through the newcomer's ears, sounded weak. She looked at the men, trying to read their expressions when they saw George. Mrs. Wolfinger had arisen from her bed, her hair awry. For the first time in days, she smiled. How was Tamsen to explain that the men had not brought relief?

The tent was crowded and warmer with the numbers. The odor of burning pine wood, of mildew, stale air, half-spoiled beef and wet hides was forgotten in the exchanged accounts of what had happened. Listening to Milt's slow story, accompanied by nods and additions from Noah, Tamsen felt sadness and despair crawling over her, and she realized how much she had hoped that the forward party had got over the pass, and that someone was on the way to rescue them. Hearing of the many fruitless attempts to cross the pass, the fate of her friends, who were as destitute as she herself was, created a mass in her throat that threatened to choke her. It was only with great determination that she managed not to cry. That would not do, with all the children here. Her good friend Margaret with no beef except the little she had "bought" from the Breens and the Graveses, Bayliss starving; the hints of quarrels, selfishness, distress made her despair. Yet, those at the lake had had no deaths. Here, there had been four. Jacob first. Then the three teamsters, Sam Shoemaker, James Smith and the fearsome death of Reinhardt with its revelations, which she would surely not disclose just now. Noah and Milford were distressed enough at the deaths of so many able men friends ....

She noticed Milt Elliott looking at their shelter, shaking his head mournfully. "What arrangements have they at the lake made for living?" she asked.

"Ma'am, you're worse off than we are. At least we have cabins."

"There weren't enough men to do anything much better in that first terrible storm ... and afterwards, Jake was so ill. We just made do. Most of our cattle wandered off, and much time was spent searching for them. Jean Baptiste has been prodding the snow for their bodies, but so far we've found nothing. We've hides left, and a little beef. I have coffee and tea and a little sugar."

"No salt? We wuz hoping you had salt left. We'd all feel a little better for some salt."

"We've mice, though," Frances said. "Mama gives us a present every time we catch one."

"They've been hiding, lately. We haven't been finding many," Georgia added.

"Who's been doing the wood chopping? ... you don't have much standing by ...."

"Betsy's boys and Jean Baptiste, when he isn't looking for the cattle ...."

"That's one thing we can do for ye, ma'am," Noah said. He brought out a piece of dried meat. "You put this on to boil and make us some soup, and we'll chop wood."

It was lucky they cut wood that afternoon. By night, yet another storm lowered, and stayed for days. Milt and Noah joined Baptiste in the wigwam across the creek, where they holed in for eight days. Then, when the bad weather abated, Noah stayed with Tamsen, and Milt returned to the lake.

Tamsen watched Milt walk along the creek. His shoulders were as bent as an old man's ... and he wasn't thirty yet. The best news was that the men at the lake were building snow shoes. Milt wanted to get home in time to join the party who was going on ... that is, if Margaret would let him go. Although it had been good to have new faces around, it was a relief to see him go. One less mouth to feed from the dwindled larder. Larder indeed!

She entered her tent. George's mind was wandering more and more, though at times he was quite lucid. "Why didn't James come, instead of sending his man, Tamsen?

I don't like the looks of that."

"Hush, George. James isn't at the lake camp. He's on his way, however. He's alive ... we know that! As soon as he can make it, he will come!"

"Where's Jake? Why doesn't he come to see me when I'm ailing?"

"Would you like me to read to you from the Bible?" Tamsen couldn't tell the direct lie. She could have said, as she was thinking, that Jake was probably in a better place than George was ... but that too was not a fact she could actually vouch for. She opened George's Bible and began reading.

MARY

The day after they left the lake camp, the snow-shoe party woke early. It was a brilliant morning, the sun glittering on the untracked snow, the summit a pillar of rosy-white, the sky blue, stretching out cloudless and clean. Mary remembered snowy mornings when she was a child. Then, she would have begged to run out in the snow, rub it on her face, fall into its softness and laugh until the cold crept through. She held out her hands to the fire, and tried not to look down to the far end of the frozen lake to the fingers of smoke beckoning from the cabins. People there were stirring probably, rising to the stale smell of the unaired fetid shelters as unkempt and hungry as she was this minute. As she remembered the blank days of staying inside and waiting, she was glad she was at least this far ... part way up the mountain, and a cloudless day to help them climb over the pass. This time, they must make it. In spite of her worry, the fresh morning made her spirits rise, and she smiled as each person stirred and woke.

Pa stood up, almost bent double. Proudly she noticed how he straightened his aching back, pulled himself to his height, pushed back his shoulders. He hadn't given up; he too felt the excitement of being on the way.

As Charlie rose, she thought suddenly that it wasn't that he was so short, but that most of the men were so tall. Pa, for instance. Will Foster, Jay, John Snyder, too, James Reed, George Donner ... all over six feet. Funny she'd never noticed before.

She took a handful of snow and rubbed her face with it until her cheeks glowed. Without her snow shoes, she managed to make her way to the spot behind a rock the women had unconsciously pre-empted for themselves and wrestled with the awkward bloomer-skirts. Then she combed her hair and tied it back from her face. She wanted to prolong the moment before she took the small inch-sized bit of beef that was breakfast. That way, she'd save strength for the climb ahead. Gratefully, she drank a cup of hot water, laced with a little coffee.

She saw the other women struggle through the snow to their small hideaway. They were still bound by modesty and old customs. There was no place for propriety now. Last night had been a restless one. The party had slept with their feet toward the fire, but in broken family groups, still divided. If sleep were to do much good, they must learn to bundle close together, huddling so that the warmth of their thin bodies wouldn't escape into the icy air. She'd talk to Eddy or Charlie about it.

When it was time to start, Mary was the last in line ... a shepherd herding sheep. But of the women, she was the strongest ... the youngest, too. If one should slip on the slick bare rocks they must climb, she could help. Everything was glaring white. The struggling black figures ahead made her think of a picture she'd seen once of a Norwegian Fur Company in single-file on an ice pack. If they were in a fur company, surely there would be food; there would be great warm fires at night, and heaps of pelts to wrap around their cold bodies. To amuse herself, she imagined this was true. It made her forget how hard it was to breathe and how the cold air cut her lungs.

Charlie was ahead with the two Indians. How could they possibly remember a trail they had taken before the snow fell last November? When snow came down in its seemingly lazy, careless way, it was being deliberately deceptive, she thought. It was disguising and hiding everything, every clue, every familiar rock, though Charlie had said he'd paid attention to landmarks, knowing he would be guiding them back. In fact, if Charlie wasn't with them, they wouldn't have known which way to start in this vast wilderness, would they? Did the rest know how much they needed him? It seemed to Mary that they were doing just what they had been doing always, thinking only of themselves, their own hunger and needs. Yet, almost every one of them had realized what a slight chance they had and had been willing to struggle rather than eat food children needed.

There were bare rocks in some places today, and they could climb without the bunglesome snow shoes part way. What a relief! Women complained of aching legs. All night long, her dreams, when she had slept, had been of lifting those cumbersome things and putting them down again, one step at a time.

They reached the top by the time the sun was straight above them. As she stood silent, stunned by the pure beauty of the scene ... the beauty that held so much cruelty, Pat Dolan said, "Better enjoy this, Mary. It's about as near to heaven as any of us will get."

Short of breath as they were, the group laughed. The triumph of their climb made the remark delicious, and the giddiness they felt at the altitude made them light-hearted as well as light-headed.

They turned one last time to look down at the slender, frozen lake below. Buried in snow and invisible, the make-shift shelters still sent smoke spirals. Beyond the lake lay the great eastern slope of the mountains and beyond that the desert over which they had toiled so many weeks ago.

"We're on top. We've made it! We're on our way!"

"Better get going, before we freeze like statues."

They started down. By night, when they figured they had advanced about six miles, the exhilaration of the pass was gone. They were bone-tired, aching, hungry, cold, and irritated.

As they cut the green logs for the base of their evening fire, Mary said, "Tonight, let's all sleep close together and keep each other warm."

Her sister said, "Mary Ann, shame. You sound wicked."

"We're too tired for wickedness, " Eddy said. "Mary's right. The colder we are, the more nourishment we waste."

Darkness came early. The fifteen people, sheltering young Lem Murphy, whose improvised snow shoes were almost too much for him, crowded together, bodies touching, their shawls and blankets spread over them. Some murmured softly, Lem cried out once, one of the women, either Sally or Harriet, moaned for her baby. Pa's heavy breathing kept Mary awake. She gazed at the multitude of stars, brilliant and sharp, like broken glass. She counted falling stars until she too fell into a light sleep, every edge of her body coated with cold.

By the third day, every vestige of elation was gone. The sunshine that had been so welcome now cut their eyes with brilliance, bringing tears and blindness. The tiny amounts of food were not enough for the energy they were using.

Mary trudged along doggedly. Once in a while she tried the trick she had used to keep the children going in the desert, saying little jingles that beat rhythmically, or she counted one-two-three-four or made little rhymes. One two, buckle my shoe, three four, my feet are sore, which made some of them smile and cheered them into walking faster; but the altitude stole her breath away, and she couldn't continue for more than a few minutes. Inside her head, though, she tried holding a count to make her steps even and steady.

As they stopped to rest, she noticed that Charlie was some distance behind. When the others started forward again, she waited for him. His slight figure seemed lost in the expanse of snow. He looked dear to her, dear and vulnerable, all alone. So he was shorter than she? He had a heart so large the world couldn't hold it. Oh, but he had aged ... he seemed so tired and bent.

She thought he would see that she waited for him, but when he approached, she saw that his eyes were closed.

"Charlie! It's Mary. I waited for you."

He turned toward her voice, looking bewildered. "I can't see you, Mary." He opened his eyes, but they were watery and red.

"Let me lead you."

"I'm almost blind."

"My dear ..." she reached for his hand. He put it to his cheek.

"How good of you to wait for me ... I'm all right, only slow. I have no trouble feeling for the trail."

She led him for a short while; then he dropped her hand. "Now, Mary, you must go ahead with the others. I promise I'll follow. If you fall behind, your father might come to help you, and he needs all his strength for himself."

"Pa knows I'm strong ...."

"He would come back, you know that. Now go on, leave me. I'll be along, never fear."

"You promise?"

"I promise."

Mary leaned toward him and kissed him. "Please, Charlie. Don't deceive me. You'll come?"

He smiled. "For a kiss, I'd follow anywhere."

Mary laughed. "You look like a snow-covered gnome."

"I feel as if I'd been kissed by an angel. Now, go on."

"If you don't come in, I'll come look for you."

"Trust me, slow but sure."

She caught up with the others just as they had decided to make camp. They guessed they had made six miles or more. "Where's Stanton?"

"Coming."

"What if he doesn't come? How will we ever find the way?" Sarah asked.

"He'll come. He promised."

It began to snow. Not hard, but there was a wind that sent sharp knives into their faces and seemed to cut right through their clothing. Mary kept her eyes on the trail behind them. Finally, an hour late, Charlie stumbled in, and her heart seemed to bloom in a great flower of relief. She handed him a hot cup of the weak coffee she had ready and whispered, "Bless you, Charlie. You kept your promise. I was so afraid!"

When they settled into the circle that night, she found Charlie was next to her, her father on her other side. Because of the wind, the cold was more biting, and the party pressed together as closely as they could. Some had arranged green logs so they could rest their feet on them and absorb more heat. They were so exhausted that in spite of the weather and their hunger, they slept. Mary felt for Charlie's hand and held it all night long.

The next day, their fourth, was like the third, an endless struggle. Snow came in quick, bitter squalls. Their feet were either numb with cold, or itching with frost bite. That day, Charlie fell behind again, but some of the time Mary could see him, black against the blinding white.

Exhausted as they were, some of the party began imagining things ... bears crossing the trail ahead, wolves following, clouds that looked like mountains they must climb. Eddy warned, "Remember when we crossed the desert? Then we saw armies marching ...."

Mary was walking a little behind when she saw smoke from a mountain cabin down in a gorge.

Stumbling ahead on the clumsy snow shoes, she shouted, "Look! Look! We've come to a settlement! See the smoke from the chimneys? Oh, at last, at last!"

She pointed. Everyone stopped to stare.

Eddy turned to her, "Mary, that's only mist."

"No! I can see it plainly. It's a cabin with smoke. Can't you see?"

"I see wisps of fog, Mary, only fog."

"I believe Mary's right," her sister said. "I see it too!"

Will Foster said, "Don't be fools. It's nothing. As nothing as everything is. Nothing!"

"Please believe me. I'll go down and prove I'm right."

Eddy took her by the arm. "Mary, you can't do that. You're imagining ...."

"Foster, let me have the gun. We'll fire a signal. If anyone's there they'll hear and come out."

"Oh, Eddy, thank you, thank you for believing!"

Foster said, "He doesn't believe you, he's just trying to bring you back to your senses ...."

The gunshot echoed, echoed and re-echoed until the canyon was full of blasting sounds. Mary watched the smoke. Nothing happened. The wisp of mist disappeared as if it had never been there. In spite of herself, Mary started to cry. "Oh, it's wicked, wicked to have things deceive you like that. It's not fair to make a body so happy and then snatch hope away ... I'm sorry, Eddy."

"You've got too much imagination," Sally Foster said. "Will, don't be so hard on her. She didn't mean to start anything."

Stanton groped forward then. "Didn't I hear a shot? Did someone shoot something?" His voice was hopeful.

"Mary thought she saw a cabin with smoke coming out of the chimney."

"It was only in my mind, Charlie." Mary's voice trembled.

"Well, it helped me find the way, so it did some good. Don't worry. I was ready for some bear steak, Eddy."

They slept that night as they had before, fitfully, with cold encasing their bodies. Now they were going downhill much of the time and the snow-shoeing was easier. They had made perhaps five miles, or so they hoped. When they talked it looked as if they were blowing smoke in each other's faces. There was less conversation at night while they ate their bits of beef and drank their hot water. They couldn't spare the energy talk required. There was only a dull realization that one more day of dogged struggling was over toward a place they had no real picture of in their minds. When sleep came, dreams were of old homes, warm fires, and boards loaded with food, clean sweet beds, and someone singing somewhere.

Just before they fell asleep that night, Amanda McCutchen started to giggle. "Mary, you're no worse than I was. I just saw my mother putting a bowl of hot soup on the table."

Lem Murphy stirred. "I want some hot soup!"

"Shut your mouths, you silly women, or I'll make soup of you," Foster said irritably.

No one said another word, but Mary heard Amanda giggle once more.

The next day was colder than before; the sharp wind continued. They climbed up from a river gorge they had been following and went over a ridge. Nothing ahead but snow, snow, snow, and more mountains. The rations were almost gone. Where was Bear Valley?

When Charlie came up that night, Mary heard him talking to Eddy. "I thought we'd be out of it by now."

Charlie said, "Bear Valley has to be just ahead ... but we won't be out of the snow, even then."

"I was afraid we wouldn't be. I see no end to it, Charlie."

"Neither do I." Charlie's voice was hoarse with weariness. She had never heard him express despair before.

"What do we do when our food gives out? We can't make it back."

Charlie only shook his head. His eyes were shut.

"How can you lead us when you can't even see? And you're far behind. The Indians don't seem to know any more than we do," Eddy persisted.

"I'm too tired to think, Eddy. Ask Foster. Maybe in the morning ... after I've rested, I can think better."

Mary took some hot-water-coffee to him. "Here Charlie. Save your strength. It'll be better tomorrow."

He turned his blinded eyes toward her. He reached out his hands, feeling for her. "Oh, Mary, Mary, what has happened to us?"

"We're dead tired. Here, take a bit of my sugar. Then come to the fire and we'll sleep."

"Let me just touch you, Mary ... to be sure it's you."

She took his hands but when she felt how cold they were, she rubbed them in her own warm ones.

"Bless you, Mary." His voice was slow and weak. "Bless you."

Listening to the wind in the trees, the crashing of branches, the crackling of the fire, Mary thought of how they were all changing. Even though they had expected hardship, perhaps death, they had not had any idea of what hardship meant. Now the cabins by the lake, smelly, dirty, crowded as they were, seemed like havens. If they had even one wall to hide behind, they would not be so cold. And the hunger ... she hadn't realized how much it drained from her, fighting through the snow and climbing up, only to slide down again. No one had told her how hunger hurt and how dizzy she felt. They had only one or two small squares of beef each to last them ... then what would they do?

Yet, when they started out, they were still part of home, of the villages they had left. Shy, embarrassed about things that didn't matter any more. Nothing but food and warmth mattered now. Modesty, the shrinking from exposing themselves, impropriety! None of that meant anything any more.

Men still turned away when they peed, and women turned away also, but they no longer had the strength to find a private spot for themselves, and they pulled at their improvised trousers without shame. What if someone watched? Well, they were just other people, facing an equality never experienced before. At night they were like a litter of kittens or puppies, bunched together for warmth, whimpering for food, crying openly when they hurt ... they had no defenses any more.

If they ever got out of the snow and back to the other life, would they also go back to the old ways, bashfulness about their bodies, stoic about their hurts? Their spirits were as thin and skeletonal as their bodies. Everything showed.

Her heart was filled with love of all of them, a strange kind of love. Struggling through this ordeal, and climbing at night into their little nests of shared love and protection. She loved them so much that when they did something selfish and cruel, the hurt was so big she could hardly contain it.

On the morning of the sixth day, as they stood around the dying fire, drinking hot water, now without any coffee in it at all, Amanda said, "It's almost Christmas. It's the 21st."

Foster said, "A fine Christmas. In Hell, out of food, lost, damn fools that we are."

"Hell would be warmer. Let's try to lighten our loads."

Mary watched as they sorted out their meager packs. Should they leave blankets? Their last piece of dried meat? The hatchet? The gun, the axe? The only thing they could not spare was hope. That didn't weigh anything.

"What are you going to leave, Eddy?" Then she saw he had tears in his eyes.

"Nothing," he said, putting a package into his sack.

"We're wasting time. Let's start," Foster said in the abrupt, angry, bitter way he'd used on the entire trek.

Mary noticed that her father groaned as he stood. Sarah was urging Jay to move. Where was Charlie?

He had not moved from the fire. He was smoking his pipe. She went to him, smiling. "Are you ready to start, Charlie?" he turned his face toward her.

"We're going now ... Will Foster has already started." She almost hated to prod him. He looked so comfortable, almost content. "Don't wait too long, dear one ...."

"I'll be coming soon."

Mary sighed and joined the others, keeping to the end of the line, as usual. He'd be later than ever today, poor man.

All day long they struggled to find where they were going. The Indians would nod their head, or shake them when they were asked. Mary thought they were guessing as much as the rest of the party. Why didn't Charlie come? He might remember some of the landmarks ... even if he couldn't see, he might remember. Little streams seemed to lead south instead of west. They left the ridge, and started down, vaguely hoping it was in the right direction.

Foster said angrily, "Why doesn't that damned Stanton catch up and help us out? He got us into this ...."

Trying to control her annoyance, Mary said, "He'll be along. He has to feel his way, remember?"

"Well, it's about time he began to lead us instead of following."

Mary flared. "He's smaller than the rest of you men. He's worn out. He looked mighty good coming into the valley that day with the load of food. He could have stayed in California, remember, Will Foster?"

Sally Foster said, "Now, Mary, quiet down. Will meant no harm. You leave him alone."

Sarah said, "Keep still, everybody. Yelling at each other ...." Jay had sat himself down in the snow.

Mary thought, I could go back and help him. Should I? Do I have enough strength left to climb back up the ridge?

"He'll come in."

As if it were a ritual, they ate their last rations. Amanda commented, "The Last Supper. Just before Christmas."

"We're like Mary and Joseph, looking for a place to stay."

"A manger would look damned good," Eddy said.

"Stop talking about Christmas! Who in hell wants to think about Christmas?" Will Foster wouldn't let them talk about anything any more without getting mad.

Lem Murphy, who seldom spoke said, "I wonder what Ma and the kids are doing back at the lake?"

They built up the fire much higher than usual, so that Stanton could find the way. They themselves, exhausted and worn, tried to sleep. Only Mary lay with closed eyes and wakeful mind, waiting for the sound of his coming. Perhaps a halloo from a distance. She said the alphabet over and over, she counted in twos, then she counted in threes, then she tried to remember every small detail about the house back in Illinois, where the dishes were, where the pots hung over the big stove, where the chairs had been, where they kept the flour ... heavens, there had been so much flour ... enough always, enough so that if any fell on the floor, they just swept it up and threw it away ... how the fire looked on dark nights, how the wood looked, glowing on the fireplace, how the bread felt, hot from the oven ... oh, she could smell it! The taste of warm bread, spread with butter and honey, the bread, the fire, the bread, the fire ... she must have slept after all, for the sky was lightening, the stars had moved across the sky, another day was coming. She sat up with a start. No, Charlie hadn't come in yet. She looked back at the path they had left behind them yesterday. Was Charlie moving on it slowly? It was still too dark to see clearly. She slipped away from the huddle around their fire. Someone groaned and her father stirred. She reached down, put her blanket over him. She ached from head to toe. Rubbing her icy hands together, she swallowed, trying not to cry. If she started weeping she would never be able to stop. Charlie had not caught up. How far behind was he, blindly searching, feeling for the trail with his hands and feet? He had always kept his promise to come before — she had taken it for granted yesterday.

As the coming day brought its light, she saw only emptiness behind them ... no little hunched, tired snowy gnome.

Out of habit, she struggled to a tree to relieve herself, combed her tangled hair, washed her face in snow. Now the others were rising and the usual abrupt, monosyllabic conversation began. This morning there was nothing to eat. No use asking them if they would wait for Charlie. They had to go on.

"It wouldn't do any good for you to go back, Mary," Sarah said. "You aren't strong enough to carry him. If he's alive, he'll manage."

If he's alive? *If* he's alive. She hadn't wanted even to think there was an if.

"Stop your eternal gabbing, you two. If you don't start out, I have a gun that may change your minds."

Eddy drew in his breath, "Foster! That's enough. Mary, you must go on."

"I suppose so." She wanted to ask if it would be like Hardcoop, but that would have stung her father. After they had gone about a mile, the snow began again. Giddy with starvation, fearful that they were indeed hopelessly lost, the party gave in, made camp, and waited silently for Stanton to arrive to show them the way. He did not come. Now the falling snow had erased their trail. Now they were alone in the endless mountains, without even the sun to point a direction, without food, without a guide, and without an idea of what they should do.

Because there was nowhere to be alone, Mary wept openly, staring at the fire that hissed with the unrelenting snow that threatened to put it out. She had tried to be brave, to be strong. Now all her hope was gone.

Statement of John Sinclair, esq., Alcade. District of Sacramento. Rancho Del Paso, February, 1847.

... From the first day, Mr. Stanton, it appears, could not keep up with them (The Forlorn Hope) but had always reached their camp by the time they got their fire built, and preparations made for passing the night. This day (the twentieth December) they had traveled eight miles, and encamped early; and as the shades of evening gathered about them, many an anxious glance was cast back through the deepening gloom for Stanton; but he came not. Before morning the weather became stormy, and before daylight they started and went about four miles, when they encamped, and agreed to wait and see if Stanton would come up; but that night his place was again vacant by their cheerless fire, while he, I suppose, had escaped from all further suffering, and lay wrapped in his "winding sheet of snow." — Bryant: *What I Saw In California* p. 251

REED & McCUTCHEN

Because this story has tried always to reflect what went on inside the women of the party, within the realm of their thinking, the author has not explained what happened to James Reed after he kissed his daughter goodbye, and bade her go back to her mother, following the unfortunate murder on the trail.

James, who had been joined by Walter Herron, left the Donner wagons, which were three days traveling time ahead of the rear party. The men alternated riding exhausted Glaucus, hunting for food as they went. James left notes for his family, and bones and feathers of the game they managed to kill as signs to his family that he had food. When even game disappeared, or perhaps the ammunition needed to kill it, Reed and Herron pushed toward the Sierra Nevada with great difficulty. They came close to starving, subsisting on only a few beans dropped by the preceding train, a bit of grease in a tar bucket, which only Herron could stomach. They made the ascent of the "snowy mountains," now in full autumn glory. The men caught up with the rear guard of Hastings' party just before they reached Sutter's Fort.

Here James Reed met Edwin Bryant, and some of the men who had been in other companies earlier on the crossing.

"I remained at the fort (Sutter's Fort) from the 27th to the 30th of October. On the 28th, Mr. Reed, whom I have before mentioned as belonging to the rear emigrating party, arrived here. He left his party on the Mary's River, and in company with one man, crossed the desert and the mountains. He was several days without provisions, and when he arrived at Johnson's, was so much emaciated by fatigue and famine that he could scarcely walk. His object was to procure provisions immediately, and to transport them with pack-mules over the mountains for the relief of the suffering emigrants behind. He had lost all of his cattle, and had been compelled to *cache* two of his wagons and most of his property. Captain Sutter generously furnished the requisite quantity of mules and horses, with Indian vaqueros, and jerked meat, and flour. This is the second expedition for the relief of the emigrants he (Sutter) has fitted out since our arrival in the country. Ex-governor Boggs and family reached Sutter's Fort today."

Edwin Bryant's *WHAT I SAW IN CALIFORNIA*, Chapter XXIX

Captain Sutter, an open-hearted generous Swiss, assured Reed of mules and food for the relief of the company behind. However, the war with Mexico had begun, and all of California seethed with this comic-opera war. With his experience in the Black Hawk war, Reed was asked to be an officer in the California troops. He accepted only a lieutenancy, promising to recruit as many men as he could as he and McCutcheon rode east to succor his family.

Reed knew nothing of the hardships of the Humboldt, or that so many of the cattle were killed, wounded, or run off by the poor revengeful Nevada Indians. When Sutter questioned Reed about what supplies remained to the party, Reed spoke only what he knew to be true when he had left ... before the depredations of the Indians had commenced. Stanton, returning with his supplies, also would have had no knowledge of the depletion of their assets. Sutter was reassuring to both Reed and Stanton, stating that the party could not be in danger of starvation with the numbers of animals they were bringing to California. All they had to do was slaughter them and wait until spring. However, he generously lent Reed horses, saddles, flour, jerked beef, and an order for more supplies from those pioneers living between the Fort and the mountains. Will McCutchen, who had been prevented by illness of accompanying Stanton on his relief trip, was as eager as Reed to rejoin his family, wherever they were, now joined with Reed in his effort.

Ominously, as Reed stood talking with Sutter, rain fell on their heads. It would become snow in the mountains. Sutter, a veteran, was not duly alarmed when he saw the tracings of early snow the next morning. Frequent slight snows often came before Thanksgiving. The heavy snow storms occurred later. There was nothing much to worry about. Nevertheless, with only a day or two delay, Reed and McCutchen started their return trip to the lagging emigration. They took with them from Johnson's Ranch (a landmark outpost) thirty horses, one mule, and two Indians to assist them. The party started for Bear Valley, the object of every emigrant's hopes, west of the spine of the mountains, the first relatively safe place on the westward push.

Snow began to fall the first day out. The next day, they came upon two people, a man named Curtis and his wife, who had stopped for some reason or other, plannng to spend the winter. Out of supplies, they were dining on their dog. "Very good dog," McCutchen pronounced it.

The snow continuing, and the horses unable to travel through the drifts without tremendous effort, Reed and McCutchen struggled on through the unseasonable snow, but could not continue without snow shoes, and returned to the Curtis cabin. They cached their supplies in hopes of a further attempt, should the snow melt.

The story of their experiences with the Curtis family is an opera bouffe: *McCutchen with his rich supply of Shakespearean oaths, Mr. Curtis with his interminable complaining, and Mrs. Curtis, a typical woman protecting her man, helping where she could and standing loyally by her useless husband. The Indians had taken the horses back to the Fort, and the foursome returned also, where Captain Sutter again assessed the problem, assuring them that no danger of starvation existed. With their supposed supply of cattle, they could easily withstand the rigors of the mountains until spring when rescue would be easier.*

Then Sutter, generous as he was, having lost men, mules, horses, and supplies, suggested that Reed go to Yerba Buena for additional men and assistance.

Who was to know what a winter that was to be! None living in California could have predicted it, since it had not happened before to their knowledge.

And who were to be those additional men not already conscripted for the mock war? At that time the number of Yankees in California was estimated at about 2,000.

There were sob-stories in the newspapers. Hints of what was happening in the mountains had been reported by Sam Brannan's yellow sheet, The Star, *and there also had been less flamboyant accounts in the Monterey* Californian.

Californians heard that there was a late emigrant party delayed somewhere over the mountains. Had it not been for the war in Mexico, there would have been more concern. They were vastly more interested in the Bear Flag Revolt (in which Edwin Bryant played a part).

It is heart-breaking to think that on the fifth night out from Truckee Lake, when Stanton was still alive, the snow shoers camped quite near the place where Reed and McCutchen had cached food for their return try. No wonder Margaret Reed felt her husband close those first days at the lake. He was within fifteen miles of her, struggling to reach her and his family, as she was fighting to reach him.

With Milt gone to find the Donners, Baylis Williams dead, Margaret and the children were without anyone to cut wood, unless it was one of the Breen boys or good-hearted but unwell John Denton. She and the girls managed to gather a pile of dead branches and small pieces of wood during the few good days. It was hard to keep the lean-to warm. The snow-shoers had left the weakest behind. There was not much visiting or communication between the various cabins. Left in the Reed section were her family, Eliza and John Denton, who divided this time between the Reeds and the Graves. In the Graves' cabin were Elizabeth, nearly fifty, 18-year-old Billy to chop wood and care for the group, six small children from 15 down to a nursing baby, and Amanda McCutchen's Harriet.

The Breens were all still together and in good condition.

Next to them, the Kesebergs and their two babies, and possibly Dutch Burger, who was despondent and ailing. With Mother Murphy at the cabin against the great rock was Landrum, 15, Mary, in her early teens, Billy, who had not been able to keep up with the snow-shoers, and Simon, 8. Her grandchildren were also there: Naomi Pike, 2, Catherine Pike, nursing baby, George Foster, son of Sally and Will Foster.

Patrick Breen believed that both Noah and Milt had perished in the long storm. "Dutch" Burger, who had turned back when the snow-shoe party left, tried to find the two men, but again drifts were too deep for him.

The next day, Breen reported in his diary:

Monday, 21 (December). Milt got back last night from Donos camp sad news. Jake Donno Sam Shoemaker Rinehart & Smith are dead the rest of them in a low situation   Snowed all night with a strong S-W wind. to day cloudy   wind continues but not snowing, thawing, sun shineing dimly   in hopes it will clear off.

Days before, Breen had reported that Spitzer was so weak he could barely move. He was not mentioned again; he died in December.

MARGARET

When the weary Milt returned to the Reed cabin, the children climbed over him like puppies. They didn't notice, as Margaret did, his pallor, exhaustion and despair.

"Ma, they ain't got anything at Donners ... nothin' but hides and mice."

"Ugh," Virginia said, but Patty asked, "Did you eat any, Milt? What do they taste like?"

A small smile flitted over Milt's face. "They didn't find any while I was there. Mizz Donner's boiled hides taste better'n ours because they still have a little pepper."

"Hides. That reminds me, Milt. When Pat Dolan left, I bought some of his hides. I think we'd better get them. Otherwise we'll have to take some from the roof."

"Who's been cuttin wood for you, Ma?"

"John Denton, some, though he's not very strong. Dutch Charlie helped too, but he's weak. The girls and I got some small branches."

"Well, Ma, at least I can cut wood. 'Bout all I can do."

With a rush of affection, Margaret said, "Milt, I can't tell you how glad I am you're back. I didn't realize how much I depended on you ... not just for woodcutting, but for your loyalty." She added the word as if it were gold.

> Thursd. 24th. Rained all night and still continues to rain poor prospect for any kind of comfort spiritual or temporal, wind S: may God help us to spend the Christmas as we ought, considering circumstances.

Milt turned away when he heard of Baylis's death. Every time his name was mentioned, Eliza cried. "He just didn't want to be alive any more," she said over and over. "He's all I had of fambly." Milt patted her back rather gingerly, looking at Margaret over Eliza's head.

"We're dying like flies. Poor fella," was all he said. Virginia said, "Milt, can I go with you to cut wood? I'm sick of this old place, and maybe I'll learn how to use a hatchet."

"If your Ma wants you to go."

"It will do her good to be out in the air ... but stay close to Milt, Puss in case of a storm. I'll have glue soup for you when you get back. The meat's mostly gone."

"Mizz Reed, I can't stand the stuff. It comes right up again," Eliza said.

"I'm sorry, Eliza. Beggars can't be choosers. Now you tidy up and shake out the blankets and fix Milt's bed for him."

It was good they chopped wood that morning, for the dreaded black clouds were low again. For the next few days it stormed with short interruptions. At night, snow fell steadily, covering everything.

"Every day we have a clean slate to start with. If I weren't so hungry I'd go out and mess it up with footsteps," Virginia remarked.

Just before when they were alone, Virginia and Patty talked of Christmas quietly so the little boys wouldn't hear. Did Mama even realize it was nearly Christmas? Maybe she'd forgotten.

"Remember last year, Patty? Mama had a new coat made for me, and a hat to wear to church and she gave me a string of beads and some hair bows ...."

"I bet you wished you had the coat now. It's back in the wagon with your beads. Remember, we walked through just a little bit of snow to the church and bells were ringing, and Papa and Mama were talking 'bout this trip, and we were excited about it?"

"I wish we were there. Grandma knitted us mittens, and we sat by the fire and sang songs 'cause she wasn't well enough to go to church ...."

"And we had three big fat chickens for dinner with stuffing in them and sweet potatoes and mashed potatoes and corn relish and apple pie and mince pie and hard sauce ...."

"Stop it, Puss. I can't stand it. You're making my stomach growl."

"And we ate so much we just lay on the carpet in front of the fire and went to sleep."

"And the little boys got tops and marbles and a ball ... and I got my little doll." She reached under her shawl. "See, I keep it with me all the time. It's so tiny. Grandma made all its clothes. These are all that's left ... the rest are all back in the desert in the toy chest."

"I wish we could think of something for Ma and the little boys."

"The only thing we could think of is food and there's just not any."

"I don't think we should even mention Christmas. It'll make the boys feel bad. Poor Papa. I wonder where he'll be at Christmas?"

"That's it, Puss! Let's pray Papa comes for Christmas ... just like Santa Claus ... wouldn't that be the best thing in the world?"

Virginia was silent. "Now you make my stomach ache ... or something ache. I wish it would be true. I wish, I wish, I wish."

"Mama keeps saying he'll come, but I don't think she believes it any more."

"Oh yes she does, Patty. Anyway, he promised me." Virginia thought back to the day ages and ages ago, when she and Milt had followed Papa's trail and found him sitting there alone in the dark. "Mama says not to lose faith, he'll come."

"I'm not losing my faith, Puss. I'm just wondering *when* it'll come true, that's all."

"He'll come if it's humanly possible, Ma says. Meanwhile, let's don't waste anything. Not one bit. Just watch how little Cash keeps alive."

"Puss! Cash eats all sorts of awful things!"

"He's alive. Even if everyone forgets Christmas, let's you and I bring in some pine branches and we can pretend it's a Christmas tree. It'll smell like Christmas, anyway."

"Don't mention smell. I can't stand how it smells. It's better in Mama's house than it is other places .... You ever been in Mr. Keseberg's house, Puss? It's so awful it makes me want to puke."

"Patty Reed! Puke isn't a nice word to use! Mama says to say 'throw up.' "

"It's all the same. When things won't stay down. Sometimes when I eat that gluey stuff it just stays and stays in my mouth and I can't make myself swallow. It's the worst stuff I ever tasted, worse'n castor oil, even."

"You want to die? Just think of something else and swallow. Pretend it's calf's foot jelly, like Grandma used to have when she was sick."

"Ugh. I hated it then, but at least it didn't taste like old cow hides. I bet I could eat it now."

"I'd rather eat six dozen fried cakes all at once."

"I could eat sixteen drumsticks right in a row."

"I could eat a whole pie and a cake and five thousand dishes of mashed potatoes."

"I could eat ten thousand helpings of mashed potatoes, with gravy all over them, in nice little puddles in the middle."

"You'd be sick."

"Maybe so, but it would be worth it just to feel full clear up to my top."

On Christmas Eve, Milt built up the fire, the glue pot was forgotten for the moment, without being quite aware of it, Patty said aloud:

"I wonder where our dear papa is this Christmas Eve?"

Without a second's hesitation, as if she too had been thinking the same thing, Mama said, "Wherever he is, he's thinking of us too, right this minute. Let's just send him our love."

That led to more talk ... of Santa and his visits. Immediately the little boys wanted to know why he wasn't coming this year, and why *couldn't* he find them here just as easily as he had, back in Illinois? That was hard to explain, when you thought of what a miraculous person he was, and the boys were not entirely satisfied.

"Santa's used to snow, Milt. He lives at the North Pole," Jimmy said logically, and a little reprovingly.

"It's too deep, brother. He can't get through it."

"You didn't write him any letter this year, anyway, Jimmy."

"There wasn't any place to mail it to him."

"See? So he *can't* come tonight. But I bet next year he'll come and bring us twice as much. If you're good boys and don't cry," Patty said.

"Next year I want a gun so I can shoot a great big bear."

"Next year I want ... let's see ..." Patty began. "I want a stocking full of oranges and nuts and candy and a punkin pie."

"A punkin pie will get all squashed."

"All right, I want a punkin pie under the Christmas tree then."

"I want a big turkey and Papa cutting it up, and Papa and Mama laughing, and another pony like Billy," Virginia stopped. She was too old to talk this way. She was talking like a little girl.

Mama had tears in her eyes, but she was smiling. "God willing, we'll have all that."

Little Tommie, who had been listening with large confused eyes while he sucked on a rag Mama had soaked in sugar water, said, "I want Papa and I want milk."

Eliza said, "Miss Reed, kin I have my say? I want to be in California and have a nice husband and some children of my own."

"That's a big order for one year, Eliza. I hope you you have your wish."

"What do you want, Milt?" Virginia asked.

"Why, sis, I ain't really thought about it. Let's see ... that I get you back to Mister Reed, I guess. And maybe ... oh, that I don't remember none of this."

"Let's hold hands and wish. And Mama, don't you cry. Papa doesn't like you to cry."

They joined hands and wished, bundled up as best they could, and slept.

The next morning the glue-pot was warmed up as usual. As Milt started up to get more wood, Mama said, "Would you bring me a fresh bucket of snow, please? And help me get something outside."

From under the snow where she had cached it, Mama brought in a big piece of frozen tripe from the last beef. She went to another hiding place and took out a small bundle of rice. Under her blanket she had secreted a cupful of beans. Behind the wall near the firehole, she had stored some dried apples, and a piece of bacon appeared from a cool place in the cabin.

It was magic! "Mama where did you get those things?" Patty demanded to know.

"Well, I'll be danged, Ma," Milt said. Eliza complained, "If I'da known they was there I'd eaten them instead of this glue stew."

"That's why they were hidden. I surprised you, didn't I? I saved these for Christmas dinner!" She went about dicing the bacon and tripe. Everything went into the pot ... not the despised glue pot, but another fresh one.

"I've never smelled anything so good in my life. Milt, you go get wood by yourself today. I'm just going to sit here and smell my dinner cooking."

"Me too." Patty took her doll and sat next to her sister. She whispered to it, "It's Christmas dinner cooking, that's what it is!"

When Virginia started to make fun of her she said severely, "Now Puss, don't you laugh at me. My doll's been with me all the time!"

Afterwards they all agreed that waiting for the food, knowing it was actually there bubbling in the kettle, was almost as much fun as eating it, but at the time they didn't think they could stand to wait for it to be done. The little boys clapped their hands over the pot, watching the bits of bacon bobbing up and then disappearing, or the rice swirl in the water. "That's my piece," Jimmy said, "and the next one's mine and the next one's Mama's" ... on through the family. Milt brought in another load of wood and sat in the far corner of the lean-to, smoking his pipe and smiling. Eliza had the table set hours before the dinner was ready, and she asked to take a turn at stirring, but Margaret waved her away. Not a bit was to be tasted before they were ready.

At last, after what seemed hours and hours, the dinner was ready. Margaret ladeled out cupfuls. They joined hands for grace.

"Now children, eat slowly; there is plenty for all."

It was better than any Christmas dinner they had ever eaten before.

"Sip the soupy part first and save the chunks for afterwards," Patty advised.

Her spoon halfway to her lips, Virginia said, "Now if only Papa were here, it would be perfect."

"Amen, sister."

"And Grandma, too."

That night they slept well. The soup pot was empty again, the glue pot hung in its place as before, ready for the day after Christmas. For once, they had eaten well. Margaret tried to remember how long it had been, then she thought, "Why spoil it by thinking of hunger? That will come tomorrow."

MARY

Christmas for the snow shoers was much different. They had eaten their last food, and the days of starvation began.

Mary Graves recalled the day later, "What to do we did not know. We held a consultation, whether to go ahead without provisions, or to go back to the cabins, where we must undoubtedly starve. Some of those who had children and families wished to go back, but the two Indians said they would go on to Captain Sutter's. I told them I would go too, for to go back and hear the cries of hunger from my little brothers and sisters was more than I could stand. I would go as far as I could, let the consequences be what they might."

Mary thought longingly of the bare ounce of food they had allowed themselves three times a day, after the "consultation" held on the ridge. They decided to go on. To return was almost impossible, lost as they were. They camped, and the next day, made three miles before snow began to fall. The storm started with such unexpected fury that once again they halted to confer. Confused, lost, starving, they were in no condition to think logically. Will Eddy was the only one of the party who seemed strong enough to make any decisions. Mary wondered where he got his strength. Her mind wouldn't behave itself, she felt sure she was losing her sanity. She saw camps ahead or signal fires, or people walking toward them, but she didn't mention them again to the others, no matter how real they appeared to her. A few days without food would not have made them insane; but they had not eaten well since the day after they had crossed the desert when James Reed had surveyed the supplies and found there was not enough to take them to California. Their bodies were so weakened by privations that the exertion of the last days was bound to be fatal to someone but who was to go first?

She thought of Charlie Stanton starting ahead with McCutchen, remembering how she had watched them out of sight. Now Charlie was surely dead, McCutchen was ill, Reed was where no one knew. She began to imagine Charlie coming toward her with steaming hot food in his hands. "That's the long and short of it," James Reed had joked as the six-foot-four McCutchen had gone off with five-foot-five Charlie next to him. It was coming on to Christmas, wasn't it? Let's see, they had started the sixteenth. She counted on her fingers. The food was to last six days, enough to get them to Bear Valley, where the trail would be easier to follow. The days mixed up in her mind. She forgot some. They were hidden in the snow. She couldn't count any more. If she thought of the blistering hot days in the desert, perhaps the snow would seem a blessing as it would have been then. They had water now ... indeed that was all they did have. Water was good, but it didn't stop your stomach from cramping in pain. Sarah was having terrible dreams and visions too. Once she thought she was walking on water instead of snow, and she saw clouds that she imagined were blankets Mama had made of scraps and wanted to climb something to reach them. Jay was far worse than Sarah. It was only her sister's strength that was keeping him on his feet at all. Sarah led him, and sometimes pushed at him to make him go forward. Foster was crazier than any of them. When he said some cruel things, Sally Foster looked so bewildered, so hurt, and tried to explain with her eyes that this wasn't her Will. Something had happened to him. He'd been a fine loyal man on the entire trip. Had he been richer or older, he might have made a better captain than George Donner. But now he was surly, mean; he looked at people as if ... as if he was thinking ... oh, she refused to acknowledge, even to herself, what he was thinking. Poor Sally ... her little brother Lem to worry about too. Sally and Harriet kept near him, helping him over hard spots, but Will was so strange, Harriet had to watch out for him most of the time. It was probably a good thing for Harriet; she wouldn't worry so much about her little baby boy back with her mother, or her dead husband. Just think, it was Will Foster and Will Pike that were ready to go ahead for relief, when Will Pike was killed! A vision of Stanton's intent brown eyes came to her, then she thought of John Snyder and wondered if she too hadn't suffered loss ... not like theirs ... or was it worse? She was confused. One minute she was glad that Charlie was beyond pain, asleep, his pipe fallen from his hand; the next minute she would have given anything to see the stocky, bundled figure groping through the snow to her. Oh, and he was bringing food! She almost cried out, then she remembered the smoke from the cabins, and she was silent. Charlie, Charlie, can't you come? Where are you Charlie? She thought she'd said it aloud, but no one paid attention to her, so she supposed she hadn't.

Somehow they were all huddled around a fire. The snow clung to the snow shoes like great masses of clay too heavy to lift; they could barely see through the whirling flakes, the wind was screaming like a crazy woman. Eddy was yelling. Somehow he got them herded into a circle. He put down blankets, made them lie on them, feet in. Some didn't want to stop; they'd rather walk anywhere than give up. Eddy pushed at them 'till they huddled together. Then he spread blankets on top of them and crawled under himself. Sheltered between his sisters, little Lem Murphy went to sleep first, bless his brave soul. Amanda said suddenly, "Mary, why did you make me leave my baby?"

"Our babies are better off where they are," Sally Foster answered for her. Harriet Pike said, half under her breath, "My Will is better off than any of us."

"There's more Williamses in this party than I can count. which one do you mean?" Will Foster said crossly as usual.

"This William isn't here to be counted. Another Will's gun killed him, and that ought to shut your irritable mouth for once, Will Foster."

"William Eddy, William Pike, William Foster, William Graves, William McCutchen," Mary counted out their names to stop the argument.

"You forgot Billy Hook and Billy Murphy," Sarah said, huddled between her father and Jay.

Amanda said, "My baby's named Harriet. That makes two. And two Sarahs in this crazy bunch."

"There's only two Marys," Mary said. "No, three. Three Marys going toward

Bethlehem."

"When's Christmas?"

"What the hell does it matter, you babbling women?" Foster growled.

"Shh, Will. What does anything matter any more?"

Mary said, "If we talk a little, it makes the time go faster. We daren't leave each other in this storm. Put your fingers in your ears, Will." When they talked, she didn't mind the wind. "There is only one Charlie. No, there *was* only one Charlie."

"What about Dutch Charlie?"

"Lucky Dutch ... back at the lake in a cabin."

"Is it still snowing?"

"Oh, my God, what do you think we're doing here, a bunch of cattle, if it isn't snowing?"

"I'm going to count to one hundred very slowly," Mary said. "And when I'm through I want every one of you to be asleep."

"Hush, Mary. What good would that do?"

"Maybe she'll find that some of the numbers are missing," Pat Dolan said in a strange, wandering voice. "I hid them yesterday. I saved them so we could eat them today. I hope twenty-five is the one missing. It's a nice number. Twenty-five tastes like burning hot soup with meat in it."

Pat Dolan ... was he beginning to hallucinate too? He'd been so steadfast. There was silence. The wailing wind tugged at their covering, but Eddy had fastened it tight. No one wanted to move; some of the heat would be lost. Antoine so silent, Pat so cheery, usually. Antoine groaned. Without some kind of food, they could not make it across the mountains. They would be found here, someday, their skeletons like the spokes of a wheel, dead and fleshless, staring. The cramps of hunger, someone called them. Pangs of hunger. What were pangs? Pangs came and went. Their stomachs were cramped with pure, unrelenting pain. When they were awake, they could control their screaming. When they drifted off to sleep, the groans came without their being able to supress them. Emptiness, churning, all their inner selves screaming to be fed. The wind screaming outside, their empty bodies screaming under this terrible, life-saving tent Eddy had somehow created for them. Maybe, Mary listened carefully ... maybe Charlie was coming. Were there steps? He would be bringing a steaming bucket of meat ... not that dried, shreddy, tasteless stuff they had no more of, but a great pail of hot meat stew, the broth salted, easy to swallow. The first sip would burn her throat when it went down. He promised he would come soon. It must be soon now ... Christmas was coming soon. Christmas couldn't help coming, and there was nothing that would keep Charlie from coming soon. Charlie had killed the big bear she had seen yesterday, and was making bear stew of it. That was why he hadn't come before. They must set the table with the best cloth, and all their good chinaware.

Pat Dolan broke into her thoughts. His voice was firm, with the warm laughter it always held. "One of us must die to save the others."

Mary's hair suddenly hurt at the roots. What was Pat saying? He was such a funny man, always making jokes. She chilled. He wasn't laughing. He wasn't wandering in his mind. He was deathly serious ... deadly serious .... Oh ugly term.

"You're right, Pat. One of us must sacrifice ...."

"Eenie, meenie, miney, moe." Mary started, trying to make it a joke.

"We'll draw lots. Whoever gets the short end dies."

"The short end of what?"

"We'll use paper, pine needles ... whatever."

Will Eddy said, "We could have a duel. We could fight to the finish."

"Damn it, that isn't fair," Foster said. "The women are the fattest. They've got to be in on this just like the men."

"You want to kill Sally, Will?"

"Shut up. One of us must die."

It was hard to concentrate. Was someone really suggesting that someone be killed? None of them were thinking any better than she was. Had they really come to this point? On and on they talked, discussing how they could choose. There was some vague plan ... they did something as silly as eenie, meenie, miney, moe. The one that lost was Pat himself, who had suggested it.

"The joke's on me," he said. "I thought it up, I get to die."

Mary heard herself say, "No. It will *not* be Pat. He left all his food at the lake for the rest. You can't do it!"

"You want to be the one, Mary?" Foster said.

Eddy said in a low unsteady voice, as if he had just awakened from a terrible dream. "Mary's right. No. We must not kill. Let God do it for us. One of us is bound to fall soon."

Mary felt as if someone had just caught her as she was falling into a great pit of horror. In the excitement of the contest, they had uncovered themselves. Some were already standing, the snow plummeting from their shoulders. With no one urging them, the rest rose and started forward, west-southwest again. Mary helped her father to his feet. He was groaning, and tears ran down his cheeks, the bones of his face standing out horribly. "Let me crawl, Mary, it's easier."

"Try to walk." Sarah had Jay, Mary had her father ... Harriet had Lem, Sally had Foster, Antoine and Pat, Amanda and Eddy, the two Indians struggled together. Pat Dolan sometimes fell, but crawled on in the path the others left. Little Lem followed him. One step at a time. One step at a time. Some super-human strength, perhaps given them by the terrible decision they had avoided, brought them back to relative sanity, and gave them the will to try once more.

They were only guessing, but when they stopped once again, they thought they'd made three miles. Oh, dear God, it felt like ten, Mary thought. They made another camp, they made another fire and huddled against the cold. By morning the snow became rain, melting snow into slush, too heavy and wet to battle any more. A weary, dreary, day. Hardly speaking, they rose and struggled, but after a few hours, they lay down, utterly exhausted. One by one they staggered back to the fire they had built the night before. They rebuilt it as high as they could, and huddled in its heat. The rain was sleet, sharp, stinging, biting sleet. Nature was against them. There was no hope. Hallucinations, nightmares, pain, scrambled memories, cold, hunger, cold, hunger. They had no idea where they were. The world had turned into a giant pit of mist, snow-fog, canyons that led nowhere, snow-covered earth that suddenly gave way with their feeble weight and let them fall into rushing icy water underneath. No path, no sun to show what direction they were going. The great fire they built up seemed a dream, a great scarlet dream of hell-fire and death. Mary remembered home when she had roasted potatoes in a fire of burning leaves. She reached out to grab the potato, and she burned her hand and dropped the potato. Now she had nothing to eat, not even the potato that burned her. It had disappeared.

"I think it's Christmas Eve. But I can't remember ... I count the days yesterday, the day before, and the days like everything else, disappear into the blanket that covers us all, and doesn't feel warm .... Let's see, yesterday, the day before, the day before the day before ...."

She awoke to miserable cries. The fire had fallen through the snow and disappeared! "Surely the hand of God," she heard Pa say, groaning. "It is His will that I die here for my sins ... I did not reach out my hand ....” Pa was thinking of Hardcoop again.

Mary looked down the hole were the fire had fallen. In the darkness, she could hear water running. Now, even Hell’s heat was gone. They were out of wood. Someone, Antoine, Foster, one of the Indians? went to cut some more. Her brain cold and sluggish, working slowly, she thought, we wasted all our wood in that great blazing fire ... and even that was taken away.

Antoine stood there, tears frozen on his cheeks. “I lost it.”

“Lost what?” Foster yelled in anger. “Lost what, you fool?”

“The hatchet head ... too cold to hold on.”

“Now we have nothing to cut wood,” Eddy said dully.

Hardly moving, the other men looked at edges of the hole turning into slush. Pa’s eyes were closed ... she touched him. He did not move. She rubbed his hands and face with snow, blew her breath into his mouth, took off her shawl and wrapped it around his shaking body. A yell went up, a faint little flag of sound. Someone had rescued a few unburned ends of the green logs, and had restarted the fire on the top of a precarious platform.

“The fire’s going again, Pa. Don’t give up. Don’t,” Mary pleaded, just as Antoine stumbled against the improvised fire and knocked it over, like a house made of toothpicks. The light and the fire was gone.

Now they would all die. Someone, was it Pat Dolan? was saying the Lord’s Prayer slowly, as if his memory were searching deep for the words. Eddy, with one more spurt of more than human strength, made another effort. Begging, pushing, demanding, he got the people out of the waterhole. Mary tried to help, but her brains were like frozen ice-cream ... they were made of slush ... there was no power in them. She heard Amanda calling for her baby; that started Harriet and Sally crying also. Will Foster was almost completely out of control, swearing words Mary had never heard him say before, asking for vengeance!

Tugging and pulling, Mary said, “Sarah, help me with Pa!”

“I don’t dare leave Jay.”

“You’ve got to. Pa’s dying. He wants you. He’s saying something ... Sarah, Sarah, please help!”

With sudden energy Sarah said, “Jay, you git up there with Eddy, hear me? Or come help Pa.”

The blanket was spread on the snow, Eddy was pushing people toward it, bullying them, slapping them as a mother would children when they didn’t behave. “Huddle. Huddle get together, close as you can. Bring Uncle Frank over here, Mary.”

“He’s dying,” Mary muttered dully.

Sarah said, “He says, remember Christ ... gave His body ...” she started and then broke down, her head on his chest. “Oh, Pa, Pa!”

Mary felt her heart wrench. “No, no, Pa.” His eyes were open, just slits. His eyelashes were covered with snow; there was snow on his balding head. He said, “Mary. Yes. Yes.”

The two sisters huddled over him, trying to warm his body with theirs. His large bones were the only reminder of what a big man he once had been. The sisters rubbed his wrists until he was gone. Then they crawled to the circle, and under the coverings. Eddy climbed in and closed the circle. There was warmth inside ... how could there be? The snow on top of the blankets had cut off the piercing wind. She and Sarah had held hands, and were surprised that their tears were hot, salty, warm salt. Mary was surprised that her freezing body was still alive. But then she remembered that they were all dreaming ... would there never be an end to this nightmare? Warmth was like a slate rag ... it wiped memory and thoughts away as if they had never been. Perhaps when they woke, it would be to no more dreams like this last horrible one.

A voice said, slowly and clearly. "I remember now. This is Christmas Eve."

"Didn't Jesus die on Christmas Eve?" Lem Murphy asked, his face looking ... Mary couldn't describe it ... unearthly, unreal, far away ....

"Christ died at Easter. He was born on Christmas Eve ...."

"In a place with animals all around, mooing," Lem said dreamily.

"He died that we might live," Mary said dully.

In the morning the storm still roared. Now it was Pat Dolan who started to go. In the night Antoine, the stranger in their midst, whose last name they didn't even know, had died. Now it was time for Pat, poor Pat Dolan. He didn't die quietly. He raved, repeated words over and over, fought to get out from under their shelter. "Raven hair — raven hair — broken bow, dead man's face, dead man's bones. Chew chew chew chew rats will get you, let's go, folks, let's get out of here before they get us. Come on Eddy, I'm going on now ... I can see California straight ahead, golden, shining, come on Eddy, you're the only one with any sense, you come with me. Got to get ready, got to git my clothes off for the glorious day I'm burning up with heat. Here's my shoes, my socks, you show me the way, the way, the way. Take off my other shoe it's in the way ... here's my shirt boys take it to blow your nose on, play a tune on it. It's only one more hour's walk to California, now Eddy, let's go, let's go, it's shining ahead."

He got free of them all, and half-dressed, he started away. Eddy couldn't stop him. Finally Pat himself returned and squatted near the shelter. "I've come back," he said quietly. They got him inside. They held him ... he became quiet ... he fell asleep, and at dusk on Christmas Eve, he died.

"Poor lonely Pat," Mary said. By now, the ones who were left, who were semi-conscious from the cold and hunger, were the only comfortable ones. If you had a shred of mind left in one piece, Mary thought, it hurts, makes you hurt everywhere.

"What is keeping us alive?" she asked Sarah.

"You and Jay are keeping me alive. Jay thinks he's back with his mother. He keeps sucking on my fingers. I'm half afraid he'll bite them in his dreams ...."

"These are all dreams, Sarah. Life could never be this bad. The lucky ones, Pa, Charlie, Pat, even John Snyder ... they're the lucky ones."

For more than a full twenty-four hours they stayed in this poor shelter, without fire or food, while the storm spit, moaned, tore at them with ragged, raging hands. Now it was little Lem, out of his head, yelling for food. He'd been such a silent sufferer all these days ... it made the screaming harder to bear.

He kept having dreams of food, and crying because no one would help him get to the food. His sister Harriet held him so he wouldn't wander away in his delirium. Most of the rest were in a stupor so deep that they hardly knew what was happening. Mary offered to help with Lem, but Harriet and Sally only looked at her with sad, uncomprehending eyes, and shook their heads. He was their brother.

The wind and sleet would put out any fire they made outside the shelter. Eddy tried to start one underneath the blanket, with gun powder. It blew up in the powder horn and burned his face and hands, and hurt some of the others, who were so nearly unconscious they didn't seem to notice. Amanda flicked one spark off her sleeve as calmly as if it had been a fly, without opening her eyes.

Finally the storm blew itself out, as if it needed rest before it could come at them again. The sun appeared in a rift in the clouds. Eddy tried once more to make a fire, after finding some dry cotton lining in Harriet Pike's cape. It was the only dry thing he could find to strike a flint into. With this bit of flame he set fire to a tall pine tree, using its hanging dead branches as wicks. Everyone crawled to the blaze and lay still, not moving even when a branch fell among them.

Five days of starvation. Little Lem in a coma now, cradled in Sarah's lap. Three gone. Who would be next?

From the whirlpool of her conscious mind, Mary heard someone make the decision they knew they must make, if all were not to die. Mary never wished to remember who had said the final word. She only wanted to live. If they all died and no one reached relief, the effort of these days would go to naught. Charlie's resolute strength, Pa's death, Pat's cheerfulness and sacrifice ... all created for nothing. For some reason she could not fathom, she knew she must live.

They cut up Pat's body, and weeping uncontrollably, roasted and ate it. All ate but Eddy and the two Indians, who moved away in disgust to a fire of their own. Lem Murphy was offered food, but he was beyond saving, poor child. They turned their backs to each other, hunched and eating like animals, but animals who cried and felt shame.

Mary felt strength coming back; the hallucinations that had clouded her mind for the last five days in a dreamlike agony, disappeared like the smoke she imagined seeing in the valley. Yet the truth now seemed more horrible than the dreams that had preceded it. Pa had said, "Eat of me." There was no way she and Sarah could do that ... no one was asked to eat the flesh of his kinfolk. As she drifted into an exhausted sleep, she thought, "Now it is done. It is something I will live with all my life."

That night a full moon shone brilliantly on the snow, making trees stand out like great black shadows, Sally and Harriet, the only two people awake, held their brother. Neither of them would ever forget moonlight on snow. Hearing a cry, Mary turned and saw Harriet take Sally's head to her heart, and she knew that Lem was dead.

In the morning they had to accept what they had done. They had to do what was next. No one spoke unless it was necessary, none let his eyes look directly into the eyes of another. They stayed at this camp until all the flesh of the dead had been eaten or dried to carry with them. A forbidden thing had been committed.

Mary and Sarah held their hands together and said a prayer for Pa. "He always said he would die before he reached California," Sarah said quietly. "He never forgot leaving that old man."

"The oldest man in this forlorn hope," Mary said. "It's up to us. We've some how been chosen to go on. Go on we must. I only hope life is worth it."

"Mama and the children must never know ... what we did."

With her voice as dull as the pewter-colored clouds, Mary said, "What we *had* to do. Let's not think of it any more." She faced west.

That night Mary had strange twisted dreams. Of her father dying, Stanton lying on a pool of John Snyder's blood, of Pat Dolan dancing on old Hardcoop's body. People she knew were dead were alive, and she was happy, then they died again. Sarah would be there, brushing coals off her shawl; Mary, you are going to burn up and she would cry let me alone I don't care if I do, it would be warm. Sometimes she would be watching Pat Dolan dancing and eating his leg at the same time and she would wake, screaming. No one paid much attention ... everyone had nightmares now. She would move and turn and hear herself groan and hear people moving about her and drift into another nightmare. What had she done that she didn't want to remember? There was always something hiding behind a pine tree that she couldn't see clearly ... "I've got to bury Pa with old man Hardcoop, Sarah, and you've got to help me!" she begged. Such a long way back to find him in the desert, how would she ever do it? I'm more of Pat Dolan than anyone else now. That made her stomach lurch and she choked back that dream. But the pain remained ... the awful pain in her stomach. It was like when Ma had the baby, her face all twisted and screaming, the little children huddled and 'Vina with her hands over her ears behind the stove ... "now, Lizzie, the pain's almost over, just let yourself go," a neighbor said. A great bubble of gas caught at her stomach and woke her again. She'd been out of her head once when she was a child. Then, she'd had dreams all mixed up, of people and scarecrows and rocks falling, and Pa had whispered to Ma, "She's out of her head," and she felt herself fly right out of the top of her body, just as Pa said, "Don't worry, she'll make it, she's a mighty strong young'un, and the purtiest of them all." Sometimes when she woke she could not remember where she was, the dream had been so real. She was at a beautiful party, in her finest clothes and the table was set with a white lace cloth and every kind of food was heaped on it, cakes and pies and steaming soup and huge roasts and bacon ... everything she could think of. She would turn on the hard ground and let tears come, she was so disappointed. If to die was to see all that food, why didn't she die?

Half-dreaming, she thought she must never think of what they had all done; she must go on dreaming all her life and never think again about the bodies, and what had happened to them. She must make it seem a part of the love she felt for everyone. Drifting again, the blood became red roses, a great bouquet of them, one from each one who had died. She would lay red roses on the grave of memory and put a stone there so that remembering could never rise again. Roses for Pa, from all the children he'd led here and died for ... a beautiful deep red rose for Charlie, one that would never die ... a bunch of tiny red roses for Lem, who had come so far without complaint, the youngest of them all ... dancing roses in the wind for Pat and his laughing face. A rose for Antoine, because no one knew who mourned for him ... strange ... all the men ... all the single men were going first ... Pa wasn't single, was he? So she, Mary must save his family for him. Did the Indians have squaws waiting for them in California, with little black-haired papooses on their shoulders? Mary's head spun with thinking for reasons. Was she doomed, now that Charlie was gone? Harriet Pike had lost her Will, but she had two little ones to struggle for. Mary must go on. She must fight for Pa, and her sisters and brothers. She would not remember the bad parts, but she would never forget their gift of life as a mass of great red roses on a burial place.

The sky lightened. There was cold under her. She tried to turn, but she was so stiff she moaned without meaning to. People were talking, far off, and she closed her eyes again. It was absolutely necessary to know what she must do before she started the day. They had done the unforgiveable, and their doing it must not be wasted, or all evil would possess them. Suddenly she felt stronger. The horror was gone. What was done was done, and they must make the best of it, make the deed a positive thing that would give them the strength to go on. It was dear kind Patrick Dolan's gift to her, his laughter, so like hers, his high spirits, his love for everyone, just like hers.

From a distance she heard Eddy say, "We must eat what we need and dry the rest. With this, we may make it, if we all try." It was the first time for many days she had heard hope in his voice. Hope was rising from horror ... what was the meaning?

"You awake, Mary?"

"Umhum. Sort of." She looked at Sarah, then looked away. Their lips trembled at the same time.

"It's awful, Mary. They're ... it's Pa, too."

For a moment Mary's whole body rebelled, and her stomach almost turned inside out. She would drift off to sleep again. It was her only peace.

"Don't you care, Mary?"

"Yes. I care."

"I guess we can't stop them."

Mary thought of Pat Dolan. “No. Say goodbye, and look away.”

Sarah was crying weakly. “Oh, Mary, Mary, what have we done?”

Feeling was tingling in Mary’s cold legs. She stretched them slowly and rose, her body stiff and aching.

“Little Lem died in the night.”

How did she know?

“They’re going to ... oh Mary, him too, and Pa, just like Antoine and Pat.”

The air was like a nutmeg grater on her face. She walked to Sarah, took her hand and said softly, “Yes, Sarah. Tell yourself yes. You have Jay to think about, and the children back there. You have to say yes. You can. Don’t look. Don’t think. Pa wanted it that way. He died saying yes.”

“Oh,” Sarah moaned. “That way?”

Strength flowed into Mary, almost as if Pat were singing or dancing to the fiddle. She must find the strength to smile, to make people smile back at her when she looked at them.

“That way is the only way. Pa wanted it that way.”

Sarah looked at her sister in amazement. “Mary ... your face! Why, Mary, you’re smiling!”

Mary picked up a handful of the hated snow and rubbed her face with it. “Yes, I’m smiling. I might as well smile as cry.”

The snow shoe party, whom McGlashan called The Forlorn Hope, named this place the Camp of Death.

PATRICK BREEN’S DIARY

(December)

Wedsd. 30th Fine clear morning froze hard last night Charley died last night about 10 o clock had with him in money $1.50 two good loking silver watches one razor 3 boxes caps Keysburg tok them into his possession Spitzer took his coat & waistcoat Keysburg all his other little effects gold pin one shirt and tools for shaveing.

Thursday 31st Last of the year, may with Gods help spend the comeing year better than the past which we purpose to do if Almighty God will deliver us from our present dredful situation which is our prayer if the will of God sees it fiting for us Amen. Morning fair now cloudy wind E by S for three days past freeseing hard every night looks like another snow storm Snow Storms are dredful to us snow very deep crust ....

Sund. 3rd Continues fair in day time freezeing at night wind about E Mrs. Reid talks of crossing the mountains with her children provisions scarce

Mond 4th Fine morning looks like spring thawing now about 12 o’clock wind S:E Mrs. Reid Milt. Virginia & Eliza started about ½ hour ago with prospect of crossing the mountain may God of Mercy help them left ther children here Tom’s with us Pat with Keysburg & Jas with Gravese’s folks, it was difficult for Mrs. Reid to get away from the children.

Tuesd 5th Beautiful day thawing some in the sun wind S-E snow not settleing much we are in hopes of the rainy time ending.

Weds. 6th Fine day clear not a cloud froze very hard last night wind S:E Eliza came back from the mountain yesterday evening not able to proceed, to day went to Graves the others kept ahead.

Friday 8th Fine morning wind E froze hard last night very cold this morning Mrs. Reid & company came back this moring could not find their way on the other side of the mountain they have nothing but hides to live on Martha (Patty) is to stay here Milt and Eliza going to Donos Mrs. Reid & the 2 boys going to their own shanty & Virginia prospects dull May God relieve us all from this difficulty if it is his Holy will Amen.

Mond. 11th Still continues to snow fast, looks gloomy Mrs. Reid at Keysburgs Virg. with us wood scarce difficult to get any more wind W.

Frid. 15th Fine clear day wind N W Mrs. Murphy blind Lanth. not able to get wood has but one axe betwixt him and Keysburg, he moved to Murphys yesterday looks like another storm expecting some account from Suiters soon.

MARGARET

Failed one more. Poor Milt, so down-hearted. If only Eliza had more staying power. Took courage for her to turn back ... did she know what turning back was like?

Now they were all turning back. As soon as she saw the smoke from the chimneys below, Margaret wished she had forced herself to go on ... but where, what direction? If she perished what would happen to the three she left behind? It was hard enough to get someone to take them.

There was nothing left but to scavenge, pick up discarded bones and boil them till they went to pieces. Even wood to make the fire to boil bones was now great effort. Bringing snow down, buckets which melted into driblets, was never-ending labor. Milt had talked of taking Eliza to Donner's camp, but he'd changed his mind.

She doubted she would make another try to escape. If Virginia's feet hadn't frozen, perhaps they might have gone on, found some trace of the trail the snow-shoers had taken weeks ago.

Well, she was not ready to lie down to die quite yet. She set out to collect all the hides that were hers. She would wash them and cook them, one by one. She would keep her eyes open for any scrap she could use.

Every day she went from cabin to cabin, seeing how the children were faring. Lavina Murphy was blind. She had babies with her and it was becoming hard to take care of them. She managed to feed them a little flour mixed with water; then she would put them in their bed to sleep. They weren't crying as much as they did, she told Margaret. Yes, Billy was managing wood for her, thank you. Eleanor Eddy looked like cheesecloth, she was so pale and transparent. She managed to take care of her children, and that was all. They were little skeletons.

When Margaret went to Keseburg's, Patty took her aside and begged her to take her back to the shanty. "Honey, there's nothing much left of the shanty. We've eaten most of the hides on the roof."

"I don't care, Ma. I can't stand it here. Ma, I'm scared."

Margaret didn't wonder that Patty was afraid of Lewis Keseburg. He no longer looked human. His beard was long and scraggly, his eyes were as wild as those of a spooking horse. "He just lies in bed, Ma. He won't walk. He screams at us if we make any noise. He hits her and makes her do all the work."

"You stay out of his way, Patty. I'll be here every day. I don't think Mrs. Keseburg would let anything happen to you ...." Yet, as she looked at the man, so handsome and straight once, who was huddled under a filthy blanket, she couldn't blame Patty for being afraid of the man.

Margaret thanked Phillipine as well as she could. Her little baby, the baby that they'd worried over on the trail, wasn't at all well. Poor misbegotten thing. Phillipine had no milk for the child. Margaret tried to force some of the glue soup between his lips but it ran out his slack mouth. "Soak a rag in a little sugar-water," Margaret said. Phillipine didn't understand, so Margaret, finding a clean rag somewhere in the dirty, unkempt lean-to, fixed it for her. "Patty, you keep a rag clean ... if there's any flour at all left, mix it with water for the baby."

"Flour! *flour!* Who has flour?" came the hoarse voice of Keseberg from his tangled dirty bed. "If we had any rags we'd put them on my foot to draw out the pain." The outburst was followed by thumps of his cane on the wall and a string of German oaths.

"Patty, do the best you can. Help Mrs. Keseberg ...."

Patty bit her lips firmly. Oh, Margaret hoped she wouldn't cry.

"I try Ma. She's good to me, but he doesn't like me at all. He yells about the kinder or something like that."

"I'll come every day. As soon as I can get us all together, I will."

She went back and helped Milt fix up their lean-to again. Until they ate all the roof, she'd keep the children.

Before the children came back, she asked Milton to help ... or she helped Milton, one or the other, and they prepared the last bit of meat. She had thought of it often ... what she would do and say, that when Milt actually killed poor skinny little Cash, she was trembling as she used to do on Friday afternoon "exercises." There was a lump in her throat. Margaret tried not to think of his trotting behind much of the way, or huddling that cold night on the salt desert, or his following Virginia and Billy when they went riding. Of course that made her remember how brave Puss had been when Billy had to be left behind. Puss had just sat silently in the back of the wagon, watching him get smaller and smaller and then disappear. Then she turned back to them all and said, "He's gone," in a little-girl voice. "He kept looking at me."

"Maybe he'll catch up tonight," Patty said in her hopeful way.

"I don't think so. I don't think I'll ever see Billy again."

"Papa said he'd get you another pony in California."

"I know. He will." She took a deep breath, and before she moved, she looked once more where Billy had been.

No one said anything more.

After a while, Puss said, "Everything about this trip has been goodbyes. I never knew goodbyes hurt so much. Grandma, Papa, Billy, my cousins, that Jackson from the other train." She began to cry. Margaret held her quietly. It was good for her to cry. Why did it take people so long to learn that? "There, there, Puss. I know." They held each other till the sobs grew easier.

If Virginia could survive losing Billy, Margaret knew she must be brave about Cash. She didn't want to lie to them, but she dare not tell them before supper. She didn't want Cash to be sacrificed in vain. Had she better explain first and wait until their grief had passed? Would their hunger overcome their revulsion? This time, it wasn't Puss she was worried about. It was Jimmy. Cash had been his pet, his special love. While she was fixing their dinner, Margaret changed her mind again and again. Would they hate her for doing this? She finally decided on saying nothing, but holding to the truth as much as she could ... temporizing, perhaps, but how else to overcome the feelings they would have?

Patty wasn't with her family. She had stayed at the Breen's. Good Peggy Breen, coarse, strong, butchering her cattle while her husband sat and prayed. She is more like a man than a woman. I trust her with children; she seems to love them all, her own and every one else's, Margaret thought.

"What smells so good, Ma?" Puss asked, putting Tommie down on the floor in front of the fire. Jimmy ran to the pot. "Can we eat right now? I'm so hungry even the glue soup smells good today."

"This isn't glue soup. This is special. A good friend sent us a present of some meat, and I've made a stew."

It wasn't a lie, was it? Not really a lie. The children ate heartily and she didn't tell them any more, until several days later when they finally realized that Cash must be lost. Margaret didn't eat a bite herself, and for the first time in months, she had one of her headaches. Cash lasted almost ten days.

I, MARGARET

Milt and I must ask Lizzie Graves for our hides, the ones I bought from Pat Dolan. They are on Lizzie's roof. She needs them too. When her roof is gone where will she go? All of us women are fighting for our children; Lizzie is too. We look into each other's eyes with understanding; we know that if we seem selfish, we can't help it. It is in us to save our children, no matter what. I wish all the children to survive ... all of them, especially mine.

Milt brings the hide. This is the last one I have. At Keseberg's and Breen's I picked up bones they had thrown out. Boil, boil, boil, over and over; after a while they make a powder. It is better than nothing. It is better than what some of them are thinking of doing. I don't think I could force myself. It was hard enough, killing Cash.

Before Milt starts back to Murphy's, where he is trying to help that poor woman with those babies, he comes inside our shack.

"Ma ...."

As always, Milt talks slowly. "Yes, Milt?"

"Ma, before I go back ...."

I nod. How worn he looks, I think.

"I want to say something to you, Ma."

No use rushing Milt. His big strong hands clench and his face is worried. I wait. I hope he won't weep. It would be shame to him to weep before a woman.

"It boils down to this .... " He twists his poor battered hat that he has worn all these months, a hat as steady as Milt ... "that I'm sorry, Ma."

"Sorry for what, Milt?"

"Losing them cattle and becuz Mr. Reed had to take up that fight for me."

"That's long ago. You forget spilt milk. No mistake you've ever made could cancel out the good you've done for us all."

"I promised Mr. Reed I would take care of you ...."

"You have. You've done fine. No one could have done more."

"You ain't got a man to help, and I'm plumb wore out, Ma. I can't go no farther."

"You'll feel better tomorrow ...."

"Ever day I feel worse. I can't do anything tomorrow, unless ...."

I wait for what he is going to say, hoping it isn't what I fear. His clothes hang on his big frame, bones have risen in his face and body.

"I'm goin' to have to eat sumthin', Ma, or I'm not going to make it."

Oh, don't say it Milt, I think. "There's still glue soup ...."

He tries not to show nausea. "I can't, any more. I don't want you to feel bad, but me and some of the teamsters are ...."

He is going to say something I don't want to hear.

"We're going to dig up Baylis or Dutch ...."

"No, Milt. Don't do that."

"I can't lie, Ma. I want you to know. You don't have to see me any more. I'll stay out of the way. I'll never touch the children. I'll lay wood next the door. Don't ever tell Puss or Patty or the boys."

If I cry, it will set Milt off. Oh, please, don't let me break down.

"I will pray for you, Milt. I'd rather you didn't ... but we've all got to do what we have to. Be as strong as you can, Milt. Hold out as long as possible. But don't ever blame yourself. It's just been all bad luck since the Little Sandy."

Milt sways, or does he? I can't tell, the tears are so thick in my eyes. I add, "I'm the one who's sorry. I told Mr. Reed I wouldn't come if you didn't drive for us."

He tries to smile. "Thank you, Ma."

He's said all he's going to say, by the final tone of his voice. So exhausted, so weary, so starved.

"Do the very best you can, as Patty's always saying. God will forgive you. I hope he gives you strength."

He comes toward me, his right hand raises, slowly, stiff as a pump handle. "My best respects, Ma. I'll do what you say."

I reach out impulsively, putting my arms around him, as if he were one of the children. "Milt ... Milt ... God bless you."

His face is ready to fall to pieces. I pray once again that he won't cry. I turn away so that he won't see that I am crying. I hear him fumbling at the makeshift door, and hear a choking sound, or a cough.

"Milt, we all love you as if you belonged to us."

I think he says "Thank you, Ma," before he leaves, but I am not sure. I've held myself in as long as I can. When the flap closes, and it is dark inside the shack, I hear my own great helpless sobs choking me until I can hardly breathe.

ELEANOR

After her baby girl died, Eleanor Eddy lay helplessly on the thin blankets she called her bed. Someone had taken the baby away. Faces appeared in her vision, disappeared, grew larger than life, shrunk to nothing before her bewildered eyes. What time, what day, what month, what year was it? Did it matter? All that was real and all that was imaginary blended into one horrible caldron of sorrow which she stirred like a wicked witch. Where was Jimmy? Sometimes Lavina Murphy's face bent above hers saying something she couldn't understand; sometimes she heard crying ... was it Jimmy, or one of the other babies? She *must* find out. She tried to raise her head, but instead, she fell into a well of dizziness, of drowning, of retching, of whirling. The fire blazed up; she saw shadows dancing on the wall. Will would be here soon, and they would dance together for joy. She heard his footsteps.

Frances Donner was told Mrs. Eddy died "deranged ... she danced until she was exhausted."

Patrick Breen's diary for February 8th, 1847 read:

"Fine clear morning wind S.W. froze hard last. Spitzer died last night about 3 o clock to we will bury him in the snow Mrs. Eddy died on the night of the 7th."

Tuesd.9th Mrs. Murphy here this morning Pikes child all but dead Milt at Murphys not able to get out of bed Keyburg never gets up says he is not able. John went down to day to bury Mrs. Eddy & child heard nothing from Graves for 2 or 3 days Mrs. Murphy just now going to Graves fine morning wind S.E. froze hard last night begins to thaw in the sun.

Wednd. 10th (February 1847) Beautiful morning wind W: froze hard last night, to day thawing in the sun Milt Elliot died las night at Murphys shanty about 9 o clock P:M: Mrs. Reid went there this morning to see after his effects. J Denton trying to borrow meat for Graves had none to give they have nothing but hides all are entirely out of meat but a little we have our hides are nearly all eat up but with Gods help spring will soon smile upon us.

MARGARET

Milt was gone now, with the others. Good faithful Milt ... gone with John Snyder and all the Donner teamsters ... why was it that the strong single men were dying first? Dutch Burger, Baylis Williams, Smith, Shoemaker, Rhinehart ... John Denton failing fast. Had they nobody to live for? Oh, but Milt had all the Reeds for his family. He even called her Ma, he called the girls sister ... had she condemned him to die when she asked him to forbear eating human flesh? She put the thought out of her mind. Now she must attend to Milt. There was no one else to do it.

"Virginia, my dear, will you go with me to help with Milt?"

VIRGINIA

Virginia went with Ma to Murphy's. Though her frost bitten feet hurt, she followed Ma across the snow to the Murphy's shanty by the rock. Auntie Eleanor had died there the day before Milt, and her little baby girl, and Landrum. She wished Milt hadn't had to stay there. People seemed to move from place to place; sometimes she had been with the Breens, sometimes she'd been with that awful Mr. Keseberg. She always thought he was crazy back on the plains when he was so mean to his wife and when he'd stolen something from a dead Indian, but he was worse now. He didn't look tall and straight and young; he looked thousands of years older than Ma, for instance. He looked like an ape or an ogre or something out of a fairy tale book she had read when she was little. Long hair and crazy eyes ... shouting and screaming and saying those German words that always sounded like cursing or spitting. In his lean-to nobody could make the least bit of noise, even the little baby. When the baby finally died, she bet he was glad the crying had stopped. The little girl, though. That was different. Poor Patty had told her how awful it was when she'd stayed with them the time they tried to get out of there.

Ma was surely in a hurry. Didn't she remember how Virginia's feet hurt? They'd bled yesterday. Ma was getting so strong; she just set her chin now and did whatever had to be done ... not like the old days when she got those headaches. Now Milt was gone, who was going to help Ma with cutting wood? Milt had showed her how but now her feet were so bad, she wasn't sure she could chop any more. And who would make people give up hides Pat Dolan had left for them? Well, no matter, Ma said they were 'most used up anyway.

Oh, the sun stung her eyes, her feet ached and pricked and itched.

When they got to Murphy's, Ma stopped. "It's bad down there. Take a deep breath and try not to think about it."

They started down the ice-steps, half-sliding, barely holding on. She hated to go to the Murphys. There were so many people there, all lying on their beds, the children crying, the smells so strong you could taste them. Ma, so fussy at home, so neat and clean, in a dress that was raggedy around the edges, her shoes cracked and split, her hair pulled back tight, her back as straight as Grandma's used to be. She wasn't pretty any more. Virginia looked at her in wonder. Would Mama's brothers recognize her if they saw her now?

"We're just going to have to forget what we're doing," Ma said.

Virginia nodded.

"We've got to take care of Milt now, as he took care of us," Ma said, and Virginia nodded once more. Was Ma trying to get her courage up? When she'd heard about Auntie Eleanor, Ma had been sad, but she wasn't as sad as she was today, with Milt gone. Stop thinking about it, Virginia Backenstoe Reed. Ma said *not* to think.

Virginia slipped and yelled. "*Ow!* my foot!"

Ma turned. "Puss, I forgot about your poor feet. Forgive me. Take it slowly."

They lifted the rug that was the door. For a time, neither could see anything, their eyes were so used to the snow outside. How many beds were there, how many people? Smoke distorted everything. Virginia's eyes burned. Mrs. Murphy was groping toward them, her hands outstretched.

"Who is it? Who is it? Has help come?"

"It's Margaret Reed, Lavina. Come to see about Milt."

Don't look, Virginia. Don't look. They had awakened the babies ... how many were there? and they started crying ... weakly like mice squeaking. Where was Milt? She didn't want to look at him. She only wanted to remember him driving the Palace Car, way back in the beginning when he was so proud.

As if in a trance, Virginia followed Mama to the bed where Milt lay. He looked pinched and gray and little. She wanted to remember his voice, "Hey there, sister, where you takin' Billy? See you watch out for snakes, hear?" And the night they found Papa, when he let her cry. And the way he harnessed Billy, so careful, patting him and stroking his smooth neck. "See, sister, no need ever to whip this feller ...."

Mrs. Murphy was shouting at Ma. "You got to git him out of here or I'll cook him for dinner. I got to keep these young'uns alive, hear me?"

Mama said something softly, but Mrs. Murphy continued to yell. "Only Mary's here, Mary and Billy ... us and all these babies. Why didn't you bring one of them lazy Breen boys to help? You think I can help carry that big feller up them stairs? You think I can do everything?"

"One of the Breen boys is coming, Lavina," Mama said, trying to calm Mrs. Murphy.

"Nobody to git me food. Just eat ever thing up!"

Margaret looked at Virginia helplessly. "Don't mind her, Puss. She's beside herself with worry, poor thing, doing the best she can."

"He'd make a nice stew. You better git him out of here quick or I'll give him to the pot. Listen to them babies. That's all I hear, day and night. I'm blind now, and all I hear is crying for food. They sound louder when you're blind. They sound louder'n the wolves outside that's waiting to eat us all up. How're a pair of you goin' to get that big man up and out of here?"

"One of the Breens should be here by now." Margaret looked at Virginia. "Do you think we ...?"

We? Could she pick up dear old Milt? The thought was so silly ....

"We can try, Ma."

Together, they pulled and dragged and managed to get Milt to the stairs, and there the air was better. He was surprisingly light after all. One of the Breen boys came and helped them pull him up the stairs. They took deep breaths of fresh air, so cold it burned their throats, and rested. Virginia didn't want to stop. If she stopped helping she'd think about what she was doing instead of trying to get strength enough to do it.

"We'd better bury him," Mama was saying to the Breen boy. "We can't just leave him here like this."

The ground was frozen, so they merely heaped snow on top of Milt, and patted it down as hard as they could. When they had covered him, Virginia said, "Shouldn't we say something, Ma?"

"We'll stand here and pray for an old faithful friend, and tell him goodbye," Mama said simply. "In our hearts forever, dear Milford Elliott."

Virginia said, "I think I can remember one of Uncle Patrick's prayers."

"Milt wasn't Catholic, dear."

"I don't think he'd mind, do you? I listen to Uncle Patrick every morning and every night, and I think I know a short one. It would seem more ... well, more what God would want." She said a short prayer, and made the sign of the cross.

When they finally were finished, both Margaret and Virginia realized that now there was no one to help them, no man at all to do the hard work. What were they to do? Looking at the heaped mound, Virginia was horrified that her feelings were as frozen as the snow ... she didn't feel anything any more but the pangs in her stomach, the hurt of her feet, the glare of snow in their eyes. She couldn't cry, and she ought to, for there lay their best friend. She hoped feeling would never come back, as it had in her feet. When feeling came back in them, she wanted to scream. Maybe someday she could bear to think of Milt with real sorrow, maybe some day she would be strong enough to cry. Right now she was dizzy from the work they'd done, and her feet felt as she were walking on knives.

MARY

When Mary remembered the last weeks of their attempt to reach Sutter's Fort, she could not separate one day from the next.

Much later, Mary wrote of the trials of the so-called Forlorn Hope: "Our only chance for camp-fire for the night was to hunt a dead tree of some description, and set fire to it. The hemlock being the best and generally much the largest timber, it was our custom to select the driest we could find without leaving our course. When the fire would reach the top of the tree, the falling limbs would fall all around us and bury themselves in the snow, but we heeded them not. Sometimes the falling, blazing limbs would brush our clothes, but they never hit us; that would have been too lucky a hit. We would sit or lie on the snow, and rest our weary frames. We would sleep, only to dream of something nice to eat, and awake again to disappointment. Such was our sad fate .... We would strike fire by means of the flint-lock gun which we had with us. This had to be carried by turns, as it was considered the only hope left in case we might find game which we could kill. We traveled over a ridge of mountains, and then descended a deep canyon, where one could scarcely see the bottom. Down, down we would go, or rather slide, for it is very slavish work going down hill, and in many cases we were compelled to slide on our shoes as sleds. On reaching the bottom we would plunge into the snow, so that it was difficult getting out, with the shoes tied to our feet, our packs lashed to our backs, and ourselves head and ears under the snow. But we managed to get out some way, and one by one reached the bottom of the canyon. When this was accomplished we had to ascend a hill as steep as the one we had descended. We would drive the toes of our shoes into the loose snow, to make a sort of step, and one by one, as if ascending stair-steps, we climbed up. It took us an entire day to reach the top of the mountain. Each time we attained the summit of a mountain we hoped we should be able to see ... a valley, but each time came disappointment, for far ahead was always another and higher mountain. We found some springs, or, as we called them, wells, from five to twenty feet under ground, for they were under the snow on which we walked. The water was so warm that it melted the snow, and from some of these springs were large streams of running water. We crossed numbers of these streams on bridges of snow, which would sometimes form upon a blade of grass hanging over the water; and from so small a foundation would grow a bridge from ten to twenty-five feet high, and from a foot-and-a-half to three feet across the top. It would make you dizzy to look down at the water, and it was with much difficulty we could place our clumsy ox-bow snow-shoes one ahead of the other without falling. Our feet had been frozen and thawed so many times that they were bleeding and sore. When we stopped at night we would take off our shoes, which by this time were so badly rotted by constant wetting in snow, that there was very little left of them. In the morning we would push our shoes on, bruising and numbing the feet so badly that they would ache and ache with walking and the cold, until night would come again. Oh! the pain! It seemed to make the pangs of hunger more excruciating."

It is a cold account, exact and carefully written, thirty years later. Details of the gruesome decision made at Christmas to survive, no matter how, are omitted. Feelings: cold, hunger, pain, are described. Inner emotions that tore at their hearts and the veneer of civilization that had been buried under scar tissue are not.

Foster's mania increased: his threats to kill either Sarah or Mary for food only because neither of them had children to live for, his determination to kill the two Indians who had suffered so stoicly, and who now kept themselves more and more separate from the rest after Eddy warned them of their peril. Sarah, led half-blind Jay. All of them straggled along without order or sometimes hardly with any consciousness that they were struggling at all. They just took one step at a time, and now they were generally going downhill. Only two men left, Eddy and Foster. You couldn't count Jay any more, nor the Indians, who disappeared, though sometimes they found their tracks ahead of them. Foster cried for murder, screamed for someone to die so he could live. Sally Pike walked with her sister and Foster. Mary and Amanda and Sarah together, Sarah dragging Jay. Eddy ahead with the gun ... there was a fight ... or could one call it a fight? One night Eddy and Foster struggled together, both so thin and tired and helpless that it would have been funny if it hadn't been so sad. Fighting like two weak animals... at least Jay acted human. He was only wearing out.

Since the Indians had left, the snow-shoers were lost in an unpredictable country ... nothing to guide them but a weak sun and the down-hill course ... even the latter fooled them often, with another barrier to climb.

MARY

At last Will Eddy gave in and ate human flesh. Mary was surprised. How could he have gone so long? He told Mary as they walked along what made him stronger than the rest ... Eleanor's gift of bear meat, secreted in his pack, which he had discovered Christmas Day, or was it Christmas Eve? Mary didn't want to know for sure, in fear she would find out that the bear meat might have saved Charles Stanton. That was done now, there was no changing it. If Eleanor had given it to him, she meant to save him, and him only. Eddy had kept them going. He said he hadn't minded human flesh, because he was doing it for Eleanor. He also told her that he had no appetite at all. He didn't feel hunger ... he had not felt thirst, either, when they crossed the desert ... he only knew that he could not go farther without food or water. He was matter-of-fact when he talked about it. Mary thought he was the only sane person in the group. He didn't have the dreams and hallucinations the others did. The only time he'd broken down was when he tried to fight Foster. The rest had to tell him that he would die if he didn't do as they had done, eat the forbidden flesh. He seemed never to think of himself at all.

He had not been selfish from the start; he was always the one who volunteered to help someone fix a broken wagon. Mary still blushed when she thought of the geese he'd divided with their family, after Pa had refused to give him food. He never spared himself. Must she blame him because he kept Eleanor's gift to himself? It had served its purpose. It had kept him going, and without his sanity and good sense, they could not have made it.

At least, Mary thought, they had not come to extreme measures with Charlie Stanton. She could still keep her memory of him, sitting by the fire that last morning, smoking his pipe. "I will be coming soon."

Although she couldn't remember exactly what day it happened, there was one sight Mary would never forget. After those unending mountains, the climbing up and the falling down, with blood in their footsteps now, like the crumbs Hansel and Gretel left behind, they saw a great wide valley ahead of them, blue-brown and mercifully flat. someone said it was New Year's Day. It couldn't have been ... there had been an eternity since Christmas.

Another downhill slide and they lost sight of the valley. Foster was now yelling at Jay to hurry. He was holding them back ... he and the women who were helping him. "Go ahead, Foster, go on!" Sarah cried in anger. "Don't wait for us. I'll bring him along as best I can." She was afraid at night to sleep, for fear Foster would steal up and kill Jay. "Mary, you're stronger ... go ahead with Eddy. We'll follow. Jay wants to stay behind as Stanton did, but I won't let him. Go on! You're our hope, you and Eddy."

They had reached a level where the snow no longer covered the ground. Earth was visible between patches of snow. Mary fell once, and so precious was the feel of soil beneath her hands that she rolled over and kissed it ... how long had it been since she had felt earth under her instead of the hated snow?

She and Will were ahead now ... the rest strung out like scarecrows in a corn field. Farthest back, Sarah and Jay. She and Eddy followed bloody footsteps ... the Indians left them ... Eddy had the rifle ... there was a faint chance of game, and anyway, Eddy feared Foster's insane threats and dared not trust him with it. Eddy, looking down, tears in his eyes. The first time she had ever seen Eddy cry. A gulping sound, inhuman, as quiet as he could make it ... pointing. Marks on the wet earth. Deer spoor. The place where a deer had slept ... the dry grass from last year still bent. Mary cried too.

"Mary, do you feel like praying?"

"I never prayed out loud in my life. Do you know how?"

Kneeling there together, they felt almost civilized again, like people brought back to their own country once more. Rising like two lost children, they felt strong, sure of themselves, calm.

Going on, their eyes searching, searching for signs of the deer. How quiet it was, after the gulping sobs and the praying! Stealthily, peering, for any movement, any sign, and every disturbance of the soil. A spot where a cluster of little black balls lay like Easter eggs. Eddy's hand on her arm. His whisper, "There! Over there!"

The proud buck stood as motionless as they, ears alert. Eddy kneeling, trying to lift the rifle into position, but so weak and shaky he couldn't. Trying again, Mary couldn't look. She felt as if she would snap in two. Her hands over her eyes, her whisper, "Oh, I am afraid ...." Eddy bringing the rifle up once more, this time resting it on his shoulder and swinging it around the best way he could ... and the shot that screamed and screamed and screamed long after the deer had bounded away ... and her cry, "Oh, merciful God, you have missed!"

"Its tail dropped. It's been hit." He was off staggering, and Mary was after him, over dry ground, falling once on an icy patch, Mary thinking as she ran how like grotesque stick-drawings they looked, thin, bodyless, inhuman ... the deer ahead, falling as Will hit it with the butt of his gun.

Eddy's knife out, and they were drinking the warm blood as it gushed from the animal, taking turns, like children at the well pump. Their faces wet and sticky with lovely warm life-giving blood. After the terrible exertion and the strain, almost more than their wasted bodies could take, resting on bare earth, the deer still warm beside them.

"That's enough for now," Mary rolled over on the ground, warm, fed, relaxed, slept ... not long ... how long had it been? Letting strength return to her body. Helping Eddy drag the deer's limp body to a place where they could strike a fire, and eat pieces of the deer cooked, as human beings cook their food ... small parts, so there would be some for the people who followed.

The fire warm on their feet. Bodies warm with food. Sleep free of dreams ... she heard Eddy fire his gun, so the others would know where they were. She thought all their troubles were over.

Later, Sarah told her how Jay had said, when he heard the shots, "Now, I will live if I can reach him," but they were far behind the others; the extra exertion was more than Jay could stand. He died on the way, and Sarah covered him with her shawl and prayed she would freeze to death and join him. She had no fire at all. The next morning, she struggled to her feet, still alive, she thought dully, only to meet the Fosters on the way to cut up Jay's body.

Sarah went on to the Foster camp, where Eddy met them with the deer, and she ate some. She could not bring herself to think of what happened next, so depraved they had all become. The deer was not enough to take seven people the miles they had yet to go. There was no pity for Sarah. With drugged, exhausted eyes she saw Foster drying both Jay and the deer; someone devoured Jay's heart as she watched, weeping.

The seven started once again for the wide valley they had glimpsed, putting pieces of thin blanket over their bleeding feet, discarding their rotted shoes. Now they were always wet. Snow turned to rain. Their poor filthy clothes had no way of drying. In a few days the last of Jay and the deer were gone. Foster so worn he had no energy to scream his threats. His mania subsiding into an apathy. He allowed Eddy to do everything, find wood, make a fire, and prod the exhausted party to their feet for another day. Then, frenzied again, Foster demanded to kill Amanda, because she fell behind the rest. Eddy and Foster fighting, a pitiful fight, both falling down in weakness, unable to talk.

One day they came to softly rolling countryside, but were unable to rejoice because of hunger, weakness, apathy. What did it matter? They were in sunshine at last, but they still left bloody footprints, like flowers in a path.

A day came when they found other bloody footprints. Foster knew at once that the Indians were still on their feet ahead of them. With a lurch at Eddy, he took the gun from him and went ahead. No one went with Foster. No one saw what happened. No one would look, but all heard the shots. "They were going to die anyway," Foster said. No one answered. From then on Harriet, her sister Sally and Foster were behind. No one wished to camp with them, for fear someone else would also be killed. Now, when they saw deer, there was no one able to kill, no one with strength to care. Only a thin needle of courage kept them going ahead.

Rain, rain, rain. Unable to stand any more, they crawled ahead on hands and knees like the beasts they had become. It was impossible to climb the slightest rise without falling. They staggered like drunken crazies, with not even the release of weeping tears.

They were following some sort of faint path, where it led they didn't know. Instinctively they felt it must lead somewhere to something.

Crawling ahead, they found tracks. Tracks! Blindly pushing ahead, they hardly knew where ... a village of Indians ... human beings, as they had once been, looking at them in fear, as if they were ghosts, apparitions of evil. Squaws screaming and hiding from human animals who crawled. Skeletons that were only bones hung with flesh that moved towards them with demented eyes.

Raw acorns for food, acorn bread. Bitter, but something to keep them going. Passing from one Indian village to another, accompanied by Indians whose fear had turned to soft pity ... the awful thought present always of what one of their party had done to other Indians. Poor Eddy, vomiting the acorns. Almost gone now, Eddy far to the rear, almost out of sight. Unable to eat, he was entering the coma that preceded death. They received strength from acorns, but he couldn't keep them down ... a handful of pine nuts, brought lovingly by some pitying Indian soul.

A final moment came when no one could go farther.

Eddy, brought back to life by the miraculous pine nuts, staggering ahead with an Indian holding each arm ... Eddy disappearing around a bend ahead of them, going somewhere they could not fathom. All of them prone. Mary held her sister's hand; it was a claw. Death so near they could see him grinning. At the end, they had done all they could. No one spoke; there was no strength. A new moon, a sliver of hopelessness. Mary saw that her sister had a blanket wrapped around her instead of a skirt. Her ragged shirt on her feet. Would they, any of them, stand on feet again? Even a new moon gave faint light. It disclosed more than Mary could bear.

A faint sound ... some bear come to feed upon them? No, to sneer and move away from something not fit to eat. Was it a deer? Some faint movement in the ground upon which she lay, ready to die ... her hand tightened on Sarah's. "Listen ... what's that noise?" Her heart made a sound too loud for her to hear. "Listen, Sarah ... it's ... what?" Did death come on that kind of feet?

Footsteps ... the moon behind the trees now. Voices, "Oh my God, Sarah! It's people ... talking! calling ... it can't be! It's a dream! You hear too?"

Foster's voice, hoarse and weak, calling back, "Here ... we're here ...." Amanda slowly lifting her head, eyes as wild as a cat's. People! Men ... with packs on their backs ... a smell of bread! Bread! Oh, glorious God, Sarah, they have come!" Tears ran down Sarah's face. Bread ... later a fire ... tea ... hot tea! Sugar! Strength flowing through them like fire flaming through dry trees ... Mary felt her hair rising on her head.

Feeling again! She was daring to feel, to think, to bless, to live! She was starting up the long trail to humanity ... how close she had come ... to becoming a howling wolf like those at night. How close she had come ... and so far to go before she could begin to live once more.

"Of the ten men and five women who had camped at the head of Truckee Lake on the night of December 16, eight men had died, and two men and all five of the women had come through. They had been thirty-three days upon the way.

George Stewart *Ordeal by Hunger,* p. 149

TAMSEN

At Alder Creek, everything was quiet, too quiet. Tamsen marked off the days on a calendar. Each morning she looked forward to penciling out another day.

Only a hide or two remained to eat. At first, she had wished that Jake and George had built their shelters closer together, but as time passed she was glad. It was easier to ignore what was going on at the other camp. Betsy had told her that if worst came to worst, she would use the bodies of the dead to feed her children. They needn't know what they were eating. She had seen the teamsters come from the wigwam and busy themselves around the spot where Rheinhardt, Shoemaker and Jacob were buried.

She would not think of it. She sent Jean Baptiste with a pole to prod again for the bodies of the oxen that had perished. He was such an unpredictable boy, lazy, impudent, mean, and yet curiously kind to the children, whom he seemed to love. She would never understand him. But no matter his rebellious looks, she was determined to make him work.

George's wound would not heal. She wondered how Mrs. Wolfinger could lie on her bed and sleep or cry weakly ... had she lost self-respect completely? Oh, she was being unkind. Adversity had made her intolerant. Poor woman, not able to talk to anyone in her own language, now that Rhinehardt was gone ... a good thing, she thought. He might have told her what he had told George. Well, George would make things right when he reached California.

There was no doubt in her mind that they would reach their goal. George would recover. He must. The other day, Betsy had looked at his hand and right in front of him, said he was not long for this world. Why did she put wrong thoughts into George's head?

Tamsen still read to the girls and to George. She made plans for each day; she refused to fall into the lethargy that lurked close to her. Still, she could not control her dreams. They were strange and disconnected. Tully, dear Tully Dozier; why he came so often in her dreams she didn't know. Sometimes he had tears in his eyes as he looked at her, sometimes he would smile that hopeful smile he always had for her. Then she would dream of rainbows and sunshine and happiness, and they would be children walking through woods with never a care, singing and laughing. How refreshed she felt then, but how disappointed when she woke! Sometimes she saw her first two daughters as they'd been before they were ill. Strange that George so seldom came into her dreams. Sometimes her father appeared ... sometimes she confused him with dear George.

Once, when she saw her babies, they were pinched and dying and she had wakened George with her scream. What a horrible dream it had been. They were lying in their small coffins, white-faced and cold, and a horrible man was standing beside them. He was sinister and hateful and meant harm. She heard Tully say quietly behind her, "Watch out for that man, Tamsen ...." Who was he? The devil?

It was always a terrible thing to wake to the darkness of the tent, feel the dampness rising from the floor, smell the thick biting odor of the pine boughs burning, the nauseous odor of the boiling hides. That smell would never leave her. She wished she could go back to sleep and talk to Tully and find out who the evil man was, what he was about to do. Tully and she had had so many plans ... he was enthusiastic, proud to help her. What was she thinking of? George too had encouraged her in whatever she wished. George thought it was a whim, a charming whim of a little girl, but Tully had treated her as a person.

One night she dreamed of her father. Then as she looked at her father, his face became George's and when she turned to introduce George to her father, he was gone. She went looking for him, through room after room, rooms she had known in many houses. She heard someone say "He has died ..." and she replied, "I knew he would, but I hardly expected it just now," and started to cry as she'd cried when her mother had died and she was only a child. She rarely dreamed of her mother, but she thought how nice to see her again ... now I remember her.

No sense in her dreams at all. Betsy said she was always dreaming of great holiday dinners and hot fires and clean clothes. Why didn't she dream of sensible things like that? She would open her eyes, and get up and mark another day on the calendar. If she did it exactly on waking, it would become a habit and she wouldn't lose track of time. It was important to know how long they had stayed in this tent. Pretty soon, after more days passed, she would start to hope again. And when George asked her what day it was, she could answer with certainty.

Cross out a day. Wash her face. Comb her hair neatly. Wake the girls. See that they washed their faces and combed their hair. Then the pretense of breakfast. Have the girls go outside, if the weather was at all favorable. See that they kept their bodies regular. Run a bit first, so they would be ready. Swing their arms, get their blood up. After that, they could come in for a little nap. The naps seemed to be getting longer and longer, or was it that darkness came so early? The girls stayed with George while she went out to her private place, and took some fresh clean air in her lungs. After supper she tried to have them sing a little. It helped pass the long nights. Too dark to read then. Lately, the singing had come so reluctantly from their throats ... weakly, unwillingly. They must try. She insisted they try. Elitha was ill, she was the weakest of them all ... but she could sing.

Then would come the dark and sleep, and sometimes moans. They couldn't help crying out in their sleep any more than she could prevent her dreams. She had tried keeping her eyes resolutely open so she wouldn't fall into another nightmare ... she told herself to rest her body without closing her eyes, but try as she might she couldn't.

Then the next morning, rise again, the dream clinging like a soft white clean nightgown, sometimes like a horrible black shroud. Cross off another day. She would corral her mind as they'd corraled the cattle on the way. It would prevent those Indians ... those bad dreams, from coming. She would walk one step after another through her days until one morning, help would come and she would be free.

MARGARET

By now, the shanty roof was eaten up. Margaret and the children moved in with the Breens. The Keseberg baby died. Lewis Keseberg stayed in bed with his lame foot, screaming and yelling. Little baby Catherine Pike was barely alive. Eliza was sent to the Graves' house to live. She could help Lizzie a little, perhaps. Eliza refused to eat the glue soup at first, but there was nothing else. The Murphy and the Breen cabins were housing more people than they could hold. The teamsters slept wherever they could; sometimes they didn't rise all day unless they had to. Sometimes someone from one of the shelters would climb out to look at the pass. In the Breen cabin, Patrick read and prayed and kept a meager, scant diary, day after day recording the weather, the bickerings and the deaths. It was good to know someone was keeping track. The children liked listening to him read the Bible aloud. The sound of his prayers was as soothing as sleep.

Margaret Reed scurried from place to place like a squirrel. If she *were* a squirrel, she would have gathered things against the winter. Would that there were nuts to find here! She made do with bones that she boiled. The dogs were gone by now, poor things. She scampered home with any little bit of treasure she found, exactly like a squirrel.

Virginia began to worry her. She had been so willing and brave the last time they'd attempted the pass. Turning back seemed almost to have broken her, and her frost-bitten feet hurt all the time. She had stopped talking about Milt or Papa or Billy ... she seemed not to care, staying in the Breen cabin, sipping the thin broth Margaret created out of thrice-boiled bones, or chewing one that had been crisped in the fire. Patty and the boys played outside in the snow when it was possible, but Virginia only watched them go with such shattered eyes that Margaret could have cried for her.

"I dreamed of Papa last night," she said to Margaret once. "I was fixing his cuts, back when it all happened at that horrible hill. I was washing his wounds and I was cutting his hair away from the cuts, and I hurt him. I made lint, just like that day, and put it in the cuts, and bandaged him up, and then I cried, and he comforted me. It was exactly like it happened!"

"You were a brave good girl to help Papa."

"He said that too. 'I've asked too much of you.' Oh, Mama, I wish I'd gone with him!"

"Whatever would I have done without you?" But Margaret wondered if Virginia had gone with James, would she have been safe in California now, or would she have died, when they were near exhaustion?

"I could see his bone in the cuts. They were awfully deep. He had blood all over his face and his arms."

"Head cuts bleed more, child. Try not to think about it."

"I thought I'd hurt him ... he said he hurt more inside."

"I know he did."

"He had to, Mama. He had to do it. John Snyder was going to ...."

"It's over, Virginia. We mustn't think of it, nor blame anyone. Papa did what he had to do ... you needn't feel ashamed."

"But people say things."

"Forgive them in your heart. That's the only way, Puss. Don't carry a grudge, or you'll be bent over all your life."

"Oh, I wish he'd come."

"We all do, pet. Now read a little. You'll forget."

"No, Ma. I won't ever forget."

"Well, forgive then. That makes you feel better inside."

Margaret knew Virginia was wandering ... she had never talked about the fight before. She could barely stand to see her thin arms and legs. Tommie and Jimmy were curled up in a ball in some blankets before the fireplace, out of Peggy's way. Well, she'd go out one more time and see if there was anything ... anything left to boil. Remembering the three beans made her sure there would be something she could find to eat. For the thousandth time she tried to figure where Stanton's mules might have wandered. If she could only find one, they would be spared. She took a long stick and kept poking it into the snow.

Everyone said the snow-shoe party must have died in the terrible storms that came after they left. If they were alive, why hadn't they come back? What was that hump in the snow? She poked at it with the stick. Only a rock. Oh dear God, she thought, please help us all. There has to be some way to live!

Almost in a frenzy she sloshed back to the Breen cabin. Virginia lay where she had left her. Poor Puss; she tried to lift her hand in a wave, but it fell back and she closed her eyes. Let her sleep, poor thing.

Peggy Breen was standing on the other side of the fireplace, arms akimbo, legs far apart, as a man would stand.

"And where might you have been all this afternoon?" she asked in the rough voice that Margaret had learned held kindness.

"Looking for lost cattle."

"You'd better be after saving strength for the young'uns."

"I know. But I thought I might find something." Her pot of glue soup hung next to Peggy's and she went to see if it was hot. "Some like it hot, some like it cold, some like it in the pot, nine days old," she thought. There was a running argument about whether the stuff was worse heated or cold, like a jelly. Margaret favored the heat. At least it would be safer. Mama had always said to boil things. The stench was far worse, though. There was not a great deal left and she tried not to look at Peggy's full kettle. One of the rules that Uncle Patrick had laid down when they had come to his cabin to live was that "ivery family for himself, and mind you don't touch any Breen food."

She had never broken her promise, though once she had taken a knife to bed, thinking that when they were all asleep she would chip off a bit of the frozen beef carcass that was stored next to a cold wall. She had lain awake until Patrick's snores started. When the time came, she couldn't do it. She would not steal. If they died, it would be an honorable death, at least. She scolded herself. "You're a simple-minded woman, Margaret." No one would blame her.

Little Tommie had to be forced to swallow the glue. "Isn't there anything else, Mama?"

The Breens didn't mind hides. Well, there were some leather shoestrings left to toast, and she'd found an old leather packet of James' in the things at the old lean-to. Tomorrow she would clean and scrape those ... maybe some pine-needles cooked with it would give more taste to the glue.

She should be glad to be anywhere at all and the Breen's cabin was much the best, though it was crowded. The boys kept Virginia and Patty laughing and teasing, and they helped Margaret with wood sometimes. She thought back to the days on the trail when the big Palace car was a gathering place for the women, and they knitted and talked and ate Eliza's biscuits and jam. She had felt more than a notch better than Peggy Breen with her bossy ways and her loud talk, and would secretly pity her for her huge arms and legs. Now she was Peggy's guest and she behaved as she should in another's home. Actually, she had begun to cherish Peggy as a friend. Her heart was kind, she didn't complain as Lizzie Graves did ... but then poor Lizzie was left with only her young children to help, and Billy Graves as rebellious as any boy that age would be. He had begged to go with the snow-shoers. Someone had told Margaret that Lizzie used to paddle down rivers in a canoe selling homemade soap ... she'd had no easy time of it.

Oh, it was easy to hate these days. Easy to let people hurt her. Easy to count grudges. If she put herself in their places there wasn't anyone that Margaret didn't feel sorry for. Lavina with that family of babies ... steadfastly trying, even if she was out of her head now, part of the time. She was so scared of Keseberg, who sometimes came to the Murphy cabin because he was too lazy or sick to build a fire in his, ranting and raving like people in houses for the insane. And look at Phillipine, often beaten, they said, whenever she raised her voice to the girl, or whenever he was angry. He screamed at her instead of talking and the words he used sounded disgusting. Losing her baby, after they'd had such a hard birth of it, back there on the Platte. Blessed thing, he was out of his misery. He didn't look strong from the first ... thank goodness all her children had been wanted.

Margaret looked down at her shoes. They were worse than any beggar's. Her hands ... she felt long strands of her hair wisping down her back. It was a good thing she had left that mirror back in the Palace wagon ... the one her friends had given her, "So you'll keep remembering to look just as pretty as you are!" Oh, if they could see her now! Shredded skirt, like a gypsy woman's. Black nails from the soot on the kettle. She smiled a little to herself, thinking of the old Margaret, protected and sheltered, that silly French straw bonnet with rosebuds ... think of it, rosebuds! on the brim. When James came, though ....

Peggy was saying, "Margaret Reed, you're day dreaming. Feed the little ones last, Margaret. It's Virginia that's needing her food first."

Margaret took a cup of glue soup and went to Virginia. How gaunt she looked! "Puss, do you think you could try to walk a little?"

Virginia's eyes were strangely glazed when she looked at her.

"I'll try tomorrow."

"Here, eat a little of this ...." Margaret put a spoonful into her mouth, but she had to catch it again, for her daughter's lips had gone lax. She gave some soup to the boys and Patty, and tried Virginia again. Patty, funny child, was holding her doll and pretending to feed it. Patty hadn't used to be such a doll lover, but now she was hardly ever parted from it. She put the spoon to Virginia's lips, but the contents ran down her chin as before ... why, that was the way it had been with Baylis when he ....

Peggy came to Margaret and said, "I'm going up for some air. Come along with me ...."

Margaret was about to say that she'd had fresh air that afternoon, but there was something commanding in Peggy's eyes, and her hand was firmly grasping Margaret's arm.

"Come along, me lady."

What was it now? Was she about to be put out of this house, too? She'd been moved and tossed from one place to the other ever since James left. She followed Peggy's broad back up the snow-steps to the air, so cold it felt like ice on her face. The sun was just about to go behind the pass. It had turned the clouds pink.

"Margaret Reed," Peggy began formally, "I think it's right you should know Virginia's going to die!"

Margaret's mouth fell open in shock. Puss? "Why, Peggy, she's strong yet! Her feet hurt, but ... Virginia die? Oh, no!"

"I've seen 'em die. She's got the look."

Margaret wanted to sink into the snow and weep till her heart broke. Did it take another mother to tell her about her own daughter? Why, Virginia was her standby.

"I thought you'd best know. Not today, but soon."

The two mothers stood, a vast silence between them, staring at each other. The snow muted all sounds and chilled the cutting edges of its knives. A sudden wind knocked against a tree which shed its weight of snow with a swish that crashed into the stillness, breaking into Margaret's agonized thoughts.

"I've been treating her as if she were a grown woman," she said finally. "She's still part child. I've been putting too much on her shoulders ... she's even cut wood!" Inside her thoughts were racing in horror, away from what Peggy had warned her of. My God, oh dear loving God, I can't spare her. Must I lose her too?

Just then a great hoarse shout came from the direction of the Murphy cabin. Whose voice was that strong, that powerful? Not even the crazed Keseberg could call out like that!

Hallooo! More shouting. Peggy and Margaret started on a trot toward the Murphy's. Margaret was praying in jerky breaths, "Oh God, let it be ... please God, let it be James ...."

Margaret tried to call back to the children, but the sounds choked in her throat. She needed the breath for running. She and Peggy ran, stumbled, once Margaret almost fell. She straightened, kept running toward the voices. Patty must have heard because she and the Breen boys ran past her ....

As she came to the crowd that had gathered at Murphy's, Margaret saw Lavina lift her arms toward the sky, as if in her blindness she was having a vision.

"Are you men from California, or do you come from heaven above?"

Seven men, each with a pack on his back, all wearing snow shoes, were standing and looking at the starved people who were raising their hands in feeble joy. Most people were weeping. Peggy knelt there in the snow and said a Hail Mary.

Margaret's eyes searched. Where was James?

"I don't see Papa ... " Patty said, holding Margaret's hand tightly.

"There's Mr. Glover ...." Margaret recognized him from those who had not made the fateful left hand turn. "And Reasin Tucker ..." a voice said behind her.

With Patty beside her, Margaret approached the men. "Have you had word of James Reed?" Then she saw, in the half-dusk, that their rescuers had tears in their eyes, and some were openly weeping. How they all must look to these great strong men ... skeletons dressed like depraved humans, death and starvation on every face. How they must smell to these men! Ragged clothes, torn, stained with the vile smelling soup.

"I'm Margaret Reed," she said, seeing they did not recognize her. "Do you have news of my husband?"

"He's just come from San Francisco this week. He's collected money for another trip. He will follow us as soon as he can, within the week if possible."

"*Another* trip?" Margaret started to say, but the children were begging for bread, and the men were handing out small bits of it. There were cries of joy and thanksgiving ... and then Margaret remembered Virginia, back at the Breen's. She and Patty accepted their portions and returned to Puss as fast as they could.

James is alive! James is alive! pounded through Margaret's head like a great trumpet blowing joy. I knew, I *knew* he had tried to find us before ... later I will know when ... I knew! Oh blessed God, I knew ...."

It wasn't the bread entirely that saved Virginia's life. It did, but without the news, the renewed hope that came with it, it would not have tasted so heavenly, nor would she have recovered so quickly. When Patty told her about Papa, Virginia's face opened into a smile of an angel.

Patty said matter-of-factly, "Well I guess the florn hope wasn't so florn after all. Here Puss, you can take my doll. I'm going back for some more bread."

For Thursday, February 18, Patrick Breen wrote:
Froze hard last night to day clear & warm in the sun cold in the shanty or in the shade wind S.E. all in good health Thanks be to Almightly God Amen.
For Friday, the 19th:
Froze hard last night 7 men arrived from California yesterday evening with som provisions but left the greater part on the way to day clear and warm for this region some of the men are gone to day to Donnos Camp will start back on Monday
Saturday 20th Pleasant weather.

This unemotional account of Patrick Breen is all that we have, first hand, except the memories of those who were there, recalled after a period of thirty-odd years.

All who were able to walk were to start the first of the week. Waiting even that long was taking a gamble with the treacherous weather. The rescuers, strong as they seemed to the emaciated party, were exhausted. None were true mountaineers, but great-hearted people who had volunteered to come. The fact that the Donners themselves were farther on also caused a delay. A guard was set over the supplies the relief party had brought, to keep the hungry from gorging themselves and dying from over-eating. The three strongest, Reasin Tucker, John Rhodes and Riley Moultry went on to Alder Creek, taking a small amount of food with them.

Noah James, Mrs. Wolfinger, and three of the older Donner children, one of Betsy's and Tamsen's two step-children were well enough to make the trip, although Elitha Donner was almost unable to walk. Both Betsy and Tamsen were able to go, but Betsy would not leave her young children, and Tamsen refused to abandon her own girls or George. Left in the Jacob Donner tent were Betsy, Mary Donner, Isaac, the baby Lewis and Solomon Hook. George Donner was not dead, but the infection had spread to his elbow. Left to take care of this group was Jean Baptiste, sullen and angry that he could not leave.

At the lake camp, all the Reeds plus Eliza were to make the attempt, for there was nothing left of their supplies. The two eldest Breen boys, Lavina, Eleanor, and Billy Graves were to go. Lizzie Graves had wished her son to remain with her, but when he promised to cut enough wood to last until the next party came, she relented. Phillipine Keseberg and her daughter Ada were included, if she promised to carry the child herself. Lewis Keseberg said he was too crippled to make the try. He then moved into the Murphy cabin. Both Mary and William Murphy were going with the party. Poor Lavina Murphy was left with only her own ten-year-old, Simon, and the helpless Keseberg to aid with the babies. John Rhodes, a particularly kind and compassionate man, offered to carry little Naomi Pike in a blanket; he remembered the pitiful face of her mother, Harriet, when she had struggled in with the Forlorn Hope.

The members of this first relief did not acquaint the snow-bound ones of the fate of so many of the snow-shoe party. To each question, they merely answered that they were in good shape. They could not heap despair on the heads of people suffering as these were; also, the news might discourage those they were escorting over the mountains.

The situation at the lake horrified these hardy men. Bodies, wrapped in blankets, lay unburied. Other dead were under the snow, many survivors were irrational. Some prayed, some cursed. The rescue party wanted to leave with their burden as soon as possible. Not an able-bodied man was among the refugees, for although John Denton was going with them, he was almost too weak to walk. Seventeen were left at Truckee Lake, two men, three women, and twelve children.

On the twenty-second of February the twenty-four, with their seven heroic rescuers started up the lake to the climb over the pass. Only a small amount of food could be left for those behind. To take thirty-one people back to Sutter's would use as much food as they had brought and more. If another storm hit them before they reached the first cache of food, they would be in a desperate situation. They knew another rescue party was on the way.

MARGARET

Margaret herded her little party along, following the clear trail left by the men coming in. No snow had fallen since they had arrived. Leading was one of the rescue party on snow shoes; all were to follow in the path he made. In spite of herself, Margaret was joyous and her spirit soared. The trail was there, clear and sharp. They would soon be free!

It was not long before her joy dimmed. The line, so compact on starting, was splintering. Elitha was struggling to keep up, John Denton lagged, and bless them, all Margaret's children needed urging. Virginia, amazingly, was doing better than Patty; little Tommie was the worst off. Margaret stayed with him, urging him to climb from one shoe print to the next, since his legs were not long enough to make the space in one step.

After a few miles, the party stopped for a brief rest. Mr. Glover, the leader, came back toward Margaret. When she saw him coming, she was afraid of what he was going to say, and her heart fell. No, no ... I can't ....

It was clear, he said, that Patty and Tommie could not make it this trip. He himself would carry them back to the cabins.

Margaret stood silently, hearing his words like the tolling of a church bell at death. Should she take them all back, should she let Jimmy and Virginia go on? They seemed to be doing well ... Jimmy would not make it if Puss failed; then who would care for him? The scales trembled, they balanced almost equally. Where was her place? What was her duty? Should she go back with Patty and Tommie, or help the able ones to make it? Eliza was not able to carry Tommie. Margaret could carry him part way, but what about Virginia's frozen feet?

Questions, thoughts and desires mingled in her mind. Through it all, she heard Mr. Glover's kind voice promise that he himself would return to bring the other children out. Could she believe him? Or would she be sending her two back to a certain death? She looked into Mr. Glover's face with eyes that reflected her fears.

"If you go on, Mrs. Reed, you'll get the older two out with you. You can carry Tommie."

The words whirled. Margaret thought suddenly of the thing that had always meant so much to James: James' Masonic insignia, which she had given Pat Dolan as security ... "Mr. Glover," she asked, "are you a Mason?"

When he nodded his head, she asked, "Do you promise on your honor as a Mason to return for my children?"

"I do," he replied seriously. Tall, handsome, strong, he was a man who had reached California long before they had. They had known him on the trail, and he had returned to help them. She made her decision. She must tell Patty and Tommie that they were to return to the loathed cabins at the lake.

Tommie was too weak and small to know what was happening; he only knew he was too tired to walk, and when the strong man picked him up, he laid his head wearily on his shoulder. But Patty fully realized what the decision meant. Oh, Lord, I have been asked to face so many things ... must you demand that I face this too? Margaret cried to herself. Her eyes blinded with tears, she took Patty's hand in hers.

Patty looked at her quietly. Margaret would never forget the sight of the tiny, spindling child, so chunky and solid a few months ago, as she reached her arms out to hug her mother. So small, so thin, so much a little mother already, saying "Don't worry Ma. Don't cry so ... we'll be all right ...." Where had the blessed child got her inner strength?

Puss was silent, holding Jimmy's hand, her eyes brilliant with unshed tears.

"Ma, do you want me to stay with her?"

"No, Puss. I need you to help with Jimmy. Children, we must all pray. Pray every day that your father will be here soon. He is on the way, Mr. Glover says ... (Oh, how she hoped she was telling the truth!) Mr. Glover and Mr. Moultry will carry you back to Uncle Patrick's ... you will be my good children, won't you?" Patty's face was so composed, so determined. Oh, had a mother ever had to do what she was doing?

The four hugged each other tightly, and in spite of her effort to be brave, Margaret dropped tears on their vulnerable necks, their thin, pitiful, raggedy clothes.

The men were waiting. The moment must be met.

"Goodbye, my darlings. We must pray for each other."

She gave Patty one more hug. "Take care of your little brother, Patty."

She would never forget the reply.

"Well, Mother, if you never see me again, do the best you can."

Eliza wept loudly, and Virginia and Jimmy watched the two men, each carrying a child, walk down the lakeside. Then they turned to follow the long line of emigrants, black against blinding snow, as they began the cruel climb. When Margaret next looked through blurred eyes, the men and her children had disappeared into the pines.

It was well that Mr. Glover and Mr. Moultry did not tell Margaret when they returned of the reception they found waiting at the Breen cabin. Before Patrick would take the children in, the men had had to surrender food for their care while they were with them. Promises that another party was on the way were made. Then they were allowed inside the Breen cabin.

Breen's diary does not mention this. The next day "they shot Towser and dressed his flesh" and later, "there has not any more returned from those who started to cross the mountains." A few days later "Mrs. Murphy says the wolves are about to dig up the dead bodies at her shanty, the nights are too cold to watch them, we hear them howl."

On Friday: ... "Marthas jaw swelled with the toothache; hungry times in camp, plenty hides but the folks will not eat them we eat them with a tolerable good appetite ... Mrs. Murphy said here yesterday that thought she would commence on Milt. & eat him ... it is distressing. The Donnos told the California folks that they commence to eat the dead people 4 days ago, if they did not succeed that day or next in finding their cattle then under ten or twelve feet of snow & did not know the spot or near it, I suppose they have done so ere this time."

The rescue party reached only the bottom of the pass the first day. Ada Keseberg could not walk, and her mother was not able to carry her. A gold watch and twenty-five dollars was offered the person who would take her out. The next day someone noticed that John Denton had not come up. Retracing their steps, two of the relief found him in a coma. They brought him in with great difficulty. One of the starved children stole the rawhide thongs from one of the snow shoes and ate them.

When the party reached the cache of food, they discovered that animals had eaten it. They faced four days of travel with the weakening children before they could reach the next cache. Four men went ahead to fetch the food. Two of these men were so worn out that they could not return. The other two brought supplies of dried meat to the party.

John Denton, with characteristic stoicism, told the party that he could go no farther. He asked them to go without him, since nothing could be done. Leaving the lone man with a fire and food they could ill spare, they went forward after cutting wood for him. Reasin Tucker left him his blanket. Poor Jimmy Reed, almost as exhausied as his brother had been, begged to be left with his friend, John, who looked so comfortable and warm, smoking his pipe.

During the night, Ada Keseberg died. Both her children dead, Phillipine could not be comforted. John Rhoads still carried little Naomi in a blanket-sling.

MARGARET

Margaret Reed pushed doggedly onward, holding her son by the hand, thinking of Patty and Tommie back at the lake, wondering if she had made the right decision and what James would have done in her place. Now that there was a definite goal, Virginia seemed to grow stronger each day. Margaret wondered how Virginia could keep up, but she managed without help.

Thank goodness, no storm had come thus far, though in a way, the trip was made harder because sunshine melted the snow crust, and the afternoons were difficult going. Children were better off ... they did not sink in the snow so easily. Sometimes they could slide. Once Margaret heard Jimmy scream with glee as he skidded down a slope. She had not heard him laugh like that for a long time. Several times she kept him on his feet by telling him that each step brought him closer to his Papa. She and Virginia would exchange glances: were they telling the truth?

On the way to the lake, the rescue party had set fire to dry trees, and the burned stumps served as markers. Margaret wondered at the bright hope those black signals held for her.

"The men say only one more day and we'll be at Bear Valley," Virginia said as they stood around the evening fire drying out their clothes.

Bear Valley ... the hope that had been held out all these months! They were almost saved! Mr. Glover held great hopes that they would meet the second relief party there. He didn't mention James, and Margaret was afraid to ask whether he would be with them. She was superstitious. She had a feeling that only a frail balance held them in life, some strength in them that could topple at any minute. She was afraid to question or think about what was to happen the next day, or the next. Hope might vanish as suddenly as every other hope had done. She could not forget Patty and Tommie in the Breen shanty. Puss seemed to thrive on action, on going ahead; she withered when she was left to wait. Patty would wait patiently ... maybe impatiently, but she would wait. Patty a waiter, Virginia a doer ... she could not do without either. If they reached safety and James was not on the way, she would go back with Mr. Glover herself.

Just then the men returned from Bear Valley. They brought food, and also information that no relief party was at the outpost. Margaret bit her lips, trying not to show disappointment. See? she thought to herself, you have been proud again, proud and demanding ... at least in your heart. Out loud she said, "They will be along soon."

Well, she was beginning to talk to herself as some of the demented people at the lake had done.

"What was it you said, Ma?"

"I was just being absent-minded, Puss ... thinking of Patty and Tommie."

"Patty will manage, Ma. Don't you worry so. Pa will come ...."

"With both of us believing, it must happen," Margaret replied, thinking how often she and Puss thought the same things. Still, as night came with dark and cold, she found herself steeling her courage against the news that James had had some sort of trouble ... else, why hadn't he come?

The next morning, their clothes stiff with ice, they all stood around the fire, chewing on their bits of dried beef before starting the morning trek. With four men gone ahead, the remainder had all they could do to manage the party. They were eager to start before the crust would melt. Jimmie didn't want to go. With reckless abandon, Margaret promised him that his Papa had a horse waiting for him in California, and he struggled to his feet.

"Today we'll take turns lifting Jimmy over the holes," Margaret said to Virginia. "Eliza, can't you help a little?"

"Mizz Reed, I'm doing all I kin."

"We must all do *more* than we can!" Puss said firmly, leaving Eliza gaping at her, shaking her head at what she couldn't understand.

"Come, Eliza, we don't want to be last!"

Virginia added mischievously, "There are lots of husbands waiting for you, Eliza, better hurry!"

Margaret was cheered. Virginia teasing again, and Jimmy laughing once in a while. Alas, they could not keep up, no matter how they tried. As soon as the crust became soft, Jimmy had to climb laboriously from one great print to another.

"Up and over! One step at a time," Margaret said, remembering how Mary Graves had urged her little ones ahead. "One more step closer to Papa." How many times since she had left Illinois had she thought to herself, "One day at a time? One week at a time ... one hour at a time?" With a hint of amusement at her own fantasies, she thought that when she arrived (if she arrived?) in California, she would do a petit-point hanging for the wall. It would say ONE STEP AT A TIME.

Just one more step, and one more step ... would she be strong enough to carry Jimmy if he fell?

Ahead, everyone was standing still ... something must have happened to the long line of straggling frozen scarecrows.

"Puss, what is it?"

Virginia's turned with a peculiar look on her face. "There's people coming ... they don't look like Indians ..." she began. Then there was a shout, and both at once heard a beloved voice cry out, "Is Mrs. Reed with you?" Margaret didn't hear the rest. She was told later that it was "Tell her Mr. Reed is here!"

She heard Virginia's cry and saw her start to run. Jimmy yelled. "Papa, here I am!" She tried to move toward that great beautiful voice of his, but she couldn't ... she couldn't take another step ... the world whirled around her, everything turned black except for a tunnel she fell into, and fell and fell ... and then, through a spinning, shining climb back to consciousness, she heard Virginia say, very close to her ear,

"Here she is, Papa ... I guess she's fainted dead away!"

PATTY

Riding on Mr. Glover's shoulders, Patty wondered what was going to happen to Tommie and her. She was so tired from the morning's walk she didn't know yet whether she was glad or sorry. The world had become so strange and undependable. All Patty had left to talk to was her doll, and it never answered back. Was she being a baby, talking to a doll? But with Puss and Mama and Milt and even silly Eliza gone, who was she to talk to? Tommie was too little to understand. He had fallen asleep in Mr. Moultry's arms. Tommie's eyelashes looked so fragile against his cheeks, he was pale and tiny ... oh dear, he wasn't going to be dead like Auntie Eleanor's little girl, was he?

Lulled by the regular lift of Mr. Glover's feet and the scrunch of the snow shoes, almost like the ticking of a clock, she finally went to sleep, and dreamed she was at a birthday party last year when all of them had been at home together ... Grannie and Puss and Papa and Mama and her aunts and uncles except Uncle Cadden. Mama had let her choose whatever she wanted for dinner and she'd asked for one of Eliza's big gooey chocolate cakes with the frosting all messy, running all down the sides and the candles put on any which way. There was fried chicken and she had a new dress and there was chicken gravy for the smashed potatoes ... smashed potatoes looked just like snow except there was a big pat of yellow butter running down the middle. Her stomach growled and she woke again, but the dream was better than thinking so she put her head down on top of Mr. Glover's big knitted woolly cap and it was almost like riding behind Puss on Billy ....

She woke when they reached the cabins again, and her heart fell way out of her when she thought that she and Tommie were alone, like once when Mama and Milt and Puss had tried to get across before. Oh, Uncle Patrick was mad as a wet hen! He didn't seem glad to see them at all. Tommie started to cry.

"Shh, don't you bother Uncle Patrick or he won't let us stay." Tommie only cried louder. "I want my mommie. I want my mommie!"

Funny that a grown man would cry like Mr. Moultry was doing. She was down off Mr. Glover's back now and she looked up at his face and he looked just as mad as Uncle Patrick.

"Haven't you a bit of pity in that black heart of yours?" Mr. Glover said, and then Aunt Peggy came out, her arms on her hips and started yelling just like a man, "What's this goin' on?" They explained all over again that she and Tommie had to be sent back to wait for the next relief. Uncle Patrick shouted some more about not having food to put in his own family's mouths, and the men talked some more. Mr. Moultry talked to Aunt Peggy, and then things looked better. Mr. Glover took some food out of his pack and said, "That's as much as I can leave you ... you've got two boys going with us, so you just think of these two as your own ...."

Mr. Moultry whispered to Mr. Glover that Aunt Peggy would make it all right with her husband. He just had to let off a little steam. Finally they were in the cabin again. It smelled even worse now that they'd got used to fresh air. The stinky old hides almost made Patty throw up. Mr. Glover gave her a piece of bread and another she was to give to Tommie very slowly, and told the children goodbye. She ran to the doorway and called, "Thank you very much, gentlemen," as Mama would want her to do. Then she fed Tommie some bread, and they hid in the darkest corner they could find so they would be out of Uncle Patrick's way.

"Don't you be a-worryin' about him. He'll get over it pretty soon. Just you keep quiet and he won't notice," Aunty Peggy said. Then she put her hand on Patty's head and added, "They say another bunch of men is comin' right soon, so you just be still and be after sayin' your prayers."

Patty whispered her prayers when she heard Uncle Patrick say his. "He does the prayin'. I does the work," Aunt Peggy said.

Patty felt better after a while, when she got rested, though she was as empty as an apple barrel inside. She liked to go outside when she could. Uncle Patrick complained a lot about his gravels ... what on earth were they? She knew enough not to ask, but she would remember and ask Mama and Virginia, when — if she saw them again.

If she saw them again? She thought that if men could make it in once, they could again, and if Papa was able, he'd be here, even if he had to crawl all the way. Cold as it was outside, it was better than inside, and she must be ready when the men came. She must be strong so she could walk better next time. It wouldn't take her a minute to get her things together. She had everything she cherished with her all the time ... her little bundle of treasures. All they had to do was pick up Tommie and start.

One day she had a bad toothache. In a way, she didn't mind, because for a while she didn't feel hungry any more. She was glad she didn't fuss about hide soup, because that was all they had after the men left. The food the men had left was gone already. Uncle Patrick always knew what day it was ... he wrote in that little book every day. She had asked him once when he wasn't cross what he was writing, and he said it was a journal. When she asked him what a journal was, he looked at her and said, "A book about what happens every day."

"That's nice, Uncle Patrick. That way you'll never forget."

Sometimes she thought he liked her, after all. It would be disappointing to have two more children when he'd just got rid of two boys. Sometimes he called her Martha, sometimes he called her Paddy. She didn't really care. He could call her anything, just so long as he didn't yell at her or scold Tommie when he cried. Tommie was thin as thin. No wonder he couldn't walk in the snow ... his legs were just sticks. She tucked him in his bed and took care of him like Mama told Eliza to do, and cleaned him up after he messed himself or was wet. There wasn't anything clean left to put on him. Oh dear, would Papa never come?

One sunny morning, she sat on the roof of the house, looking up the lake to the mountains where the others had gone. It was so bright she could hardly see. Yesterday an Indian had come all by himself past the lake and had left some kind of a root for Uncle Patrick, and Aunt Peggy had cooked it. She gave her a spoonful to taste, and she shared it with Tommie. It tasted sort of funny, but nice, sort of like a sweet potato. What do you suppose it was? She wished there was more.

Oh, there was something on the lake trail that was moving, something black. Oh dear, do you suppose it is a bear? she thought. Or is it the wolves Mrs. Murphy was always so afraid of, coming to eat up the people that had died? ... but she had seen ... no, she wouldn't think of what she seen the last time she went to the Murphy's. She bet it wasn't the wolves at all that had done that to poor Milt. She bet it was that awful Mr. Keseberg, yelling like an animal, screaming and saying all those bad words and looking so much like the devil ... bad words like John Snyder said that day ... at least they sounded like them. She squinted her eyes to shut out the glare, so that she could see if what was moving down by the lake was a bear or a wolf. Then black figures came out of the trees ... they hadn't gone toward Murphy's, they were coming right this way toward her. They weren't wolves at all! They were men! Big strong men, one of them 'way ahead of the others, walking as fast as he could. Oh, Tommie! Oh, goodness! Heavens! Her hair tingled hard on the top of her head.

She jumped off the roof and started to run. Oh! she knew she was dreaming! Oh, my! It was ... it *was* Papa!

"Papa! Papa! I'm here!" she called with all her strength, and then tripped and fell. Big strong arms picked her up and Papa kissed her hard and then said, "Where's Tommie?" And she said, "Is it really you, Papa, is it? Tommie's down there, sleeping," and it was the happiest moment of her life up till then.

Papa held her hand and they started down into the shanty. At the doorway, he stopped, and went in slowly, as if he was blind. She heard him say, "Oh, my God!"

"He's over there."

Poor Tommie didn't have any idea who Papa was. Papa looked like he was going to cry.

"Who dat man, Patty?"

"It's Papa, Tommie, come to save us and take us away!"

"No." Tommie turned his back to Papa and put his thumb in his mouth. " 'Fraid."

Tears were running down Papa's face, he felt so bad. "No, Tommie ... look, see? See, he's not anybody bad, he's our Papa!" She turned Tommie's head around. "See? I wouldn't say so if it wasn't true."

Slowly, tentatively, Tommie reached out his arms and Papa picked him up. Goodness gracious, Papa was sad. His face looked as if it were coming to pieces.

"If you've brought food, Papa, he'll get fatter."

Papa reached into his pack and brought out bread. "I baked this myself. Don't eat too much at first, Patty. There isn't a great deal. Give Tommie some, and then I'm going to trust you to give little pieces of bread to every little child. Do you think you can do that without eating it all yourself?" Papa's voice was deep and rough, she supposed because he was sorry he'd cried. Men didn't like people to see them cry very much. Oh, she was the happiest girl in the whole wide world! And she could make everyone else happy too! Wouldn't old Mrs. Murphy's face light up when she brought bread for those babies ... oh dear! ... oh my! she'd have to tell Papa ....

"When I go to the other cabin, Papa, will you go with me?"

"I want to clean up these children ... don't you know the way?"

"Yes." She took a deep breath. "Yes. But Milt's there, between us and the Murphy's ... and ...." Papa was looking at her. She had to finish. "Milt's all cut up ... his legs and his arms ... and his stomach ... just his face is there ...."

"Oh my God!" Papa said again, and this time he held her very close and hard. "My poor child ... my poor little girl ... what you've had to suffer, at your age ...." She could see him swallowing hard as she did when she tried to keep from crying out loud. Poor Papa. He didn't know all the things that had happened.

"You take care of Tommie, Patty-girl. I'll go to Murphy's place myself," he said. "Tommie will have time to get used to me that way. I'll be back soon ...."

Uncle Patrick was saying some prayers, and Aunt Peggy said, "The blessings of the Lord be upon ye, Jim Reed," as he went out.

"... at the Murphy cabin conditions passed the limits of description and almost of imagination. In the noisome huddle of filth and unspeakable things deep below the surface of the snow, Keseberg lay almost helpless. Old Mrs. Murphy was even worse; she had become childish, and laughed and wept by turns. Her boy Simon was old enough to take care of himself a little, but the two small children, the sons of Eddy and Foster, lay helplessly in bed crying weakly and incessantly for food. Reed and McCutchen [who had arrived with Reed] on their arrival at the cabin found Stone, the rough frontiersman, busily engaged in the domestic task of washing out some of the children's clothes. The condition of the two little boys was past telling, for they had lain in bed for days, unwashed and unchanged. Although Stone had already given them something, Reed was so moved that he even risked their lives by giving them more.

Then he and McCutchen warmed water and began a clean-up. First they took off their own clothes and laid them on the snow outside to avoid danger of infection with the vermin which now swarmed in the cabin. They then took up the children, soaped, washed and oiled them, and wrapping them in flannel, returned them to bed in a fairly comfortable state. Afterwards, the two comrades washed Keseberg, the man who had once raised up his wagon tongue for Reed's hanging. The irony of the situation was not lost upon the German, and unnerved he even pled that some one other than Reed should wash him. Such a returning of good for evil was more, he said, than he could bear.

As they worked, Reed and McCutchen could not remain insensible to what had recently been happening in the cabin. Only a week had passed since the departure of the first relief party. No one had died in the lake cabins, and yet (so close was the contest between starvation and rescue) that brief period had seen the bitter struggle for existence pass to another stage. Perhaps the feeling that relief was so close at hand had made life seem at once dearer and more precarious. A certain tone of desperation seems to run through the last entries of Breen's diary.

— George Stewart *Ordeal by Hunger* p. 213

The last entry in Breen's diary was:

Mond. March the 1st So fine & pleasant froze hard last night there has 10 men arrived this morning from Bear Valley with provisions we are to start in two or three days and cash our goods her there is amongst them some old they say the snow will be here untill June.

The roster of the second relief, led by James Reed and William McCutchen, contained names familiar to the Donner Party. Hiram Miller and Brit Greenwood had traveled in the same emigration. The "some old" is curious. Caleb Greenwood, 83, a true mountain man and the father of Brit by an Indian woman, had attempted the rescue but was not up to the strenuous climb and stayed at a lower camp. However, his advice was of great value. He is not generally thought to have been at the lake.

It seems strange that after the frequent prayers in Patrick Breen's diary that both entries concerning the arrival of the relief parties lack his usual thanks to God, Amen. Doubly strange that in no account does he mention James Reed or William McCutchen, nor does he acknowledge Reed's loyalty in returning to help those who had cast him out. In fact, Patrick Breen resisted returning with the relief parties, saying that he had enough hides to last him until spring.

PATTY

Papa wouldn't even sleep in the cabin that night. He and the other men, cold though they were, slept in the open air. The next day some of the men went with him to the Donner encampment. Papa would never tell her anything about that trip. When he came back, Mary and little Isaac and Solomon Hook were with him. Oh, she was so glad to see Mary! They had always been good friends. It was almost like having Puss with her. Solomon Hook was a big boy, fifteen years old, and he acted crazy. Mary told her that he'd tried to get away and over the mountains, all by himself, a while back, and when he came back he was snowblind and "crazy as a coot." Mary also told her other things ... awful things, that had happened at their place ... things like what happened to Milt. Finally Patty couldn't stand it and said, "Stop it, Mary Donner, stop it! I don't want to hear another word!" Mary had cried then and said, "Yes it was awful, but we couldn't help it, Patty! Mama wouldn't, and she's going to die!" Patty couldn't help wondering how the Reed family had been so lucky. Aunt Betsy was such a nice lady, the nicest lady in the world almost, and Auntie Tamsen was too. She wouldn't leave Uncle George. He was awful sick, Mary said, and was going to die any day now. Aunt Tamsen just stayed right with him, trying to make him believe he wouldn't die. It was Mary too that told her Aunt Tamsen's three little girls were going to stay until another relief party came in ... Auntie didn't want to divide the family till she had to. It took Patty a long time to forget the things Mary told her, and though she felt sorry for Sol Hook, she was a little afraid of him too. He didn't act at all like he used to, when they played games and had good times back on the prairie.

Papa, when he got back, was pleased with what the men had been doing. They'd hidden all the people's things in a cash so they could come get them when the snow was gone, and they'd got everyone all ready to leave the next day. Papa was nervous because people wouldn't hurry. He hated to be pokey, and he kept worrying about more snow storms.

People couldn't decide what to take and what to leave. Mrs. Graves had some money she wouldn't give up. Then she decided to take Jay Fosdick's violin because it was so valuable. All the rest of the Breens were going to go. Aunt Peggy and Mrs. Graves were going to carry their babies. It was like a Sunday School picnic, Patty thought ... all little kids except for the Breens and Mrs. Graves. They could make play ice cream out of the snow. Papa's face didn't look as if it was a party at all.

They didn't get started till noontime, and they only got half-way down the lake before dark. That night Uncle Patrick took Mrs. Graves' violin and played pieces on it and sang, though most of the children just looked blank and tired and still cried that they were hungry. The men were careful about making camp, and for once there was a fire big enough to keep everyone warm.

They felt pretty bad about not taking the two babies that were still at Murphy's, but they weren't well enough, Papa said. Patty was glad she knew exactly what she was going to take and was ready to go. She had what she wanted, and no one knew.

Patty heard Papa say to Big Mac that they'd never get this bunch of children up and over the pass, they were going so slowly. The men carried the little children most of the time, but Patty wanted to show Papa how brave she could be, and she wouldn't let them help her. Papa couldn't push them as far as the pass even by the second day, so he sent some of the men ahead to bring back more food from the place they'd hidden it on the way up.

Uncle Patrick wouldn't stop playing the fiddle the next night either, though they were all too tired to pay much attention. Patty heard one man say he was "going to bust that damned fiddle over Breen's head ... there was more at stake than that consarned noise ... he'd best help his family through the snow."

Papa looked at the clouds and shook his head. It was getting stormy looking again. Now that the men had gone ahead, there weren't quite enough men to help the children over the snow banks. Papa looked a whole lot happier when everyone finally started moving faster. At last they were over the pass.

Oh it was lonely that night! Patty stayed with Tommie all the time, because he still wasn't absolutely sure about Papa, and Papa was so busy cutting logs and getting people settled down to sleep and passing out pieces of meat and trying to keep the children covered that she hardly had time to talk to him at all. Papa had told her that by now Mama and Virginia were safely down in the valley, where there was a Navy man and a camp and supplies for everyone.

It was a terrible storm, as bad as all the rest. Worse, because they didn't even have a lean-to or a shanty to get inside. They all huddled down in blankets and Uncle Pat didn't play the violin any more ... he started praying again. That scared the children. They weren't as used to his praying as she was. Children seemed to cry louder when they saw that the grown-ups were scared. She busied herself with Tommie. There wasn't much food that night, just some flour to mix with water. Papa was expecting the two men who'd gone for food, but they didn't come. Papa and Big Mac and Hiram Miller cut wood as fast as they could, but my goodness, how frozen they all looked!

Reed had been keeping a diary during his expedition, and toward the end of this terrible day, crouched somewhere beneath the snow, he made his entry for March 6. As a courageous and self-contained man he allowed himself only one expression of his emotions, the simple statement — "I dread the coming night." At the end, he wrote ominously: "Night closing fast, and with it, the hurricane increases ...."

George Stewart *Ordeal by Hunger*, p. 225

PATTY

She listened to the wind howling. It was hard to sleep. thank goodness, Tommie finally drifted off. He lay next to her. Papa kept coming and going with wood, and each time he would look at her and ask with his eyes if everything was all right and she would nod yes. To Patty it was more restful to watch Papa and Big Mac than to sleep when her feet were so cold. Finally Papa came and lay down with the rest. He was rubbing his eyes, and he didn't seem to see her. She watched until he fell asleep. Even though everything was quiet except the wind and the fire, she still couldn't sleep. All of a sudden, with a funny rattling sound, the fire just disappeared! It had gone right down through the snow.

What a confusion of voices, everybody screaming or yelling and praying and Big Mac got mad and said a lot of words that sounded bad, but they weren't really. "Get out of my way, you Irish virago!" Papa slept right though it, and then Mac yelled at him, and pulled him up to the fire they'd managed to get started again and started rubbing his hands and feet ... it took a lot of rubbing. He and Mr. Miller kept saying, "Wake up, Jim Reed! Wake up, open your eyes .... You can't die now ... wake up!"

Papa die? Patty was so scared she could have cried, but she didn't dare ... there was enough crying as it was. She said her prayers quietly, as hard as she could. She was afraid to close her eyes, though, because she was wishing Papa would wake up and she wanted to know when he did. It took an awful lot of rubbing and trying to make Papa warm again. Finally he opened his eyes, but he didn't seem to know where he was. Oh, she was frightened! Patty had been so sure that as soon as Papa came, they would all be all right, and here they were with the Breens yelling that they were all going to die!

Oh! that awful storm seemed to go on forever! It just blew and never stopped, and there was nothing at all to eat. The little children started crying again. Patty was really scared, but she tried not to let Papa know. The men hadn't come back with more food. Papa's face was dark and tight, as if he had to keep his face straight and not give up.

Then the worst thing of all! One morning when Patty and Mary Donner woke up, there was Mary's little brother, Isaac, dead, between them. And they didn't even know! Patty thought that she was getting mighty used to people dying if she could be lying right next to a dead person and not even feel the difference. Then she began to wonder if Mama and Puss had really reached the place were there was food. Maybe they had been caught in this storm too and little Jimmy was dead between them. She didn't mention this to Papa ... she knew he thought they were safe. He had enough to do without thinking bad thoughts like those, so she just said a prayer to herself, quietly, not loudly like Uncle Patrick did.

Poor Mary ... she was so cold and numb that in the night, she put her feet right into the fire and burned them before she felt anything. Everything became confused in her mind. Mrs. Graves died too ... before or after Isaac? Mary cried, not because of her feet, though they hurt all the time, but because she was so sad about Isaac, and she'd promised Aunt Betsy she would get him to Sutter's safely. She wasn't used to Uncle Patrick's loud prayers, either. He would yell God All Mighty, save us, save us, if it be thy will, Amen, as if he yelled loud enough, maybe God could hear him. Mama had always said God hears us even if we whisper, even if we just *think* prayers. "Why does he yell so much?" Mary would ask.

Papa and Big Mac and Hiram Miller said it was madness to stay there any longer, and that anyone able to go on should make a try at it. No use to stay down in the snow-hole like animals. Uncle Patrick said he and his family would stay right where they were. God had brought them this far, and he'd see they got the rest of the way. Papa said he was facing death if he did, but Uncle Patrick wouldn't budge, just the same. Papa asked Uncle Patrick to say that in front of the whole company, so he wouldn't be blamed for leaving them. As for the rest of the men, they would go on. Uncle Patrick said it again.

I, PATTY REED

Oh, I felt so sorry for Mary. We had to leave her with the Breens ... she couldn't walk, even though she tried and tried, and she was too big for anybody to carry. I kissed her goodbye and told her that I'd see her when we all got down safely. Her brother Sol was going to stagger along with us.

The men piled up stacks of wood for the Breens, but there wasn't a single scrap of food to leave for them ... not one bite for anyone. I don't think the younger kids knew what was happening because they were so hungry, and crying all the time. Papa wanted to carry me, but I wouldn't let him. Mr. Miller was carrying Tommie. Papa had enough to do without carrying me.

It was hard walking at first. Then it was funny ... it started getting easier and easier. The snow was so bright I closed my eyes and then I was flying over the snow, easy as pie! Oh, I thought, this is beautiful! I'll get there before anyone else! The white snow was so clean and over it I flew like a bird. Like a big white bird. Then there were lots of white birds, but when I looked I saw they were angels. Real angels flying beside me, swooping and turning and going up to the stars and there was such a lovely light just ahead ... I'd never seen such a light before. It was so beautiful I couldn't catch my breath, and I wanted to cry with joy!

'Way far off I heard Big Mac's voice say something to Papa. They were miles away, down on earth, and I began wishing they would fly too, as I was, we'd all get there so much faster ... the angels were lifting me up, up, up.

Papa put something in my mouth. It tasted almost as good as the angels flying ... but then I stopped going up, and very softly swooped down, and Papa's voice was right next to my ear and he kept saying, over and over, "Patty, Patty, dear, wake up. Wake up!"

Finally I did. I hated to leave that bright, beautiful sky and the angels, but suddenly they were gone and there I was down in the cold snow again.

I was sorry because the angels made walking so much fun, but I wanted to tell Papa about what I'd seen, too.

Then I heard Papa say, "She's all right, but that was a close one ...."

The men all cheered as if I'd done something wonderful, and I felt glad I was with Papa and not flying away from him.

Big Mac said, "Now is the winter of our discontent made glorious summer! An Angel! Or if not, an earthly paragon!" and slapped his leg and smiled ... he wasn't a bit angry to see I had made them stop when we were all so much in a hurry. Papa looked at him and smiled for the first time in days. "That's the happiest Shakespeare I've heard from that mouth of yours, Will McCutchen, my good friend!"

Papa told me later that he'd scraped some crumbs out of the empty bread sacks and put them in his mitten for an emergency. That was what had tasted so good and made me wake up. "You never know what little bits of food will do," Papa added.

"I do, Papa. Mama was always saying that. We knew about your beans."

Papa put me in a blanket and carried me on his back. I felt sorry he had to do that, because he was awfully tired. I tried to be brave and not make him ashamed of me. Then pretty soon we found what maybe those angels had left for us, except Papa said it was the two men that had gone ahead for food. At the first cash, they found the animals had eaten everything up, so they went on to the next place. The storm hit them too, and they just hung a bunch of food in a tree and we all found it hanging there .... Oh how good it tasted, and how I wished the Breens and Mary were with us. We camped right there and rested and I saw our footsteps all with blood in them, like roses in the snow. All the men had frozen feet, but they didn't seem to mind they were all so happy. One of them even said he wished old Patrick Breen was there with his fiddle and they'd dance right on their bloody feet with joy.

Papa said that everything was about over. We'd be out of the snow, horses would be there to ride the rest of the way, and pretty soon we could eat all we wanted again. Mama and Puss and Jimmy would be waiting for us at a place called Sinclair's, waving and as happy to see us as we were to see them ... and it did happen that way. Puss said Mama had been watching for us almost all the time, looking up the trail.

Later on, poor Mary got out and she told me how it was to be left in the snow-hole ... they called it Starved Camp ... and how Uncle Patrick had sort of gone out of his mind and Aunt Peggy had tried to stop him, and that there was a wonderful man named James Rhoads who helped all of them get to Bear Valley, and I was glad she was safe, but I had to ask her not to talk about what had happened because it made me sick. "Maybe later I can think of it again, Mary, but right now I just want to be happy ... all our family together for the first time since way last summer." I was glad she made it out, and all the Breens did. The ones that didn't made me sad until I remembered flying around with the angels in all that light. I told Mary about what had happened, and I said I'd never be afraid to die if it was like that.

I showed them all that I'd brought from the lake. They laughed at me. Mama and Papa had tears in their eyes, though. Puss said, "Oh you funny Patty ... there's the lace from Grandma's dress and a lock of her hair and that little doll you've been talking to .... You are a dear sweet little silly."

Poor Mary. Her Pa was dead before she left, and Isaac died on the way and when she got to Bear Valley she heard about her half-brother Billy Hook eating too much and dying, but she knew her brother George was safe. Oh, how she hoped her Ma and the babies would come out with the next people! They didn't though. Aunt Betsy, Lewis and the baby died so there she was, left with nobody but queer Sol and George. Pa and Ma said she'd always have a home with us, and that made her feel better.

TAMSEN

Even though she herself had made the decision, when Tamsen saw James Reed start toward the lake camp without her girls, she suddenly wanted to call to him to come back and take them. Had she made a mistake? There was still time to run after him. Before she could make up her mind, he had entered the trees and was gone from sight. She had forgotten how fast well men walked; he had said he was in a hurry; another storm might mean a disaster.

He told her George's other girls were safe at Sutter's by now. Should she have sent her three girls? Oh, but they were pitifully young to go alone! She stood quietly, thinking, thinking. What should she have done? James said Margaret and two of his had got through, and he was taking Patty and Tommie with his party. No, she decided once again. The girls couldn't go without her help as James said, and she couldn't leave George to die by himself.

James had asked her not to tell Betsy that Bill Hook had died, but Betsy pried it out of the two men who had come with James. In the short time they were there, they moved Betsy's tent to a cleaner location and made her as comfortable as they could. Tamsen had offered to care for Betsy's two remaining children so that she could go with Isaac and Mary, but Betsy decided to stay with the little ones.

By the time James reached Tamsen's tent, he was grey and tired, close to breaking down. At the other encampment, he had seen what they had done to Jacob and the three teamsters. He looked as if he could stomach no more.

"I loved Jake. He was like a father to me, Tamsen ... it shook me to see ... how is George?"

Without a word, Tamsen led him to the palette where George lay. He had not been able to rise from bed for two weeks. She heard James' quick intake of breath. "George, old friend, how did you get this wound?"

In his voice which was now little more than a hoarse whisper, George said, "Jake says he slipped with the axe, but I think I caused it myself. It's not much of a cut, but it just won't heal ...."

"I've soaked it, poulticed it, given him every remedy I have."

"I'm a goner, Jim. Take Tamsen with you."

"I will. I'll leave two men here to care for him, Tamsen, till the infection subsides. I wish there were men enough to carry the children for you. They are too small to manage unless you go with them. There are too many youngsters to carry as it is. You are strong enough to go with them, Tamsen."

"I won't go."

"Tamsen, the men will care for him as you would ... think of your girls."

George's voice came again, with effort. "Please, my dear, go. Take the girls and go."

"... leave you here alone? Out of the question. I belong here with you."

George bit his lips, trying to avoid groaning with pain. "Sorry, Reed. The whole arm seems swollen. Gives a man a twinge now and then."

Bending over his friend, James saw the red streaks going up his arm. "It's a nasty wound, George. Don't hold back a yell." He turned to Tamsen. She saw his eyes sending her a hard message. "Will you and the girls go with me?"

"I'll keep them here with me, if you're sure about another relief coming." The thought flashed across her mind that if George would still be alive, she must send the girls out alone. "Then, if I must, I will pay someone to take the girls to California."

"Your other girls made it. You're well enough to go. Much better shape than Lizzie Graves, for instance. She's going."

Tamsen didn't answer. What Lizzie did made no great difference to her.

George raised his head with effort. "Tamsen, I know I haven't much longer. I beg you to go with friend Reed while you are still able. Death is very near, waiting for me. Tamsen, I beg you ...." He fell back, exhausted.

It was as if she hadn't heard him at all. "I will say here where my duty is."

"Your duty is to your daughters. Your husband asks you to go with them."

"We will all stay together."

James shook his head, and said his farewell to George, taking his good hand in his. "Keep up the good fight, George." When he reached the tent opening, he turned once again. "Tamsen, if you change your mind, be quick about it. We leave tomorrow. George, thank you for all you have done for me. You're a good brave man."

Tamsen followed him outside. When they had reached the snow level, she saw he had tears in his eyes. "This has been almost too much ... seeing Betsy and what happened to Jake ... and now George. I'm proud of you, Tamsen. Your tent is neat and cared for ... not like those others .... Don't give up, my dear."

"I will not, James."

"I will ask you once again. George is very near death. You must think of your daughters. God only knows if there will be another chance for them to get out."

"Don't ask me again."

"Well, Tamsen, it's your decision. You owe strength to your children as well as to George."

She didn't answer for a moment. Then she said, "A way will open up. No, I simply cannot."

James patted her on the shoulder, gently. "I promise to look after them as well as I can, Tamsen, for all of your sakes. If worse comes to worse."

"Goodbye, James, and God be with you."

"And with you, Tamsen."

Heartsick, far more unsure than she wanted to admit even to herself, she watched him walk away. She put out her hand as if to beckon him back. Another relief would come. Then, if George had ... she couldn't put the thought back into her mind much longer ... died, they would reach California together, as it should be. How was one to know her duty when things became so complicated? Tamsen had always prided herself on being able to decide things quickly. She took a few steps forward, then stopped. James was gone and the other men with him. She was alone once more.

She had sometimes doubted God's wisdom. She was a believer, but she simply couldn't imagine what God was thinking of to make things so hard. It tried her patience. She and George were loyal church-goers. She had even joined George's church, so much stricter than her own liberal New England one, had abided by His ways, had done good whenever she saw it ... hadn't she nursed poor Luke Halloran, hadn't she taken that German woman in, given her a home when her husband died? Mrs. Wolfinger was safe now, too, and Mary Donner on her way with Isaac and George, Jr.

Had she failed God? Hadn't she and George given thanks to Him for His care? If God would show her her error, she would try to atone.

Was it that they had been richer than the rest? Was George another Job? Was it true that it is easier for a camel to go through the eye of a needle than a rich man to enter the gates of Heaven?

Now it was too late. No use worrying over whether she should have taken her girls and gone with James Reed. But dear God, please remember that I have been loyal and true and stayed with my sick husband. I have lost my loved ones before ... is it fair that I should be forced to do it once again?

Before she descended to the dark tent, she stood looking at the mountains ahead, and at the great swale of meadow that had looked so tempting months ago when it was filled with grass ... a rich valley where they felt they could live if they couldn't go forward. Were they meant to lie down in green pastures ...?" only they weren't green then, but brown with dry thick grass "for thou art with me ..." but God had sent snow so deep that they couldn't even find the cattle that had wandered away.

It *must* come out right. She supposed James Reed couldn't understand why she wouldn't leave George. Did she herself understand it? Then she remembered how James had had to leave his wife and children. Once again a question came into her mind. If she and George had been with the train when the tragedy occurred, would they have been able to divert the tide of anger that had sent him off alone ... probably, they thought, to die? Still, if James hadn't gone ahead, would he have been able to bring help to them? Contradictory statements always bothered her. She liked things clear and definite, with Duty and Honor and Conscience on one side and Evil and Dereliction of Duty and Irresponsibility on the other.

Oh, it was hard to have on her conscience that George was the leader and hadn't been with the party when they needed him There was no one so good as George, but for the thousandth time she wished he had never been chosen captain. Not that it made that much difference until trouble came. George was easy-going on one hand, and stubborn on the other ... another contradiction and how she hated them!

Well, it wouldn't be much longer. She would keep the children in shape to go with the next party. Right now they must go with that Jean Baptiste, who rolled them all in one big blanket so they could watch him while he chopped wood. Lazy Baptiste, rebellious at not going with the party today. But he loved the children, and he made them laugh once in a while. She would write in her diary and read to the children. George seemed never to get enough of the Bible. As she started down the steps, an arrow of long-necked wild geese went honking by. It was an omen. She rejoiced. Spring? It could not come soon enough.

James had left a little food; with care, there was enough to keep them until the next party arrived. He had mentioned a man named Woodworth, who was "slow but sure." By that time George must be well enough to go. She must teach the girls what to say and do, in case they might have to go on alone.

In her mind was the sight of her two stepdaughters, Leanna and Elitha, dressed as warmly as she could manage, walking up the trail behind the men in the first relief party ... Elitha almost unable to walk, lying down ... probably fallen, and seeing Leanna help her up. Each had a blanket they wore as a shawl. They would use it to cover themselves at night. All alone ... half-orphans already, and about to be completely alone .... James said they were safe. Safe? Girls 14 and 12 in a strange country?

Within a few days after James' visit, a man named Stone had walked up from the lake camp. Tamsen didn't quite understand why. Probably to see how the two men who had been left behind, Cady and Clark, were faring. Since Clark was out following the trail of a bear he had wounded earlier, Stone talked to Cady. What were they talking about? Tamsen wondered. Finally they came to her and she listened to what they had to say. Perhaps she had been wrong in keeping the girls with her. Oh, her mind was a weather-vane, going first this way and then another! She hadn't sent the girls with James Reed, and now she was sorry. She *must* listen to what these men had to say ....

What happened when Stone and Cady talked to Tamsen is known only from reports *of the three girls themselves, Frances, the oldest, was eight. Georgia was six, Eliza only a little more than three years old. They recalled later that their mother offered the men $500 to carry them down to the California settlements. Mama put a few of their keepsakes and some silver spoons in the men's packs. She dressed them in their warmest clothes, combed their hair, put woolen stockings and their strongest shoes on them. Their red cloaks, like Red Ridinghood's, were to make them feel brave enough for the trip. Mama took them to the bed where their Papa lay, and they said goodbye. His face was flushed and twisted in pain. Was it from the hurt, or was it because they were gong away? Then Mama told them what to say when they reached Captain Sutter's. "We are the children of Mr. and Mrs. George Donner."*

In Georgia's own words: "The men came. I listened to their talking as they made their agreement. Then they took us, three little girls, up the stone steps and stood us on the bank. Mother came, put on our hoods and cloaks, saying, as if she was talking more to herself than us: 'I may never see you again, but God will take care of you.' After traveling a few miles they left us on the snow, went ahead a short distance, talked to one another, then came back, took us as far as Keseberg's cabin, and left us." Letter written by Georgia Donner in the Bancroft Library at University of California, Berkeley, McGlashan Collection

Not long after the three girls left with Cady and Stone, another of the ferocious mountain storms roared across the wide meadow and through the trees. Those left at the lake camp huddled in their shelters, hoped that the wood would last, and prayed for those who had been caught in the snow and sleet without protection.

When Clark awoke on the morning of the third day, the tent was literally buried in freshly fallen snow. He was in Jacob Donner's tent. Its only occupants besides himself were Mrs. Elizabeth Donner, her son Lewis, and the Spanish boy, John Baptiste. George Donner and wife were in their own tent, and with them was Elizabeth's (Betsy's) youngest child, Samuel. Mr. Clark says he cannot remember how long the storm lasted, but it seems as if it must have been at least a week. The snow was so deep that it was impossible to procure wood, and during all those terrible days and nights there was no fire in either of the tents. The food gave out the first day, and the dreadful cold was rendered more intense by the pangs of hunger. Sometimes the wind would blow like a hurricane, and they could plainly hear the great pines crashing on the mountainside above them, as the wind uprooted them and hurled them to the ground. Sometimes the weather would seem to moderate, and the snow would melt and trickle in under the sides of the tent, wetting their clothes and bedding .... When the storm cleared away, Clark found himself starving like the rest .... Just as the storm was closing, Lewis Donner died, and the poor mother was well-nigh frantic with grief. As soon as she could make her way to the other tent, she carried her dead babe and laid it in Mrs. George Donner's lap. With Clark's assistance, they finally buried the child in a grave cut out of the solid snow. Charles McGlashen, *The Donner Party*, p. 165

Nicholas Clark again made a search for the bear he had wounded, and by a miracle, brought back its cub. Now there was food. For Betsy, it was too late. The death of yet another of her children broke her brave spirit, and nothing could entice her to live. Samuel, the child Tamsen was caring for, died a few days afterward. The three graves in the snow were side by side. Of Betsy' and Jake's seven children, only Mary and George Donner and Solomon Hook survived.

TAMSEN

Tamsen did not think that suffering could be any worse than it was during the days of this prolonged storm. She was sick with worry over what had happened to her girls. George was delirious most of the time. Betsy's visit had left her aching with loss. When Clark came to tell her that her sister-in-law too had died, Tamsen was grateful that she didn't have to tell Betsy that her other son was almost dead. At least Betsy had known that Elitha and Leanna, her sister's daughters, had reached safety.

Tamsen was wild with regret for having been so foolish as to send her own three out, perhaps only to perish in this last violent storm. She was determined to send Mr. Clark to the lake for news of them.

On his return, Tamsen learned that the girls still lived. When she heard Clark out she became more frantic than before. He told her that the girls had been abandoned by Cady and Stone in the filthy Murphy cabin, without friends or champions, since there lived there only the crazy man, Keseberg and the now blind and mentally confused Lavina Murphy and some neglected, crying children. Clark had found the girls huddled together, weeping, trying to hide in the shadows of the dark cabin, lying on a pile of pine branches far from the fire. If they so much as whispered, Keseberg screamed at them.

Tamsen swallowed hard. They were alive; she should rejoice. Still, there was something unspoken in Clark's report that frightened her. He had said, when she asked him if they had food, that there was a danger of a death much worse than starvation.

Clark told her then that he and Baptiste intended to make a try for Sutter's Fort. She drew in her breath and looked at them in disbelief. That meant she would be here alone with George, who was becoming incoherent. They were to start the next day. She would have only a few hours to make her way to the lake camp to rescue her girls. Would Clark and Baptiste wait until she returned? She couldn't leave George alone.

They agreed to remain, and Tamsen quickly set out through the punishing snow to find out what hideous thing was happening that even Mr. Clark could only hint about. In her heart she knew it must have something to do with Lewis Keseberg.

Meanwhile, a third relief party was slogging through the drifts toward the lake. Four men, among them the barely recovered Will Eddy and William Foster, both desperate to see if their sons lived or had died. They had planned a swift dash from the summit to the lake and back in one day. They started at four in the morning, and reached the lake camp by dawn.

Even though James Reed had prepared them for the deplorable conditions at the lake cabins, they were sickened by what they found. Almost hidden by deep snow, the shanties were littered with filth and refuse of every kind. In the fetid Murphy cabin, Lavina Murphy was near death, and unable to care for the children, who were whimpering in the near darkness.

Only four children remained alive. Their sons were not among them.

When they recovered sufficiently to hear the stories the Donner girls told, Foster had to restrain Will Eddy from killing Keseberg. The death of the last remaining member of his young family under such sordid conditions was more than he could bear without striking out. The two men looked at the miserable creature, more animal than man cringing before them and turned away in loathing. Death to this man would bring him surcease Eddy would have welcomed for himself. Let him live. But one day ....

Since they had brought little food with them, they must start back as soon as possible. They made Mrs. Murphy as comfortable as they could, left her a pile of chopped wood, and prepared for their return to their summit camp. Each man would carry a child. Simon Murphy was able to walk some of the time as was Georgia, but the other two Donner girls would have to be carried all the way. They fashioned a blanket sling for Eliza.

They must leave before yet another treacherous storm arrived.

As they were making their preparations they saw in the distance a figure of someone moving toward them through an open space in the pines.

TAMSEN

Mr. Clark had told her it was five-six miles to the lake camp. Whatever it was, it was hard following his footsteps. Tamsen's anxiety made it endless. She had never felt so completely alone. She hurried on. No bear would frighten her, no wolf, not even the clouds building up ahead on the high ridges. She was strong. She wasn't hungry; after what she had endured this last week, she never wished to think of food again. She would walk, step by step until she found her children. She had not realized it was so far. What Mr. Clark had warned her about in the Murphy camp had at first sickened her with its possible meaning; now she writhed inwardly in horrible fear. She knew, but she did not want to know what he meant. She must get to her daughters. What she was going to do when she got there was not clear in her mind. She only knew she must get the girls away from Keseberg. The night his son was born still hung in her memory. He was inhuman, capable of cruelty when he was sane; when insane, there was no limit to what he might do.

Now, as she took step after step, having to reach and stretch to match her stride with Clark's prints, she tried to unravel Lewis Keseberg. Of all the people in the entire party, he was the only one she actively disliked. What was it in him she distrusted? Some people had thought he was evil. More tolerant than they, she had said nothing, waiting for him to declare himself ... misunderstood or villain? Even the night of his wife's birthing, his behavior could be caused by anxiety, worry, fear. She had never met anyone she thought was wholly bad ... perhaps because she was so sunny-natured, as George used to say. His bright little happy child, his darling. Of course she was sunny to George. He didn't believe in evil, either, although he stubbornly believed in the Devil. Who and what the Devil was he never said. While she, with customary optimism felt that if God was Almighty he would not allow the Devil to exist. Oh, dear, now she was getting into those confusing contradictions again. Would she ever be strong enough to go ahead, after these months of horror, knowing to what extremes man could go? There had been heights of courage and depths of depravity. Could she ever be her strong self again?

Step by step she went on.

When she mounted a small slope that Clark had taken, she saw ahead of her Truckee Lake for the first time. Narrow, flat ... a long white plain, with dark spots where the ice had melted since the storm. It looked calm, deserted, untouched. Where were the shanties and the lean-tos and the cabin she'd heard about? There were no signs of life ... only Clark's footsteps going straight down ... he said he had gone straight to the farthest cabins ... that of the Breens' and Murphy's ... the Graves' cabin was higher to her right. His prints would take her to her girls. With a lurch of her heart, she thought ... what if they aren't ...? She could not finish the thought. On she went, but in her anguish she hurried faster than her strength would take her. Stopping on the rise where she could overlook this place she had never seen before, she rested. Dizzy from the hurried walk, she almost lost her balance. "Steady, Tamsen, steady," she heard herself say. "You're just giddy ... you're not dying." She was too strong to die. Still the world whirled and tipped. With an extreme effort she kept her stinging eyes on the path Clark had left, and waited until the scene righted itself.

Only a little farther to go, Tamsen, she encouraged herself, only a little farther.

When she had joined George's church, she accepted, in words at least, that God granted grace to those chosen ones. But how did He choose? Why was she here, alive, when Betsy was not? Why had Betsy's children died, and hers survived? Why had Reed triumphed? Both Donner brothers believed equally; both wives had obeyed their husbands, attended church, given to the poor, helped the needy, kept the commandments. "In sickness and in health until death doth you part." She had accepted that. Oh, but God did not want you to be willing to accept only what you wanted, you must accept *everything* ... and she had always had doubts, horrible doubts ... was that why she was being punished? Think of Job, she said to herself. Tamsen, think of Job. He lost all his children, all his cattle, his men-servants and his woman-servants, all his wealth ... then received them again, because God could not budge his beliefs. Her mind always recoiled at the story ... not because of Job, but because of the wives and the children and their souls. Weren't they also children of God? Didn't they also deserve grace? Did they only serve as instruments to teach poor stupid Job a lesson? Was there justice?

Deep inside herself she heard her heart saying over and over, "My God, why hast thou forsaken me?" And it was the voice of agony, the voice of that first terrible loss ... the dying scream, the dying scream ... and as she recovered her balance, the world seemed to stop falling away from her, and she asked herself, a dying scream ... of what? What has died within me?

As soon as she felt able, she began walking toward the lake, shielding her eyes from the glare, towards that fearsome place ahead where her children waited. She felt strong again. She didn't put into words what her strength really was ... God, or George, or her love for her children, or her intelligence, or duty or survival. She just went on, as fast as she could.

It was as bad, if not worse, than Nicholas Clark had described it. Tamsen clenched her teeth together to stop a scream. The hovel was like nothing she had ever seen or imagined. The Donners had suffered, but something remained of order and civilization. Here was only filth of the worst kind, vermin, an open acceptance of cannibalism (she must not avoid the word any longer, nor the fact) bodies bare on the snow, their hearts cut out, sometimes with their poor recognizable faces left intact ... out of what kind of respect, she wondered? Legs and arms sawed off ... her three innocent girls here in this hell? The stench was so strong and foul it brought bile up to her mouth. James Reed had said he had cleaned things up as best he could "under the circumstancs," but she had never imagined anything like this. The horror if it hit her with all the strength of a storm. She would not have recognized Lewis Keseberg if she had not been told he was there. Where was the tall, handsome, straight German? A creeping, bent dwarf, with a full dirty beard crawling over his face, hair that was matted with filth. Oh the foul odor of the man! Lavina Murphy, the kind woman of the plains (could it really be she?) half-dressed, in tatters so dirty they looked like the rags of the wretches in Dante's Inferno ... babbling and laughing and screaming and crying, saying words Tamsen had heard no woman say, accusing Keseberg, pointing her finger at him, spitting, then laughing again. Poor demented woman. How could her girls have stood this place? They slept here with these distorted ... she could not call them humans. Oh no, no, no! Where would they sleep this night? When she said she would take them to the Breen's now empty cabin, Georgia said, "He'll follow us there, Mama. He sleeps with the little boys to keep them warm."

"Then they die!" Lavina screamed. "Then they die, don't they, you blackhearted devil? Like Jimmy, last night." She pointed at Keseberg. "Don't they die, you ogre?"

"Jimmy Eddy?" Tamsen asked. Had Will Eddy lost him too?

Frances said, "Mama, his papa came this morning and cut him down. Mr. Keseberg hung him by the door when he died."

Tamsen had too much. She ran up the snow-steps, retching.

When she at last regained control of herself, Tamsen began putting the pieces of the puzzle together, although her first wish had been to die rather than hear any more. The girls told her of the arrival of Uncle Will Eddy and Mr. Foster, and that they were going to take them all out of the mountains.

Will Eddy here? She sighed in relief; there would be one sane person to steady her in this nightmare. Oh, but Will had lost everyone! How could the man face life again?

When they met she managed to say, "Will, I am sorry." What was that to this man who had lost everything he had in life, his wife, his two beloved children?

Will took her hand slowly. His eyes were tired, tortured, puzzled. "I wanted to kill him, Mrs. Donner. I don't know why I didn't ... maybe because death is too good for him. This is a nightmare and I can't wake up. I hoped that little Jimmy at least ...."

Did she dare ask him to take her children when he had expected to take his own? She must. After a pause, she began tentatively, "Will, I have $1500. Will you take it and my children to the settlements in California?"

He looked at her as if she were speaking some strange language. He said wearily, "Money? to take out your children, Tamsen? No. I cannot carry money, but I can carry children. Our men will see that they get out. But not for money. Money is a heavy burden, children are not."

She could only say, "Will you are a good man. You are good."

"Will you be going with us?"

"Can you wait while I go back to George? Perhaps I am free to go."

Again his look was strange. For some reason she remembered the story of Niobe and her pride. Had she not learned yet? She must be punished further.

"Another storm may come. We dare not wait."

Will Foster nodded his head in agreement.

She stood silently, the wavering light from the fire against the great rock patterned her face. Her body, still firm and lithe, able to go, able to help these two men who had lost children, who were to take hers with them. The three little girls she had brought into being, had taught their letters and to read and spell, to behave ... were they equipped to go forth to a new world alone? Three-year-old Eliza looked at her with great frightened eyes, but eyes more innocent than those of Frances and Georgia ... mere children, going across the mountains to a new life. Will would get them there. Will was a good man. James Reed had said he would care for them if he could. What would it be like for them? She had parted with them once, forever, she thought. Now she must do it again. This time it would be forever unless —

Will Eddy and Will Foster would carry them out. She ... why? ... would go back to that bleak open place on the creek, where, as soon as she had returned, the men would leave her alone with a dying man. Oh my God, she cried in rebellion, you cannot do this to me! You cannot break my spirit as the Romans tore the Christians apart! Ripping their bodies in two until they died in screaming agony.

"You start when you must. I will follow when I can. I will bless you both until my dying day." In her confusion and weariness she looked at Will in the dark of the dirty, lice-crawling, urine stench, fecal odor, dead-body rotting reek ... with these horrors staring him in the face, she saw Will Eddy plain, with a halo around his head. She knew it was a dream-figment, but there he stood, sainted and good.

Strong as she was, she felt her body sway. She would just let go, just this once. She and Eddy had held on to their sanity. He stood with the memory of this morning's horror in his eyes, sane. She would let go. She could not fight any more.

In a calm, controlled voice, she heard herself say, "I will follow if I can, Will. I will pray forever for you. Take my girls, and God be with you."

She could not believe it was she talking. In a sort of out-of-focus dream, she said goodbye once more to her and George's three girls. "Be good children, and do as Uncle Will says, and be sure to remember that you are the children of Mr. and Mrs. George Donner."

She dared not look at their faces nor their eyes. She would never see them again. She walked to the door and up the steps of the ice tunnel. At the top, she turned, "God bless you all!" she said, and started away, steadily, one step after another, across the barren snow, toward the east ... where George was, by Alder Creek. She did not turn once to look back. Had she turned, she would have been lost. Then, as if she were a bird, she saw her lone figure, black against the snow, disappear into the trees.

By the time the four men and their charges reached the foot of the pass, it was already nearing dusk. Suddenly through the trees ahead of them, they saw two men bearing packs on their back. They recognized Jean Baptiste Trubode and Nicholas Clark. They had left the Donner cabin long before Tamsen returned. Poor Tamsen was left alone with George at the upper encampment.

Their excuses were flimsy. They were afraid of a new storm, there would be fewer people to feed, another relief was on its way.

Foster and Eddy could not help but remember the slight, determined figure disappearing in the trees. Eddy shook his head sadly. "You should have waited till she got back."

"She knew we were leaving anyway. She'll manage."

When they discovered what was contained in the packs, Eddy could only stare in disgust and disbelief. They had looted the cabins. The weight they carried was far heavier than a child would have been. Exhausted by the day's horror, Will Eddy was silent. He thought he had lost everything. These men had stolen more than guns and silver. They had also taken what little remained of his belief in his fellow man.

TAMSEN

When Tamsen reached the camp on Alder Creek, she found it silent. She was alone with George. There was no one to cut wood, to hunt for food, to help her with George's wasted body. A week wore on, then another. When Tamsen crawled out of the tent to find wood, the bleak landscape frightened her. Snow was melting once more, wood was easier to find and less was needed. She continued to mark the days on her calendar. The damp floor of the hut no longer bothered her. George lay on his bed as he had done for these many months, groaning occasionally, always with a weak smile for her when she went to his side. She closed her mind to the smell of his body, to the details of his illness.

Half-formed thoughts raced dream-like through her mind, like children freed from school after a long day. They tangled with each other, pummeled and punched, yelling as boys used to do when lessons were over. Every day she tried to get outside, move about, keep herself ready. She used the small amount of bear cub meat sparingly; she boiled the bones over and over. Each time the broth was thinner and less nourishing.

It was eerie to be alone. Walking in the deserted landscape, she had a sense of being outside herself looking in, wondering sometimes what kind of being she was, why she was here, even wondering if she actually existed except in her own mind. Sometimes, terrified, she ran back to the tent, woke George from his half-coma, talked to him, read the Bible, held his hand in hers tightly, anything to make her feel not so alone.

Sometimes in the night when she could not sleep, she looked toward the man who was dying so slowly. How gaunt he was. No youthful flush on his cheeks, no hearty laugh, no hand to chuck her on the chin, or pull at her escaped locks of hair ... nothing but a sort of goodness flowing from his face, as it always had, no matter what happened. Once a funny, twisted smile appeared. She saw he was watching her, his eyes glazed. He raised his good arm. "Come, Tamsen. Come to me."

She rose from their pitiful fire, their sad symbol of home, and knelt by his bed, close to his face.

"I want you to go, Tamsen."

He didn't realize that everyone had gone.

"No, George."

"You must. For the sake of the girls. For yourself ... you're still young." It was hard for him to speak ... his booming voice was only a whisper. "I'm done for. I know it. I don't mind thinking about it. I want to die. I want you to go with Jim Reed."

She shook her head, unable to tell him Reed had gone long before.

"Will Eddy ... he's a good man. He will take you with him." She had told him about the girls. She was surprised he remembered. The pressure of his hand on hers was the only thing she felt for a few moments while he struggled to say more.

"For my sake, Tamsen."

"No, my dear. No."

He closed his eyes. Tears ran from under his lids. She could not bear to see his eyes begging her. He turned his face away and she smoothed his hair.

The fire needed some more wood, or it would perish. She might not be able to start another. She went to the door and brought back a handful of half-wet branches and some chips, and threw them on the darkening coals.

"Whither thou goest, I will go," she whispered to herself ... or to him? She would not give in to his persuasions as she had last spring when he had asked her to take this trip. This time, she would stay.

When he died at last, she laid him out, washed his face, closed his lids over his blank eyes, folded his hands, and put a clean blanket neatly over his thin, wasted body. When she had finished, she gathered up whatever she could carry. She put on warm clothes, blindly selecting whatever might be useful. There was only one thought in her mind: to go to her children. For the second time she crossed the long slope leading to the lake. She was frantic with haste. As before, going as fast as she could, she was forced to stop by a cramp in her side. Strangely, it was where she had stopped that first time. This time the shelters and the cabins were visible, and she saw, with an explosion of joy in her heart, that a thin wisp of smoke came from one of them. By the time she reached the lake, it was almost evening. Spring was evident: the ground was plowed by small animals underneath, the earth was spongy with melted snow-water, the ground was exposed, though snow remained in shaded places, hard and crusty. Birds moved and flew, she saw a squirrel pop up and look at her, the air was sweet with spring. There were fellow humans here! Who remained in this place? She would find out, and tomorrow after she had rested, she would start over the mountains to find her daughters. Snow still glinted pinkly on the pass, from the sunset.

She knocked before she entered. A gutteral voice, as unused to speaking as she herself was, growled something at her. So Keseberg remained.

She opened the door flap and went in.

When the June sunshine gladdened the Sacramento Valley, three little barefooted girls walked here and there among the houses and tents of Sutter's Fort. They were scantily clothed, and one carried a thin blanket. At night they said their prayers, lay down in whatever tent they happened to be, and, folding the blanket about them, fell asleep in each other's arms. When they were hungry, they asked food from whomsoever they met. If anyone inquired who they were, they answered as their mother had taught them: "We are the children of Mr. and Mrs. George Donner." But they added something they had learned since. It was, "And our parents are dead."

Charles McGlashen: *History of the Donner Party,* p. 204

Note From The Author

I have struggled with Tamsen, fighting her all the way, woman to woman. Like Sacajewa, Tamsen is a legendary heroine. This heroine is hard to understand. I end not knowing if I have ever understood the real Tamsen, although at times, while walking and pondering her, I have had clear thoughts.

From the first I saw Tamsen as a high hurdle. To understand a woman who could allow her small children to go alone into a strange land without protectors, money, nor help, boggles my mind, especially since her dying husband is pleading with her to go with their girls. To me there is something more here than meets the eye.

If the promise 'till death do us part' holds, then the values of motherly love and survival do not. So many unknowns are part of Tamsen's character: intelligence, discipline, goodness, courage — the attributes of a model woman. Yet, to me, there is a 'shadow of a doubt.'

She loved and cared for many people: Luke Halloran, the lonely consumptive, Mrs. Wolfinger, who wept in another language. Tamsen strove for order and reason in lives that would have been empty without her. No one casts doubt on her goodness. Am I too simplistic to understand her, or am I not simplistic enough?

Nagging details tangle in my mind. A suggestion in one text that she was a little finer than the other wives, the peculiar remark in her letter to the Springfield editor about George — "George Donner is himself yet. He crows in the morning and shouts out 'Chain up boys, chain up,' with as much authority as though he was 'something in particular'" — the fact that she offered money sometimes instead of love. By her own admission, she did not believe in Hastings' fairy tales, yet sent her three daughters, 8, 5, and 3 years of age through the snows to California without any assurance of their safety in a raw country. She paid to have them carried out; they were abandoned, yet she later offered money again for their passage. Luckily, the three survived and lived to good ages. In adulthood, they accepted their mother's actions as right.

For me there is an unexplainable mystery in Tamsen. I have weighed the loss of her first family by an epidemic, probably cholera; I have considered the fact that she was much more educated and much younger than George Donner, and I admire her indomitable spirit and courage. I have also wondered if there was not a great deal of disillusionment hanging over her at the end. Why did the Donners go ahead when the traveling was hard, and leadership needed? Was she happy with George's decision? Did she realize what she would face in California if she had gone with her girls, which by all accounts she was perfectly able to do? Was she just too exhausted by life to want to start over a third time? Although she willingly sent her two stepchildren, one who was grievously ill, with the first relief, she kept her own with her until it was almost too late.

She remains a mystery as her death was. Where her bones lie, no one has ever known. Her daughter Eliza, 3 years old at the time she left her, years later took Lewis Keseberg's hand in her own, looked into his eyes and was convinced that he had not killed her mother. Even the man who saw her last gave no clue.

I do not doubt Tamsen's heroism and goodness. But what she was, what she thought and felt that was not expressed, I have only understood in fleeting flashes of understanding.

THE ICEBERG BENEATH
— NOTES—

LANSFORD HASTINGS

Who was this Hastings?

Irene Paden, in *Prairie Schooner Detours,* p. 10, says, "A great deal has been said and written about Lansford Hastings' ambition and selfishness. Most of it is no doubt true. He was young — only twenty-three; a lawyer, and had the most unbounded confidence in himself, never hesitating to dominate a situation." Ralph Moody, in *The Old Trails West* says, "The Donner tragedy ... was brought about largely by the chicanery of Lansford Hastings. Ambitious, dishonest, and a clever propagandist, Hastings had arrived by sea in 1843, when the first surge of Oregon migration was at its crest. He was quick in observing the weakness of the Mexican Government, and equally quick in divising a scheme for turning it to his own advantage ... he believed he could overthrow the Mexicans, set up an independent nation, and establish himself as ruler ...."

In Dale Morgan's *The Humboldt,* the author continues the story: "California now seemed ripe for the plucking. Bring here a great company of American emigrants, long rifles ready to their hand, and a man would need nothing but the spirit to act. He might yet be president of California .... To publish his lyrical picture of California (Hastings' *The Emigrant's Guide to Oregon and California*) he had traveled to the length and breadth of Ohio, lecturing upon the evils of intemperance ... it paid for his book." Moody again: "With practically no knowledge of geography, and no investigation he invented the Hastings' Cut-off, and assured prospective emigrants that by taking it they could reach California quickly and easily. They would simply turn their wagons away from the Oregon Trail at Bridger's Fort bearing westsouthwest, to the Salt Lake; and thence continue down to the Bay of San Francisco."

In *The Year of Decision,* by Bernard De Voto, this comment is found: "Anyone who studied a map at Fort Laramie, intending to go to California, would look with loathing on that detour (the arc northward through Fort Hall) which was one side of a triangle." The Hastings' Cut-off would "reach the Humboldt almost exactly where a line traced due west from Fort Bridger would have reached it." De Voto's last comment is ominous: "On June 27, 1846, no map ever drawn had filled in the country between Fort Bridger and Great Salt Lake — no map showed what the Wasatch Mountains were like. And no map filled in the country between Great Salt Lake and the north bend of the Humboldt River ...."

THE PALACE CAR

Possibly in the entire western movement to California there was no larger wagon than James Reed's Pioneer Palace Car, so-called by his daughter, Virginia. A cabinet maker, Reed spent much thought on the vehicle that was to carry his cherished family west. It loomed above every other wagon starting from Independence in May of 1846. Because his wife was often unwell and his mother-in-law was in failing health, he strove to make it as much like a home as possible. The living quarters were spacious, furnished with easy chairs, carpets, and even a wood-burning stove. He planned his storage well, adding special chests for the children's toys, space for some good old wines, another for cherished family possessions. This was foolish of him, perhaps, but he wanted the best for his Margaret and their family. He had no real idea of the difficulties of the trip. Perhaps by the time he was forced to abandon the cumbersome vehicle on the white sands of the Salt Lake Desert, he had already realized that the Palace Car was doomed. In any event, there is no record of complaint on his part when he cached the wagon with all of its luxuries left behind.

WAHSATCH, WASATCH, WAGON, WAGGON

I have chosen the older spelling of Wahsatch to invoke the age. In using wagon instead of waggon, I have used the more familiar spelling, although Tamsen used waggon in her letters.

GLAUCUS

Proof readers have difficulty with the name of James Reed's silver-gray blooded mare, Glaucus. George Stewart's witty remark on the subject bears repeating: "He (James Reed) dashed back and forth upon his prized gray racing mare, called in fine defiance of Latin gender, Glaucus."

STANTON AND McCUTCHEN, STANTON AND PIKE

A poll of references mentioning the men who accompanied James Reed when he went ahead to overtake Hastings show an almost equal division on their identities. J. Quinn Thornton and Charles McGlashan state that Pike was the man and Bernard De Voto agrees with them. Later in his history Thornton reverses his decision in favor of McCutchen. George Stewart indicates that it was McCutchen. Even in the Reed family, memories do not agree. James Reed and Patty say McCutchen accompanied him and Stanton. Virginia Reed says it was William Pike. While reading George Stewart's neatly penciled notes, I realized that he too had noted the discrepancy. He comments that the two men, Pike and McCutchen were of the same height and of similar builds and coloring and comes to the conclusion that surely Reed would have remembered correctly. This is perhaps the only place in my research that I have taken an opposite view from Stewart's. William McCutchen had joined the party only a few days before, having been delayed by an illness which had forced him to drop back to join the Donners. To me, it seemed unlikely that he would leave his young wife and child to strangers under these circumstances. Also, McCutchen read McGlashan's account and agreed that it was, on the whole, correct. being an honest man who called a spade a spade or something worse, I doubt that he would have allowed the error to go by without comment. Relatives of McCutchen could shed no light on the matter, either. One must take into account that Pike later was willing to go forward at Truckee Meadows when he was accidently shot, so he can be reckoned as a man who might have volunteered earlier. It is one of those points that drive a researcher crazy.

THE FORLORN HOPE

Whether the forlorn hope existed as a proper title at the time is problematical. Patrick Breen's diary refers to the group as the snow-shoers, but he has not a man for poetic symbolism in his diaries. I have not capitalized it, although my feeling is that it was indeed a proper name. During the many crossings emigrants named camping places of particular interest, possibly because it was a way of establishing special events. Independence Rock was so named because an early party had celebrated the Fourth of July there. In the Donner Party, one of the miserable camping spots in the Wahsatch Range was named Mad Women's Camp. The second relief named one of their stopping places Starved Camp. Another name, Camp of Death is the saddest of all. A letter from Georgia Donner refers to the snow-shoers as the Forlorn Hope. This was written thirty years afterwards, and may have been picked up in conversations.

$10,000 DOLLARS IN A DONNER QUILT

Historians have frequently mentioned a sum of money Tamsen sewed into a quilt. That the Donners were liberally supplied with money is not to be denied ... however, I believe the quilt story to be a charming myth. Since it has no real bearing on the events, I have chosen to ignore it.

RICH DRESS ON THE PRAIRIE CROSSING

In a recently reissued book, "The Gentle Tamers," by Dee Brown (see bibliography), the author comments that during the gold rush era, women frequently went, or were taken west to be prostitutes. They were easily identified by the gaudiness and richness of their clothing. It is a provoking thought.

ARRANGEMENT OF THE PRAIRIE SCHOONERS

In the book "Women of the West," by Cathy Luchetti and Carol Olwell there is a charming letter written by a young woman describing in great detail just how her wagon was arranged for the trip across the plains. Too long for inclusion in this book, it is delightful supplemental reading, and explains much of the necessary planning and organizing required for living in a narrow covered wagon.

HIRAM O. MILLER

I was almost finished with this book before I began noticing a "mystery man" hovering in the background of many accounts of the saga, Hiram Miller. Apparently more than a teamster, he was also a good friend of both the Reeds and the Donners. Tamsen mentions him particularly in her letters to Mr. Francis, the Springfield editor.

With Edwin Bryant and others, Miller left the party to go ahead on mules. In Bryant's book he figures often, as he stayed with him and was in Fremont's 'conquest' of California. Miller also saved Reed's life when he was overcome in a storm. Not only that, but he was one of the four men who made the forced march into Truckee Lake to try to rescue Foster and Eddy's sons. Later he was appointed guardian of the Donner children's property recovered from the lake and from Keseberg. He carried the three little Donner girls with him. Little Eliza was angry at him for promising her sugar if she would walk for a while, only to tell her there wasn't any. Georgia remembers the comfort of riding on his shoulders on the trip out. William McCutchen, describing the events of Starved Camp to McGlashan says that when Reed was overcome by exhaustion "Hi Miller and myself took over ... Hi Miller being a man of Herculean strength and endurance," was the savior of the party. Later he adds "Do not fail to mention the name of Hi Miller as being altogether lovely in the relief party." Lovely seems a strange word for the direct-speaking McCutchen (the writing is unclear and he may have used a similar word to express admiration.)

Virginia Reed tells McGlashan that Hiram Miller was always their friend and welcome in their home. He is buried with many others of the party in San Jose's Oak Hill Cemetery.

BRYANT'S LETTER AT FORT BRIDGER

Although Tamsen and the others looked for word from Bryant at Fort Bridger, it was not discovered until later that indeed their friend had left a letter urging the party on no account to take Hastings' cut-off, but to turn north at Bridger on the old Oregon Trail to Fort Hall. The letter was not delivered. Traffic through Bridger had been threatened by Greenwood's cut-off; the little fort depended on Hastings' new trail, known only by hear-say, to keep it solvent. Vasquez, Bridger's partner is usually blamed for the failure to deliver the letter to the Donners.

JOTHAM CURTIS

In the roster of the first relief appears the name of Curtis, who, with his wife, was brought complaining all the while, down from the mountains by Reed and McCutchen. Lest his name go down in glory for his participation in the rescue, it should be mentioned that as soon as the relief reached his snow-buried cabin, Curtis and two other men decided to go no farther.

BIRTH OF KESEBERGS' SON

That the Kesebergs' son was born on the crossing is certain. Phillipine Keseberg was obviously pregnant when their wagon tipped over on the Little Blue. The Kesebergs started with one child and arrived at the lake with two. That no mention is made of Lewis Keseberg, Jr.'s birth is not remarkable. The many diaries of pioneer women rarely mention childbirth. One diary goes on at length about every occurence of a certain date in great detail. At the end the off-hand remark is made that her baby was born that day.

JACKSON STRONG

This young man is a pure invention. If there was a Jackson Strong, I did not know it. I felt that if this young man had not turned up, Virginia Reed would have invented him herself.

THE RELIEF PARTIES

Although this narrative ends when the last woman has met her fate, an entire book could be written about the heroics and knavery of the various relief parties. The first was made up chiefly of big-hearted men, inexperienced in such conditions, who had volunteered through altruism. These were Aquila Glover, Riley Moultry, Joseph Sels (Sells), John Rhodes, Daniel Rhodes, Captain Reasin Tucker and Ned Coffeemire (Coffeymire).

The second relief was headed by James Reed, Big Mac McCutchen and Hiram Miller, with Brit Greenwood, son of the famed mountain man Caleb Greenwood, then in his 80s, guiding them with his experience. The part the infamous Selim Woodworth played in this rescue is a saga of cowardice and frustration.

The third relief in which William Eddy, William Foster, Hiram Miller and William Thompson took part was a quick dash of one day from the summit to the lake camp and back in a futile effort to save the two sons of Eddy and Foster. They brought all the remaining children to safety, including Tamsen's three youngest daughters.

About the fourth relief there is a considerable mass of evidence, both good and bad. The men were hired to go, for a part of the property recovered. Any of the complete accounts, McGlashan's or Stewart's will provide the interested reader with details. Only Lewis Keseberg returned with these men. The *California Star,* Sam Brannan's San Francisco newspaper, carried frequent bulletins during the months of the rescue efforts.

CANNIBALISM

A cannibal is defined as a animal who eats his own kind, and to cannibalize is as much a taboo now as it was then. To my nine-year-old mind, it was the ultimate horror that possessed me for years.

Wanton cannibalism is still forbidden, but in cases of survival, understanding turns to forgiveness. In an age when people willingly accept hearts, livers, kidneys or other organs of the dead, the stigma has become moot, to say the least. Judge not, that ye be not judged.

FRANCIS PARKMAN

Francis Parkman and his cousin Quincy Adams, both of Harvard University, were traveling in this area in 1846 and described Fort Laramie.

"Fort Laramie is one of the posts established by 'The American Fur Company' which well-nigh monopolizes the Indian trade of this region. Here its officials rule with an absolute sway; the arm of the United States has little force, for when we were there, the extreme outposts of her troops were about seven hundred miles to the eastward. The little fort is built of bricks dried in the sun, and externally is of an oblong form, with bastions of clay, in the form of ordinary blockhouses, at two of the corners. The walls are about fifteen feet high, and surmounted by a slender palisade .... Within, the fort is divided by a partition: on one side is the square area, surrounded by the storerooms and apartments of the inmates; on the other is the *corral,* a narrow place, encompassed by the high clay walls, where at night, or in the presence of dangerous Indians, the horses and mules of the fort are crowded for safe keeping."

Parkman also gives an unforgettable picture of a train of emigrants approaching Fort Laramie, seen through a friend's "spy-glass." Although these travelers were not the Boggs Party, they were just ahead of it, perhaps with the deposed Owl Russell among them.

"... a few moments elapsed before the heavy caravan of the emigrant wagons could be seen, steadily advancing from the hills. They gained the river, and, without turning or pausing, plunged in, passed through, and slowly ascending the opposing bank, kept directly on their way by the fort and the Indian village, until, gaining a spot a quarter of a mile distant, they wheeled into a circle ...."

Parkman does not give a complimentary picture of the emigrants. "A crowd of broad-brimmed hats, thin visages, and staring eyes, appeared suddenly at the gate. Tall, awkward men, in brown home-spun, women with cadaverous faces and long lank figures, came thronging in together, and as if inspired by the very demon of curiosity, ransacked every nook and corner of the fort." Later, their curiosity satisfied, the emigrants settled themselves to the job of trading useless articles for useful ones, or buying supplies outright.

"They (the emigrants) seemed like men totally out of their element, bewildered and amazed like a troop of schoolboys lost in the woods. It was impossible to be long among them without being conscious of the bold spirit with which most of them were animated. But the *forest* is the home of the backwoodsman. On the prairie he is totally at a loss. He differs as much from the genuine 'mountain-man' as a Canadian voyageur, paddling his canoe ... differs from an American sailor. Still ... (we) were somewhat at a loss to account for this perturbed state of mind. It could not be cowardice .... Yet for the most part they were the rudest and most ignorant of the frontier population; they knew absolutely nothing of the country and its inhabitants; they had already experienced much misfortune, and apprehended more; they had seen nothing of mankind, and had never put their resources to the test."

However, later, Parkman describes a man who definitely was "Owl Russell" (who may have gone ahead to Laramie for more excitement than Fort Bernard afforded.) In an effort to rid themselves of excess whiskey, Parkman states, "he was drinking it on the spot."

"In the middle of the room a tall, lank man, with a dingy broadcloth coat, was haranguing the company in the style of the stump orator. With one hand, he sawed the air, and with the other clutched firmly a brown whiskey-jug, which he applied every moment to his lips, forgetting that he had drained the contents long ago. Richard introduced me to this personage, who was no less a man than Colonel R, once the leader of the party. Instantly the Colonel, seizing me by the leather fringes of my frock, began to define his position. His men had mutinied and deposed him .... As the Colonel spoke I looked around on the wild assemblage and could not help thinking that he was ill-fitted to conduct such men across the deserts to California .... Fearful was the fate that, months after, overtook some of the members of that party ...."

Francis Parkman, *The Oregon Trail*

CACHE, CASH

"The word cache occurs so frequently in this history that a brief definition of the process might not be amiss. The cache of goods or valuables was generally made in a wagon ... if one was to be abandoned. A square hole, say six feet in depth was dug in the earth, and in the bottom of this the box or wagon bed containing the articles was placed. Sand, soil or clay of the proper stratum was filled in upon this, so as just to cover the box from sight. The ground was then tightly packed or trampled to make it resemble ... the earth in its natural state. Into the remaining hole would be placed such useless articles as could be spared such as old tins, cast-off clothing, broken furniture, etc., and upon these the earth was thrown until the surface of the ground was again level. These precautions were taken to prevent the Indians from discovering and appropriating the articles cached. It was argued that the Indians, when digging down, would come to the useless articles and not thinking there was treasure further down, would abandon the task." C.F. McGlashan, *History of the Donner Party,* p.38. The Indians, however, were not often taken in by such a ruse. Many spelled cache as it was pronounced, cash.

AFTER WORDS

The survivors who straggled into Sutter's Fort had ended a horrible part of their lives. Now they were faced with beginning again in a strange environment, and with negligible resources. Most wished to put memories behind them and forget their sufferings and losses.

Ten women survived, all of them mothers, with the exception of Mary Graves. Some had lost children, two had come across the mountains with their families intact. Among the twenty-nine children there were sixteen orphans (including Mary and Billy Graves, who were in their late teens). Eight men survived, all fathers with the exception of Noah James and the young Juan Baptiste Trubode. Although several fathers of families had perished, Jacob and George Donner and Franklin Graves were in a group then considered elderly. Of the mothers who died, only Eleanor Eddy was young. Betsy Donner, Tamsen Donner, Elizabeth Graves and Lavina Murphy were all nearing fifty years of age and were probably worn down with frequent child-bearing and care, although starvation was usually given as the cause of death. Tamsen's sudden end remains a mystery. She had been considered to be in better condition than most; however, she had not been seen by any survivors for more than a month. Keseberg reported her frenzied appearance the night before her death; certainly the last days alone with her dying husband could not have been easy on her usually strong constitution.

There were three orphans in the Murphy family, six in the Graves family, three in the Jacob Donner family, and five in Tamsen and George Donner's family. Mary Donner had badly burned feet, her little brother George was only nine years old, and her half-brother Simon Hook had been 'strange' since his solitary attempt to walk out by himself.

The Murphy and Graves orphans had older siblings to help them on their way. The eight Donner orphans had no blood relatives in California. At fourteen, Elitha was the eldest of her sisters and cousins.

As they rejoined each other at Sutter's Fort, the Donner children were dependent on the kindness of strangers for the most part. Through the guardianship of Hiram Miller, they received a portion of the proceeds of what was recovered from the Donner tents by the Fourth Relief and also the money Keseberg had obtained. It is almost certain that much of the coin contained in the Donner wagons was not accounted for, but there is no answer to that mystery. Even the sums the family were rumored to have with them cannot be entirely established. In June, only a few months after her rescue, Elitha, 14, was married to Perry McCoon, a man fated to be killed by a runaway horse not long afterwards. In 1853, she married Benjamin Wilder. Elitha did all she could to help her younger sisters, and later assisted in sending Frances and Georgia to a seminary to be educated. It is probable that Leanna lived with Elitha much of the time before her marriage at eighteen to John App.

The two younger girls, Georgia and Eliza, were befriended by a loving Swiss couple with the symbolic names of Mary and Christian Brunner. The two lived with their 'grandma' and 'grandpa' near Sutter's Fort until the Brunners removed to Sonoma County to live, taking the children with them. Frances Donner lived with the Reed family until her marriage in 1858 to William Wilder, possibly her sister's brother-in-law.

The daughters of the George Donner family were resilient, reflecting the training Tamsen had given them. Two were present at one or the other of the two dedications of the Donner Monument, and Leanna came close to living a full century.

Of the Jacob Donner family, Mary, seven, George, nine, and their half-brother Solomon, fourteen survived. Mary's burned feet required months of care in San Francisco after which she was adopted into the James Reed home. Later in 1859, Mary became the bride of Sherman O. Houghton, an ex-mayor of San Jose, but within a year, she died in childbirth, leaving an infant daughter to bear her name. She is buried in the Reed-Lewis plot in San Jose.

With the close pattern of relationships continuing, Eliza Donner, then about seventeen, married Mary's widower in 1861 and brought up his daughter as her own. Sherman Houghton went on to become a United States Senator.

As might be expected of the resolute Reed family, they survived, prospered and continued to help others. They remained at Sinclair's, then went on to the Napa Valley where they stayed for a time with George Yount before moving to San Jose, where Reed bought land. When gold was discovered, he went to the mines, where he prospered. His investments made him once more a well-to-do man. Reed's terse diaries and his later reports of the tragedy, while occasionally tinged with bitterness, blame no one. His reserve remained with him, as did the scar he received from Snyder, until his death.

Both Margaret and James Reed's characters are reflected in the many letters exchanged with C.F. McGlashan. Although Virginia often evidenced spurts of indignation, they were quickly regretted and dispelled. Both daughters abided by their parents' admonitions to call no man villain. That Margaret wished bygones to be bygones is part of their rich inheritance from her. In San Jose, Reed named streets for the family: Margaret, Virginia, Martha, Reed, and to honor his wife's mother, Keyes.

Influenced by the piety and the daily prayers of the Breen family, and true to a promise she made to herself in the mountain cabin, Virginia became a Catholic. In 1850 when she was fifteen, she married J.M. Murphy and bore him nine children, three of whom died early in life.

As one reads her letters, her humor, romanticism and joy of life are evident. Although her spelling never improved to Tamsen's standards, her written words express a certain childish glee that had not been destroyed by her dreadful experiences.

To C.F. McGlashan she wrote of herself, "I know you would never stop to criticize a little weed that does not pretend to be even a wild flower," and again, "I alone am responsible for all my many faults. I am constantly running off in all directions, trying to crawl up somewhere and become a butterfly." She speaks of her memory: "I remember many things distinctly. I think it would have been better had my memory been druged (sic)." "I loved Mary Graves, and do still ...." and "I will not be bitter."

Patty, or Mattie, as she was called later, was married Christmas Day in 1856 to Frank Lewis. They had eight children, the last being born three years before her husband's death. The Lewises lived in San Jose, then moved to Santa Cruz, where, after Patty's death the little treasures she had carried across the plains and over the mountains were discovered. They are presently in the museum at Sutter's Fort. Strangely, the practical Patty wrote in a style one would not expect from her calm behavior as a child. I give an example from a letter written to C.F. McGlashan:

"You, have proven, yourself, to be, a noble! True! & faithful! friend! Never! to be forgotten! The name of C.G. McGlashan is engraven, so perfectly, upon the mind of 'Patty Reed' that, Time! can, never, deface, or errase it there from."

During their lives both daughters were greatly concerned for the reputation of their father in the Snyder affair. Without malice toward Snyder himself, only with a certain sense of inevitability, they recounted their version of the story. In an interview with a college friend, Mary Balch Kennedy, I was told of her being taken, at ten years of age, with the other children to visit Mrs. Lewis (Patty). "We were ushered into the parlor, and were introduced to this tiny little old lady who was standing to greet us. Her hair was pulled back severely from her face and in a knot at the back. The adults then left. We heard later that she was reluctant to talk ... but had agreed because we were young and could tell our children and grandchildren what she was going to tell us .... She showed us her doll. I have since seen it in the museum at Sutter's Fort. It looked like a wooden one and had a bit of material, faded and worn, wrapped around it. The things she impressed upon us were 1. that although her father had killed a man, it was in self defense; 2. that her own family had not engaged in cannibalism. She said that they chewed on leather and it did not taste very good and 3. that her father came back and saved them."

Margaret Reed, the steadfast, determined, loving wife, lived only until she was sixty-one. From C.F. McGlashan's HISTORY (p. 242) comes this quote: "Mrs. Reed died with her entire family gathered about her bedside, and few deathbed scenes ever recorded were more peaceful. As she entered the dark waters, all about her suddenly seemed bright. She spoke of the light, and asked that the windows be darkened, but a moment afterward she said, 'Never mind; I see you cannot shut out the bright light which I see.' Looking up at the faces of her husband and children, she said very slowly, 'I expect, when I die, I will die this way, just as if I were going to sleep. Wouldn't it be a blessing if I did?' The last words were uttered just as the soul took its flight."

On a rainy winter day I visited the Pioneer section of the Oak Hill Memorial Park in San Jose. Many of the party are buried there: William McCutchen, William Eddy, and Moses Shallenberger, who lived the winter of 1844-45 in the cabin which sheltered the Breen family.

Thirty gravestones are contained in the Reed-Lewis plot. Among them are Mary Donner Houghton, Willianoski Yount Reed, 1850-1869, Sarah Adams Reed (1850-1891), a Charles Cadden Reed (1848-1927), and a Charles Cadden Reed, Jr. 1873-1929), Little Jimmy (James Frazier Reed, Jr.) and Martha Jane Reed Lewis and her husband and their many children. Under Martha Jane's formal name is written **Little Patty Reed.**

Margaret W. Keyes Reed and James Frazier Reed lie together. It is said that their coffins touch.

Mary Graves was the last of my three women to die. Her life seemed haunted by tragic events. In May, shortly after her ordeal with the Forlorn Hope, she married Edward Pile. Six months later he was killed by a Spaniard who dragged him to death on a lariat behind a horse.

Sometime later she went to San Jose, where she was the first female teacher ever employed there in that capacity. In 1852 or '53 she married J.T. Clarke, and about ten years later they moved to White River, Tulare County, California.

Alvin S. Trivelpiece, a correspondent for the *Bee* newspapers, in an undated article, stated that there were seven children born to Mary and Thomas Clarke, three that died young. According to the *Tulare Times*, March 12, 1891, at her death Mary Graves Clarke was survived only by a son and a daughter. Whatever the number of children there were is not as significant as the fact that her son James died soon after birth, Belle at 11 years, and Louis and Daniel did not reach maturity.

Trivelpiece writes "Mary Graves was a skilled practical nurse and aided many Tulare County children into the world. Her descendents say she never failed to answer a call for aid .... Historians describe Mary Graves at the time her family moved westward as 19 years of age, 5 feet 7 inches tall, slender and with olive skin, full red lips and wavy black hair ... a perfect picture of young girlhood. Her grandchildren remember her as a very serious woman who deeply appreciated the security of her home. She once told a grandchild, 'I wish I could cry but I cannot. If I could forget the tragedy, perhaps I would know how to cry again.' She steadfastly declined to return to the horror scene at Donner Lake." Trivelpiece reports that Mary was engaged to John Snyder, and adds "Charles Stanton, who became her ardent admirer on the trip to the west, died of hunger and privation."

Her obituary in the *Tulare County Times* adds other details. "Mrs. Clarke was a woman of indomitable will and energy, and her heart was ever as tender as that of a child. Wherever sickness or want was, there would she be found to administer to the needy."

To me, most poignant of all were two obituaries located in the *Tulare Times'* legal notices:

CLARKE — At Traver, March 5, 1891, Alexander Russell Clarke, a native of Tulare County, and son of Mr. and Mrs. Thomas Clarke, aged about 26 years.

From the same source: CLARKE — At Traver, March 9, 1891, Mrs. Mary A. Clark (sic) aged 64 years, 4 months and 8 days.

When I started writing *LEFT HAND TURN,* I began my story with these two deaths. That first sketch does not appear in this book.

Charles Stanton was described by various members of the party as about 5 feet, 6 inches, a quiet man who spoke little, a botanist with 'tolerable' good education, slow, easy-going. Virginia Reed states in her letters that "Stanton did all he could for us. Noble."

With his usual thoroughness, McGlashan wrote to Stanton's family. They reported that although Stanton's early education was limited, he tried to improve it by his own efforts. The family speak of 'Mary': "How I would like to see her and talk with her face to face." Stanton's brother sent a picture of Stanton to Mary, for which she expressed gratitude. The unusual use of the familiar Mary instead of the more formal Miss Graves or Mrs. Clarke suggests that Stanton may have written his family of her, although to their knowledge he was not engaged.

William Eddy who lost so much, remarried and had children, two of whom were named Eleanor and James. He died Christmas Eve 1859 in Petaluma, still a young man. Later his remains were removed to the Oak Hill Cemetery in San Jose.

The Breen family settled in San Juan Bautista, where they raised their large family. As quoted in *The Early Inns of California,* by Ralph Herbert Cross, J. Ross Browne stopped at the United States Hotel and tavern in the mission town in 1849. Browne writes:

"The only tavern in the place was the 'United States' kept by an American and his wife in old adobe house .... The woman seemed to be the principal manager ... she struck me as an uncommon person — tall, raw-boned, sharp, and masculine — with a wild piercing expression of eye, and a smile startling and unfeminine. The man was a subdued and melancholy-looking person, presenting no particular trait of character in his appearance save that of general abandonment to the influence of misfortune ...." It was young James, only four at the time of the tragedy, whose appearance in Truckee and his subscription to *The Truckee Republican* inspired C.F. McGlashan to start research for his remarkable *History of the Donner Party.*

The Murphy family survivors settled in Marysville, which was named after Mary Murphy Covilaud. Harriet Pike married M.C. Nye a year later.

With the exception of Mary Graves, most of her family made their homes in Napa County. Eleanor Graves married William McDonnell in 1859, her sister Lovina married John Cyrus, a member of an earlier party.

There remains only Lewis Keseberg to account for. He was variously described in the replies to C.F. McGlashan's queries to survivors as tall, slender, light complexioned, with blue eyes having a hard, stern expression, and as being brutal in his treatment of his family. One said "You'd think he was a gentleman unless you saw his dark side."

Georgia Donner twice says that Keseberg "did heart-sickening things to the boys" when they were abandoned in his cabin; her sister Leanna describes him as tall, with blue eyes,"as fair headed a scoundrel as ever lived."

On his late arrival at Sutter's Fort, the last person to be brought out, the stories of his cannibalism had preceded him. Further details were added by the Fallon party, only one of whom, Reasin Tucker was tolerant of him. Their stories are the basis for much of the frightening legend that has grown up about him. Later, Keseberg brought a suit against Ned Coffeemire for his statement that Keseberg had killed Tamsen Donner. The suit was settled strangely: an award of $1 to Keseberg, who was ordered to pay the costs of the trial.

Later, John Sutter hired Keseberg to captain his schooner plying between Sacramento and San Francisco. Eddy, in San Francisco when the craft arrived, was about to kill Keseberg as he had promised to do, but James Reed and Edwin Bryant managed to talk him out of it.

For a complete account of Keseberg's defense of his actions at the lake, one may read in McGlashan's history an interview in which Keseberg denies murder and wrong doing. It is indeed a pitiful story of misery, baseness, insanity and depravity. Keseberg does not deny cannibalism in her case, nor in any of the others of which he is charged.

In the *California Quarterly* (Volume XI, #2) Dr. John Lyman has written an account of a Dr. Victor Fourgeaud who crossed the plains in 1846. Fourgeaud chartered a launch from Sutter's Fort to San Francisco on two occasions. Both times the craft was navigated by Lewis Keseberg. Dr. Lyman, quoting the other doctor says "He (Keseberg) couldn't forget that orgy of flesh .... It was a nightmare that exerted a terrible fascination .... Sometimes at night Dr. Fourgeaud would overhear him telling the crew of his horrible repasts, describing in minute detail the delicacy of what he considered the choicest bits. Hands with long fingers seemed to be favorite portions ... sometimes he screamed in his sleep. Blood curdling yells would awake the doctor. The babbling kept the passengers awake."

Whether Keseberg was the villain he is painted or not, he was almost certainly insane much of the time. Although he prospered for a time after his arrival in California, suffering and persecution followed him wherever he went. He and his wife had other children, two of whom were mentally retarded and could not be left unattended. After Phillipine died, Keseberg was left to care for them alone. He died in poverty.

As for the rumored mistreatment of his wife and family, Virginia reported to McGlashan a story told her by an acquaintance of her child being hit by Keseberg while she was playing with his daughter. Virginia added "I knew enough. I did not want to heere (sic) any more about him unless it was something good." and later, "His treatment of his wife was anything but right. She was a pretty little woman, humble and unassuming, proud of her husband and afeered of him ... she made excuses for him .... Poor Keseberg. I feel sorry for him. What a forlorn, miserable life."

Whether he killed Tamsen Donner or not cannot be established. The members of the Donner family differed among themselves. In the end, there is no answer.

Keseberg's words to Charles McGlashan were "I beg of you to insert in your book a fervent prayer to Almighty God that he will forever prevent the recurrence of a similar scene of horror."

Jacob Wright Harlan, in the party just ahead of the Donners, said of Keseberg that he knew him on the prairie crossing, that he was a man of much eccentricity, unsociable, unpopular and was "predisposed to derangement of mind.", but that he didn't believe Keseberg killed Tamsen Donner.

While researching his novel, *Wheels West,* Homer Croy located a document in the records of the Sacramento County Hospital.

Hospital Number	11029
Name	Louis Keseberg
Nativity	German
Age	80
Sex	Male
Occupation	Brewer
When admitted	June 7, 1892
Disease	(left blank)
When discharged	September 3, 1895
How discharged	died
Remarks	A last survivor of the Donner Party

BIBLIOGRAPHY

Although there will be readers who will be glad to be done with this sad story, there may be others who wish to know more. I would like to comment on the bibliography that follows.

For those interested in the era, none could do better than to read Bernard De Voto's *Year of Decision.* His text includes a running account of the Reed-Donner story, set against the history of the time.

The first comprehensive book on the party is *The California Tragedy,* by Jessy Quinn Thornton, taken from his book *Oregon and California in 1848,* published in 1849. Thornton and his wife Nancy were members of the large party that started together from Independence with whom the Reeds and Donners traveled until the parting at the Little Sandy Creek.

It is evident that Thornton wrote from conversations with survivors, many of whom he knew personally. Much of his evidence stems from statements made by William Eddy although there is solid evidence that he reflected statements of many others, particularly McCutchen and Reed. Eddy, still close to the devastating losses he sustained undoubtedly expressed in one way or another the bitterness and prejudice he felt against those he felt had dealt unfairly with him, but this is understandable in a man who lost everything he had, and who had brought the Forlorn Hope across the mountains in order to save those in the stranded party.

Thornton probably talked to some members of the various relief parties, some who gave him detailed descriptions of the conditions found at the mountain camps. As in all histories, there tend to be divergent points of view, some honest, some motivated by personal likes and dislikes. No historian, however, should set aside as valuable a document as this one is. Thirty years later perhaps survivors would wish to repress some grim details. At the time Thornton wrote his book it was an act of courage to include the frank details. Even the rough-and-ready Fallon of the Fourth relief could not find words for some of the horrors he found at the all but deserted camps.

As a personal comment I add that when Fallon and later Bryant and Kearny viewed the camps, snows had melted. Anyone who has visited even the best ski lodges suddenly laid bare by a thaw will be able to imagine how shocking the refuse, bones and rotting bodies of the dead, heretofore mercifully covered by twenty feet of snow, looked on bare ground. You may be sure that animals had also been at work on the grim burial grounds. No wonder Kearny and Bryant, the latter who had known these people so well, burned and buried the gruesome remains. One wishes only that Bryant had remembered Tamsen's diaries.

Thornton's book is explicit, but it is lightened by the hilarious story of Reed and McCutchen's encounter with the stranded Curtis family while on their first attempt to reach the party.

In the foreword of the *California Centennial Edition,* Joseph Sullivan says of Thornton, "The author was a creature of his times and while no one will challenge his heroes, he was too severe with his villains."

Another of the first hand records is contained in the classic *What I Saw In California,* in my opinion the most interesting and informative books written of the overland crossing. Long neglected after the furor of the gold rush had abated, it contains more accurate, detailed descriptions of the trail — its flora, fauna, scenery, road conditions and weather — than any other single account.

Born in 1805 in Massachusetts, Bryant moved to Lexington, Kentucky and became a newspaperman and editor. He also studied medicine and was an avid botanist. He planned his book deliberately as a factual guide, making careful notes as he went. He traveled with the body of emigrants that contained the Reed-Donner group, as well as ex-Governor Boggs of Missouri, Thornton, Colonel Russell and Andrew Grayson. From the very begining Bryant was troubled by the slow progress of the cumbersome train. He finally broke off from them near Fort Laramie, trading his wagon for mules. A party of men without wagons, using Hastings' infamous short-cut, his was possibly the first group to reach California that year, arriving at Johnson's Ranch August 30 (at approximately the same that the Donner Party finally cut their way through the Wahsatch).

Bryant joined in the California war, traveled with Fremont, and with Reed, recruited troops. Later he was named the first Alcade of San Francisco during the town's days under its new name. He held that office only a few months before he returned to Kentucky, traveling with General Kearny's troops. He was present at the burials at the camp sites.

T.H. Jefferson, traveling with the Harlan-Young contingent, just ahead of the Donners, has left a map showing Reed's general route, to accompany a guide that was written to save future travelers costly mistakes. Harlan's memories and William Graves' report, although first hand material, were done much later, which may excuse their inaccuracies.

Another writer who spoke directly to survivors was Eliza Farnham, whose 1856 book *California Indoors And Out* dealt with the experiences of the women of the party. Mrs. Farnham was an early-day feminist who used few actual names, but her informants are easily recognized.

Except for casual and fragile stories in various local newspapers, the Reed-Donner epic might have been largely forgotten, since the survivors, shamed by what had happened, yearned to forget. Others less sensitive bragged that they had belonged to the party when they had not. Exaggerated, inaccurate tales passed from mouth to mouth. In 1871, Reed and McCutchen made statements published in the *Pacific Rural Press* ad in 1877 in the *San Jose Pioneer* in order to refute these floating rumors.

In 1973, an Englishman, James Hewitt published *Eye-Witnesses To Wagons Trains West,* a summary of all first hand accounts. It is an interesting compilation, and many of the Donner Party participants are represented.

If it had not been for Charles Fayette McGlashan, the story as it is known today would have been largely forgotten. Bancroft had dismssed it summarily in his *History,* but after seeing McGlashan's careful documentation, bowed to his detailed study.

Born in 1847, McGlashan crossed the plains with his father and sisters, the mother of the family having died in childbirth. After a hard persistent struggle, he obtained an education that equipped him to earn a living in almost any field he desired. He was a defense attorney skilled in cross examination, a practiced observer and judge of character, and adept in journalistic interviewing, "especially of men — of women he was inclined to Victorian chivalry and idealism" a comment from M. Nona McGlashan, his granddaughter, (and adopted child after the death in childbirth of her mother).

His championship of labor earned him the reputation of being "the Clarence Darrow of the west coast." In addition he was an entomologist, and prominent in educational fields. Fate put him in Truckee, California, where he was a principal and superintendent of schools, practiced law, and bought and became editor of the *Truckee Republican.* In 1878, the Donner tragedy was not forgotten, but information was vague and confused. To quote from McGlashan himself in an article in the *Grizzly Bear* in 1918, reprinted recently in Nona McGlashan and Betty H. McGlashan's collection, *From The Desk Of C.F. McGlashan,* published in 1986:

"In 1878 ... a distinguished looking stranger came into the office of the 'Truckee Republican' and asked me the subscription price of the paper, and being told it was six dollars per year, paid me that amount and directed that the paper be sent to James F. Breen, South San Juan, San Benito County, California. Expressing my surprise that he should want a little country newspaper sent so far away, he told me that he was a member of the Donner Party, had been up to Donner Lake trying to locate the cabins, and that he should like a paper published near the lake. I had been seven years in Truckee, as teacher, lawyer and editor, and from the best information I had then been able to acquire believed the Donner Party consisted of four people: Donner, his wife, a Dutchman, and somebody else, and that the Dutchman ate the others up."

From this small seed grew one of the most valuable books ever written about the tragic event. The newsman's quick mind saw a 'story,' and his insatiable intellectual curiosity was aroused. Mr. McGlashan's announcement that he planned to write a full account of the Donner tragedy brought response from people from everywhere. Thirty years had passed with no decisive effort to sift the true from the false.

Surprised, McGlashan devoted himself to the task, applying his many skills to the work ahead. His promised articles mushroomed into a serialized narrative, then into a book, which in turn called for corrections and revisions as information began to pour in from all over California.

It was as if a forest fire had been kindled by the striking of a match.

C.F. McGlashan had a character consummately adapted to gaining the confidence of those he interviewed. Straight, dignified, a practiced listener, unbiased in his thinking, he was able to make firm friends of the people who stepped forward. In spite of the fact that various versions of the incidents did not always agree, he remained just and accepted corrections and criticism with an equanimity that made both sides sense his inate integrity. Reading some of the letters his informants sent him, one would think he might be provoked to anger. This was not the case; he was too professional to be contentious. He was discreet and careful never to violate a confidence.

Twenty-four of the twenty-six survivors who were alive in 1878 gave him their version of the tragedy. Of these, three had been mature at the time and probably able to recall most events. Two were infants who spoke from lore repeated through the years rather than from self-memory. Ten were children from six to twelve; nine were from the fourteen to eighteen age group.

McGlashan laced direct quotes from those he interviewed. With some, he revisited the site, only three miles away from Truckee, and discovered remaining artifacts. Others of the party were adamantly opposed to see the place again, and wished the whole event forgotten.

There are a few differences in various editions that were difficult to resolve. One concerns the romance of Mary Graves and John Snyder. Mary Graves Clarke was one of those to whom McGlashan applied for assistance. Writing perhaps from Thornton's account, recorded only a year or so after the events, McGlashan stated in the first edtion that Mary Graves and John Snyder were engaged to be married. This drew a violent reaction from Mary, who denied any 'romance' existed between the two. Interestingly enough, Mary's first letters to the editor are well composed and written in a neat, organized style, as one would expect from an ex-teacher. In her protestations over the 'romance' the handwriting becomes uneven and careless and reflects only emotion. Since other first hand sources have also stated that Mary was engaged to John, the mystery deepens. Why did Mary react so furiously? She reproves McGlashan for his statement, saying:

"Was surprised to see myself the subject of fiction." Later she adds in a completely different style of spelling and writing, "Freind, ples drop that trarsh, false trarsh out and insert some more usefull history where you got falst idear (is strange) and that must have been from some child acount. It was all real life of a sterner type ...." The letter is carelessly scribbled, far from the careful penmanship she had used in thanking him for a picture of Charles Stanton.

Virginia Reed, writing to McGlashan, had noticed that Mary's engagement to Snyder had been deleted. She comments, "Who gave you that false information in regard to

Mary Graves and John Snyder? It seems too bad to have that little romance left out."

The actual deletion follows. In the beginning of Chapter IV, McGlashan had written:

"Life, thirty-three years ago, was not vastly different from life now-a-days. It was impossible that so large a train could cross the great plains without the occurrence of love episodes. Perhaps the tenderest and most sacred of these in the Donner Party was the betrothal of John Snyder and Mary Graves. Mary was one of the sweetest and bravest girls in the company, and was as good as she was sweet. Everyone knew of the engagement, and everyone heartily approved. Whether during the long horseback rides ahead of the train, or amidst the young folks, clambering over the cliffs and cutting their names in the rocks, or yet in the joyous circle about the evening campfire, John and Mary were ever and always the happiest couple in all the train. The weariest day was brightened by visions of the little home they would build in the land of the sunset. They had been playmates from childhood; had come from the same town in Illinois, and Snyder drove one of Mr. Graves' teams. Always near each other, every wondrous landscape, every dainty, unfamiliar wild flower, was appreciated the more because seen by both."

Whatever Mary's reasons for objecting to the passage, the historian must choose sometimes, and to spare Mary embarrassment, McGlashan removed this paragraph from his revised edition.

Certainly thirty years can alter memories. Reading the letters McGlashan received which are preserved in the Bancroft Library, one cannot help but be surprised at the hatreds that still seethed in various families. Because of altercations on the Humboldt, the Breens and Will Eddy became enemies. Whether or not Eddy aggrandized himself in his stories to Thornton, or whether Thornton himself made the errors does not seem to justify the epithets heaped upon Eddy, who among them all, lost the most. For instance, it took a great deal of carefully documented proof by McGlashan to convince the Breens that Foster and Eddy had indeed returned to the lake for their sons, both of whom were found dead. It is also touching to note the love and loyalty the Breen sons had for their hard-working resilient mother. Over and over in their letters, they ask that McGlashan say no wrong of her, a request that was easy for him to honor. The Breen family had a copy of Thornton's account, but the children were not allowed to read it.

Both J.Q. Thornton and C.F. McGlashan should receive homage for their accounts, which reflect truth and not prejudice.

Following McGlashan's *History,* few historians failed to mention the tragedy. The Gold Rush, however, was uppermost in many of these books and references to the tragedy are sketchy and incomplete. Yet to skip a single item is to risk missing a clue to the truth.

I come now to George Stewart, whose book *Ordeal by Hunger,* is still in print. Stewart was an open-minded man who weighed every fact or rumor and condensed the history into a compact, gripping story. Besides being a "poet and precisionist" as he has been called, he was also a novelist, and the reader will sense his efforts to keep the novel contained in the history from breaking loose. To read his penciled notes in the California Historical Society's library is to realize what precision means. Born in Pennsylvania, a graduate of Princeton, with post-graduate work at Columbia, teaching at the University of Michigan and other colleges, he came finally to the University of California where, apparently, California and western trail history became a major interest in his life. His many books have added much to California literature. Besides his epic *Ordeal,* his book *The California Trail* adds much to the understanding of those people who came in such multitudes to the Golden State.

In *Year Of Decision,* Bernard De Voto says, "I owe much to George Stewart's *Ordeal By Hunger* ... anyone who writes about the Donners today necessarily owes much to

Stewart and necessarily uses him repeatedly."

A little-known book is Dr. William Stookey's *Fatal Decision,* published in 1950. Written from Utah, Stookey's book adds much local information about the disastrous dry drive across the salt flats of Utah, and posits a reason for the hostility of the Nevada Indians. This was a daring thing to do, for it involved a hero among mountain men, Joe Walker, and also reflects the attitude of the time toward Indians as a race.

Washington Irving's *Adventures of Captain Bonneville,* Francis Parkman's classic, *The Oregon Trail,* and James Clyman's diaries also add facts that serve as a back drop for the trials of the unlucky party, as well as being good reading on their own. A recent book, published in 1982 by John D. Unruh, Jr. deserves to be placed among the best of these books. It is a pity that this young man did not live to write more history such as this.

Both Julia Altrocchi's *The Old California Trail* and Irene Paden's *The Wake Of The Prairie Schooners* and *Prairie Schooner Detours* have traced the actual routes of the emigrants, and Dale Morgan's *The Humboldt* adds important data to the Nevada route. The list of writers who described the many routes contains many authors: Turentine Jackson, William Johnson, Ralph Moody, Jay Monaghan, Francis Farquhar, and both Royces, Josiah and Sarah.

If the reader ventures into fiction on the subject, there are two books well worth reading based on the Reed-Donner Party. Homer Croy's *Wagons West,* written in a breezy manner from James Reed's point of view, has excellent original research, marred only by his mistake in confusing two James Reeds, both from Springfield and both in the Black Hawk War. The second is *Grim Journey,* by Hoffman Birney, speaking for the hapless Will Eddy. Many of the other fictions are over-worked and emotionalized.

And now for the women. In the past few years there has been a spate of diaries, letters, and accounts written concerning women and the west. My favorites among these are Sandra Myres' *Westering Women,* Cathy Luchetti and Carol Olwell's *Women Of The West,* Dee Brown's *The Gentle Tamers,* and from a later period, the delightful *Shirley Letters.* Eliza Farnham and Lillian Schlissel seem a little hard on the men in my opinion, but contain much of interest. I mention Sarah Royce again in this category, and Edward Dunbar's *First Women Over The Rockies.*

For my purpose these were primary sources, revealing more about women than any generalizations can do. Letters were written for loved ones at home, and therefore possibly slanted toward the intended reader. Diaries reflect more completely what the woman really felt about life.

Reading these letters and diaries I was first taken by their word usage. They used the language as carefully as they could. Only the casual phrase and the style of their time make these letters different from letters we ourselves might write to far-off friends.

Women being what they are, there can be no simplistic picture that emerges, although some interpreters like to find one anyway. There are women who complain, are disappointed or discouraged and tired, whether at home cooking dinner, at a super-market shopping, or working side by side with men in the marketplace. By the same token there are women who take things in their stride, endure, and sometimes manage a laugh at a calamity. There are women who have good days and there are women who have bad days. There are women impatient with men and women who are far too patient. Reading what these women took the trouble to write after a long day's travel and trial, you cannot help putting yourself in their place and laugh, despair or complain with them.

One thing you cannot do is to categorize them, for few women will stay neatly in a compartment without protest. Thank goodness these women went west with their husbands and children. Many of them didn't want to go, or if they did, regretted it after they discovered what they were facing. However, only one or two had actually to be tied inside the wagon. Only a few chose to stay at home and wait it out with their parents or alone. They went, unwillingly, some of them, but they went. And having gone, most bore what they had to and made do with what they had. And they added the comfort of home to some degree at least, and they did give men the will to go on, for in the case of the Donner Party it was the single men who gave up first.

One must be careful about making judgments about women. As a rule, they are unpredictable; sometimes they cry when they shouldn't; other times, they laugh in the most trying of situations. My women of the Donner Party were not all alike; they were as unpredictable as women always are and as strong and brave and enduring.

BIBLIOGRAPHY — HISTORY

Altrocchi, Julia Cooley: *The Old California Trail.* Caldwell, Idaho, Caxton Printers 1945

Archuleta, Kay: *The Brannan Saga.* San Jose, Smith McKay, 1977

Atherton, Gertrude: *California, an Intimate History.* Freeport, N.Y., Books for Libraries Press, 1971

Bancroft, Hubert Howe: *History of California* Vol. 5 1846-1848. Santa Barbara, Wallace Hebberd 1950

Beebe, Lucius and Clegg, Charles: *The American West.* New York, E.P. Dutton Co., Inc. 1955

Bird, Isabella L.: *A Lady's Life in the Rocky Mountains.* Oklahoma, University of Oklahoma Press, 1960

Billington, Ray Allen: *The Far Western Frontier.* New York, Harper and Row 1962

Breen, Patrick: *Diary of Patrick Breen.* Berkeley, University of California Press 1910

Brewer, William: *Up and Down California.* Berkeley, University of California Press 1949

Brown, Dee: *The Gentle Tamers.* Lincoln, Nebraska 1958

Brown, Dee: *The Westerners.* New York, Holt Rinehart & Winston

Bidwell, John: *Life in California Before the Gold Discovery.* Palo Alto, Lewis Osborne 1966

Browne, J. Ross: *A Dangerous Story.* Ashland, Oregon 1972

Bryant, Edwin: *Rocky Mountain Adventures.* New York, Hurst and Co. undated

Bryant, Edwin: *What I Saw in California.* Palo Alto, Lewis Osborne 1967

Camp, Charles L.: *William Allen Trubody and the Overland Pioneers.* San Franciso, Lawton R. Kennedy, 1937 Reprint from the *California Historical Society Quarterly*

Camp, Charles L. *Yount and His Chronicle of the West.* Denver, Old West Publishing Co. 1966

Caughey, John W.: *California.* New York, Prentice Hall Inc. 1953

Clappe, Louise: *The Shirley Letters.* New York, Alfred A. Knopf 1949

Clark, Thomas D., editor: *Gold Rush Diary.* Lexington, Kentucky, University of Kentucky Press 1967

Cleland, Robert Glass: *History of California, the American Period.* New York 1939

Cleland, Robert Glass: *This Reckless Breed of Men.* New York, Alfred Knopf 1952

Cleland, Robert Glass: *From Wilderness to Empire.* New York, Alfred A. Knopf 1944

Cleland, Robert Glass: *Pathfinders.* San Francisco, Los Angeles, Chicago, Powell Publishing Co.

Clyman, James: *Journal of a Mountain Man.* Missoula, Montana, Mountain Press 1984

Coy, Owen Cochran: *The Great Trek.* San Franciso, Los Angeles and Chicago, Powell Publishing Company 1931

Cronise, Titus Fey: *The Natural Wealth of California.* San Francisco, The Bancroft Company 1868

Cross, Ralph Herbert: *Early Inns of California 1844-1869.* San Francisco 1954

Dana, Julian: *Sutter of California.* Press of the Pioneers, New York 1934

Dick, Everett: *The Story of the Frontier.* New York, Tudor Publishing Co. 1941

Dillon, Richard: *Fool's Gold.* New York, Coward McCann 1967

Dellenbaugh, Frederick S.: *Breaking the Wilderness.* New York, London, G.P. Putnam's Sons 1905

Dellenbaugh, Frederick S.: *Fremont and '49.* New York, G.P. Putnam's Sons 1914

De Voto, Bernard: *Across the Wide Missouri.* Boston, Houghton Mifflin 1947

De Voto, Bernard: *Year of Decision.* Boston, Little Brown and Co. 1943

Drury, Aubrey: *California, an Intimate Guide.* New York, G.P. Putnam's Sons 1905

Drury, Clifford Merrill, editor: *First White Women Over the Rockies, Vol. III.* Glendale, Arthur H. Clark Co. 1966

Dunbar, Edward E.: *Romance of the Age.* New York, Appleton and Co. 1867

: *Eldorado County, Historical Souvenir of.* Oakland, Paoli Sioli 1883

Eldredge, Zoeth Skinner: *History of California, Vol. III.* New York, D. Appleton and Co. 1912

Fahey, Frank M. and Fahey, Marie L.: *Chapters from the American Experience.* Englewood Cliffs, N.J., Prentice Hall 1971

Farnham, Eliza W.: *California, Indoors and Out.* Facsimile of 1856 edition. New York 1856

Farnham, J.T.: *The Early Days of California.* Philadelphia, John Potter 1860

Farquhar, Francis P.: *History of the Sierra Nevada.* Berkeley, University of California Press 1965

Field, Matthew C.: *Prairie and Mountain Sketches.* Norman, University of Oklahoma Press 1957

Foote, H.S.: *Pen Pictures of the Garden World.* Chicago, Lewis Publishing Co. 1888

French, Joseph Lewis: *The Pioneer West.* New York, Garden City Publishers 1937

Frost, John: *Pioneer Mothers of the West.* Boston, Lee and Sheard 1875

Ghent, W.J.: *The Road to Oregon.* New York, Tudor Publishing Co. 1934

Graves, William: *Crossing the Plains in '46.* 1877

Graydon, Charles K.: *Trail of the First Wagons Over the Sierra Nevada.* Gerald, MO, 1986

Groh, George W.: *Gold Fever.* New York, William Morrow and Co. 1966

Gudde, Erwin G.: *Bigler's Chronicle of the West.* Berkeley, University of California Press 1962

Gudde, Erwin G.: *Sutter's Own Story.* New York, G.P. Putnam's Sons 1936

Hall, Carroll D.: *Donner Miscellany.* San Francisco, Book Club of California 1947

Harlan, Jacob Wright: *California, '46 to '88.* San Francisco, Bancroft Company 1888

:*Harper's Encyclopaedia of United States History.* New York, Harper and Brothers 1915 Vol. I

Hastings, Lansford Warren: *The Emigrant's Guide to Oregon and California.* Princeton 1932

Hewitt, James: *Eye-Witnesses to Wagon Trains West.* New York, Charles Scribner's Sons 1973

Hine, Robert V.: *In the Shadow of Fremont.* University of Oklahoma Press, Norman, OK 1982

Hinkle, George Henry and Hinkle, Bliss McGlashan: *Sierra Nevada Lakes.* New York, Indianapolis, Bobbs Merrill Company 1949

Hittell, Theodore Henry: *History of California.* San Francisco, N.J., Stone and Co. 1885 Vol. 2

Holliday, J.S.: *The World Rushed In.* New York, Simon and Schuster 1981

Horgan, Paul: *Josiah Gregg and His Vision of the West.* New York, Farrar Straus Giroux 1979

Houghton, Eliza Poor Donner: *The Expedition of the Donner Party and Its Tragic Fate.* Chicago, A.C. McClurg and Co. 1911

Hunt, Thomas H. and Adams, Robert V.H.: *Ghost Trails to California*

Hulbert, Archer Butler: *Forty Niners.* Boston, Little Brown and Co. 1931

Hunt, Rockwell and Ament, William: *Oxcart to Airplane.* Los Angeles, Chicago, Powell Publishing Co. 1929

Hunt, Rockwell and Sanchez, Nellie Van DeGrift: *A Short History of California.* New York, Thomas Y. Crowell Co. 1929

Irving, Washington: *The Adventures of Captain Bonneville.* New York, London, Cooperative Publication Society, undated

Jackson, Joseph Henry: *Gold Rush Album.* New York, Charles Scribner's Sons 1949

Jackson, W. Turrentine: *Wagon Roads West.* New Haven, London, Yale University Press 1952

James, George Wharton: *Heroes of California.* Boston, Little Brown and Co. 1910

Jefferson, T.H.: *Map of the Emigrant Road from Independence, MO to San Francisco, California* (and guide instructions) Drawn in 1846, Introduction by George Stewart 1945

Johnson, William G.: *Overland to California.* Oakland, Bio Books, Centennial Edition

Kelly, Charles: *Salt Desert Trails.* Salt Lake City, Western Printing Co. 1930

Kloes, Donald R.: *California, Land of Contrasts.* San Francisco, Fearon Publishers 1959

Knowland, Joseph R.: *California, A Landmark History.* Knowland 1941

Lamar, Howard L.: *The Trader on the American Frontier.* Texas A & M University Press 1977

Lewis, Martha Jane (Patty) Reed: Letters written to C.F McGlashan, bound volume in Bancroft Library
Lewis, Oscar: *Sutter's Fort.* Edgewood Cliffs, N.J., Prentice Hall Inc. 1966
Luchetti, Cathy and Olwell, Carol: *Women of the West.* St. George, Utah, Antelope Island Press 1982
Markham, Edwin: *California the Wonderful.* New York, Heart's International Library Co. 1914
McGlashan, C.F.: *History of the Donner Party,* various editions;
Truckee, California, Crowley and McGlashan 1879 (first edition)
Sacramento, H.S. Crocker Co. 1907
San Francisco, A. Carlisle Co. 1927, paperback
Stanford University Press, 1940 (Introduction by George and Bliss McGlashan Hinkle)
McGlashan, Charles Fayette: C-B 570 Boxes I, II, III and Cartons I, II, University of California, Bancroft Library, donated in 1956 and 1959
McGlashan, M. Nona and McGlashan, Betty H.: *From the Desk of Truckee's C.F. McGlashan.* Fresno, Panorama West Books 1986
McGlashan, M. Nona: *Give Me a Mountain Meadow.* Fresno, Pioneer Publishing Co. 1981
Monaghan, Jay: *The Overland Trail.* New York, Bobbs Merrill 1947
Moody, Ralph: *The Old Trails West.* New York, Thomas Crowell Company 1963
Morgan, Dale: *The Humboldt,* Rivers of America Series. New York, Toronto, Farrar & Rinehart 1943
Murphy, Virginia Reed: *Across the Plains in the Donner Party.* Palo Alto, Lewis Osborne, no date
Murphy, Virginia Backenstoe Reed. Bound Letters from Virginia Reed to C.F. McGlashan In the McGlashan papers at the Bancroft Library
Myres, Sandra: *Westering Women.* Albuquerque, University of New Mexico Press 1983
Norton, Henry Kittredge: *The Story of California.* Chicago, A.C. McClurg and Co. 1913
O'Brian, Robert: *California Called Them.* New York, London, Toronto, McGraw Hill Book Co. 1951
Older, Mrs. Fremont: *Love Stories of Old Caifornia.* New York, Coward McCann, Inc. 1940
Paden, Irene: *Prairie Schooner Detours.* New York, Macmillan Co. 1949
Paden, Irene D.: *The Wake of the Prairie Schooner.* New York, Macmillan Co. 1943
Parkman, Francis: *The Oregon Trail.* Boston, Little Brown and Co. 1900. Illustrated by Frederick Remington
Parkman, Francis: *The Oregon Trail.* Heritage Press, illustrated by Maynard Dixon
Parker, Rev. Samuel: *Journal of an Exploring Tour Beynd the Rocky Mountains.* Ithaca, Mack, Andrus and Woodruff 1842
Peck, J.M.: *A New Guide for Emigrants to the West.* Boston, Gould, Kendall and Lincoln 1836
Pomeroy, Earl: *The Pacific Slope.* New York, Alfred A. Knopf 1965
Prendergast, Thomas F.: *Forgotten Pioneers.* San Francisco, The Trade Pressroom 1942
Regnery, Dorothy F.: *The Battle of Santa Clara.* San Jose, Smith and McKay Printing Co. 1978
Robinson, Edna Minter: *John S. Minter, Survivor of the Donner Party.* San Diego Library
Roddy, W. Lee: *Remarkable Californians.* Lee Roddy 1970
Rolle, Andrew F.: *California, a History.* New York, Thomas Y. Crowell 1963
Royce, Josiah: *California.* Boston, New York, Houghton Mifflin Co. 1886
Royce, Sarah: *A Frontier Lady.* Lincoln, University of Nebraska Press 1932
Sale, Randall and Karn, Edwin D.: *American Expansion.* Lincoln and London, University of Nebraska Press 10th Printing
Schlissel, Lillian: *Women's Diaries of the Westward Journey.* New York, Schocken Books 1982
Soule, Frank and Gihon, John H. and Nisbet, James: *The Annals of San Francisco.* 1884
Starr, Kevin: *Americans and the California Dream.* Santa Barbara, Peregrine Smith, Inc. 1973
Starr, Paul: *Social Transformation of American Medicine.* 1769 version, revised by Gunn, Starr
Stegner, Wallace, Laxalt, Robert, et al: *Trails West.* National Geographic Society 1979
Stewart, George R.: *The California Trail.* New York, McGraw Hill Co. 1962

Stewart, George R.: *Donner Pass and Those Who Crossed It.* San Francisco, San Francisco Historical Society 1960

Stewart, George R.: *The Opening of the California Trail.* Berkeley and Los Angeles, University of California Press 1953

Stewart, George R.: *Ordeal by Hunger.* New York, Henry Holt and Co. 1950

Stewart, George R.: *U.S. 40.* Boston, Houghton Mifflin 1953

Stewart, Elinore Pruitt: *Letters of a Woman Homesteader.* Boston, Houghton Mifflin 1914-1952

Stookey, Walter M. M.D.: *Fatal Decision.* Salt Lake City, Deseret Book Co. 1950

Stone, Irving: *Men to Match My Mountains.* New York, Doubleday and Co. 1956

Taylor, Bayard: *Eldorado.* New York, Pennsylvania, Alfred A. Knopf 1949

Thompson and West: *History of Nevada County.* Berkeley, Howell and North Books 1970

Thornton, J. Quinn: *Camp of Death.* Olympic Valley, Outbooks 1978

Thornton, J. Quinn: *The California Tragedy.* Oakland, Biobooks Centennial Edition

Triplett Frank: *Conquering the Wilderness.* New York, St. Louis, N.D., Thompson and Co. 1885

Unruh, John D., Jr.: *The Plains Across.* urbana, Chicago, London, University of Illinois Press 1982

Walsh, Hebry L. S.J. *Hallowed Were the Gold Dust Trails.* University of Santa Clara Press, Santa Clara, CA 1946

Watkins, T.W.: *California.* Palo Alto, American West Publishing Co.

Webster, Paul: *The Mighty Sierra.* Palo Alto, The American West Publishing Co. 1972

Wiley, Bert: *The Overland Emigrant Trail.* Wiley, 1979

Wood, Coke, and Bush, Leon: *California History.* San Francisco, Fearon Press 1963

Wright, Elizabeth Cyrus: *Early Napa Valley.* Napa, Napa Historical Society 1979

Wyman, Walker N.: *California Emigrant Letters.* New York, Bookman Associates 1952

BIBLIOGRAPHY — FICTIONS, POETRY

Altrocchi, Julia: *Snow Covered Wagons.* New York, The Macmillan Company 1936. Poetry

Anderson, Edna Mae: *Tamsen.* Fort Washington, Chipmunk Books 1973. Juvenile

Birney, Hoffman: *Grim Journey.* New York, Minton Balch Company 1934

Bonner, Geraldine: *The Emigrant Trail.* New York, Duffield and Company 1910

Croy, Homer: *Wheels West.* New York, Hastings House 1955

Fisher, Vardis: *The Mothers.* Chicago, Swallow Press, Inc. Sage Books 1943

Galloway, David: *Tamsen.* San Diego, New York, London, Harcourt Brace Javanovich Press 1982

Harte, Bret: *Gabriel Conroy.* Boston, Houghton Mifflin 1871-1903

Headon, William: *Beyond the Pass.* New York, Vantage Press 1955

Keithley, George: *The Donner Party.* New York, George Braziller 1972. Poetry

Lofts, Nora: *Winter Harvest.* New York, Doubleday and Company 1955

McDonald, Kay L.: *The Vision is Fulfilled.* New York, Walker and Company 1983

Pigney, Joseph: *For Fear We Shall Perish.* New York, E.P. Dutton and Co. 1961 *

Rhodes, Richard: *The Ungodly.* New York, Charterhouse 1973

Sutton, Margaret: *Palace Wagon Family.* New York, Alfred Knopf 1957. Juvenile

Whitman, Ruth: Tamsen Donner: *A Woman's Journey.* Alice James Books, Cambridge, MA 1985

Wilbur, Marguerite Eyer: *John Sutter, Rascal and Adventurer.* New York, Liveright Publishing Co. 1949

Wagner, Harr N.: *Pacific History Stories.* San Francisco, N. Harr Wagner Company 1918. Juvenile

* This is sometimes classified as history. Its prejudice caused me to classify it as fiction, although the bibliography and research are valuable.

BIBLIOGRAPHY — Periodicals, Newspapers, interviews, tapes, etc.

Alter, Carol: Review of James Bridger's book. *California Historical Quarterly* Vol. IV, p. 290

Andrews, Thomas F.: *Satire and the Overland Guide.* California Historical Quarterly, Vol. XLVIII, June 1969

Bagley, Harry P.: *Along the Trail of the Donner Party. Sacramento Bee,* March 1942

Bagley, Harry P.: *The Donner Party.* Feb. 18, 1939. Illustrated by Newton Pratt

Bee, the Modesto: John Quincy App's death. October 22, 1957

Bee, the Sacramento: Where Death Stalked the Donner Party. Oct. 11, 1941

California Historical Quarterly, various issues

Vol. IV #3 Review of book by James Bridger.

Vol. V #4 Dec. 1926. Review of James Clyman's Diaries.

Vol. V #2 George Lyman, M.D., article concerning Dr. Fouregeaud, second physician in S.F. who crossed the plains in '46.

Vol. XII, December 1933. Gudde, Edwin, translation of the Memories of Theodore Cordua concerning cannibalism and Keseberg.

Vol. XIX #2: The James and Elizabeth Gregson Memoirs.

Vol. XXVIII, December 1949: The Burrell Letters.

Campbell, David. Manuscript. *Porterville Weekly Review,* 1899, copied by Glenna Blout

The Californian, Monterey, California Vol. I

The California Star, Yerba Buena, California. January 16, Feb. 13, Feb. 26, Feb. 27, March 20, Apr. 10, 1947

Chapman, Dr. C.W.: *Grizzly Bear,* May, June 1918

Clark, Brian: *Donner Lake, Modesto Bee,* July 18, 1985

Clarken, George Gerard: Donner Lake Monument Dedication, *San Francisco Call,* undated. (Today, June 10, the Native Sons Monument was dedicated)

Crouch, Alice Spires: Obituary. *Weekly Calistogan,* undated

Donner Memorial State Park, State of California, Department of Natural Resources and Parks Pamphlet

Donner Memorial State Park: *The Longest Journey,* video tape.

On the Donner Trail, Sunday supplement and pictures and recap of Walter Stookey article. Undated and unidentified. Possibly *Salt Lake Tribune.* California Historical Society files

Durney, Maxine Kortum: Biographical material of the Graves family.

Edmonson, Maude Harlan: Interview. Mrs. Edmonson is a granddaughter of one of the Harlan parties who were just ahead of the Donner Party with Hastings as their guide.

Fallon, D'Arcy: Researchers Dig up New Facts about Fate of Donner Party. *San Francisco Examiner,* July 6, 1986

Fairchild, Edna Sherwood: Reprint of a story told by Edna Sherwood of her grandmother's memories of the Donner Tragedy. *The Calistogan,* Friday, June 14, 1940

Fennelly, Mrs. Joseph C.: Letter in reply to questions re William McCutchen. Jan. 27, 1984

Francis, J.D.: *The Donner Party Tragedy.* San Diego Historical Society Quarterly April-May 1931

Frederick, Donald J.: Californa Dig Discovers Donner Party Artifacts. *Chicago Tribune,* August 26, 1984

Gibbons, Boyd: *The Itch to Move West. National Geographic,* August 1986, Vol 170 #2

Grass Valley Morning Union, June 26, July 10, Sept. 4, 1938

Graves, Mrs. Joseph Thomas Clarke (Mary Graves) Obituaries: March 5, March 9. Obituaries

Graves, William: A Survivor of the Dopwner (sic) Horror of 1846-47. *Russian River Flag* 1895

Gray, Alice Worth: *A Turgid Rehash of the Donner Tragedy:* Unidentified newspaper. Marked Review, July 3, 1983

Japenga, Ann: Tracking Down the Truth of What Happened to the Donner Party. *Los Angeles Times,* May 11, 1986

Keithly, George: *Along the Donner Trail.* San Francisco Chronicle, January 30, 1972.

Kennedy, Mary Balch. Interview and letter concerning a meeting with Mrs. Frank Lewis (Patty Reed)

King, Marsha: *The Westering Women.* Seattle Times, Seattle Post Intelligence, Sunday, August 21, 1983

Kinyon, Edmund G.: Observations and Experiences. *Grass Valley Morning Union,* June 26, July 10, Sept. 4, 11, 1938. Selim Woodworth

Mann, Henry Rice: Diary, 1849. Unpublished manuscript in California Historical Society

Marshall, Emma Seckle: Information on Donner Dedication. *The Grizzly Bear,* June, July 1918

McCutchen, William: Statement of the Donner Party. *San Jose Pioneer,* May 5, 1887

McCutchen, Edward: News Item of a race from the Donner Campsite to the office of McCutchen, Doyle, Brown and Ensenare in San Francisco. *Modesto Bee,* May 29, 1983

McGlashan, C.F.: Why the Donner Party was Written. *The Grizzly Bear,* 1918

McGlashan, M. Nona: Interview and correspondence

Moultry, Riley: Interview. *Santa Cruz Sentinel,* August 31, 1888

Oregon-California Trails Association: Fourth Annual National Convention, Carson City, Nevada August 20-24, 1986. Maps and articles.

Reed, Frazier O.: Interview. October 2, 1984, San Jose, California

Reed, James Frazier: An Unpublished Report of the Battle of Santa Clara. *San Francisco Chronicle,* Sept. 4, 1910

Reed, James: Statement of the Donner Party. *San Jose Pioneer,* April 28, May 15, 1877

Richardson, Donald M., George and Jacob Donner cabin site. *Sacramento Bee,* July 24, 1950

Roach, James. 95th Birthday is Observed by Mrs. John App (Leanna Donner) *Modesto Bee* December 5-6, 1929

Road to Survival, Video tape of T.V. Program

Saarni, Clarine: Location of the Donner Camps. *Sacramento Bee,* July 24, 1960

Extracts from Virginia Reed's article in the *Century Magazine,* July ____

Picture of Mrs. Frank Lewis, (Patty Reed), Mrs. John Murphy (Virginia Reed), and Frances Donner Wilder, *San Francisco Daily Call,* June 10 undated

Saxton, Ruth: *A Search for the Past.* Interview by unidentified writer. At Mills, published by alumni and friends of Mills College

South Lake Tahoe Reporter: Sierra Peak Named for UC Professor (George Stewart) undated

Article on the Dedication at Donner Lake. *San Francisco Daily Call,* June undated

Monument Unveiled. *San Francisco Examiner,* June 6, 1918

Sherwood, Mary Cyrus, (Lovina Graves Cyrus' daughter). Obituary. *Weekly Calistogan,* no date

Skaar, Sven. U.S. 40, Route of the Old Donner Trail. Tourist map

Stokes, Frederick: The Last Man Out. *Touring Topics,* February 1929

Stone, Wella: Unpublished manuscript and map of Salt Lake cut-off

Stone, Lois C.: Andrew Jackson Grayson. *The American West,* Summer 1965, Vol. II, #3

Stookey, Walter, M.D.: Ninety Years After. *Salt Lake Tribune,* Sept. 15, 1946

Springfield Journal, Extracts from April 23, June 4, 1846

Stewart, George: Original Documents Concerning the Donner Party. *California Historical Society,* San Francisco

Sutter's Fort Historical Museum, Sacramento, California various documents and memorabilia

Review of Trail of the First Wagons Over the Sierra Nevada. *Weekend Prospector,* Friday, Sept. 26, 1986

Trivelpiece, Alvin S.: Donner Party Survivor's Life had Few Parallels in Fiction. *Modesto Bee* undated

Wells, Evelyn: The Donner Party. *San Jose Evening News,* 1926. Series of articles clipped and pasted in album. 1926. San Jose Public Library.

Werner, Jacobsen: Hope Among Hardship. *California Historical Courier,* Dec. Jan. issue 1986-87

ACKNOWLEDGEMENTS

For their criticism and comments:

James Algar, Lorene Cuneo Greuner, Martha Knight, Roberta Stimmel, Lolita Seguin, Dena Boer, Colleen Bare, Dr. James McGinnis, Dr. Anne Maino Alvarez, Dr. C.R. Maino.

For their encouragement:

Arlene Mattos, Aileen Jaffa, Mary Ruggieri, Vera Jensen, Blanche Lorenzen, Lois Bunce, Marian Barker, Margaret Bell, Ali Smaalders, Irene Chadwick, Marnelle White, Heidi Warner, Phyllis Ohanian, Judge Runston G. Maino, Dr. C.B. Maino, Dr. Curtis Grant, and those descendants of the Donner, Reed, Graves, Breen, and Murphy families who have written to the author.

For art work: Isabelle Schrock Barnett

For Maps: Shirley Elke

For special assistance:

Mr. and Mrs. Frazier O. Reed, M. Nona McGlashan, Carrie Hunniwell Safley, Helen Mosier, Audrey Traugh Blackinger, Roy D. Baker, Vivian Leek Stallkamp.

For her example of perfection: Margaret Painter

The Bancroft Library, University of California, Berkeley

The California State Library, Sacramento

The California Historical Society Library, San Francisco

The Stanislaus County Library, Modesto

The Stanislaus Historical Museum, Modesto

The San Jose Public Library, San Jose

The San Diego Library, San Diego

The Edwin Langhart Museum, Healdsburg, California

Bookstores everywhere

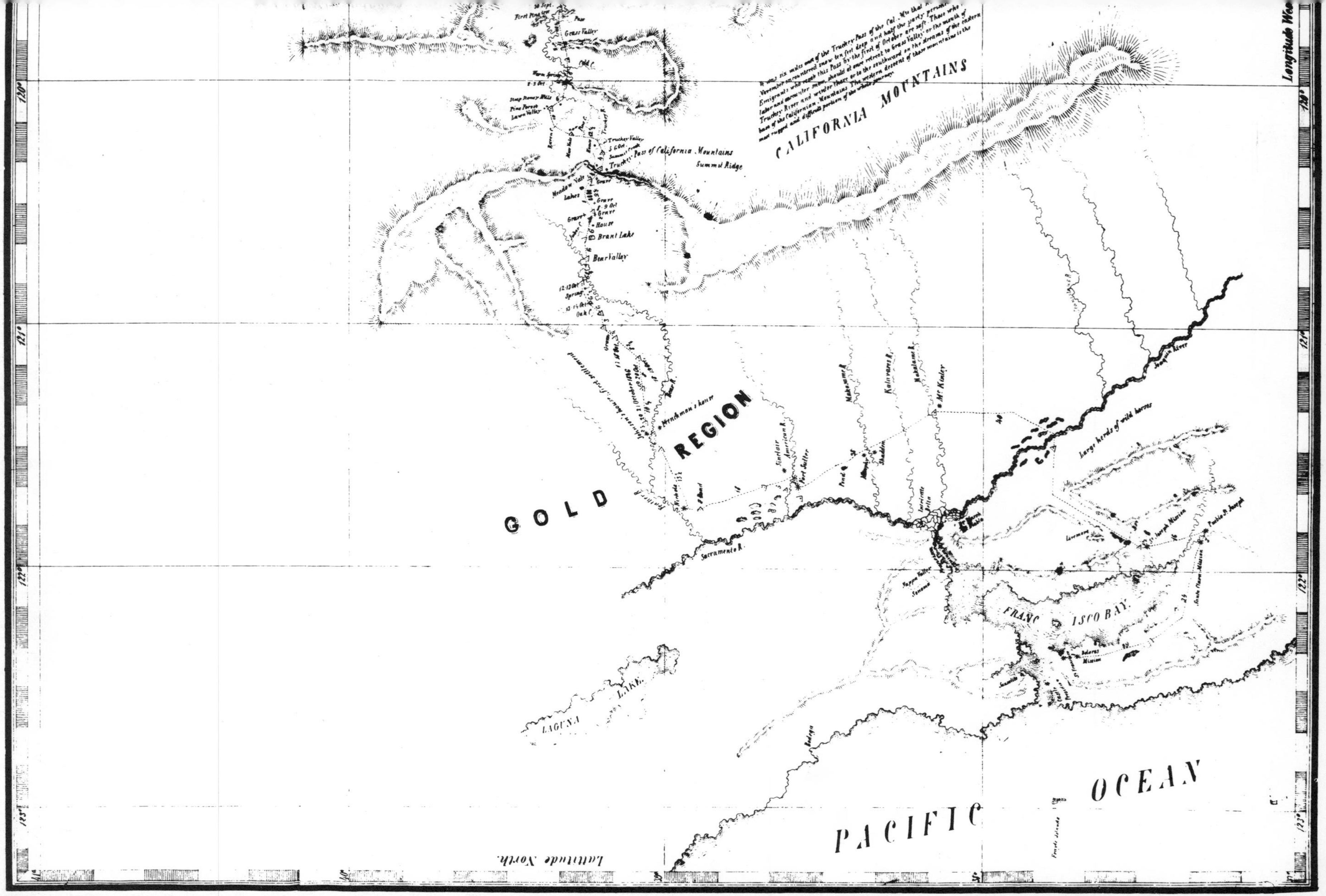

GOLD
REGION
PACIFIC
OCEAN
CALIFORNIA MOUNTAINS
FRANC ISCO BAY.
LAGUNA LAKE.
Lattitude North.
Longitude Wes
Truckey's Pass of California Mountains
Summit Ridge
Grass Valley
Truckey Valley
Brant Lake
Bear Valley
Frenchman's house
Sinclair
American R.
Fort Sutter
Sacramento R.
Pond
Makesame R.
Kalavares R.
Mc. Kinley
Shadden
Large herds of wild horses
Joaquin River
Nappa Valley
Sonoma
Livermore
St. Joseph Mission
Pueblo St. Joseph
Santa Clara Mission
Dolores Mission
Bodega
Farralo Islands